PIERCING THE DARKNESS

ALSO BY KATHERINE RAMSLAND

Dean Koontz: A Writer's Biography

Prism of the Night: A Biography of Anne Rice

The Vampire Companion: The Official Guide to Anne Rice's
The Vampire Chronicles

The Witches' Companion: The Official Guide to Anne Rice's
Lives of the Mayfair Witches

The Anne Rice Reader

The Roquelaure Reader: A Companion to Anne Rice's Erotica

The Art of Learning

Engaging the Immediate: Applying Kierkegaard's
Indirect Communication to Psychotherapy

PIERCING THE DARKNESS

Undercover with Vampires in America Today

Katherine Ramsland

HarperPrism

A Division of HarperCollins*Publishers*

HarperPrism

A Division of HarperCollins*Publishers*

10 East 53rd Street, New York, N.Y. 10022-5299

Printed in the United States of America

First Printing: October 1998

Designed by Kyoko Watanabe

Library of Congress Cataloging-in-Publication Data

Ramsland, Katherine M., 1953–
Piercing the darkness : undercover with vampires in America today /
Katherine Ramsland
p. cm.
ISBN 0-06-105062-8
1. Vampires—United States. I. Title.
GR830.V3R36 1998
398.2' 097301—DC21 98-7784
CIP

Visit HarperPrism on the World Wide Web at
http://www.harperprism.com

98 99 00 01 02 ❖ 10 9 8 7 6 5 4 3

For Pelli Wheaton and Richard Noll,
Who helped me keep perspective,

For Jim Kerr,
Whose phone call to me inspired this book,

And for Huckleberry

CONTENTS

Preface   ix

Note   xi

ONE   The Vanishing   *1*

TWO   In the Beginning   *18*

THREE   Vampires Online   *32*

FOUR   A Delicate Balance   *59*

FIVE   The Well-Read Vampire   *70*

SIX   Vampiric Diversions   *87*

SEVEN   New York by Night   *102*

EIGHT   Different Tastes   *119*

NINE   The Vampyre Mystique   *138*

TEN   In the Heartland   *156*

ELEVEN   Blood Ties   *173*

TWELVE   I'm Okay, You're a Vampire   *188*

THIRTEEN   Let the Games Begin   *208*

FOURTEEN   Vampires Intercontinental   *221*

FIFTEEN   The Disarticulated Soul   *235*

SIXTEEN   Interview with a Vampire   *251*

SEVENTEEN   The Vampire Underground   *269*

EIGHTEEN   Vampire Crimes   *289*

NINETEEN   The Glorious Exit   *309*

TWENTY   The Tao of the Vampire   *331*

Epilogue   341

Acknowledgments   347

Bibliography   349

Resources   355

Index   359

PREFACE

On July 16, 1996, a thirty-six-year-old reporter from Nutley, New Jersey, named Susan Walsh suddenly disappeared while investigating Manhattan's vampire cults. Although she danced regularly at a go-go bar and brushed against a wide range of nefarious characters, suspicion was immediately cast upon those people who dyed their hair black, painted their faces white, and wore fake fangs. Some of them were questioned by police, but the mystery of what happened to Susan Walsh remained unsolved.

Several media people called to ask me if I could shed any light on the story. Since I had written Anne Rice's biography and several books of analysis on her vampire novels, I was considered something of an expert on contemporary blood-drinkers. In fact, in 1989 I had written an article for *Psychology Today* on our culture's fascination with vampires. At that time, "real" vampires around the country were few in number and they kept mostly to themselves. Yet during the subsequent decade, I watched as increasingly more people assumed the vampire identity, and it seemed to me that this so-called emotional contagion said as much about our culture as about the individuals who chose to adopt this unusual lifestyle. Behind the media-enhanced images of "bizarre" and "pathological" characters lay a full-blown subculture with its own rituals, relationships, and boundaries.

Although the idea was daunting, I decided to pick up where Walsh had left off, to go more deeply into this subculture and see what these people had to say. I knew that meant being faced with tough decisions, such as whether to take mood-altering drugs, give or drink blood, and go places after dark that could put me in serious danger. It also meant I might come in contact with potential stalkers, fantasy-prone personalities, and perhaps even killers. Yet it seemed worth the risk to gain a genuine sense of the psychological richness of this community. Most of them, I knew, were harmless. So as a real-life "Daniel," the fictional reporter in Anne Rice's compelling novel, *Interview with the Vampire*, I sought out vampires—people who claimed to live by a vampire's code.

The question was, however, just what would be the nature of my involvement? Should I approach it like Diane Fossey in her *Gorillas in the Mist*, observing and recording without disturbing the field? Or should I look to the more dramatic example set by John Howard Griffin in *Black Like Me*? In that book, he described how he ingested dangerous chemicals and stained his white skin dark to pass as a black man in order to place himself in a position to truly understand racism and black culture. So what would it be? Observe—or immerse?

The answer came from my own training in clinical psychology. There I had been exposed to a technique called phenomenological bracketing, which involved setting aside one's personal beliefs in order to comprehend another's experience by going as far as possible inside that person's world. The best example I heard was that of a therapist whose client believed that if he walked out into the street, the buildings would fall on him. Rather than point out to him that there was no real cause for alarm, the therapist adopted the perspective of the client: What would it be like to really believe that the buildings were going to fall on him? By immersing himself in this worldview, the therapist developed enough sympathy for his client's fear to win his trust and eventually to help him.

I'd used this technique myself as a therapist, and it seemed to me a good approach for entering a community of people who were naturally suspicious of journalists whose primary aim is usually to show how weird such people are. Thus, I decided to forget *Vampires in the Mist* and go with *Dark Like Me*. I had some idea what to expect, but I soon discovered that my original assumptions were based on images and definitions that were already passé. There was more to vampire culture than I realized. A lot more.

NOTE

As vampire culture has grown and spread over the past decade, it's become more diverse. Within months of my initial research for this book, I realized I couldn't hope to cover it comprehensively. There are now so many different ways to define what a vampire is, to appreciate it, to act out its manifestations, and to develop a vampire identity, that one book could never be representative of the culture as a whole. Realizing that, I sought out what I believed were representative voices from various sectors. Inevitably, I will neglect certain prominent people; and most certainly, I will fail those who view themselves as vampires but whose stories were not captured in these pages. I made no attempt to develop an encyclopedic catalog of the manifestations of vampire culture. Others have done that, and I include those books in a bibliography. Nor am I presenting an academic or historical analysis. Others have done that, too. This book is not about vampire fiction, per se, but about vampire culture—how the image and mythology of the vampire has been translated into contemporary culture, and who the people are who actively engage in it in some fashion as part of their lives. This is the story of my own journey into the vampire world, and inevitably, it reveals my own preferences. As such, there will be those who will say that I didn't get it right. Some will think I didn't include the "right" groups or individuals. I can only say that I talked to many people and offered to listen to anyone who approached me. The stories I included were those that seemed to me from my actual encounters to best provide a broad view of how the vampire has affected people in recent years and where the culture is going.

I gave each person the choice of using his or her real name or a pseudonym. In order to protect the privacy of a number of individuals who spoke with me and who preferred not to be known, I altered identifying details to the extent I deemed necessary.

CHAPTER ONE

the vanishing

I

Where to begin? Obviously, I had to find out what Susan Walsh had been doing when she disappeared. From photos, I could see that she was a pretty blonde, tall and thin, with pale skin and long hair, and she had a way of getting people to talk. However, few of her acquaintances wanted to discuss her disappearance for fear of further endangering her should she still be alive, or because it was still an active investigation. One person, who refused to be identified, thought she had some serious mental problems. Only days before she disappeared, she had complained of mood swings. Don't bother with her relatives, I was told. They won't talk. So I had to do some digging.

In the *New York Times*, on August 10, 1996—some three weeks after her disappearance—reporter Frank Bruni decided to interview some vampires to see what kind of people Walsh had encountered. He went to the East Village, where she often hung out, to keep an appointment with a twenty-year-old vampire who calls himself Ethan Gilcrest. Surrounded by blood-red drapes of silk brocade in Ethan's apartment, Bruni took the typical (and tiresome) journalistic approach of playing up the sinister atmosphere by writing lines like, "There are sepulchral notes in his laughter and undercurrents of menace in his smile"—a smile that revealed elongated canine teeth. Ethan was quick to point out that he is not immortal and takes no prey, but he's "definitely" part vampire. He likes blood—which he calls "liquid electricity"—and dislikes the sun. He also has an unusual overbite.

In this article, Bruni went on to estimate the vampire population nationwide at several thousand, composed mostly of people under thirty. For some it's just a game, he wrote, for others a religion or a kinky sort of sexual identity. Briefly he described the custom-made fangs, Goth jargon, vampire clubs, bands, clothing, and special-effects contact lenses.

The only thing I learned from the article that might provide clues about Walsh's activities was the fleeting mention of her research—including an article on vampires that was never published. Eventually I would meet people whom she had interviewed, but for the moment, I had little to go on.

I heard from mutual acquaintances that Walsh had been talking with some vampire "squatters" in an East Village park for the article that was subsequently rejected (allegedly for being too sympathetic to the vampires). Although she was trying to change her life by breaking into journalism, she had danced in a New Jersey bar where she could have run into trouble, and she sincerely believed that dangerous people were after her. She told friends she was being followed, her phone was being bugged, and "they" were closing in. A few people thought she was just being paranoid. Others who had met with her on a regular basis perceived some truth in what she was saying. In her unpublished article, I learned, she had extensively quoted a man who ran a local vampire theater. I needed to find him.

Before she disappeared, Walsh had delivered her research notes to Sylvia Plachy and James Ridgeway for their book called *Red Light: Inside the Sex Industry*. They worked for the *Village Voice*, where Walsh was trying to place her own article. The book was about the pornography trade, seen through the eyes of insiders. It was easy to assume that Walsh's contributions had been for the chapter on "Blood Sports," as well as those about the go-go scene. In fact, the authors named Walsh as an invaluable guide into this transgressive arena and included several photographs of her. From these pages I learned not only about the kinds of people she had met, but also much more than I had known before about the lower circles of this realm of dark energy and heat.

The sex industry provides fantasy and atmosphere—which draws people of all kinds who seek the trappings of altered identities and a heightened sense of life. They can explore hidden aspects of themselves and fully indulge in whatever they discover. It goes just as far as the numinous edge of one's fantasies. *Red Light* presents the vampires simplistically (and incorrectly) as Goths in their mid-twenties, white, middle class, and having a taste for pale makeup and Victorian clothing. They hang out in clubs, predominantly in New York or San Francisco, where they congregate in back rooms and slit one another's skin to offer—or take—blood. For the most part, this is seen as an exchange of life energy. It's not so much about blood per se as about intimacy and excitement. Some of these vampires even form communities and screen new members for their HIV status.

In this book, Walsh described the go-go club as a place where the tensions between the sexes were dramatic. She admitted that she hated the way she was viewed and treated, and that her fantasies increasingly featured men she could mutilate. To her, it was a conflict between desiring power and also wanting the more familiar lack of power that came with being female. She both craved and despised the attention. She seemed confused.

Nothing in this book offered clues about Walsh's whereabouts, except perhaps a cryptic remark from one manager of a go-go club to the effect that the girls you "don't see around anymore" are the ones who "found something out that was going down." In other words, there are some dangerous customers, and dancers who get too close may end up sorry . . . or worse.

I was soon to learn from asking around in Manhattan's East Village that Walsh had been friends with a man named Christian, who had some association with the vampire world. I eventually read an article that he had written about vampirism that warned, "If you begin to hunt for vampires, the vampires will begin to hunt for you." He mentioned that Walsh had been trusted by the vampire community because she took them seriously, yet he thought that it was that very lack of skepticism that eventually had worked against her. He explained that she had revealed her activities among the vampires to club patrons who in turn confided to her that they were assassins for the Mafia and were involved in a government-connected vampire conspiracy that secretly controlled the world. According to Christian, they filled Walsh with paranoid thoughts and exploited her gullibility.

Even so, Walsh grew ever more fearful, believing she had access to dangerous secrets that someone wanted. Then a customer at the bar where she danced began to stalk her. She thought he was a vampire connected with this conspiracy, and she talked to friends about going into hiding. She made calls only from pay phones and narrowed her sphere of trusted associates. Then on that fateful day, she walked down the block from her home to go make a call . . . and never returned.

According to Christian's account, since her disappearance, Walsh had been seen by streetwalkers who claimed she had said she was hiding from the vampires. Another person, who also wanted to remain anonymous, told me she had been seen being shoved into a car. After asking around, I discovered that many in the vampire community are certain that she's alive, and some even think she's safe, while others insist there was some basis for her paranoia—although not about them.

The vampires, they insist, were Walsh's friends. They cared about her. There were others who were after her. Yet I did find people who warned me about another possibility: that the vampires created the rumors about Mafia figures and drug runners to deflect attention from themselves. Most of these vampires will admit there are some predatory types among them, and none to whom I spoke really knew anything concrete about Susan Walsh—or at least would not reveal anything. I wasn't sure what to believe.

The police investigated and cleared the vampire community on the Lower East Side, but entertainment and talk shows like *Sightings* and *Jenny Jones* continued to play up the danger: If you seek out vampires, you'll come to harm. Beware. There may be no evidence against them, but there's no evidence that entirely absolves them, either.

What really happened to Susan Walsh? And would my own hunt for vampires provoke them to hunt for me? More important, where *were* they?

2

The next step was to get some interviews. I was eager to go wherever necessary to find provocative stories. Since I lived near Manhattan, this seemed the logical first choice, but I was hesitant to venture into a city park late at night to talk to homeless drifters who reputedly attacked people for blood. Not alone anyway, although I soon learned that the solitary approach was best.

I did locate someone on the Internet who claimed to be rounding up real vampires to form a coven in the Manhattan area.

"Are you a vampire or a vampire hunter?" he asked.

"Neither," I said. "I'm a writer."

End of contact. That lead dried up. I knew I'd have to take a more stealthy approach. Go undercover, as it were.

I soon discovered a New York phone number called the Vampire Access Line. It promised information about "all things vampire," so with some trepidation—lest they trace where I lived—I dialed the number. The message was some five months old. The speaker was a woman, and she gave a long spiel about the vampire accessories she had for sale—fangs that will bite through a tin can and contact lenses of every possible vampire style ("Lost Boys," Cat, Wolf, and the like). She mentioned a cable access television show for vampires only and then went on to name some of the vampire types—Bloodists, Genetics, Classicals, Nighttimers, and Inheriters—and to discuss how vampires could meet their own kind. If I was among these, they wanted to hear from me. If I was merely a Goth or an entertainer, I was instructed to leave a message. I did so, but no one called back.

I realized that in order to find these people, I'd have to go to them. I was certainly not going to achieve any meetings through an Internet or telephone exchange. I wasn't bothered by the idea of face-to-face encounters. I'd successfully conducted many such interviews in the past. People usually sensed from me that I was sincerely interested in their stories, so it was just a matter of finding out where vampires congregate.

I was inspired by the example of Jennifer Toth, a graduate student who ventured into the abandoned subways beneath Manhattan to find out what the underground homeless culture was like. Braving the pitch darkness, the maze of tunnels, and the criminals and crack addicts, she discovered a rich and diverse population, and came out with stories about down-and-out artists, displaced families, socially disaffected intellectuals, and just plain folk struggling to get by. Her book, *The Mole People*, opens up a world otherwise inaccessible. That's what I wanted to do, even if it meant encountering dangerous elements. So I began my hunt, and it wasn't long before I was invited to a vampire club.

3

On Washington and West 14th Streets is a club called Mother. Once a month on a Wednesday night, the club's owners, Chi Chi Valenti and Johnny Dynell, cosponsor with Sabretooth, Inc. a private party known as the Long Black Veil. It's run by a tall, good-looking man in his twenties with long brown hair, high-octane energy, and an unrelenting smile. He goes by the name Father Sebastian, and he's a fangmaker by trade, as well as a highly ambitious entrepreneur. Through Sabretooth he sells jewelry, corsets, and eerie contact lenses to help his customers enhance their vampire activities. He found me through my Internet site and politely requested my attendance for the night—an evening that would last "till first light." I agreed to come. This would be my first real-world adventure into the Gothic unknown. Into the night.

I was a little nervous. Manhattan was not my territory and I wasn't too keen on going alone late at night—particularly straight into the very community that Walsh had been investigating. I decided to take as my escort a friend whom I called Outlaw (he sounds dangerous, but he's not). To my mind, he was a true Innocent. He had only the barest awareness of vampire novels, and knew little of the fetish world, but he was eager to learn. Since I already knew something about this scene, I thought that seeing this event through his eyes would help me get a different perspective. Also, he had read the story about Susan Walsh in the newspapers, and convinced she was being tortured somewhere, had become obsessed with finding her.

He was six foot four with a substantial build and an easy manner, so I felt safe. (My friends were not so sure. They all believed I would perish in some horrible way before my research was finished.) I was an invited guest, after all, and just prior to this event, a few members of the vampire community had assured me that, though they knew Susan Walsh and had spoken with her frequently, they were innocent of anything related to her disappearance.

At the Long Black Veil, Goths and vampires mingled with other "fringe" types, drinking, talking, and watching rock bands. The requested attire was "Dark Fetish, Goth, Arthurian, Edwardian, Vampire, Rubber, or Victorian." I wore black.

I should make it clear that Goths are not necessarily vampires, nor necessarily interested in vampires, and vice versa. Many people confuse the two groups. For that reason, there is some tension between them, though they do share common interests in black clothing, images of death, music, and developing an "outsider" style. Goth culture is an entity unto itself, and my purpose was to follow vampires, so I mention Goths only where they intersect with the vampire community.

Chi Chi and Johnny had designed Mother, and Johnny had done much of the artwork decorating the inside. He was happy to discuss its inspiration with me, and I found him and Chi Chi completely engaging. They gave me some copies of their magazine, *Verbal Abuse*, and offered to show me around. As we walked in, I saw a stage to the right for the bands coming later that night, and moved past the bar into a corridor that took us to a room in which a full-sized open coffin with satin lining served as a centerpiece. For that night, spiderwebs, rats, and flying bats provided ghoulish atmosphere. On the cream-colored walls of this "Versailles Room" were, as Johnny pointed out, xeroxes of famous Italian Renaissance etchings, washed over with a sponge-painted coating to give them an authentic and eerie cast, and overhead around the room was gold ornate molding with a fleur-de-lis pattern. Paintings of cherubs and clouds against a blue sky adorned the ceiling as in an Italian palazzo, and hanging iron lace lamps provided dim lighting. Against the wall stood upholstered chairs of eighteenth-century French design, and there was a small bar in the back over which hung a huge oval mirror with a gold antique frame. A European salon for Those Who Dress in Black—and several hundred came in and out that night to hear such bands as Cult of the Psychic Fetus and Stiffs, Inc.

Chi Chi was dressed in a black hoop skirt and velvet jacket, with a black top hat over a white-blond bundle of perfect pipe curls. She's a gracious hostess, well known on the fetish circuits as a lively emcee, and quite pleased to sponsor vampire events in her establishment. Click 'n Drag on Saturdays was another such event. She introduced herself, invited me to get a drink served by a cute, shirtless, long-haired bartender with fangs, and then went off to see to club matters that needed her attention.

Immediately a man dressed in a black frock coat and snowy white cravat addressed me. His hair was black and he had a dark line of facial hair running from his ears, over and around his lips, which curled slightly over a set of small white fangs. His cheeks were shaved clean. I guessed him to be in his mid-thirties. His fingers were sheathed in ornate silver.

"I'm a construction worker by day," he explained, after telling me that he simply loved to dress in the clothing of a past era. "But I identify myself as a vampire."

"Do you wear your fangs to work?" I asked.

"Sometimes," he said with a wicked smile that showed off those sharp teeth to advantage. "It has an effect. But I don't care what people say. I enjoy this and it doesn't matter to me what anyone thinks."

Behind him, a couple came in. The young man wore a red silk shirt and in his right hand carried a short black whip, while the girl was decked out in a daring lace-up corset from which she bulged over the top, and black fishnet stockings. She had long black hair in a mass of curls, and I thought I'd never seen a tinier waist. At her partner's command, she bent over a chair, exposing her rounded, fishnet-covered cheeks for his attention. As we all watched, he slapped her with the multiple leather fringes of the whip, alternating between vertical and horizontal lashings. She flinched a little, but made no sound as he repeatedly smacked her bottom. This was my first exposure to the overlap between the vampire world and the dark fetish culture—bondage-and-discipline, sadomasochism, dominance-and-submission.

Not all vampires adopt these sexual practices and not all fetishists are vampires, but there is a small percentage of each population that moves between both worlds—as I would see at the vampire fetish ball a month hence. It was a world that Susan Walsh had known intimately. She had been exploring this very overlap when she had disappeared.

When the guy in red silk finally stopped his "discipline," his "submissive" stood up with a smile. I walked over and asked her why she liked this experience. Her grin was broad and sincere. "It makes the endorphins flow," she explained. "It's like a runner's high. The longer you endure the pain, the more you get pushed into this state where it becomes like a trance and it gets very pleasurable. I'm addicted to it now."

They invited me to try my hand. The man handed me the whip. I took it and felt its leather grip. It was hefty, but I wasn't ready. I couldn't whip this girl. I handed the whip back, little knowing that I would not escape my time at the helm. But not that night. At the moment, I was merely a voyeur.

My cohort, Outlaw, had meandered over to a fellow seated in one of the upholstered chairs to ask him some questions. The guy wore nothing but lace-up leather sandals and a tiny black leather thong. His slender body was covered from neck to ankle in tattoos of every color and design. Decorating them here and there were silver studs, spiked into the skin, and long silver prongs sticking out from numerous places on his body. His face and ears were covered in piercings, and there was a thick silver ring at the base of his throat. I could detect the form of the wire just under the skin, which made me touch my own throat to be certain the skin was lying flat. His nipples were also pierced. He had shaved his head, save for a thin line of hair that grew long, and he had a sad look in his eyes. I made a mental note to ask Outlaw about him afterward.

As I looked around at the scene before me, I saw that this was no world of white makeup and fake blood, as the media like to portray, but of people whose aesthetic tastes run toward leather, velvet, and romance, and who prefer to take shelter against the world in the symbols of darkness. The dress code at such clubs quite often is black, and candles or dim lights enhance the mood. Males often carry walking sticks and wear brocade coats. Females sport fantastic gowns, corsets, hats, and hair styles. It was a mosaic of studded chokers, platform boots, tight black jackets, black lipstick, dagger tattoos, streaked hair, top hats, frock coats, belly rings, silver claws, skull shirts, and rubber clothing of every kind. There was nothing cheap or chintzy here.

I saw a thin woman in a long black dress with a wide-brimmed hat covered in a black veil that hid her face. I assumed she could see through it, but I could not see her. Another wore tight black pants, lace-up high-heeled boots, and a rubber corset. Some wore vampire makeup—a bit of blood at the corner of the mouth to suggest a recent meal—and many sported fangs, but a few simply let their true faces be known. Each person sought to express individual desires and interests without judgment. They could do that here. It was a fantasy. Anything goes that bespeaks the vampire.

That night I met a young woman with honey-blond hair and cheerleader looks, dressed in a low-cut black chenille that revealed large pink welts, each from three to six inches long, that ran in rows across her chest. She saw me looking and invited me to touch.

"I love it when people stroke them," she said with a gesture toward the swollen scars. "It feels good." Not to be impolite, I swallowed my revulsion and ran a finger across one, trying not to cringe. I could only imagine the pain she must have endured.

I'd already heard of scarification. That's where people voluntarily cut themselves or submit to someone else's scalpel. They do it for body decoration, for bloodletting, for performance art, or for the heightened experience of the sensation of pain. Apparently, I was looking at the results of one such ritual.

"You cut yourself?" I asked.

"Yes." She pulled at her shirt to give me a better view and it turned out that her welts took the shape of a large bird with outstretched wings. "It's a phoenix," she said with pride. "Actually, my boyfriend did the cutting, but it's the design I wanted."

"Didn't that hurt?"

"Oh, the real pain came after, when I had to take care of the cuts. Try washing out a cut like these with alcohol! Wow! And it took weeks to heal, but I'm glad I did it." She said all of this with a huge smile. "I really like it. It took a long time, because we didn't do it all at once, and each time he cut, I learned things about myself. It was a spiritual experience, which I hadn't really expected."

I nodded as if I understood, but I probably didn't. She was twenty-one, she told me, and I had to ask, "But what if you get to be thirty-five or forty and decide this was a mistake, that you don't want this on your chest?" To me it appeared that she had marred her beauty.

With great self-assurance, she said, "I'll accept that this is who I was at this time."

I went into the other room to watch the bands for a while, amazed at the level of seething anger the singers expressed. People danced to these heated lyrics in a strange slow motion, and the females reminded me of saplings in the breeze, their feet firmly planted as their arms flowed outward in broad gestures and their slim bodies writhed in response to the music's soul. People arched every which way, bending and swaying to some private fantasy of interpretation. It was like watching performance art.

I was soon beckoned into the cellar, where a film crew asked to interview me for a cable access television show called *Vampyre Dreams TV*. Asif Murad and his partner Morella produced this weekly late-night Manhattan-based show. I talked about my work with Anne Rice and hoped I was delivering what they wanted. I couldn't really see them very well.

At 4:00 A.M. I left with Outlaw. It was a balmy night and we walked the city streets—never thought I'd see Seventh Avenue nearly empty—while he told me what he'd seen and felt.

"I couldn't believe all the fangs!" he said. "Someone told me they cost about seventy-five dollars a pair, so that room was full of hundreds if not thousands of dollars' worth of fake teeth. Almost everybody was pierced. And tattoos—lots of people with tattoos. But I thought it was strange that some of the women were dressed in white. That just seems so unvampiric. One young woman looked like a lacy bedroom curtain, but with red dribbles down her neck. You know what she told me? 'Every vampire needs a victim.'"

"Did you get much from talking to them?" I asked. I was eager to hear the deeper story.

"Someone named Matt or Mike, who was dressed in white frills and had hair down the length of his back. He's writing a screenplay. He intends to take the myth of the vampire where it has never gone before—just like every other theater student. Still, he had such enthusiasm! And the quest for eternal life through art . . . it sort of works here."

"Anyone else?" I wanted to hear about the tattooed man.

"A young Morticia," he said with a laugh. "She hovered around me. Some kind of black spider's lace adorned her arms. Her hair, her lipstick, her army boots were all black, and she had ink-black tattoos on her skin. What was increasingly apparent to me was that these kids aren't unlike me twenty years ago; they're just as heavily involved in the mating ritual. Boys and girls are still courting each other, flirting with dark-lined eyes. Not with me, of course, despite my sexual magnetism." He smiled. "At my age, I must seem like one of the living dead to them."

I laughed. He looked pretty good to me.

"What was strange," he continued, "was that they don't touch. Not even when they slow dance. They stand in place or nearly in place and trace the shapes of their partners through the air. Their arms are like gigantic brushes. There's no embrace."

I nodded. "What did you think of the music?" I asked.

"It was angry, hateful. It made me think of that group, Johnny Rotten and the Sex Pistols. The same kind of spit and vitriol. Kvetch,

kvetch, kvetch. And yet did you see how the lead singer in this group stopped to introduce his mother? Twenty years ago, I saw the same thing at CBGB. It was the beginning of punk rock. That was the first spiked hair and all the clothing was black and ripped. The female singer had 'F*** housework' printed in bold red across her bosom. In what was supposed to be the darkest den of young despair, she stopped her set to introduce her middle class mother. I'd bet today that same singer has a child old enough to be at the vampire club. I'd also bet she's done a lot of housework since that night."

"That one guy caught your eye," I said, urging him toward the one in whom I was most interested. "The guy with all the tattoos. What was his story?"

Outlaw nodded. "The first thing I noticed was that his tattoos seemed fierce and frightening. He'd pierced his face at least thirty times. He was sort of Hannibal Lechter–esque. I was afraid he might eat babies, but to me he was the most riveting person in the place. He kept to himself. Or maybe everyone kept away from him. 'This is the real thing,' I thought to myself. 'This is the vampire.' He was scary. But when I asked his name, he spoke so softly I had to ask three times.

"He hailed from Germany and he had an extremely delicate sensibility. He said he was a Ph.D. student in applied mathematics at NYU. There's probably twenty people in the world who understand the concepts that he works with. I couldn't help but think of the contrast between the rigor of his field and the chaos of his outward appearance. My heart told me that he was a nice person. My brain was less open-minded. I decided never to be alone with him. But he admitted, actually, he was afraid of the future."

"You're kidding," I responded. "This sounds like just an ordinary conversation."

"It was. I said to him, 'Pardon me for saying this, but you don't appear to be someone searching for security.' A sad look came into his eyes, and then he said, 'You think because I look like this that I wouldn't be afraid? I could bullshit you and pretend that I'm strong . . . but why? What would I be proving? I need to feel secure like the next person.' I felt like holding him close to comfort him."

Outlaw went on to tell me that this young man was intensely lonely. I couldn't help but think that his appearance put people off, but that opinion was due to my lack of savvy in this new world I was discovering. He wasn't that different from many others I was to meet over the next few months who had chosen some form of in-your-face body decoration as their personal statement. Outlaw came away feeling privileged to have been exposed to this culture—although I never could get him to return with me. He thought that perhaps, given the life transitions he was experiencing, a culture like that might absorb and disorient him. It was too intense . . . and too inviting.

Yet his perspective had been valuable. I left the club that night with a growing awareness that there were countless stories to be found in this community and I'd never be able to collect them all—or even a good sampling—to show the variety. I'd just have to do what I could.

4

Go hunting for vampires and the vampires will hunt for you.

It wasn't long before I was contacted by a self-described "real" blood-drinker who sought the vampire experience by stalking "prey." Contrary to media presentations, the majority of people who participate in some way in vampire culture do *not* drink blood, and many even find the notion unappealing, if not altogether unsafe. Some went so far as to call it psycho; yet it cannot be denied that a growing number of people do drink blood and find within the experience something mystical, sexual, or energizing.

My first connection with this vampire happened online through e-mail. I'm easy to find if one goes through the various Anne Rice links, and many people certainly explore that access. I had no idea at that time that my mysterious correspondent would become a significant contributor to my vampire story files. He didn't say who he was, but he signed his early notes with a simple initial, W. I saved his e-mail like all the rest and gave it little thought at the time.

"I've heard what you're doing," he wrote. "You seek to know the true heart of the vampire and I know something about that. I'd like to tell you about what I've done, but I don't want you to know me."

I wrote back and invited him to write again. Very quickly, he did. He confessed to a habit of drinking blood and said he was trying to find out more about the dark things inside himself that fed this hunger. He was conflicted about it, but would not say why. He thought I might be able to help.

After his admission that his vampire activities revolved around rituals involving the moon, I asked him to describe one in detail. He explained that he had a special ritual each Halloween that he had performed over the past decade, and he was willing to divulge the details of one of those. I urged him to send it, not knowing at all what to expect. Soon I was reading it.

"This was a few years ago," he wrote. "Halloween was only two days away and I had not yet found my prey. I never pick them until just before the actual day, because part of the ritual is the challenge of finding the perfect person just in time. I happened upon this one quite unexpectedly. As it should be. I was walking along the beach late in the evening and I noticed bare skin glistening in the distance in the pinkish light of the setting sun. As I closed in, I confirmed what I had suspected: a perfect male specimen. He was wearing thin white baggy shorts that hung loosely from a muscular frame. He was waxing his car, and though there was a cool breeze blowing, his body was wet with sweat.

"I made sure that he wouldn't hear my approach until I was very near. Then I deliberately startled him with a comment about his car. He brought a pair of powder blue eyes to my gaze and I saw the unmistakable dilation. He thought me attractive. His hair was sun-bleached blond, and pieces clung to his damp forehead. I decided on the spot that he was there for me. He was the one.

"As we conversed, I watched his breathing patterns change and his bare nipples contract. The breeze? I don't think so. His white cotton shorts, soaked through, revealed his growing interest. He was eighteen and helplessly lusty. I kept an intimate distance between us to tease him. The ritual requires a full seven days of abstinence prior to the sacrifice, but this boy seemed an unstable artifact and I had to alter the rules. The only way to secure him was with the promise of an unparalleled experience."

Okay, I thought as I read W.'s account, this is good. It has the right measure of eroticism. This "vampire" had now revealed that he was attracted to males, so he was part of the large percentage of gay and bisexual culture that was into vampires. Anne Rice and other vampire writers had an enthusiastic gay following, in part because they view the vampire as transcending gender and lacking in culturally imposed prejudice with regard to choice of victim. Vampires also captured the unrelenting sensuality that gay men have told me they love. I took a breath and continued to read.

"He finished his car and offered me a lift to where he lived in an upstairs apartment in his parents' house. They were away, so he invited me up. We popped tops and I slumped on the couch while he excused himself to go take a shower. I seized the moment and followed him in. Drinking beer, I watched him through the glass door. I was ready with a towel when he stepped out. Surprised, he stood still as I blotted his clean, tanned skin. I enjoyed the play, but all the while I was thinking only of Halloween—that I had to prepare him. Timing is key. And anticipation.

"I kept the sexual contact simple—mostly just erotic—to study his drives, desires, and curiosities. Then the next day, I shadowed him. I introduced him to exotic ideas he had never heard of, which kept him interested in me. By Halloween night, he was overpoweringly curious.

"We dined early and by ten we were at the hottest club on the strip. Uncharacteristically, I sensed myself falling for him. I usually keep things hot, but dis-intimate. Yet this boy was so vulnerable and willing to please. We returned to his apartment for what I promised would be a night he would never forget. We lit candles and incense, which filled the air with a warm tingling of arousal. We drank a fine Italian red wine with a perfect bouquet. Then the ceremony:

"First we shared psyche. This means we told each other our stories, our deepest, most private fantasies and dreams. I told him the meaning of the ceremony to me, the annual feeding of my Hunger. He was enchanted, charmed, and deliriously curious. We undressed and began to lick each other's bodies, taking care to avoid the most sensitive areas. That was for later. I sat up and gestured for him to follow me into the next room, his bedroom.

"I erected a pole and told him to spread himself on it in the form of a crucifix, which he eagerly did. I tied him to it. I performed several erotic acts on him, working his desire into a frenzy. Then I picked up a sterilized razor blade and deftly sliced through his left nipple."

I stopped reading and sat back. For some reason, this quick, shocking act sent a chill through me. I almost felt that cut. It seemed an outrageous trespass, and certainly not something that *I* would have been prepared for. But as I read on, it was clear that the other boy enjoyed it.

"He winced at the sharp prick, but was soon writhing in pleasure as my lips touched the wound and I began to suck. Occasionally I lifted my lips to his mouth to give him a taste. He grew wild and confessed that he'd never felt anything like this before. He felt that he was leaving his body somehow, that he didn't know himself anymore. I pressed against him with my own nakedness as I drained him a little more and teased him with my tongue, from his nipple to the base of his neck, as if to plunge my teeth into him there. He seemed a little anxious, but also excited by the possibility.

"He was right on the edge, so I untied him, calmed him, and took him outside into the night breeze. It was nearly midnight. We traipsed barefoot across the damp grass to the oak trees nearby. I then forced him against the rough bark and we kissed deeply, probing with great urgency, and stroked each other to ejaculation. The blast of hot fluid sealed our bodies together and we moaned together in the ecstasy of the moment.

"The mingling of blood and semen represents my hunger at the core of my being. It's about me, who I am as a male with a great need for another's life force, blood cell to blood cell. I'm always tempted to return to the one I chose, but it breaks my own rules. I have to have strange flesh and these boys, once I'm done with them, are no longer strange. They are intimately mine. I know them. I need an Other. Blood is the source of life and death, a price of redemptive sacrifice. I use blood in my ritual as a symbolic reconciliation with myself. There is no greater stimulus than the line between pain and pleasure—the very sight of blood stirs the loins. I believe that we always long to look into the abyss, every one of us, even if it terrifies us."

That was it. The end of his account. I felt somewhat drained when I finished reading, but also energized—just the way someone might feel in the presence of a vampire. I quickly sent back some questions, but heard nothing in response. I sent my phone number and urged my elusive correspondent to call. He was bold. He was the very type of person I wanted to talk to. He could be a psycho, but I already knew this project would involve risk, and this man, I believed, had a story. I sensed it. I knew it.

When I heard nothing from him right away, I figured he was pondering the wisdom of making these revelations to me. Such a reaction is not uncommon after disclosing things one has kept hidden. He didn't really know me, after all. So far, he hadn't told me how I could find him, and I didn't know his name. He was still safe within his secret world. Then my requests returned as "undeliverable," and I realized I had lost him. He'd closed that e-mail account.

So I picked up on other leads and hoped for another opportunity at some other time. Eventually it came, and what I learned from my contact with this vampire was that the world into which Susan Walsh had entered did indeed have some genuine dangers. But for the moment, "W." was far away.

CHAPTER TWO

in the beginning

I

One thing I picked up right away was that many participants in vampire culture used some sort of disguise. They selected names that would yield a specific impression, such as Satan, Fang, Dementia, or Lord Byron. I decided it might be best for me to adopt one as well. Too many people knew my associations with Rice, which could influence their presentation. A pseudonym freed me to say and do whatever I wanted without worrying about my reputation, and allowed me to participate more fully in the scene. Early on, I foolishly believed that I knew the limits of this culture and wouldn't get in over my head.

I wanted a pseudonym that would have some sinister overtones, but also be clearly female, so I choose Malefika. With that persona, I entered the chat rooms online. I expected a bit of jargon-heavy repartee, but not what actually took place.

I quickly learned that those chat rooms that were named something like "Vampire Spa" or "Vampire Castle" were for role-players only. I went into one and saw people spelling out their activities in this manner: *Demigod: :: Crossing room and taking Spiderlipz in his arms and kissing her with force::.* To address one another, they seemed to rely on medieval phrases picked up from romance novels. I typed in a sentence to the effect that I was looking for vampires, and was redirected by a friendly "bartender" to the room for "Real Vampyres—no role-players." I thanked him and moved on.

(I subsequently learned that a faction of vampire culture uses the spelling "vampyre" instead of "vampire" to distinguish themselves as "real.")

In the "Real Vampyres" chamber, my new name did seem to have some force because I was quickly singled out by a man who claimed he was seeking a powerful female vampire for a highly erotic experience. He was even willing to pay me. (Wow! I could actually make money at this!) But what he requested wasn't exactly what I'd anticipated.

He would meet me anywhere, he assured me, completely on my terms. He'd been on several wild goose chases, traveling the world to find just the right one, and he sensed that I could be *it*. I wasn't sure why exactly, but I decided to draw him out.

"Why are you seeking a female vampire?" I asked.

Because, he told me, it was required in his religion to be drained nearly to the point of death so that he could move spiritually to a higher level. Yet he wasn't quite sure how it worked. "I've never been with a vampire before," he admitted. "I've met people who've told me they were, but it turned out to be nothing. They were just playing games. What is it you'd do to me?"

Okay, I was in the fantasy now. I had to go with it. "That part is not for you to know," I said. "If you indulge in anticipation, it could develop into guardedness. And I haven't yet decided that I'm definitely going to do it. I have to believe that it's worth my while."

"What would you require?" he asked.

"Maybe nothing." I wasn't quite ready for this, but keeping the book in mind, I added, "Maybe simply to hear you tell me exactly what you experience, in detail. But to do this I have to go outside my circle. I have to talk with the others first." I didn't have any "others" to talk with, but I'd heard this notion of a feeding circle, so I used it to add a little mystery.

"Of course," he agreed. "My Elder will also ask me to describe my experience when I arrive to take my Five Precepts. I'm only asking how it works so that I can feel more comfortable. I'd like to know if there's any pain involved, how it is to be inflicted, and if there's a meditation to block it."

"Pain is part of the experience," I told him. I could see I had the makings of a real dominatrix. This was almost too fun. I was tempted to really meet him and play it out. "I don't chew on skin, if that's what you mean. But you are not to try to block any sensations. Otherwise you'll lose the spirituality of it. Yet one thing disturbs me about you. You say you need a vampire to do this, but you seem to know so little about vampires. The logic of your quest escapes me."

"Vampires are the closest to the Shamess in India, who basically are vampires in their country," he explained.

"But what do *you* actually know?" I pressed. "What do you think you're pursuing? Don't you realize how dangerous this could be?"

"I'm aware of the dangers," he responded. "I've been around a little. If you're sincere, we can discuss it, but I don't want to argue over semantics. I'm accomplished in my own right as an Acolyte of my religion, one of only seven in this country in this particular sect. I'm a teacher in an ancient form of combat and psycho-spiritual studies." He gave me some exotic details.

I had no idea what he was talking about, but he seemed so sincere, I was beginning to feel a little guilty. Still, I decided to continue. "I wonder if I have what you really want."

"One is never entirely certain of anything," he responded, "as reality is only that which is perceived. This is a screening for both of us."

That vexed me a little. I wasn't about to let him take the upper hand, or even to become my equal, so I cut him off. "You say you want a vampire to drain you, but you seem to seek a complete transformation, and you may not get it. The experience is as much about you as about what I might do."

"I'm willing to take that chance. Sometimes the seeker must fall before walking is an option."

It struck me that if this guy was for real, he could really put himself in harm's way. Any unscrupulous woman (or man) on the Net could tell him to bring the money, leave it in some specified spot, and just walk away. Or worse. I could be a killer trolling for gullible people. His preoccupation, if it was real, was making him terribly vulnerable. I mentioned this, but he didn't seem to care. He was willing to do whatever was necessary to get to the next spiritual level. I told him that before I'd consider his request, he'd have to send me a complete description of this religion, because it seemed a little odd to require members to be drained by real vampires. He agreed, but I never received it. And that was a relief.

Was he just a role-player? A fanatic? A true seeker? I have no idea.

I did eventually meet a Real Vampyre in a chat room like this. What he desired was an "offline" encounter, and in pursuit of a good story, I agreed. I didn't tell him what I was doing. I just arranged to meet him.

2

So how did I get into this? What was my first introduction to the vampire realm and why was I pursuing this in-depth study? Those are the questions that people inevitably ask, so I'll answer them now. Then I'll introduce the Vampyre.

Like many kids, I read Bram Stoker's *Dracula* at an early age, around twelve. I had thrived on monster movies and had been thrilled by Bela Lugosi's interpretation of the aristocratic vampire. I wanted to get as close to that bloodsucking predator as possible, but not as Mina or Lucy. I wanted to feel what *he* felt when he went after his prey. I went to bed each night with my arms crossed over my chest in the hope that I would awaken as a vampire. I told people I was 403 years old. Without knowing how to articulate it, I sensed there was some visceral quality in the vampire's experience that would enhance life and make me feel as if I were part of something much larger than myself.

In the late sixties, the leap into *Dark Shadows* was a natural, with the agonized Barnabas Collins and his plethora of mesmerized females. That television series gave me the chance to look at the details, day by day, of a vampire's existence. It was nothing like Stoker's presentation. It was much more human. Although I didn't care for Julia, the vampire's confidante, I wanted to be in her position so I could ask him endless questions. Thus, when in 1980 I spotted Anne Rice's *Interview with the Vampire* on a drugstore rack, I grabbed it. The title alone spoke to me and the story plunged me right behind the vampire's eyes—exactly where I wanted to be.

And I wasn't alone. You might say that the collective cultural subconscious was building toward the day when many of us would identify with the monster, who in earlier vampire tales had to be annihilated as the Evil Other. We were beginning to understand that to take out the vampire with a stake through the heart was to kill a part of ourselves—a part that might yield some real treasures.

A teacher once told me that to pick up a book was to gamble with your life, because you have no idea how it may affect you. That happened to me when I grabbed *Interview with the Vampire*. I had no idea in that moment that I'd someday write books about Rice and her writings, or that I'd be on the receiving end of confessions from people who wanted to discuss their own blood-thirst and its moral consequences. All I knew as I read that novel was that I felt at home in the vampire's point of view. Louis de Pointe du Lac, formerly a refined New Orleans aristocrat, was an intellectual vampire who felt isolated and alone, and who had difficulty coming to grips with the moral and spiritual ambiguity of the universe. He also possessed mystery and powers, and shared a bond with others of his ilk that was tenuous, anxious, and unpredictable. In other words, erotic. I went on to read the rest of Rice's vampire novels, although it was Louis with whom I felt most attuned. I understood his restrained despair and his struggle to keep going when there was no certainty of making sense of his existence.

In the meantime, I went on to get a master's degree in clinical psychology and a doctorate in philosophy, specializing in existential ideas. Yet at no time did I lose my fascination with the conflicted energy of those who resonate to darkness, or with their mythological accoutrements.

By the time I read Rice's third vampire novel, *The Queen of the Damned*, I was convinced that a biography was needed. I wanted to analyze how she managed so gracefully to combine philosophical issues with what had come to be nothing more in our culture than a genre image that signaled a quick read, visceral horror, hackneyed plots, and mediocre writing.

I wrote *Prism of the Night* with Anne Rice's cooperation, and followed that with *The Vampire Companion*, a guide to the characters, themes, places, and symbols found in her novels. During the course of that experience, I wrote an article for *Psychology Today* on the psychological aspects of the vampire image, and soon began to hear from people who believed I would offer a sympathetic ear to their own identification with the vampire—and not always the vampire as presented by Rice. I attracted people who wanted me to help them sort out things they would not dare to tell to a more mainstream practitioner.

I also talked with Carol Page, who was writing a book called *Bloodlust: Conversations with Real Vampires*. She sent some of the transcripts and asked for my comments. From her research, there appeared to be a few individuals, mostly in New York or California, who claimed to drink blood and practice what they viewed as a vampire's lifestyle. Among others, there was Jack, who sucked blood from his brother; Countess Misty, who claimed that a couple was trying to steal her "vampire eyes" from her; and Vlad, the rock 'n' roll vampire from Chicago. The stories were fascinating and detailed, and Carol revealed some incidents to me behind the scenes that convinced me these people took their lifestyles quite seriously.

Norine Dresser, a folklorist at UCLA, also wrote a book that year called *American Vampires* in which she documented the plethora of vampire images in advertising and the media, and described the effects on people she met who claimed to be vampires, or to be in love with vampires. At that time, vampires showed up in television ads touting everything from mouthwash to nail polish, on Sesame Street, cereal boxes, candy bar wrappers, cartoons, cookbooks, greeting cards, rock videos, and as sponsors for blood drives. There was even a grammar book called *The Transitive Vampire*. Dresser also documented the strong *Dark Shadows* subculture, with its newsletters and conventions. She sent out a questionnaire, and out of 574 respondents, 27 percent admitted to a belief in vampires. (I tend to think that percentage would be higher today.)

I soon met Jeanne Youngson, author and president of the Count Dracula Fan Club, and Eric Held, who had offered a correspondence-type newsletter since 1979 through which he operated the Vampire Information Exchange (VIE). Both of them introduced me to a small, but growing, subculture of vampire enthusiasts, and I toured Youngson's amazing Dracula Museum. She said her fan club had several thousand members, although many of them were scholars who studied *Dracula* as a literary form. She herself led tours overseas for fans of *Dracula* who were interested in seeing the sites in Britain and Romania relevant to the story.

I located a vampire pen pal network and The Vampire Studies Society. Interviews with vampires were available from the Unquiet Grave Press, and Vampire Esoteric Encounters promised to introduce me (and any other client) to self-proclaimed vampires—sort of a dating service for the undead. One book offered six easy lessons for becoming a vampire.

And I heard from Stephen Kaplan, who operated The Vampire

Research Center and who claimed to have tracked real vampires across the country since 1981. He was a bit fanatical in his attempt to prove that the American government embraced numerous vampires (no surprise), and he wanted a government grant to finance the giving and analyzing of a ninety-nine-item questionnaire for members of Congress, to determine just how many there were. I was skeptical that real vampires who controlled a country would answer such a confrontational survey honestly. I mean, why would a senator say, "Yes, I'm a vampire and here's my method for taking blood from my victims"? Yet as a vampirologist, Kaplan claimed to be able to say with accuracy that there were some fifty or sixty true vampires in the country, and some five hundred worldwide. The average male vampire is five feet ten inches, with blue eyes and brown hair. The average female is a bit shorter and has green eyes and blond hair. (This data changed with each survey.)

"People who call themselves vampires are on the rise," Kaplan insisted, and it turns out he was right. Although he died a few years later (not from a vampire attack), his work has been continued by others, and there are estimates that vampire culture is now in the tens of thousands for hard-core participants, and ten times that number for people with a mild or part-time interest. Kaplan wrote a book called *Vampires Are*, in which he documented his various encounters, including the baffling case of Elizabeth, who claimed to be 493 years old. Kaplan also described his own experience of trying to bite one of his staff members to see if it was really as sensual and satisfying as his unusual clientele claimed. After chewing on her for a sufficient amount of time to break skin, he decided there was nothing thrilling about the salty taste of hot blood, and she decided it was definitely not erotic.

It soon became clear to me from talking with these people that some individuals were deeply entrenched in the mythology, to the point of filing their teeth permanently into razor-sharp weapons, sleeping in coffins, being active only at night, avoiding the sun, and dressing exclusively in black. Some of these individuals knew one another and had formed small groups to exchange blood in secret. And within several of those groups, rituals had developed so that each participant could indulge his or her blood-thirst without feeling like a deviant. Since AIDS was a growing threat to the blood community, a "feeding circle" was a practical idea as well.

I found these examples of actual vampirism to be fascinating. They were consenting adults, not hurting anyone, and completely caught up with the desire to experience a vampire's existence. They claimed they wanted their chosen lifestyle to be tolerated, like any other minority. They even went on talk shows to plead their case, and I watched them being drilled by horrified members of the audience. Under glaring stage lights, they looked absolutely unhealthy. They were put on the defensive in every way, and made to look like satanists who wanted to steal babies and eat them. It was an extremely unappealing circus act—and this was in the days before it had become obvious that talk shows were nothing *more* than idiotic displays of dysfunctional America. It completely missed the point that they were *not* in fact dangerous to anyone, and I found myself feeling sympathetic, although I personally saw no appeal in drinking actual blood. I wasn't that savvy in vampire culture at the time, but I knew enough to see that media distortion was probably inevitable when people claimed to do things that offended the mainstream populace.

I was interested in how someone could actually develop a bloodthirst, but I was glad that it was Carol Page and not me who was talking with someone like James Riva, who killed his grandmother with golden bullets in order to drink her blood. I was really more interested in the fictional aspects of the vampire, particularly when Carol confessed that she felt pressured to get more involved with her subjects than she wanted to be. She had just wanted to write a book, not be anyone's confidante.

Well, okay, that got me a little more interested. If it was true that people were confessing their darkest secrets and seeking help sorting that all out, then I wanted to get a little closer to that world.

Not long afterward, I read a case written by psychiatrist Robert McCully of the Medical University of South Carolina. He described an adolescent boy who had punctured his carotid artery and forced it to spurt in such a way as to be able to catch it in his mouth and drink his own blood. This form of autovampirism was highly erotic for him. Trying to comprehend this behavior, McCully researched vampire lore from ancient cultures and concluded that "some long forgotten archetype somehow got dislodged from the murky bottom of the past and emerged to take possession of a modern individual." He speculated that the vampire image has been contained in the "psychic substance" of humanity since the dawn of history. On the positive side, the vampire's promise of renewal offers transformation; on the dark side, the predator survives at the expense of another's sacrifice.

I started a correspondence with McCully. He told me that he thought the increase in interest in vampires in the late eighties was due to the culture's tendency to "extravert" our shadow side—to project away from ourselves those aspects of being human that we want to eradicate. Noting the strong component of sexuality, he said, "The vampire is surely a vivid symbol for the sadomasochistic side of evil." Collective movements, he believed, are like individual obsessions, and the form an obsession takes depends on the way nonconscious elements have been activated. It is what we *don't* see in ourselves that provides the currents of psychic energy. The increase in interest in vampires, he said, is related to a certain cultural self-blindness.

I wasn't going to forget that observation. Don't look at the vampire to understand it; look at the ground from which the vampire arises.

I wasn't sure exactly what that might involve, but it was clear that vampire-fascination was widespread and growing. So what was drawing people to the vampire? Obviously, it had something to do with the larger-than-life figure who casts a sexual allure via mystery, power, and sensuality. And it was also the blood. Blood represents life, connection, warmth, and kinship. The loss of blood is the loss of life. The sharing of blood is a bond. Fear makes the heart pump hotter, jolting us to the edge. The veins throb, the blood heats up. The vampire is the perfect embodiment of dangerous sex.

I asked some authors of vampire fiction what they thought, since they were in the business of keeping their audiences hooked. Stephen King, who wrote the 1975 *'Salem's Lot*, said, "Vampires live forever. They don't have steady jobs or punch a time clock. They can stay up all night and sleep all day. They enjoy a highly sexual nature in which impotency is never a threat, since their sexual urges are completely oral. For many of these reasons, vampires are particularly interesting to teenagers, who are sexually insecure and *very* interested in partying all night."

"Vampires are a link to an old-fashioned era," said Robert R. McCammon, author of the classic *They Thirst*, "but they're also a force that knows few limits. I think that appeals to people."

Ellen Datlow, who gathered vampire stories into an anthology called *Blood Is Not Enough*, explained her take: "Vampires have traditionally exuded sexuality and power, a mixture hard to resist. In recent years, the vampire in literature and film has developed from a creature ruled entirely by instinct and the need for blood into a complex being with an inner life. Sometimes evil, sometimes heroic, the vampire has become a romantic figure these days."

For Anne Rice, the appeal had a spiritual quality: "I think the vampire is a romantic, enthralling image. It's this person who never dies and who takes a blood sacrifice in order to live and exerts a charm over people; a handsome, seductive, alluring person who captivates us and then drains the life out of us. We long to be one of them, and the idea of being sacrificed to them becomes romantic."

3

As for an involvement deeper than just writing about fiction or interviewing authors, it started sporadically. I'd meet someone who had read one of my books and who wanted to talk. Or I'd get a letter. Usually these conversations lasted over the course of a few exchanges, but I filed the letters and thought more about the growing fascination with dark images. Particularly the vampire. I raised the issue with Rice, but her interest was rooted in mythology, not in real people who claimed to practice vampirism. I was on my own in that regard. I spoke to a few psychologists, but for the most part, the nascent vampire culture was fairly quiet. Rice was gaining steam as a best-selling writer, but that did not necessarily influence all of those who wanted to *be* vampires. Or victims.

I read the books that came out, watched films, collected more letters, and pondered what it was all about.

Then things shifted. Around 1991 White Wolf created a vampire game, "The Masquerade." They sent me their first game book, an elaborate presentation of vampire clans, legends, and game rules. The popular "Dungeons and Dragons" game had lost some steam and this was a wonderful new outlet for supernatural fantasy. People could pretend to be vampires, not just online or in some sort of intellectual format, but in person, dressed in whatever garb they desired, since vampires could span the world's entire history. There was no limit—other than the rules of the game—to what they could create for themselves and with one another. The game was to take off in a phenomenal way, and not just in America, but worldwide.

Whether or not game participants had initially been interested in vampires, they began to learn about what a vampire is . . . and what it could become. They created new dimensions as well, and began to reshape the vampire into something that met the needs of a new generation. Anne Rice's appeal increased, along with that of other authors who captured the vampire in historical scenarios, and all of that fed back like an eternal loop into the imaginations of the gamers.

Some of those who role-played a vampire became engrossed in the feeling of power and wanted it for real. They broke away and created a vampire lifestyle. Others who never got involved in the games, but who appreciated the opportunities afforded to make themselves known to kindred souls, formed vampire covens or coteries. Fantasy and reality mingled, with lots of crossover, though boundaries were set by the purists in each camp. That started some feuds.

All the while, other vampires exploited the media attention on those who dressed in costume and powdered their faces or splotched themselves with blood, to continue their own covert activities undetected. How do I know? Some of them have told me.

In short, over the span of a decade, vampire culture has grown from a handful of isolated individuals that a researcher in Queens, New York, managed to document in his files, to vast numbers of people whose appreciation for the vampire takes a multitude of forms. For me, it provided a way to access the psychological aspects via many routes, each providing its own message and none necessarily superior to any other. Susan Walsh's disappearance gave me the perfect way to get more deeply involved, and I made the decision to go to places I had never been. Whether someone wanted to drink blood or merely read about someone else drinking blood, whether someone wanted to exert a hypnotic influence over others or be the one to fall into the swoon, whether someone just wanted to be a vampire once a week and then put it aside or live the feeling of it with every breath, it mattered not to me. I was prepared to listen to the stories of vampires, donors, victims, experts, chroniclers, hunters, readers, writers, musicians, magicians, strippers, squatters, dominatrixes, role-players, criminals, divas, entrepreneurs, fetishists, conventioneers, and any other person who manifested some aspect of what I call vampire culture. It's as diverse a group as any subculture gets, and anyone who thinks that it's nothing but what the television news flashes on the screen at Halloween, or what the talk shows portray, is missing the richness and complexity of the responses that the vampire has generated in recent years.

So that's how I got my start, and when I began to follow in Susan Walsh's footsteps, I discovered things about this culture that I had never expected.

4

Back to my "offline" encounter. I'll call this vampire Diogenes, because he claimed to be seeking an "honest" experience. I wasn't sure what he meant by that, but it seemed to be about living on the edge. I had met him as Malefika and had told him I wanted to learn about the vampire experience. He'd invited me to be "screened." He resided in Manhattan, which made it easy, although I requested that our first meeting be at a place where I would feel safe. He suggested a restaurant, because he spurned the Goth-oriented clubs. Too noisy, he said, and not the kind of scene he wanted.

"How will I know you?" I asked.

"I have long black hair," he said, "and it's natural." He laughed, because in the vampire world more people dye their hair black than in the "normal" world, where blond is in vogue. "I'm about six feet tall. But I'll know you. Curiosity makes people stand apart from the mundane world."

On the appointed day, I went to the restaurant at around nine o'clock at night. Diogenes wasn't there. I turned to go wait outside and found him standing behind me. He was tall and when he smiled, I saw the fangs.

"Permanent," he said.

"Some dentist actually agreed to do that?" I asked.

He only smiled as if to say, "How convenient to be able to use a role-player's disguise these days." His eyes were dark, almost black, but I knew well enough that one could get contacts to achieve this effect. His voice came from the gut, deep and authoritative. I guessed his age to be around twenty-five, possibly thirty. He wore all black—black jeans and a black shirt unbuttoned halfway down his smooth chest. There was a hint of beard shadow on his face. If anyone was born to be a vampire, it was this guy.

We sat down across from each other at a table in a shadowed corner. He rested his hands together on the table in front of him. I pulled out a tablet for taking notes, and he said, "Not that way."

"But I want to get it right," I told him.

"You will," he assured me.

I shrugged. After telling him that I was interested in knowing more about his experience, he said, "I had a vampire mother."

"A real one?"

"What's real? She loved vampire stories and she thrived off of her children. I learned it from her."

"A psychic vampire, then?"

He shrugged. "Whatever."

"And your father?"

"He was in jail most of the time for some petty crime or other. Which was fine with us, because when he was around, he liked to take out his frustrations on us."

"Us . . . ?" I pressed.

"I have a sister. She's not a vampire. She's a nurse."

He went on to tell me a bit about his childhood, which was unremarkable, but replete with escape into supernatural fiction. I found it interesting that he did not try to convince me that he was really six hundred years old, could fly, and was immune to all diseases. It appeared that his vampirism was not framed in fantasy but was a real part of his life. He talked of how he'd first tasted blood at the age of ten, when he'd cut his wrist and that of a friend's for a ceremonial blood-oath, and he'd found that he enjoyed it. From there, he indulged with those with whom he became intimate, but it did not become a regular practice until lately, when he'd become part of a small circle. He did not want to describe their activities, he said. That was something I would have to see for myself.

As he spoke, his dark stare was unwavering. Unnerving. It was as if the irises of his eyes were all pupil. I'm sure he had no trouble drawing sexual partners, because sexual desire registers in the enlargement of the pupil, and the appearance here was that he was ever ready. Besides, he was attractive. *Really* attractive.

After half an hour, he stopped and asked, "Would you like me to drink your blood? So you can see what it's like? We could go somewhere right now."

Okay. First confrontation with this question. I wasn't prepared.

"How do you know I'm safe?" I asked, stalling.

He snorted. "What does it matter, really? Are you afraid? I thought you were interested in the Life."

"I'm just not sure yet that it's what I want to do. Or maybe you're not the right vampire. Could I see you do it with someone else first?"

He considered this as he stared at me.

"If you want to see more," he said, "meet me at the west end of Tompkins Square Park. I'll take you to the place where I . . . let's just say, *indulge*."

Tompkins Square Park. That's where the vampire squatters were, I'd heard. I wondered if he knew of them or if this was the group he was going to show me. He obviously wasn't homeless himself, but who knew the kind of people with whom he hung out?

He suggested a date and time a few weeks hence, and then rose from his seat with a Mona Lisa smile and walked out.

I figured I had time to learn more about this experience before he confronted me again, so I was relieved that we wouldn't meet right away. In fact, I was to experience quite a lot as I encountered a few more vampires in other ways before I had my next date with Diogenes.

CHAPTER THREE

vampires online

I

I continued to explore the vampire resources on the Internet. When I first did a search, I was astonished to find more than thirty thousand sites that mention vampires. There were chat rooms, journals, stories, essays, international sites, catalogs, guides, and links to games and author discussions. *Dark Shadows. Dracula.* Anne Rice. *Forever Knight.* Buffy. Vampirella. You name it, it was there. Angie McKaig even offered the "Pathway to Darkness Newsletter" to keep vampire fans up to date. I worked my way through many of these sites and found a lot of repetition, but a few stood out.

One site provided a list of the varieties of vampires, written by Virgil Greene, which included "the insane," real people who thought they were vampires; "cultists," or blood mystics; "the cursed," those who lived evil lives and became vampires; "the seduced," becoming a vampire to be with someone else; "victims," who become vampires automatically; the "diseased," from infected blood; mutants or aliens; and the vampires created by science or sorcery.

A "Nosferatu" site offered Goth databases, Black Pages, links to other Gothic sites, vampire fiction, music, and poetry, a "Necrophyle's Home Page," a link to "The Dark Side of the Net," a "Nightmare

Factory," and various other "Gateways to Darkness."

I liked the site that offered a "Vampire Probability Test," on which a real vampire might not get a perfect score, "but it should be high." Among the one hundred listed questions were: "Do you prefer the night?" "Do you like the sight of blood?" "Were you born over 120 years ago?" "Has a vampire ever bit you?" "Have you ever considered robbing a blood bank?" "When you wake up, do you often feel like you've risen from the dead?" "Have you ever been buried?" "Do you frequently get bloodstains on your clothes?"

It seemed to me that if you answered yes to these questions and *weren't* a vampire, you might have other problems.

If you get a high score, but don't view yourself as a full-fledged vampire, you can move on to the "Vampire Vulnerability Test": how vulnerable are you to *becoming* a vampire? If you test high, you might be a vampire without even knowing it! I didn't take the test, just in case.

More than a few sites promised to reveal the "full truth" about vampires. On one, there was a long essay on the modern vampire in which the writer insisted that vampires are everywhere, riding on the bus, teaching your children, shopping in the supermarket—perhaps even entering your home as a friend. They don't skulk through dark alleys at night, harm people, worship Satan, or drink blood. In fact, most vampires are nurturing and empathic.

Initially I was ready to dismiss this perspective, but it was the first of many opinions I was to hear that indicated a real shift in conscious-ness regarding vampires and the youth culture. These creatures were changing. Always malleable, they provided this new generation of vampire devotees with alternate possibilities. Now the vampire could walk in daylight, eat food, survive without drinking blood, eat garlic, steal souls, and display any number of other abilities heretofore beyond its reach. Vampires could have sex and raise families. Vampires were compassionate! Some believed vampires were not even immortal and could contract diseases. These were new traits, and taken alto-gether, made the vampire nearly unrecognizable to me. I didn't know if I liked these shifts, but I thought I'd better put aside my prejudices from an earlier generation and think about what they meant.

On another site, a full list of vampire traits was spelled out—bio-logical, spiritual, physical, and mental. By the time I was finished read-ing through all this material, and had moved on to other sites that completely contradicted it, I was thoroughly confused about what a "real" vampire is. I'd better hope to just meet one and ask. I thought about Diogenes and wondered if I'd get some answers when I saw him again.

I figured it was possible to lure a vampire into a discussion online, and when some friends challenged me, I showed them how. One evening, they met me in a room that I labeled "Realvamps." Within moments, a female vampire came in who said she was acquainted with only a few others of her kind. "One vampire knows another," she told us, "because we have a smell that others do not have. It's a musk-like smell." Okay, now we were learning something. She also said that vampires can eat food (but not processed cheese) and that vampire blood tastes much better than mortal blood, like fine wine compared to cheap wine. Being a vampire, she told us, was a genetic defect, but not one that anyone would notice physically. "My fangs do not show unless I choose for them to," she said, and admitted that there were days when she definitely wished she were not a vampire. She explained to us what fiction writers had wrong about vampires, like the idea that vampires are immortal or can turn into bats, and then insisted she must leave. We were about to close down when a vampire named "8rats" came in. I left my friends to entertain him.

Clearly, there were a lot more people now than ten years back claiming to be vampires and who had a context all worked out. They didn't need the supernatural trappings, but they wanted the vampire identity. My task was to listen to the various presentations and take seriously the message, even if some of the things they said seemed illogical or even silly. There was nothing silly about the longing within them that led them to this place.

2

Soon I found the Vampirism Research Institute, run by Liriel McMahon in Seattle, Washington. She had been profiled in a book called *Something in the Blood* by Jeff Guinn with Andy Grieser. She is a twenty-six-year-old "home-schooled volunteer for simplicity," who has worked as a computer technician. For several years, she had published the *Journal of Modern Vampirism*.

According to the information at her site, she conducts research through surveys, interviews, and correspondence, and does analysis by graphology, psychology, and astrology. "In essence, the VRI uses whatever method or source that best finds answers to the questions of Pseudo Vampirism." That is, she's not looking for information about mythological monsters, but about people who "display behavior associated with vampires: Blood-drinking, psychic or emotional draining, a preference for living at night or in the dark, vampiric relationships with others, etc."

I contacted her and she agreed to answer some questions.

"I'm interested in knowing why you started this organization," I said, "and what you've been able to do with the research you've collected."

"Most simply," she told me, "I started the VRI because I was curious. It seems to have really started when I stumbled onto a paperback copy of *Vampires Among Us*. I was looking to spend the first extra money I had from working at my first office job. What really caught my eye was that the book was in the nonfiction section at Target, and I was thinking, 'What is this? Something serious about vampires?' I picked it up and started reading right there, and after few moments I thought, 'Oh my God, I'm not the only one!'

"The thought of not being alone in my desire to become a vampire blossomed into a whole idea of finding out more about vampirism. I got inspired by Anne Rice's idea of the Talamasca—'We collect data; we correlate, cross-reference, and preserve information.' I also was inspired by Colin Wilson's works and those of Umberto Eco. In September of 1991, I wrote a declaration of foundation of the VRI, on lined paper and with a ballpoint pen, and stuck that paper on my bedroom wall. I've been doing research since that time."

I could just see her earnestly doing this very thing. "What do you do with it?" I asked.

"The research I've collected has provided insights into many areas of vampires and vampirism. I would like to think that the VRI could be useful to others who seek answers, especially if they're serious fans of the vampire, a victim of vampirism, and most especially self-proclaimed vampires."

"How did you come up with the questions for your survey?"

"They just occurred to me as being appropriate."

I found it amusing what she took for granted. How does one decide what's "appropriate" to ask vampires and their victims? It seemed so clear to her. Obviously, she hadn't gotten too entangled in the morass of conflicting claims about vampires throughout the Internet.

"Previous to starting the VRI," she continued, "I was a member of a Duran Duran fan club, called, I believe, the Secret Society of the 7th Stranger, based out of Wisconsin. In their newsletters they printed the members' questionnaires and I was fascinated with the differing answers to the same questions. I modified the format, along with advice from Dr. Jeanne Youngson and others, and then formed the first survey."

One thing I really wanted to know was about her choice of phrasing. "Do you find that some people are put off by the word *pseudo*? I know what you mean, but it does have pejorative connotations."

"Oh, I imagine a few professed vampires are put off by the term *pseudo-vampire*, and I've gone back and forth as to whether to keep using it or not. But there's been some confusion in those contacting me as to what I'm really researching. I am not researching real vampires, or in other words undead, night-dwelling creatures that drink blood as the only means of survival. Instead, what I'm researching is vampirism—people who claim to be vampires and to engage in vampire-like activities, but most plainly are not undead."

I liked her matter-of-fact approach: If you are undead, don't stop off here! "I take it from Guinn's book," I said, "that you consider yourself a pseudo-vampire. Is that true?"

"I used to. I was fifteen at the time, and it was actually after reading *The Vampire Lestat* [by Anne Rice] that I first was entranced with the idea of becoming a vampire. I would sit in my bedroom writing in my diary with candles burning and occasionally looking out my bedroom window. I'd sit there and realize that the world was a marvelous place and I wished I had the time to see it all. And how it would be so much easier if I was immortal and didn't really need to be dependent on others in order to see it all. I was drunk on the sensuality of Lestat's world. I most literally wanted to be him.

"Later on it became clear that real life doesn't work that way, at least not in the way of becoming something one is not ever going to be, like undead—how absurd to think that's physically possible! Emotionally undead, yeah, spiritually, that too; but physically undead? I just can't believe it could happen. That realization didn't fully dawn on me until 1991, and I was approaching the age of twenty. At that time the economics of living crept up on me and I kind of realized that I wasn't getting any closer to becoming Lestat. Then it dawned on me that Lestat didn't represent blood-drinking at all, he represented defeating adversity in the face of incredible odds. At least that's what I got out of being up close and personal with vampirism."

Liriel seemed so sweet in her declarations. Yet I knew people much older than she was at the age of twenty who still believed they would become Lestat. She seemed to have some common sense, anyway.

"You mention being sensitive to strong emotion," I remarked. "Others tell me the same. Do you find in your research any correlation between high sensitivity and attraction to vampires?"

"Certainly!" she responded. "Fictional vampires strike me as highly dependable creatures, predictable in the sense we know what they want. They want blood and a dark place to sleep during the day, and perhaps the occasional opportunity to use a mortal for some clearly defined purpose. From a Sensitive's point of view, it seems to me that humans are much more unpredictable. What they want is not only food, but good food; not only company, but pleasing company; not only love, but knock-you-on-your-ass love; and that opportunity to use other people—forget it, history books are riddled with the possibilities. It seems to me like there are too many undefined variables. On the other side of the coin, would someone who's highly insensitive be attracted to vampires? Yes, in the sense that a very self-centered corporate executive would be attracted to reading Alexander the Great's biography."

"Are there any other traits that stood out to you among people who responded to your survey?"

"In the broadest sense they are all individuals. That said, here are some interesting traits that I noticed in my last survey: most feel creatively inspired (81 percent) with a preference to write fiction (50 percent of the 81 percent); few feel they have low self-esteem (19 percent); most felt a close childhood relationship with their mothers (51 percent) as opposed to their fathers (37 percent); most have few regrets about the choices they've made in life (64 percent); and most are comfortable with their sexuality (82 percent). Those are just a few of the statistics that will be eventually published when the research is complete."

3

Liriel proved to be a great source, but looking for someone more clearly immersed in the vampire lifestyle, I found "Vampyres Only," run by Brad. I asked him to tell me about his site. It turned out he'd spent a lot of his free time working on it.

"Well, back in the late summer of 1994," he explained, "there wasn't much—if anything—of a vampyric presence on the Internet. There were some scattered files on FTP and Gopher sites, but nothing on the Web yet. It existed, but there wasn't much happening on it.

"I first started 'Vampyres Only' (VO) as a means for teaching myself HTML, and I figured if I was going to have my own site, I might as well make the subject interesting enough for me to want to design it. I was a fan of the shlocky Hammer Studios films, so I wanted to gather as much vampyre stuff as I could, and put it all in one place. My initial concept of the site was to have a main 'doorway' with a sign reading 'Vampyres Only,' much like an 'Employees Only' room in a restaurant. The name really stood for the content within; it wasn't meant to exclude 'breathers' by declaring this a site 'only for the Undead.' Because of the name, it was assumed that I, of course, was claiming to be a vampire. I thought I'd play along with it for a while, so I took the nickname Vlad III, after Vlad Tepes the Impaler [on whom Stoker had based Dracula]."

"What happens while you're running this site?" I asked. "Any interesting contacts?"

"One of the first e-mail discussions I was involved in was with a woman who claimed her boyfriend was a vampire. She had written a story which I had come across, and after contacting her, we ended up e-mailing back and forth. In one of her messages dated October 30, 1994, she said, 'I hesitated to become a vampire myself, because I am afraid. My friend told me that it can sometimes get very lonely. I don't want to become one unless I have another who will stay with me for a while. But now it has gotten to me. I want to become a vampire because I want more time to do all that I want in life.'

"I'm not one to refute anything unless it can be proven other-wise," Brad went on, "so her comments started to really interest me. However, after a short while, she no longer responded. Perhaps she got her wish? Anyway, it was after this conversation that I really dis-covered the power of the Internet—virtual anonymity. You have this e-mail account that was like a mask to hide behind, and it certainly helped open people up. This way, you could 'test the waters' with your ideas, with little personal embarrassment.

"It was pretty quiet for a while, and then in 1995, I received what is still one of my favorite e-mail messages, only because of its true bizarreness. I've edited it to cut out the more explicit parts:

"'i want your tongue to caress my ear tenderly i want to feel your breath, hot on my neck i want your hands to rip my clothes off my body as i scream then you will throw me over your shoulder as i am writhing to get out of your strong grasp i scream stop stop no i feel you inside me consuming me filling me with all of your being as our lust consumes the fire between us we come to climax of our embrace taking my opportunity i begin to suck on your neck feeling the warm flesh with my tongue i pull my head back opening my mouth baring the long sharp teeth which jab into your neck spilling the warm life down my cheeks in my mouth down my throat i have reached the end of my passion and . . .'"

"In a way," Brad said, "this message was much like the first, albeit a little more intense. Here we have two people expressing something online that they'd probably never do in real life. Although virtual anonymity has its downfalls, I believe its pluses have led to the ever expanding online vampire culture that we see today.

"As 1996 came around, VO got busier, and I eventually had to upgrade my account so I could allow for more hits to my site. I felt something big was happening, because the Web was being heard all over. The number of people using my online Guestbooks increased exponentially and this traffic spawned greater interest in my site, which made me want to continue to make it better. But it was getting time-consuming. Thankfully, a CGI programmer in California offered to help, and she's still with me today, along with another in the Midwest who handles all the user problems with the chat areas. We did have to introduce security, because more and more idiots were showing up in the chat areas, making trouble. I could only laugh off so many nasty messages before I questioned why I kept VO going. Then, just when I'm about to 'hang up my fangs,' I'll get a message like this, dated November 21, 1996. I call her Carmilla:

"'The Inn, or FC, has been a wonderful place for me to hide from . . . myself. I have met some wonderful friends there. Through these meetings, I have come to grow and change . . . for the better. Many, while sweet and enjoyable to talk to, are only acquaintances . . . not so close. We remain "Vampyres" . . . dark, and unknown to one another . . . but that is enough for each. You, my dear . . . I trust, admire, and appreciate . . . for all you have given me, probably without knowing. Sort of the vampyric nature of the net . . . feeding off of one another to sustain oneself . . . gaining nourishment from friendship! Does that sound horrible? I do not mean for it to, because I believe this relationship is mutual to all who come to the Inn . . . searching for something, usually companionship. I am finally finding my way again. I was quite unhappy for a very long time. Now that I have found some direction, I have purpose, and perform all aspects of my life with more enthusiasm and hope. You must receive many letters from those who find your place. I am sure this opens up many roles for you which you did not necessarily bargain for . . . Father confessor, teacher, mediator. You have always been most gracious to me, and I appreciate you more than you know.'"

Brad was obviously moved. "I don't think I could sum up the online culture any better than Carmilla did," he admitted. "I'm not quite sure if the word *phenomenon* fits, but it will have to do for now. I tend to downplay the significance of my site, especially since there are now hundreds of vampire Web sites out there. But I still think it's pretty unique, and every now and again, just when I feel that I can't stand to keep it going, the same day I'll get a message like Carmilla's, and I'll be good for another six months.

"It's been four years, over 260,000 hits and 36 awards and articles later, and VO is still going. Our conversation areas have over 360 subscribers, a far cry from the half dozen back in 1994 (although some are still around today). And even though there is not one spot on VO where I claim to be a vampire, I still get about one request a month asking me to turn that person into one. I think you actually have to spend some time online before you can really grasp the vampire culture here. It's like nothing else anywhere in the real world."

4

I did exactly as Brad suggested, and checked out many of these vampire chat rooms. Often I came away with a sense that the actual content of what was said was irrelevant. Most of it was repetitive and quite often no one even mentioned vampires. But they did seem to know one another, greeting each entering person with cyber hugs and kisses. Clearly, there was a community, shared in the spirit of the vampire.

Yet in one chat room, I got a real shock. I came in and saw names like Riverstyx, Soulchains, and Vampyrhuntr. Several people were discussing Anne Rice's vampire characters as if they really existed. Louis, Lestat, Marius. They tossed these names around as if referring to old buddies. Two of the participants insisted they wanted to meet them. Then someone mentioned *my* name—Katherine Ramsland.

"Yeah, she's one of them," said another. "One of the Immortals. She knows Louis and Lestat. You can tell from her writing."

The others agreed that I was probably a vampire, sitting around somewhere with those boys, discussing the vicissitudes of immortality.

I wish.

5

A site created by someone called NiteTrain drew me. It turned out that he presented two sides of himself—NiteTrain and WidowMaker—and he had an unusual story to tell about his journey into vampirism that drew on several different mythologies, such as the Lost Continent of Atlantis, and the Jekyll/Hyde personality split.

"So you want to know my story?" he writes on the site. "Well it's a long one indeed, and would include several volumes of literature. I shall give you the condensed version. I am Vampire. Although I can probably guarantee you've never met nor heard of one such as I. When was I born? I can't really recall myself, it was so long ago. And due to the different calendars to spring up over the last hundred centuries, plotting an exact time is difficult. I will tell you though, it was approximately 20,000 years ago, give or take a few centuries. A great continent once occupied a major portion of the north Atlantic region, and a considerable portion of its southern basin. It was never named, probably due to the fact it is no longer there. I was born there. I was born into a great society. Only now, thousands of years later, is mankind approaching the quality of living and technology we were at.

"I lived to the age of 124, and then died of natural causes. During the course of my life, I had done much work in the area of genetic manipulation, and gained much recognition in the process. I remember my death. I left the physical world, and began my journey to the after life. Mere moments after entering what you mortals would now term Purgatory, a spirit snatched me up. The spirit took me into itself, and transformed me forever. I was then and forever one of the Vampyric Spirit. WidowMaker was born. I spent around 200 mortal years in the spiritual planes, learning from my creator. I learned there were but ten of us, including myself. We roamed all areas of existence and fed on the life of others. Not blood, mind you. I was then in the spiritual realms. We fed on everything. Fear, love, hate, and the energy essence of spiritual beings themselves. And then I was taught I could return to the mortal world whenever I wished. My heart had long lusted for a return to the flesh."

He describes how he was born into several incarnations and gained more enlightenment with each. Yet he had to deal with his other side.

"It was as if there were two beings within me. And WidowMaker was definitely the violent one. He would come out and wreak havoc. He developed a lust for blood. For blood is the essence of life. I spent the next one thousand years learning to control WidowMaker. And to this day, he is not totally under control, just subdued. He only comes out when I am angered."

He goes on to discuss some historical events that he witnessed and then says, "The only way you might spot me is by my eyes. They are always changing color. I love the sunlight. My kind is not denied it. For the majority of my incarnations, I must admit, I have chosen to be male. I was originally born male. And the mortal female can be oh so seductive and alluring."

His evil counterpart has this to say: "I am the malevolence that lies within every soul. I am the part of existence that all fear. Brought to the surface by a fellow Vampyric Spirit, I will not be tamed. I feed on your fears. I will hunt you, stalk you, feed upon you. I will do as I please.

"NiteTrain is weak. He insists upon looking for the good in mortals, where I see them only as to serve me. NiteTrain believes he can live among them, as an equal, whereas I know they are inferior to me. My passions drive me. My desires damn me. I am evil incarnate. NiteTrain can never suppress me. It is I who will suppress him. My enemies fall before me. You will not defeat me."

I decided to contact the person behind the persona to see how much of it he actually believed. He responded that he did not give interviews to the media, but he knew my other books and so he would consider it. A week later, he told me part of his story via e-mail, and while there was some overlap with what he told on his site, there were also some real differences. His name was Charles and he lived in the Southwest. He expressed distaste for the way the vampire image has been romanticized and popularized. Then he told me the following:

"Since my birth into this body on July 6, 1972, I have been haunted by visions, and I've always had an overwhelming sense of intuition. I was born an empath, who can sense the emotions and feelings of those around him.

"In February of 1994, I decided that my work in this world had ended, and I determined to take my own life. Understand that this choice was not made out of desperation, depression, or of any factors surrounding my life at that time. It was simply the desire to move on. I took ninety-eight sleeping pills. I did die. I left the physical world and entered a portion of the spiritual. My entry was blocked by a soul I know I had always known. Only now, in this spiritual realm, did I finally, once again, understand everything.

"I was a vampire. Not as portrayed through literature, movies, or television, but one of spiritual nature. This explained my empathic abilities. I had had several existences in the flesh. I moved through the physical world and fed on the emotions and desires of those around me. I also learned there was another, such as myself, waiting for me on earth, although she was unaware of me or of her true abilities.

"With this, I plunged back into my body. I searched, and three years and three months later, I found her, on the opposite side of the continent. Within a week, I left my home and went to where she was. There is an undeniable link that holds us together. As time progresses, I will show her more of her abilities."

He included his phone number in this note, so I called him. He asked that I use his nickname, Chuck.

"Everyone who has contacted me has done it for exploitation, like talk shows or local news," he told me. "I've had television shows use my home page without permission. I'm annoyed by a lot of it. I'm not looking for attention, and I'm concerned that the vampire image is losing its value."

I understood what he meant, but I was more interested in his personal circumstances. "How do your friends react to your story?"

"My friends don't usually believe me, or if they do, they just accept it as me. But I met this woman—my soul mate—and she stayed with me for four days and then left. Five days passed and I went to her and have been with her ever since."

"But before that all happened, I would just blank out and have visions. Sometimes I knew what they meant and sometimes I didn't. It was always the future or something that was going on in someone's life around me. My mother and grandmother are both very spiritual. From my earliest days, they would talk to me about it. They're big into [the spiritualist] Edgar Cayce. My grandmother moved to Sedona [a town in Arizona considered to have great spiritual power] because of the energy she feels there. I had just been there on a visit, and soon thereafter met my soul mate, who was from Arizona."

"What made you think she was your soul mate?" I asked.

"At first it was difficult. I saw her and knew, but things were in the way. She was married. She lived far away. I fought it for a long time and no matter what I did, it just came back. There was no denying it. She felt the energy, too. We both have a dark side and are very spiritual. We share things that normal people don't share. We feel whatever the other one feels."

"But that sounds romantic," I interrupted, "and yet you say the vampire shouldn't be a romantic figure."

"What I mean is that it's become pop culture and the fascination is the romance and the Goth style. They're seeing only one side of it."

"What's the other side?"

"It's different for everybody. For me, it's all spiritual. It doesn't have to do with blood. It doesn't have to do with eternal life. It's how you relate. It's your eternal soul."

"What makes that vampiric?"

"I'm different than other vampires you'll talk to. For me it's all about energy."

"You're a psychic vampire?" I was seeing this idea on numerous Web sites and I'd made a note to explore it more fully.

"No," Chuck responded. "That's not what I mean. For example, when I'm with this woman, I don't require sleep, or if I do, it's only an hour a day. When I'm not around her, I need eight hours. I've gone weeks around her with very little sleep, but she doesn't get tired. I don't actually take from her. We share it. We create it. The body limitations fall away when we're together. Everything's about energy with me. People don't realize how powerful it is when you can totally focus yourself and shut off the world around you. You can do anything."

"On the day you took the sleeping pills and died, did anyone know?"

He acknowledged that, yes, someone found him, and despite what he'd said in his letter, he admitted that, indeed, it was partly a response to a bad point in his life. "I was twenty-two. I was a little depressed. I was staying with a friend and just decided to do that because I wanted to move on, and he found me. After I'd gone back into my body and was making a lot of noise trying to walk, he asked me what I had done and I remember thinking that I wasn't going to tell him. I tried to lie, but I was too drugged to lie and I gave him the box and he took me to the hospital and called my parents. I was in the ER for a couple of hours and then in the hospital for two or three days.

"There is no easy way to die. No matter how you do it, it's very painful. I can remember it. I had taken pills because I thought it would be easier on my body. Then you lay there and you know you're going to die and there's nothing you can do. I felt my body start to shut down, piece by piece. I just felt heavier and heavier. After ten minutes, I was totally paralyzed, but still conscious. And every part of my body hurt. That went on for ten minutes before I died. It was like being in outer space, but not. There was blackness and pinpoints of light, millions of lights and millions of voices. I could hear them all, but I *couldn't* hear them. It was there, but I couldn't go all the way. I was being held back, and that's when I was reminded of what I am.

"It's like going into the light, the way people describe, but it wasn't like I walked into it. I was drawn, pulled into this place, and I think it was an earthbound spiritual realm. It's hard to explain. It's a 360-degree image, like being on the ocean. It's all around you."

"Were you afraid?" I asked.

"No, not by then. I wasn't afraid when I was dying. It was just unstoppable, a point of no return, and that does something to you."

"How has it changed you?"

"I don't drink anymore. I don't take drugs. I don't sleep around. I quit a lot of things. It cleared my head. It showed me what I could do with my mind. Thoughts are very powerful, and I could think people around me into doing things that I wanted them to do."

That got me interested. "Can you make *me* do something?"

He was silent a moment. I waited, but didn't feel anything different. Then he said, "It has to be a desire that I really want. The connection between me and this woman is so strong that while we're having sex I can think to her, 'orgasm,' and she will. Or if she has pain, I can touch her and make it go away."

"But you were empathic before this happened. Is it more enhanced?"

"Yes. I could be in pain if I was near someone in pain, but I have it under control now. And the more linked you are with others, the more powerful your senses are."

I then changed the subject. "Do you ever encounter others who call themselves vampires?"

"A lot of people. It's my opinion that there are over one hundred different kinds of vampires on this earth. All are very different."

That surprised me. "How do you come up with that?" I asked.

"They're each unique. There's not one vampire. There's not one race. There is the spiritual kind, that I know I am, and there are the kinds that desire blood. They're all different. I have trouble explaining it. There are vampires in the Carpathian Mountains and those are totally different from vampires you'll find in other parts of the world. It's like different races of humanity, I suppose. It's pop culture now, and a lot of people want to be vampires, but I did meet one real vampire when I was twenty-one. She alluded to it without saying it. She was darker than I desired to be. She was into drinking blood, and I let her do that. She was real. For so many others, it's just a game. You know when they're bullshitting you."

Chuck's opinions seemed pretty well formed, as if his identity as a vampire meant a lot to him. I thanked him for his story and moved on.

6

After NiteTrain, I went through the contents of one site after another. I most enjoyed the sites that extrapolated a bit, such as Sabine's "Vampire White Pages." (She didn't like to define herself in depressing colors, so she made her classified Yellow Pages—called the more vampiric Red Pages or Black Pages by others—into White Pages.) When she designed an Internet site, she asked herself, "What do vampiric people want the most?" The answer seemed to be, "To know that they aren't alone in how they feel." So she decided to set up a way for vampires online to contact one another.

She created links for "Vampires Seeking Vampires," "Mortals Seeking Vampires," "Vampires Seeking Teachers," and "Common Bonds." Whoever wanted to could become e-mail pen pals. She also listed numerous businesses, publications, and clubs that catered to vampiric tastes.

There were many vampires seeking other vampires on the list. Most of them were role-players who named their clan from the popular vampire role-playing game, "The Masquerade." For the most part, I was sure this was all quite safe, but there had been a news report in March 1997 about the arrest of an Air Force man who allegedly had lured a fourteen-year-old to meet him from an Internet vampire chat room. It reminded me that the desperation with which some people seek companionship can make them vulnerable.

"Vampires Seeking Teachers" interested me, so I went to see if anyone had signed in. There were about twenty-five "lonely immortals who yearned for guidance."

"I am a vampire," one of them said. "I've turned [made a vampire of] one of my friends and don't know what to tell him."

"Please help me," said one young woman. "I don't know if I can go on any longer without help."

"I'm not sure if I'm a vampire or not," said another. "I hate not knowing what I am and where I belong."

Apparently, it wasn't so easy to find someone who actually offered to teach others the ways of vampirism. There were many people seeking teachers, but not many master vampires seeking protégés. Eventually, however, I did locate a "vampire" who offered lessons.

7

I'm tempted to call him Yoda for his enigmatic manner, but he called himself Vergil. I assumed he meant that he was the guide into the Inferno. He was a clean-cut man who looked to be in his late twenties, with brown hair and eyes. He asked that I not mention here how I found him, as he liked to be approached only by those who worked at it. He said he's given instruction to several people, both male and female, but he found young males to be the best students because they were eager for the eroticism. He liked to put two males together who were not gay, to heighten the tension. He also knew of females who could mentor a young vampire, and he agreed to tell me about one of his own encounters with eager young seekers.

"The boy was twenty," he said, "and had implored me to meet

him. He had sturdy shoulders and biceps like knotty pines. His black eyes were set deep and there was the slightest hint of adolescent fuzz sprouting along his jawline. He was articulate, but ended nearly every sentence with 'It's all good.' That seems to be the catchphrase of the youth these days. They just don't know that it's *not* all good. He said to me, 'I want you to make me into a vampire like you.'

"'How do you know I'm a vampire?' I asked him, wondering if he knew the difference between role-players and real blood-drinkers.

"'I know,' he said. 'I've been told you're the best. That you could share with me the mystery of my blood.'

"He spoke the truth. I could share the mystery of blood, but I had some reservations. 'He's so young,' I thought to myself. 'What have I to do with setting a youth on the road to destruction?' While I pondered this, there was a knock at the door.

"The boy, Kyle, said he was expecting a friend whom he'd told he'd be there learning the truth about being a real vampire. My heart fluttered at the notion of another young soul—two of them together. It was more than I'd hoped for. I dismissed my concerns about their youth and looked forward to the adventure."

"That's all it takes for you to dismiss your moral responsibility?" I asked, a bit incredulous.

"Apparently so. Kyle opened the door to his friend, who sauntered in, wearing a cocky grin. Extending a hand, he said, 'I'm Chance and I am honored to meet you, sir.' Then he kneeled and kissed my wrist. A nice entrance, albeit a bit overplayed. 'I hope you don't mind my dropping in like this,' he said. 'I was told that you are the only one to whom one may apply for the truth about being a vampire.'

"'Both of you boys stand against the wall,' I commanded. When they obeyed, I said, 'Now . . . there's much to the life of the true vampire. Real vampires do not advertise that they are vampires. The real vampire consumes what he needs from others without detection. Vampires live behind the veil, beneath the mask. I'm not the one to give you the answers. This must come from within each true vampire, for each creates himself. Real vampires aren't made by others, but born from within.'

"After I made my speech, I ordered each boy to undress the other, slowly and with sensual movements. They were a bit hesitant, which excited me. As the two stood naked facing each other, they grew more excited. I sat in a chair and watched the energy pass between them. I didn't know if they had any preference for their own gender, but I suspected that they'd go along with anything that got them worked up. I said, 'Now you are to touch each other as you would be touched, each in turn stroking the flesh of the other as though you were caressing your own skin. In this way, you will begin to move inside of one another, into the psyche, and learn sensuality.'

"I paused while they hesitated, and then started. Chance made the first move with a delicate swipe of a fingertip over the crest of Kyle's chest. Kyle quivered. I was enthralled at the play unraveling before me, a theater of lust.

"After a few minutes of exploring each other's bodies, I interrupted: 'Now, Chance . . . reach behind you and take the knife in your hand. I want you to gently slice into Kyle's left thigh, then slide your tongue along the surface and drink from him.' Chance did as he was told, passing the blade deftly but superficially through the moist flesh, and licked at the bright red drops. Then Kyle took the knife and, without being told, opened a shallow canal along Chance's neck and bent over to suck the pooling blood. The act excited them, but before they could play it out any further, I quietly moved alongside them and whispered, 'Now you have started your walk towards a life of true vampirism, each learning to provide what the other needs in order to feed. Likewise, you must provide what your victim needs so that he can please you and quench your thirst. The bonding of your lives tonight sets you apart as fluid feeders of the night, hunters who harvest from the lost and devour from the proud.'

"I then left them there alone, aware of having fed a passion that could easily consume their hearts. I'm sure they stayed there and explored each other further, but all they'd needed was someone to sanction for them the blood ceremony. I went home thinking about my own passions, and the dark secrets of the vampire's life that have consumed me."

"What do you mean?" I asked. "You had regrets?"

"Some. I hunger for this experience, but when it's over, I wonder how wise it is to turn young people toward it. I don't know what those boys will do now. Maybe that was enough for them. Or maybe they'll do someone harm. No teacher can know what the students will do with the power he gives over into their hands."

"I'm sorry," I interrupted, "but I think that's a cop-out. You're not exactly teaching them math."

He shrugged. "I don't do this often. I may never do it again. But of those I've turned out into the world, I know that some may be using their gift in a negative way. It's not a question of *wanting* to turn boys on to vampirism. It is only that I feel no conflict in responding to seekers. These boys are looking for alternative spiritualities to bring substance and meaning to their boring lives. They are checking out the vampire now and they're going to walk that way until they're tired. If I'm sought out in this way, I will assist in a reasonable manner. They are not going to be dissuaded at this juncture, so I offer a healthy approach balanced with cogent warnings. I have found that you can almost never alter a GenXer's momentum. I think it is best to walk beside and steer it. This is how I've tried to respond. I left them with warnings. They'll have to choose their own path. I think I provide a moral compass, even though some would say that I should convince them to abstain. But this isn't a realistic approach with GenX vampiric obsession."

I had to admit that, to some extent, he was right. As a college professor, I'd encounter so many people in their twenties and thirties who despaired of having any sense of direction and who wanted to experiment with anything that promised a transformative experience. Certainly, the vampire image did that. But I still felt uneasy about vampire mentors teaching kids how to cut themselves and surround their blood-drinking with an aura of sexual excitement. I knew from extensive reading on the subject that this is the way that serial killers who also drank from their victims described it.

8

I also wandered through the various chat rooms that seemed to have dark themes—Goth sites, "cemeteries," vampire taverns. As I perused the listings I noted such shared online interests as "Amputee Love," "Southern Subbies," "Favorite Mutilations," and "Jedi Cantina."

I entered a vampire room and looked through the profiles of the people involved. Some claimed to be vampires, while others either wanted to be transformed or had broad-ranging Gothic interests. One of them, who said he was a real vampire, noted in his profile that to give a name to himself would be like describing the face of death. "Life," he wrote, "is a road that runs to nowhere but a dead end."

I found chat rooms for vampire fans of all types, and through one I discovered private classes for learning about what vampires really are. I requested a "seat" and was given the name of the room in which the class would meet, late on a Saturday night. A woman who called herself Seeker, Kitty, and Night Poe (among other names) sent me the first notice.

"Welcome to Vampires 101," she told me. "Beginning next Tuesday you shall receive a lesson once a week that will deal with the separate races of Vampires. The information is derived either from my personal friendships with Vampires or extensive research conducted by myself and the staff of the VAL. The first three classes will cover Classicals, Inheriters, and Nighttimers."

Ah. I'd heard these names before on the Vampire Access Line. The VAL. Now I had some context. These people were in Manhattan.

"Classicals," she went on, "are anyone who says they are a Vampire, immortal and are dead, or undead and made a Vampire by one who was already a Vampire. Inheriters are anyone who says they are a Vampire and born into their lifestyle, usually immortal, meaning either unable to actually die or living a tremendously long life span compared to human life spans. Nighttimers are a sort of genetically altered human. Vampires, for the most part, consider us humans, humans consider us Vampires. We do not consider ourselves Vampires. We are not immortal in the usual sense of the word, but we do live longer than humans, look much younger than our years, and have many of the same problems as Vampires.

"We will cover all three in detail. Please feel free to save the lessons.

"For those who are new to these boards, I am Night Poe, your teacher. I am a Nighttimer. I teach 'Vampire/Humanism,' 'Psychic Self-Development,' 'Psychic Defense,' and 'Thought Projection.' I host my own TV show on public access cable TV in New York and I direct the Vampire Access Line.

"I am not, by any means, a leader. I am not the end-all authority on anything, especially Vampires. I do not presume to speak for all on these Boards. It is not my intention to try. I am simply a teacher; I speak truths. If you wish to listen, if you wish to learn, I am here to serve you. If you do not wish to learn, do not waste our time . . . and go in peace. This class is not a forum or a debating parlor. If you wish to disagree or make comment you are most welcome to do so.

"Four of you in this class are Vampires. If they wish to make themselves known, they are free to do so but it is not a requirement. There is one Genetic Vampire, two Classicals, and at least one Inheriter in this class now, and one who says they are not a Vampire [that would be me], but I have my doubts [about me?]. I think there are two Inheriters here. Enough said. Join us Tuesday when we begin on Classicals."

I sent a note to her asking how many there were of these various types of vampires. She told me three thousand in the tristate area, and seven thousand worldwide. She herself was married to a Classical, whom she had met in her own chat area. She told me that the Real Ones had divided New York City into several areas, and that there was a lot of rivalry and betrayal among the various vampire factions. She warned me about role-players and fakers, and told me not to fall into the wrong hands. She also said that no real vampire would "turn" me. If that's what I was after, I'd be disappointed. She was sure I didn't know what a true vampire is, so I said I'd be happy to take the courses.

Five of us were present for this revolving class, consisting of half a dozen lessons across six weeks. Seeker, a.k.a. Night Poe, conducted the class. Her Web site online showed a photo of her as a youngish woman with long black hair, although she claimed to be in her sixties.

She began by drilling us in the information we had received earlier about the various types of vampires. No one answered, so she began to call on us, just like a teacher in a junior high class. Eventually we were allowed to ask questions, so I ventured one about the illogic of something that had been said in the papers she had sent beforehand, and was immediately silenced.

"My question made sense," I insisted. "If they are *made* into vampires, they cannot start as vampires."

"And why not?" Seeker asked.

"If they are already vampires, why would they then be made into vampires?"

"If an Inheriter came from both parent vampires, then they could indeed. Only Classicals are made."

"But are all Classicals already vampires?"

"There are several races of vamps," she said, as if that closed the case. "Now, who has read the information on Nighttimers?"

I was puzzled. She had completely sidestepped my question.

"Nightvision," she said to another student, "you tell the class the difference between Classicals and Nighttimers."

There was some banter among the participants—not very serious or informed. When no real answers were forthcoming, I said, "Nighttimers have only consensual feeding partners." I was a good student.

Seeker seemed impatient with that. "But there is a more basic difference," she said.

"Nighttimers don't live as long—only a tenth as long."

"Well," piped up Hadit, another student, "do you mean a tenth as long as a vamp or as a human?"

"As a vamp."

"How long does a vamp live?"

"Okay," said Seeker, interrupting us and directing us back to the issue of essential differences, "then why is that?"

"Nighttimers are not as physically strong?" I ventured.

"If you had read the classes you would know."

Whoops. Wrong answer.

"Vampires live to different time spans," she hinted.

"It's a genetic malfunction from crossbreeding," I offered, but I was getting tired of this review. I couldn't see the point. I wanted to learn something more than was in the notes.

Seeker went on to tell us that Nighttimers have actual vampire blood DNA structure in their cells but it is vastly weaker than true vampires. She herself had been tested and irregularities had been found in her blood. Hadit wanted to know more about that, but abruptly, the class ended. Seeker was ready to quit. She told us to read about Genetics, PsiVamps (Symbiotics), and sexual vampires. Yet I still had questions. I remained online while the others signed off and I found myself alone with her.

I used the opportunity to ask about the New York scene and she said that someone would screen me to see if it was appropriate to bring me further into the vampire community. She would not say much about this person, only that he was the "overseer" for the tri-state area. Since that was a dead end, I decided to see if Seeker had ever heard of Susan Walsh. I was startled when she said she had. That got my interest. I was back on my original track.

"We were good friends, but she disappeared," Seeker told me. "I knew her lover, too. We run 'missing person' announcements for her on our show."

"Is her lover a vampire?"

"Yes, a psychic vampire."

I remembered. The one who had written the article I'd read.

"Do you have any ideas about what happened?" I asked.

"I know exactly what happened and what is still happening."

"What? You mean someone has her somewhere? She's alive?"

She declined to discuss it. There was still an ongoing police investigation, she said, so she didn't want to say anything, but she did assure me that the vampire community was not involved. "At first the police thought she was murdered and everyone was investigated, even me. They took the article that Susan was writing—but there's a copy of it in a shop in Soho."

I asked a few more questions, but she stood firm, like many others with whom I'd spoken. I finished the rest of the courses, but we never had another opportunity to discuss Walsh. I did go to the shop that Seeker had mentioned, but didn't find the article. It reminded me, however, that I needed to contact the guy who ran the vampire theater. He, too, had known Susan Walsh.

9

It was two o'clock in the morning when the phone rang. Several months into my study, I was feeling more nocturnal, staying up later and later in order to be included in this vampire world. These people were doing things mostly at night and when they wanted to talk to me, they expected me to answer the phone at any hour. And I always did.

"Hello?" I asked, trying to sound as if I was awake and would certainly never consider hitting the sack till the sun peeped under my shades.

"I went to the boardwalk looking for a boy," said a quiet, male voice. "Not just any boy, but a boy with searing blood. It had to be that. It's a hot night down here."

It was him. The guy who'd signed his cryptic e-mail with "W." I was sure of it from the way he just plunged in, as if he knew that I knew him. And what a voice! Sexy, throaty, with a soft accent that I couldn't quite place, but thought it could be Virginia or even Georgia. I decided in that moment to call him Wraith, because he came and went like a spirit, but there was something more sinister in his approach than that of a mere ghost.

"Down where?" I asked, hoping to pin him to a location.

He ignored the question. "When I walked into this bar, I felt a strong sense of nostalgia. It was where I first met *him*. Christian."

"Christian? Who's Christian?" I asked. I wondered if it was the Christian associated with Susan Walsh.

"I'll tell you later," he whispered, as if we were in some kind of conspiracy. "This bar is a cool hangout for vampires, or at the very least . . . for blood-curious boys."

"Blood—" I wanted to explore that, but he continued.

"I saw a pretty boy sitting at the bar sipping a Coke. He was young, too young to drink. Probably sixteen. Studying him for a few minutes before leaping, I walked over and introduced myself. I said, 'I'm your friendly vampire. Interested in giving blood this evening?'

"He laughed and said, 'Hi, I'm Ricky. Depends on where you take it from.' He was ready. He was easy. I told him I'd do whatever he'd like. So I bought him another Coke and we started talking. I could see he was excited. He kept pulling and squeezing at his crotch. We left together and slipped around the bandshell, stepping downstairs and out of sight into the shadows. It was dark and he was breathing heavy, a little frightened, I thought. He sat there while I used a sharp little knife to slit the flesh behind his ear and reassured him that I would not hurt him. The blood trickled slowly, too slowly for my taste. I made a deeper wound and his blood began to run from his neck. I sucked and sucked, kissing his neck and ear. He went into a swoon, and I knew I could do whatever I wanted. I reached down and used my free hand to caress him. He got increasingly excited. As I finished with his neck, making sure the wound clotted, I leaned down to suck him hard and fast, so he'd know the total excitement of the blood. To get the most from it, you know, it must be mixed with sex. We finished up and he asked me when he could see me again. He wanted me to come over the next night and slip through his bedroom window after his parents had gone to bed. Like a vampire. I took his number and told him I'd call."

I was nearly breathless at his description. "And did you?" I asked.

"No. I just let him believe I would. It's the anticipation, you know. That's part of it. But there's never any guarantee, and once I've conquered them, I'm not interested anymore. I leave them with the longing."

"Do they think they become vampires?"

"Sometimes. If it's hot for them to believe that, I let them."

"You let them?"

"I'm whatever they want me to be. Whatever makes the experience the best it can be. I enter their fantasies."

I had an opportunity now, so I grabbed it.

"How did all of this start?" I asked. "When did you first decide to drink someone else's blood?"

He was silent for a minute. Then, to my surprise, he decided to give me an answer. He told me about a group of children he'd played with growing up.

"We played every day together, all of us, especially during the summers. My best friend was Terry. We were inseparable. When all of us hung out together, Terry and I always paired off. In fact, I considered Terry to be my brother. He was fourteen and I was ten, but we shared the same dreams and fantasies.

"Terry was devilishly cute with sun-streaked blond hair and gracious green eyes. His nose and lips were small, but perfect. My favorite parts were his arms. They were thick and strong, bronzed flesh stretched across rippled muscles. He could lift me off the ground with one arm. I would wander over to his house in the evenings after supper and just wait for him.

"We'd run across the road and into the swamp-woods, hunting for signs of trespassers in 'our' woods. The trails were covered with thick vines, rope-like strings hanging from the tops of trees—and we loved to swing on them.

"One day while we were playing in the woods, all of us decided to take a swim. We stripped naked and climbed to the top of an abandoned crane, slid down the cable, and swung ourselves into the murky green water. It was late in the afternoon when me and Terry huddled up in the crotch of an old oak tree after a day of swimming. He was playing with his pocket knife, pretending that he was going to cut off the lucky wart that was home just inside of his right thigh, when the knife slipped and Terry sliced off not only the wart, but a ripe chunk of his leg. Without thinking, I bent over and began to suck the wound, licking the blood and swabbing the exposed flesh with my tongue. Terry looked surprised, but he was relieved. I asked, 'Does it hurt?' and he said, 'No . . . not at all. What are you doing?'

"'Nothing,' I said, 'just licking the blood off.' Terry asked me if the blood tasted good and when I told him it did, he suddenly leaned over and kissed me. Our tongues locked. When he pulled away, he said, 'Yeah, I do taste good.' Then he unzipped his pants and started playing with himself. I was amazed at his breathing. It looked like he was having some kind of heart attack. Then he started pissing on me. I loved the warm sensation running all over my body. He started to moan, then shot lines of hot, white fluid onto my chest. I felt really close to him at that moment.

"We made a pact never to reveal the true nature of our relationship, and began to meet for regular blood exchanges. Our second time together, Terry made a thin slice in his arm and asked me to drink it. I did. Soon we were sticking sewing pins into our groins and sucking each other's blood. It wasn't long before I was hooked on the taste of it, and so was Terry.

"Our most daring and intimate sharing came when Terry slit his wrist with a razor blade. All of the times before were just small amounts of blood, like what would come from a minor cut or scrape. Now we wanted to drink more directly from each other. I put my mouth to his wrist and sucked gently, as I had learned by then not to create too much vacuum. It hurt when I did. I can still remember how it felt to taste his blood—it was so delicious to me, hot and silky in my mouth. Terry had his cock out and he came while I was drinking from him, but then he got very light-headed, so I stopped.

"Me and Terry played around like this until he moved to New York when I was about fourteen. The day he left Terry hugged me and whispered in my ear, 'I will always love you.' I still cry when I remember that moment—how he smelled when he nuzzled against my ear, the press of his lips quietly to my neck. I will never forget him. He was the beginning of my vampire experience. But there were others. I'll tell you about them sometime. I'll have to tell you about Eric."

"I want to meet you," I said.

He hesitated and then said, "I don't think you should."

"Why not?"

"Because . . . because I . . . I think maybe I'm sick."

"Sick? Sick how?" Now I was alarmed. The big question that always popped up in vampire culture was the question of AIDS. How do they avoid it? Aren't they afraid?

"Sometimes I think I'm sick. I can't really tell. But I think my destiny is . . . eventually . . . to go mad. I know it, but I don't want you to make me see it in your eyes that *you* know. Sometimes I'm afraid. I'm not always sure what I will be or do in someone's presence. I don't know what I might do to you."

Okay, this sounded serious. Personal, even. But I wasn't willing to let go. "Well, we could meet in a safe place."

"Well lighted?" I heard the sarcasm in his voice, as if to say vampires don't go into the light.

"Well, a dark restaurant or a bar. Something public."

"You don't know me yet. You shouldn't ask. It could be more dangerous than you think. I'm always reinventing myself in order to survive. I can live this way among normal people as a tolerated outsider, playing into their projections. I can become whatever they want me to be. They're easily charmed. I always change in order to prey. And my prey want that."

That scared me a little. I wondered if anyone had spoken to Susan Walsh like that. Tried to lure her, but had spooked her instead. "All of them?" I asked.

"Yes, all of them. I might even make *you* want me to make you my prey. I can do that. It would be very easy."

This was a little exasperating, but I thought I might be able to get him to cooperate if I just kept him talking. "What do you mean exactly?"

I heard nothing on the other end of the line.

"Are you there?"

But there was only silence—not even breathing. Then there was a click, and he was gone. Presumably flowing into the night. A fluid fiction.

CHAPTER FOUR
a delicate balance

I

I had learned the concept of fluid fiction from another gay man who also indulged in vampiric activities, but with an interesting "shadow side": he was a minister, working in a conservative church in the Midwest. I had been alerted to him by a mutual friend, and through a series of complicated arrangements, had managed an appointment. He asked that his identity be disguised, so I'll call him Michael.

There certainly are religious and spiritual aspects to vampire culture. Some people view the vampire as a dark angel, the shadow side of God, and even as a replacement for God. I've seen many vampire poets and artists draw parallels between Christ and vampires, and certainly Anne Rice makes connections from her vampires to ancient Egyptian deities. She even views vampires as "angels going in another direction." To her they have a celestial quality, and her vampire Lestat compared his own experience to the Catholic Transubstantiation—the turning of mundane substance to spiritual via consecrated blood. So it didn't surprise me as much as you might think to find a practicing minister attracted to vampires. That he passed himself off as a normal heterosexual conservative minister was something else, and it was the philosophy with which he framed it that yielded some insights into vampire culture—and possibly into how Susan Walsh had been hoaxed.

He was a young man just out of divinity school, blond with hazel eyes, and he admitted that he was attracted to suffering. His parishioners knew nothing of his sexual proclivities or his occasional indulgence in taking blood from his partners, whom he viewed as prey. Yet, much as his various secrets burdened him, he felt no need to be released.

"I'm a frightening paradox," Michael said. "I was drawn to the healing power of ministry and I think I still serve in that capacity as a form of redemption—to compensate for my secret lives. I have an intense desire to *know* other lives deeply. I can do that as a counselor *and* as a vampire. I'm drawn to minister with the same intensity of force I use to draw my prey, and if you serve their needs, they'll see you how they want to see you. It's easy to dominate them. All ministers know this feeling of power."

"I thought ministry was about serving others with humility," I said. Not that I was that naïve, but I wanted to see how he'd respond.

He smiled. "I enjoy power. I'm a manipulator. I use my abilities to assist in all of my deeds—good or evil."

"Evil? That's how you see your vampire activities?"

"Often I do. The doctrines of my Church would never tolerate it, but then again, the faith I placed in the Church and in God have only served to squash my spirit. The Church became a vampire—sucking me dry, just like it sucks the life from hundreds of people every week. It's supposed to infuse life, not supplant it with its fetid liturgy. So I'm just acting out what they do to me."

"You sound disillusioned."

He shrugged and nodded. "I am. I always wanted to be a minister, ever since I was a kid. I also always wanted to be a vampire. And I knew quite young that I was gay, and that felt like an evil thing. I thought there was evil in me that I had to eradicate some way. I felt unacceptable, even to my family, who were very devout. But it didn't make sense. It just seems like someone who has a gift that can help others shouldn't be barred from using it just because he has different life practices than other people in the Church. So I pass myself off as being what they want me to be, to get what I want *and* to serve others."

This seemed a little much, but I wasn't there to make judgments. "How do you live with these different identities?" I asked. "I mean, and still have integrity?"

"That's been one of my most relentless struggles, creating a balance between my worlds, the blood-lust and the spiritual. There have been times when I've leapt from some sinful embrace and gone straight to the 'holy' cloth of service to others. I've spoken in front of congregations and felt totally alone—alienated by my secrets, unable to be honest. Even so, my dark side is helpful in spiritual counsel. I understand the conflicts of sin and desire."

I nodded. I, too, understood this from my own years as a counselor and psychologist.

"I think of the vampire as I think of gay males," Michael offered, "as a fluid fiction."

I was perplexed. I'd never heard the term before. "A fluid fiction? What does it mean?"

He explained to me that the inspiration came primarily from the works of Oscar Wilde, whose *Portrait of Dorian Gray* exposed and flaunted the gay charade. The Irish writer spent his days like Dorian: meandering among the idle rich, while his nights were spent in depravity. Wilde was eventually arrested and it soon became impossible in England to deny that buggery was a regular behavior in the salons of the stylish nobility. In short, *Dorian Gray* was a novel about widespread social self-deception.

"Wilde's fiction reveals his belief in the forgery of the self," said Michael. "That is, in a fluid fiction. Wilde sought to unravel the notion of a static self, to show the duplicitous layers of charade performed all the time merely for the moment. That's how it is to live a secret life. One has to change constantly to survive. The fiction with which gay men portray their presence is fluid, perfectly alterable for any occasion. Wilde was a pioneer who recognized the charade as reality."

"Okay," I said, "but how does that apply to you?"

"I first started to create myself when I realized I was gay, around the age of thirteen. Then when I dabbled in vampirism, the fiction became more intricate and elaborate. Trust and continuity are factors in most relationships, but not in vampirism. That's about the one-night feeding, which doesn't require a solid frame. I have to create myself for the prey. As a result, who I am has become a constant mystery even to myself."

"And you like that?" I asked. "You like not knowing who you really are?"

"All of us are engaged in the conscious creation of our identities, inventing profiles and personalities that fit our fantasies. From the California surfer who bleaches his hair and wears baggies to the New York businessman selecting power suits, we all use techniques to artificially inflate ourselves. The modern self is a contrivance, a mask behind which often lies a desperate desire to find our real selves."

"Sounds rather postmodern." I meant that a little sarcastically, because it was all beginning to sound a bit too conceptual. "And now you're saying there's a real self?"

"People think there is. But there isn't."

"Maybe you're just saying that because you're immersed in a form of gay culture that has to believe that."

He shrugged. "The fluid fiction of gay life, while humorously showcased by drag queens and Hollywood's token fags, is a basic tenet of survival. The fabric of the gay public image is constantly being cut, trimmed, dyed, and reshaped to create alternate 'outfits.' We also use a chameleonic approach in our personal relationships, and vampire culture is the same."

"Wait," I said. "I need to ask this: When you're presenting a false persona that you *know* your target audience will attach to you as a truth, don't you feel a twinge of conscience? Or any sense of disintegration at replacing a truth about yourself with a false impression that could become a permanent part of your identity?"

He looked amused. He had a nice smile. "Why do you think identity is permanent?" he asked.

"Well, I mean, continuity. That you could identify yourself from one moment to the next as the same person, as someone about whom you would say 'this is true' and 'that is false.'" Oh, God, now I sounded like a philosopher.

"I have never felt a prick of conscience when I assumed a role," he responded. "It's like being an actor who assumes the character's interior life. The actor is able to assimilate the part into himself in order to give genuine life to the being. I, too, assimilate the role required to serve a parishioner or lure a blood donor. But you're right. A person with my ability to play out many fantasies can't keep everything separate forever. Soon, characters begin to run together, partly because some of those created characters fascinate more than one's own personality. I'm afraid of what my heart knows. I'm trying to never lie to myself, but this is a real challenge."

"Then doesn't this do a number to your head or disturb you in any way? How do you maintain honesty with anyone, or achieve intimacy?"

"I'm not supposed to know myself in a static way. Who really is knowable in any solid sense? Even if I were to consciously construct myself as a solid character who maintains set traits, I would revert to fictionalizing myself in moments of need. It becomes desirable for what I do to permanently integrate the behavioral quirks of ghosts."

"And this works for you as a vampire as well?"

"It's within this very recycling that the vampire finds his place. Vampires are themselves fluid fictions, immortals who reinvent their identities for each new experience. The vampire's charade is to appear harmlessly charming and erotic, a point-by-point response to his prey's every nuance. He seduces his victim through the lure of his mask.

"There is a vampire in the fiction of every modern gay boy—a Jekyll and Hyde beautifully rehearsed. The monster and the man transmogrify, dissolving back and forth into one another. The vampire inhabits even the compassionate queer who helps the old lady with her groceries. He may sit with dying friends in clinics and wards, make contributions to charities, feed the homeless, and volunteer in soup kitchens. Vampires even donate blood. But at night, these same boys pound their brothers into submission in smoky red basements, shifting into their monstrous other life. I've seen it. I've done it.

"There are many true stories, from the West Side docks of Manhattan to the warehouse catacombs along Frisco's Folsom Street, of gay vampires whose adventures into sadomasochism led to suffocation, mutilation, dismemberment, and even death. Men attach their nipples to battery-charged jumper cables, dangerously electrifying their orgasms. Some tie their testicles with leather cords, twisting and stretching while a stranger's fist and forearm are plunged so deeply into the bowels that their fingers feel every contraction of their beating hearts. Other boys puncture holes in the groin and arteries, sometimes slicing the nipples, drinking and sucking the blood of their brothers while thrashing towards orgasm. A vampire lurks in every gay presentation and it's only a matter of time before he begins to prey upon his brothers, and then on strangers."

"How did this begin?" I asked. "I mean, what made you want to live this way? It's really a mystery to me why you would want to even start."

"The first time I used deception to acquire what I wanted felt powerful. I was not in the least bit upset about lying to achieve my goals—not when I saw how well it worked."

"Even though you were a minister?"

"I remember acknowledging to myself that I was doing wrong by lying and manipulating this person, but I reminded myself that everyone drapes themselves in fiction to some extent. Even animals use deception."

"But you're not an animal. And you have certain responsibilities."

"I wanted to be successful in all my worlds, so in order to do this I had to develop the art of impression management. It's as simple as that."

"Impression management," I said with a laugh. "Now you sound like a politician."

He acknowledged this with a nod. "The irony is, I had wanted to be a man of truth, like Lincoln. But then one day I read that Lincoln used deception, and I was crushed, no . . . laid utterly waste. That was the true beginning. Finding out that even those held up to us as people of great integrity used fictions for their own purposes."

"But what's the payoff?" I asked. "Aside from the power surge of the moment."

"There is no *real* payoff . . . only the charade, the immediate reward. Deception is an approach, a method that has proven effective, that's all. It's more a process than a lie."

I felt comfortable enough at that point to get a little personal. "At the heart of this, isn't it possible that you're afraid that you might not be loved just for who you really are? You don't want to put that on the line?"

He acknowledged this without embarrassment. "I do sometimes wonder if my fear is of my real self. I have always believed that people will not love or even like the real me. I still believe this. I once tried to be a man of truth, but nobody wanted me. If I told my congregation that I'm gay or a vampire—or both!—do you think they'd want me to marry them, bury them, or baptize their children? I've spent hours fighting for truth behind closed doors with fools who have their own version of truth. Everyone has his own idea. Truth is very valuable, but it's lost in our lives and will never be restored to its brilliance until Jesus returns and clears the board."

That was a little startling, hearing a man who indulged in "deception management"—my term—and blood-drinking refer to a fairly fundamentalist doctrine, but I had to remind myself that he was a minister because he believed in a religion. Even so, I wasn't altogether convinced by his sincerity.

"But you do actually enjoy your secrets, don't you?" I pressed.

He nodded. He seemed to be amused by these questions. "I enjoy retaining my darkest secrets, yes. I think the individuality and unique nature of being human requires that we remain mysterious, at least partially. So, while I would like to be known more deeply, I don't want someone to possess complete knowledge of me. I don't think anyone wants that. I once thought that Jesus Christ could maintain my soul, and if the conditions were carefully adhered to, one could come very close to soul perfection. But it hasn't worked. So I hunt for lovers who can fill my emptiness and relieve my loneliness. I subconsciously draw them into my sphere and remove some of their energy. I try and repair myself with their essence. I really have to hunt to keep myself in this world.

"I used to believe that my ministries would save me, balance me out, redeem me in some way. I even practice my vampirism as a sanctified ritual that sets apart a time and space to formally acknowledge to myself and to the other participant *who I am* and *what I am*. For me, it's an existential atonement, based on Old Testament rituals. It's an affirmation, perhaps a celebration. I do fear damnation, not so much from God, but from a morality within the universe. I exploit fellow human beings, and this is a transgression. I have tasted where I need not taste for meaning, and now I'm unable to wash it out of my mouth. Psychically, I'm branded."

2

I thought a lot about this idea of fluid fiction—the theatrical character of it. A huge part of vampire culture involves role-playing, both official and unofficial. It's a way to escape, and a way to have fun. For some, like Michael, it seems also a way to avoid mature self-development—although I'm sure he wouldn't see it that way. Whatever the purpose, I've been amazed by the high degree and detail of the fantasy involved in creating complex traits and realms for a diverse range of supernatural characters. My impression was that vampire culture drew people who had a real facility with fantasy—which is not to say that everything told to me was fabricated. What I mean is that from a basic mythology that has been repeated for many decades in our culture with little variation, we are only now seeing dramatic permutations on an image that was always capable of yielding them. Novels, film, games, music, and many other manifestations indicate that people with imagination have entered vampire culture and exploited its fertility. Because of that, someone like the minister can indulge his fluid fictions as a natural part of the cultural dynamics. A concern might be whether, with the growth of vampire culture, this attitude could feed back into the culture at large and contribute to its own increasing fragmentation.

One of the questions that arose for me as I listened to people's stories was how much of this was entertainment and how much the indulgence of a certain type of personality known as "fantasy-prone." A subculture in which a supernatural creature figures as a primary icon would probably draw those who could tell a story about themselves as if it were real. Yet the label seems a poor name for a rather rich and dynamic characteristic. I know from my own experience as a therapist with people who have strong fantasy lives that imagination can yield great creativity. I also know that people who spend a lot of time in fantasy are generally dismissed in a culture that prizes logical thinking and rationality. I needed to be sure that I did not fall into that habit, while also remaining aware of how much "fluid fiction" was in play among those I sought out.

I did some research and learned about people in experiments who could imagine unreal images as vividly as if they were real. For example, they could make their own bodies produce physical manifestations just from the suggestion of something—skin blistered, warts were cured, orgasms occurred, and allergies were created without the presence of actual physical stimuli. I can't even fathom how someone's skin can blister merely from the thought that some benign plant held near it is poison ivy! The critical element in these experimental results was the strength of the belief in the reality of an event, and the ability to facilitate the imagination long enough to produce the physical effect. I can't do that, but obviously some people can.

Those who can vividly fantasize like this have certain characteristics in common: They tend to have had a parent who encouraged fantasy when they were children. They also report vivid memories of their early years and had imaginary playmates. They feel extreme sympathy with others, may view themselves as healers, tend to focus well and to daydream, and show a profound response to sensory events. As adults, fantasy remains central, but they tend to keep it secret. They seem to be easily hypnotizable, have a greater range of tolerance toward paranormal events, and a vulnerability to certain personality disorders. Many were also abused as children and learned to dissociate into a fantasy world in which they could find some control.

I know someone who is an expert on the imagination, so I consulted him. Dr. Leonard George, author of *Alternative Realities: The Paranormal, the Mystic, and the Transcendent in Human Experience*, is a psychologist, writer, and broadcaster in Vancouver, British Columbia. He has researched the many different ways that humans process and interpret their world, and he wrote a wonderful article on the history and politics of the imagination for *The Anne Rice Reader*.

I asked him about his work on the fantasy-prone personality because I was sure that many of the stories I would collect from my encounters could be erroneously—and scornfully—dismissed with this label. What it means, according to Dr. George, is an ability to become deeply involved in fantasy, but not necessarily to be trapped by it.

"I'm intrigued by the idea that fantasy-proneness defines a subgroup within every human culture," Dr. George told me, "a sort of human resource pool. But *fantasy-proneness* sounds so pejorative. One could devise other labels, such as *fantasy-virtuosity*, which more closely captures it.

"Depending on the cutoff used, perhaps five percent of the population could be classified as dramatically fantasy-prone. It seems likely that such people have existed in every culture. This raises the question of the interaction between fantasy-proneness and society. Conventional modern culture is largely negative about the imagination. While we value creativity and imaginativeness when it serves the status quo, our support for imagining outside the grid of permitted thoughts is low. We're careful to define fantasy as 'an experience of the unreal,' and those who take imagining seriously are often viewed as impractical, or even mad. Consequently, we have no formal, culturally sanctioned means of identifying the fantasizers, and no institutions to harness their potential for the benefit of all."

"Are there any societies that do?" I asked.

"In many hunter/gatherer societies, children between eight and twelve are monitored for signs of a 'shamanic calling'—visions, voices, recurrent dreams, or strange illnesses. These are the sorts of experiences that fantasizers in our society report from their own childhoods. Once identified, these people are trained in ways of mastering their powers, generally understood as access to a world of spirits. The result is the shamanic vocation, an important organ of healing, guidance, and group memory among these cultures.

"In more complex societies, the fate of the fantasizer has depended on the prevailing worldview and the political economy. The imagination has been typically regarded either as a resource of great value or as a menace—or both at once. The old Babylonians valued it: On their equivalent of Halloween, they would hire fantasizers to spend the night on the roofs of Babylon, where they would visualize themselves as mighty star-gods, protecting the city from the air raids of sorcerers. Yet orthodox Christians of the later Middle Ages became so fearful of extravagant imagining that any public sign of it could get you killed as a heretic or a witch."

"And in our own time?"

"The fantasizers are an invisible tribe," Dr. George responded. "They move, untagged, through the labyrinth of modern society. They're not randomly distributed. They tend to cluster in two sectors. First, in areas where their imaginal talents can be exercised, as artists and healers and various types of religious professionals. Second, in subcultures where they can stretch, allowing more intense expressions of fantasy than are acceptable among normal society. The Goth/vampire subculture appears to be a classic instance. These socially marginal regions can be the sources of ideas that transform society in positive ways, such as with scientists who were once viewed as weirdoes. But the fantasy zone can also breed tragedy, such as with [suicide cults like] Heaven's Gate. As the circumstances of a society shift, so does its relationship with its fantasy-prone citizens, and we may be leaving a great human resource shunned or unrecognized."

What Dr. George said made me think a bit differently about Diogenes, Wraith, NiteTrain, and others I had met. I wondered how much of their vampire experience was fed by fantasy, and whether it even mattered if I knew. Fluid fiction. Fantasy-prone. Role-playing. Impression management. The vampire is a malleable image that relies on mystery. Those who want to be vampires, think of themselves as vampires, or just depict vampires, have a wide-open canvas.

It does seem, from the fantasy-proneness experiments, that fantasy is more continuous with reality than we in this culture tend to believe, so the stories told to me—whether real with aspects of fiction, or fiction with aspects of the real—may amount to the same thing. The vampire minister may present himself as a fiction to lure his prey, or he might have been a fiction for me—telling a story to create an impression. In the end, I felt, it hardly mattered. Playing a vampire or being a vampire, they're rooted in the same cultural source, and if I wanted to know the heart of the vampire, as Wraith had put it, I had to respect each and every story for its essence.

Then again, the difference between someone playing a vampire and being a vampire has a little more significance if you're going out alone at night to meet them. It would not be long before I'd meet Diogenes and I was sure there would be others for whom I might not be prepared. I could be fooled. Perhaps Walsh had been fooled. Somewhere, some vampire might convince me I was safe when I wasn't. The best defense, I believed, was to gain a deeper awareness of vampire culture—their inspirations, their boundaries, and their desires.

the well-read
vampire

Modern man must rediscover a deeper source of his own
spiritual life. To do this, he is obligated to struggle with evil, to
confront his own shadow, to integrate the devil.

—CARL JUNG

I

Most people who become fascinated with vampires do so through
films or fiction, and much of that was inspired by Bram Stoker's 1897
novel, *Dracula*. Okay, we had the nineteenth-century tales of Varney,
Carmilla, and Lord Ruthven before that, but they didn't make as
much of an impact. *Dracula* has never been out of print, and has
inspired countless films, stage plays, and vampire novels. It's a morality play about a Transylvanian count who arrives in England to find
new blood, and the valiant men led by Van Helsing who drive him
from their virtuous women and destroy him. That novel, and the 1931

film of it starring Bela Lugosi, formed in our minds what vampires are: They're repelled by garlic and crucifixes, show no reflection in the mirror, must be invited into a home, and can be dispatched with a wooden stake driven through the heart. They must sleep in their native soil, can turn into bats, wolves, or mist, and have hypnotic powers, superhuman strength, an Eastern European accent, and a classy presentation (black cape and tuxedo).

To some extent, this image was influenced by Eurocentric ideas about peasant superstitions. I even ran across an authentic Vampire Killing Kit that confirmed this. It was manufactured in England during the nineteenth century for tourists traveling to Eastern Europe, and contained a crucifix, holy water, a wooden stake, a pistol, silver bullets, a magnifying glass (to focus intensified rays of the sun onto a vampire), and powdered garlic. Even so, Stoker made up more than a few of his conventions.

In 1954 Richard Matheson published *I Am Legend*, about vampirism as a disease, but not much else of note came out in book-length fiction for some time. Dracula was even defanged with humor in the Abbot and Costello films. With the television series *Dark Shadows* introducing Barnabas Collins in 1967, interest in vampires picked up, including mine. Well, I didn't like Barnabas so much because he always forgot his lines, but Quentin, the ghost, was a babe. That show gave us a sympathetic vampire who regretted doing what his nature dictated.

The mid-seventies brought the new wave of vampire antiheroes, Stephen King's more Dracula-like *'Salem's Lot* notwithstanding. In *The Dracula Tape*, Fred Saberhagen presented Dracula as an okay guy and Van Helsing as a self-righteous oaf; Chelsea Quinn Yarbro was shopping around the first of her romantic Saint-Germain series; and Anne Rice published *Interview with the Vampire*. After that, vampires were never the same. In the eighties, *Vampire Tapestry*, *Fevre Dream*, and *The Hunger*, among others, brought the vampire center stage and stripped it of many superstitious clichés. Then, in 1985, Anne Rice wrote a sequel, *The Vampire Lestat*, and another one three years later, *The Queen of the Damned*. By the end of that decade, vampires were an industry.

The bloodsucker as the Evil Other has had a shakedown. Now it's more the shadow of our own selves than something "out there." Anne Rice created her guilt-ridden, lonely, self-aware vampire named Louis in what became a best-selling novel and cult underground hit. Louis tells his story to a mortal reporter, taking him back to the late eighteenth century and describing how a vampire named Lestat transformed him and cast him into an unending philosophical twilight. He still could not answer those existential questions that had always plagued him regarding truth, God, and the devil; and on top of that, he now had to take the lives of others to survive. To assuage the loneliness, he helped his vampire Maker, Lestat, create a child vampire, Claudia, and with her he searched the world for others of their kind who might know something of their function in the larger scheme of things. He met the equally clueless, four-hundred-year-old Armand in Paris and lost Claudia. Nothing worked out quite right and he resigned himself to a beleaguered existence of endless nights and slippery truths.

This seminal novel turned into *The Vampire Chronicles*, with the inclusion of the two Lestat sequels named above and four more books: *The Tale of the Body Thief*, *Memnoch the Devil*, *Pandora*, and *Armand*, with more to follow. In these, Lestat became the focus. He told his own story, recasting from his perspective the facts that Louis had described, and presenting himself as a new vampire for a new age. He was ready for adventure, though he'd not asked to be a vampire, and he took his mother, Gabrielle, with him. With all the brashness of his youthful soul, he sought out and found Marius, who told him about the vampire origins in ancient Egypt.

With the emergence of Lestat as a new type of hero who embraced his vampirism, how we understood the vampire changed. We learn that vampires defy the limitations imposed by social expectations and can therefore realize their utmost potential. They possess heightened perception and strength. They can cultivate great focus, passion, and awareness of life. They form mental bonds that allow them to read minds; fly, project astral bodies, move fast, and jump great heights; transcend gender categories; heal themselves; fully surrender to the flow of life; and defy death. Often they are young, beautiful, and vitally seductive, like gods of ancient times; yet even when ugly, they possess wisdom and power. Vampires feel everything with the amplitude of the Romantic poets. They know isolation, need, and the craving for meaning, but also the bond of unity with other minds. They seize the intensity of experience that many of us covet, and challenge us, if we dare, to take it for ourselves. In short, the vampire shows us what it means to live the extraordinary life. Now readers want to *be* vampires, not kill them.

To write *The Vampire Companion*, I spent many hours over several years in conversation with Rice, getting the details of her supernatural universe right. She had started writing about vampires on a whim, and when she saw that her own desire to experience the monster's perspective matched that of a large and growing readership, she continued to explore the possibilities through numerous characters. "Seeing through Louis's eyes," she told me, "allowed me to write about life in a way I hadn't been able to do in a contemporary novel. I was able to describe reality through fantasy."

She was interested primarily in the way good and evil both flow into strong character development, so I asked about her use of opposition in her work.

"I don't usually create pure opposites who interact as such," she responded. "The tension between opposites is not a violent clash of objects so much as a mixing in each individual character. I'm not talking about creating sympathy for the evildoer, and I'm not maintaining that understanding evil will eradicate it. I'm speaking about the need to go into evil's complexity."

Rice's understanding of vampires shows them to be more cerebral than animal, as she sensed from the vampire's presentation in *Dracula*. "I always saw them as angels going in another direction. They had become finely tuned imitations of human beings imbued with this evil spirit. I always saw vampires as romantic and abstract. The vampire image is powerful. It calls forth something in us that goes back to the ancient gods. They've transcended time and transformed themselves. They're like dark saints—beings who transcend the corruptible. They're creatures outside the human sphere who can therefore speak about it. I gave them conscience and intelligence and wisdom so they could see things humans aren't able to see."

What fascinates her with the character of Lestat, in contrast to Louis and the original story, is that he knows right from wrong and still does his vampire thing. He's energized, bold, and refuses to lose, so he has to go with what his nature dictates, even when that plagues him with guilt. "Lestat is undefeatable. I love to write from that point of view."

2

Rice makes her home in New Orleans, where vampire culture has found a niche. It's the site of the Westgate Museum of the necromantic arts, the Marie Laveau voodoo shop, Ghost Tours, and even tours of Rice's vampire settings. (There are clubs where Real Vampyres meet, but those in the know requested I not name the places. Yet anyone who hangs out long enough can find them. Hint: Think religious settings.) New Orleans is one of the principal locations of Rice's vampire novels. Even when they run off to London, Paris, or San Francisco, they seem always to return here. It's a vampire's city, with its sleazy French Quarter, aboveground cemeteries, violent crimes, omnipresent hauntings, Gothic churches, and Euro-Caribbean textures. Even the homeless might ask for your blood. To go to the Big Easy is, for some, like making a pilgrimage to a sacred place. Many of Rice's fans have moved there just to be close to where her characters "reside," or because they claim to feel a deep affinity with the place. Personally, I go for the parties.

New Orleans is known for its extravagant parades and celebrations, and in 1995, Anne Rice's Memnoch Ball was among them. That was to mark the publication of the fifth of her vampire novels, and she had invited six thousand friends and fans to attend. The costumes were lavish and the setting unique: St. Elizabeth's, once a former girl's orphanage and now Rice's pet real estate project. This was the largest of the annual parties thrown by her fan club since 1989, and may remain a legend around town.

Despite the difficulty of squeezing through doorways and maneuvering stairways so crowded they'd inspire claustrophobia in the proverbial two peas in a pod, the ball was eye candy of the finest variety to even the most experienced masquerader. In a city where thousands of dollars are lavished on costumes for every occasion, including the two-week Mardi Gras period, people turned out in their best. Historical costumes, Ricean characters, religious figures, S&M getups, and vampires of every stripe roamed the halls and grounds of the former orphanage, which Rice and her staff had decorated with ghoulish themes that changed from room to room. She needed two rooms to showcase her vast and impressive doll display, and the huge chapel floor had been buffed for a troupe of professional dancers to set the tone of eighteenth-century elegance. There were bands, tarot readers, lectures, Broadway tunes, and an assortment of activities to entertain and engage the awestruck attendees.

Jana Marcus, who went to the Memnoch Ball, was so impressed with the stories she heard from some of Rice's fans that she decided to do a special photography book to collect images from the party.

Published by Thunder's Mouth Press, it was called *In the Shadow of the Vampire.*

At her request, I met with her before the ball to hear what she had in mind. She was a pretty, black-haired woman with expressive dark eyes and a lot of enthusiasm. She had done some photography work in the fetish scene and wanted to explore a new subject. I asked her about her inspiration and she said, "As a photojournalist I'm fascinated with why certain things influence our culture as we move toward the year 2000. Anne Rice is a phenomenon as a writer. Her devoted followers and their fanatic admiration fascinated me. I wanted to investigate this Rice-vampire culture and discover the source of her popularity, her readers' fascination with the vampire icon, and last, Generation X's delve into dark narcissism."

"Has Rice's work affected you as well?" I asked.

She admitted that it had. "I read my first Rice book in 1976, at age fourteen. Her books opened up a world of philosophy and beauty to me unlike any other I'd read in my young life. I wanted to be like her characters . . . living life to the fullest and appreciating the here and now. I also loved the fact that the world she presented could be probable, and it made me look at things in a new and different way."

During the process of writing the book, Marcus asked me to write an introduction with a Jungian slant on the vampire archetype, so I did. When it was all finished, packaged, and published, I asked her whether among all of her interviews she had come across anything interesting.

"Overall, the people I interviewed were all very nice," she said. "I may not have agreed with their lifestyles personally, like the blood-drinkers, but they explained their practices in a very intelligent fashion and I could understand the basis for why they practice their rituals. I interviewed over one hundred people and only forty appear in the book. Toward the end of my research I was really trying to get the 'dramatic' life-changing stories, like the person you hear about who got off heroin because of Rice."

"Now that you've done this book," I said, "what's your own take on vampire culture?"

"I don't believe vampires are anything other than mythic creatures that reflect our dark natures back at us. The vampire is an archetype that allows us to see the human condition in another realm. Vampire culture is yet another subculture where youth can express themselves in a unique voice and vision to reflect our times. Through the vampire archetype, we come to appreciate life through the study of death and looking at our own mortality."

3

Rice's readers typically name her vampire protagonists as their favorite characters from all of those she offers. They read the stories over and over, create new scenarios, role-play her characters, sign up for online chats, and join fan clubs. One person, Susan, told me how she'd been hesitant to even read Rice, but after devouring her novels, wrote one of her own, for her own entertainment, using Rice's characters.

Rice fan Sarah Faye Starr, age seventeen, sent me an e-mail saying that she was attracted to vampires because they are powerfully sexual. "They can have any person they want, when they want them, and not meet any resistance. The mere idea of such power is captivating to me. I am so powerless in my own life due to emotional problems which make it impossible for me to accept rejection, while causing me to fall in love with people who will always reject me, that the idea of a creature who has the power to make others love him, fear him, and generally do whatever he says to do is monumentally wonderful for me. I have the power to truly shock with my black clothes and 'got blood?' T-shirt. Perhaps this is my way of appropriating some of the power of the vampire."

With the rise in popularity of the Internet, Anne Rice chats attracted her fans. Lisa Rowe has run one such list. "I've run the mailing list for over a year now," she says, "after two years as assistant administrator. During this time, it's split into two lists, one to deal just with book discussion, and one to encourage and handle the community that's built up among Anne's fans online for news, movies, and gatherings. The two lists together have about 1,500 members. It was started by Laurie Salopek back in 1994! It picked up speed with the release of the movie, *Interview with the Vampire*, and served to bring together people who'd been reading Anne's works for a long time. I've always been big on hunting down news about Anne, and Laurie brought me on as assistant. I also run the AnneRice channel on EfNet Internet Relay Chat, which has been going strong since 1995.

"The most interesting thing about all of this has been how people have come together, finding a common element in their 'fandom.' I've seen weddings . . . and divorces! In fact, I met my husband on the IRC channel. People from both the list and the chat channel have met in real life many times, from gathering in New Orleans for the ball, to just getting together in different parts of the country. There's a true community. While we have our share of 'young Goths,' we span in age from mid-teens to over forty-five years old, with the average user around thirty. It's an extremely tolerant group too, with alternative sexual lifestyles well represented. We're as close a cross section of America as I've seen online."

Many Web sites were created to provide news for Rice fans, such as the one by Lillith and Darryle Toney. "Our page, 'DarkRose Manor,' has been online since September 1997," they told me. "There are four sections which are vampire related, one of which is 'The Library,' where we have a collection of Anne Rice fan fiction. All involve the characters created by Anne, and in some cases, new characters. They are written in Anne's style, and for the most part follow the canon Anne has set forth."

(It should be noted that Rice does not endorse the use of her characters in the various role-playing games or fan fiction scenarios. She is not always aware of the Internet sites that pay homage to her in this way, but she owns the copyrights and prefers to keep her characters in her own domain.)

The "Black Rose" Web site, unrelated to "DarkRose Manor," is an active role-playing site for fans who take on the personas of Rice's characters. Donna Askren told me about her group:

"The idea for the 'Black Rose' came about after viewing several role-playing games currently active on the Internet. It centers on *The Vampire Chronicles*, *The Witching Hour* series, and *The Mummy*.

"The game is more than a hobby; it's the outlet for an all-consuming desire and obsession with the world that Anne Rice has created. The time required is considerable, starting with choosing a character and knowing this character intimately enough to actually 'become' the character for a few hours every day.

"We currently have approximately ten members. All of our lives go on normally, with school, work, or raising children, but always in the back of our minds we know that there is a special place, a world all our own, dark and enticing. And when this world of harsh reality we live in becomes a burden, we can run and hide, if only for a little while!"

"What I love about Anne Rice's vampires," explained another player, Joe Petty (Santino), "is the sensuality. In Santino, I can be mysterious, sensual, and dangerous. Santino is my alter ego, the man I always wanted to be, but was afraid of."

Sometimes identification with a specific character has psychological benefits. "Pandora" saw the movie *Interview with the Vampire* over ninety times. "When I found the RPG [role-playing games] on the Net," she said, "I knew I finally had found a place where I belonged. I have a great fear of death, and playing Pandora gives me the escape from death. I'm also able to act out my own frustrations, anger, and desires in ways that are not acceptable in real life."

"Natalie Mayfair," a.k.a. Yasmine Voglewede, was twelve when she became fascinated with vampires. "I was born with a handicap, a disability that prevented me from walking. My newfound 'immortality' allowed me to feel what it was like to walk on the hot sand, or climb a mountain. Vampire powers opened a doorway into a realm I might never have in reality."

I actually participated in one of these role-playing games with another Rice-oriented group who invited me in. I decided to go in as Louis, since he's my favorite of Rice's characters. I found the experience to be a real test of my knowledge of the finer details of Rice's work—and I had been immersed in all of that for seven years! The idea was to create a scenario with the others without breaking character. In other words, if Louis had never read Dostoevsky, I couldn't have him quote something from *The Brothers Karamazov*. So I had to know him pretty well to play him, because we weren't just acting out scenes from Rice's novels. We were interacting in entirely new ways. It was a fun exercise, but not something I wanted to do every week—let alone every day.

4

Some of Rice's fans are captivated with vampires on a more serious level. She inspires a vampire lifestyle. Nina C. from Canada told me that vampires have intrigued her since she first heard about Vlad Tepes as a small child. "I am not a role-player," she insisted. "Part of my ancestry is Romanian, and some of the folklore and myth surrounding Vlad the tyrant managed to filter through my great-grandparents, who emigrated to Saskatchewan, Canada, after the turn of the century. The vampire as an archetype has figured hugely in my fantasies and fiction."

I asked her whether she recalled any of those fantasies in which vampires played a part.

"Yes, I used to believe that there was a shadow-vampire in my room, and the only way to combat it was to make sure my room was totally dark.

"When I was around ten years old I began to identify with my Transylvanian ancestry in a campy way, showing my schoolmates my eyeteeth to prove real vampire blood ran in my veins. I believe that as a symbol, the vampire can become a means of confronting dissociated traits and characteristics within ourselves. However, the vampire in its negative aspect is a feeder, a parasite, like a human sociopath. I do, however, love the Gothic fashions and opulence of literary vampires, and adore dressing up."

"Is there a vampire in fiction that fits the type of vampire to which you feel most attracted?" I asked. "Or have you met real people like this?"

"Actually, I have met people who fall under the sociopathic vampire category, but a celebrity I really identify my vampire myth with is Trent Reznor, mastermind of Nine Inch Nails. He embodies many qualities I find admirable in vampires. In fiction, Lestat wins hands down. I was attracted to him because I felt as though I encountered a character of mine in the guise of a vampire."

"How was Lestat a character of yours?"

"When I was a child I created many male characters who embodied qualities that I could not develop in myself due to social conditioning and some very real safety issues. I couldn't act out my real responses in the real world because to do so would have been harmful to me. When I first read Interview with the Vampire, it was like meeting my characters. The longing, the ferocity, the need to challenge God, the need to prove that 'see there; there is really nothing out there, what we found our lives on is a lie.' All of these questions that birthed my characters were to be found in Lestat. He even physically resembled one of my favorite characters."

"I'm intrigued with your idea that the vampire can be a means of confronting dissociated traits. Can you say more about that?"

She was happy to do so, although she said it was much more complicated than she could explain at the moment. "In the Victorian era, for example, dissociated traits were more than likely the natural sexual inclinations of individuals. The vampire was a means of personifying forbidden sexual energy. After all, the energy of the libido has to go somewhere. I believe this is still true to some measure today, one hundred years later, because even though we are bombarded by sexual images in every form of media, there is still an underlying taboo towards transgressive attitudes and behaviors. Gender roles are challenged, but are still to some degree static. The vampire embodies freedom from gender stereotyping. In essence, the vampire is beyond the law. Human, but not human. The vampire can become akin to a shamanic figure, a powerful being that understands human realities, but lives in a place beyond human limitation. The vampire actualizes the so-called dark half."

5

Another Rice fan actually saw himself as a vampire. Online, he is one of the many who use one of Rice's characters for a screen name, and he has darker secrets, which he was willing to share with me:

"If I had to summarize in a few words what has been Anne's influence on me I would say something like this: From the day I opened *The Vampire Lestat*, Lestat became me, or I became Lestat, I don't know which. I discovered another side of my personality, and it was there, revealed in black and white. *The Vampire Chronicles* became a part of my existence . . . and I am not saying that lightly. I see the world in a very different way now. She took the vampire mythology to another level, a most desirable one, more attractive to me perhaps. The character of Lestat must be me. We have so much in common that if he was real, I would be him.

"I'm a real vampire, or close to being one. It all depends on the many definitions the word *vampire* carries. I do not believe in vampires as they are often described in fictional novels. I do not have fangs, I am not an immortal, but I drink blood and it comforts me. My life story is quite complicated. Even though I am only twenty years old, I already went through quite a lot, and my vampiric nature revealed itself through the painful events I have witnessed."

He told me he'd been born in another country to parents of different races. "My grandmother did not accept my mother and she used witchcraft to drive her away from my father. My mother resisted her, but became possessed from time to time. As a result I lived in a very violent and disturbed environment.

"My mother turned her rage and despair on us. She would hit us with phenomenal strength. I tell you, it was hell. The house itself became haunted. Not by ghosts, but by spirits. This environment left me in a perpetual state of fear. And strangely, I turned to blood to comfort me. I myself don't really understand the reason for it. When my mother would beat me up, I'd bleed, and one day, when I was still a child, perhaps six or seven years old, I don't really remember, I started sucking the blood coming out from my wounds. It was the feeling of comfort, the taste of it maybe. Well, from that day on, I found myself cutting my arms to drink my blood. Not much, of course, just for the feeling, the pain, the taste.

"When we moved to another city, my mother tried to escape from my grandmother's spells. Things got better, but I guess it was already too late for me. While moving away from my grandmother, my mother started studying with Jehovah's Witnesses. I even went from door to door preaching for them. The thing was, I was still drinking my blood, and to them, it's one of the cardinal sins! 'Thou shalt not drink blood . . .' One more reason to hide this habit. Then we moved to the United States and I dropped the religion. I'm currently a college student."

I asked him whether he drank blood from other people.

"It happened, once," he admitted, "from a willing partner. She was my girlfriend and knew about my little habit. I have strange desires, though. I'd like to try from an unwilling partner, but this could get sick. So I'll keep it as just a desire. Don't mistake me for a Goth. I look normal, I have normal friends, but I am a vampire. I drink blood. I even prefer living at night and sleeping during the day."

He told me that he plans to move to New Orleans.

6

Rice's enormous influence on vampire fiction and vampiric identities notwithstanding, there are other authors who have made a definite mark, and who have a following of their own. For a while, vampire literature seemed to take one of two routes that branched off in the mid-seventies. The evil vampire followed Stephen King's lead in *'Salem's Lot*, while Rice, shadowed closely by Chelsea Quinn Yarbro, developed a more romantic and historical angle. Some authors tried to mix the two, and a few, like Les Daniels, P. N. Elrod, and Brian Lumley, developed their own vampire series. There was a backlash to Rice, and some horror writers claimed that the vampire had been demystified and defanged. F. Paul Wilson, author of *The Keep*, said, "I can't buy trying to romanticize that type of creature." Nancy Collins, creator of the vampire Sonja Blue, agrees that the vampire is "everything that is bad with humanity." In that tradition, the vampire often becomes nihilistic and excessively brutal. Yet try as they might to supplant Rice, no other vampire author has gained the widespread appeal that she had amassed for their own versions of the story.

Some vampire authors have a particularly avid fan base, such as that of Chelsea Quinn Yarbro. She gave the vampire a completely different angle with her beloved character, Le Comte de Saint-Germain. Her first novel in the series, *Hotel Transylvania*, came out in 1978; but she is not, as some may think, a post-Ricean fantasist. Her story development had a long and involved evolution, originally inspired by *Dracula*.

I first met Yarbro when she was president of Horror Writers of America. She's a strong and vocal redheaded woman with remarkable presence, willing to serve on various committees to help improve the quality of fiction and bring good fiction to the attention of potential readers. She has many friends among other writers, and the day I met her, she was with Suzy McKee Charnas, Les Daniels, and Charlie Grant. They all gave me quotes for an article I was writing. The next time I saw Yarbro was at the Dracula '97 conference, and she was once again helping to coordinate a rather complicated international gathering. She seems indefatigable, and she has left a definite mark on the world of vampire fiction. Her protagonist has endured through twice as many novels as Lestat.

In a speech presented at the 150th anniversary conference commemorating Bram Stoker's birth, Yarbro said, "I believe no vampire story written in English after 1920 is free of Stoker's influence, for that book and its theatrical and cinematic stepchildren have imbued the culture with icons and clichés to such an extent that whether or not a writer has actually taken the time to read Stoker's novel, he—or she—has his or her creative landscape littered with Dracular images that are inescapable."

Her own first encounter with the novel occurred when she was fourteen. She became fascinated with the female figures, linking them in school projects to Macbeth's Weird Sisters. In later years, she researched vampire folklore and the structure of fictional roles. When she returned to *Dracula* to try to analyze just how Stoker had so successfully made his novel compelling to one generation after another, she realized that to write a contemporary vampire novel meant taking a very different approach. "Stoker had done the manipulative seducer as well as anyone could," she said. Yarbro did more research to build for herself a universal paradigm from which she could develop her own vampire character profile. She asked a lot of questions about the vampire/mortal relationship and decided that, contrary to the tradition, the vampire could serve as a metaphor of humanism; i.e., could seek to be part of human experience—particularly in the erotic realm. It did not have to be about seducers and prey; it could also be about lovers, closer to the conventions of historical romance.

Then she moved her vampire milieu from the nineteenth century to Louis XV's Paris, and did research on the historical Comte de Saint-Germain. She noted that he dressed in black and white, never ate or drank in public, claimed to be many centuries old, kept his origins and nationality a mystery, was an occultist and alchemist, had multiple aliases, and was wealthy, elegant, intelligent, and cultured. The perfect vampire! Yarbro worked on his character across eleven novels, having him interact with real historical personages, and she sees no end in sight for all the possibilities. He's a humanist, not a monster, and exercises few of the supernatural powers often associated with vampires. Saint-Germain is a natural for readers' fantasies.

Lindig Harris puts out a newsletter on Yarbro. "I'm interested in Yarbro's Comte de Saint-Germain," she says, "whom she uses as a deus ex machina to comment on humanity from a true outsider's point of view. She has taken the vampire as a symbol of true otherness, modified him to be vampiric but not horrific, and made him a substitute for authorial omnipotence. I started a newsletter about her because I think she's a better writer than many others and is stuck as a midlist 'cult' author. I thought a newsletter would be a way of spreading the word about her and her fans and the wide range of her work: e.g., military science fiction, westerns, romance, and mysteries. Her fan base varies so widely, it's difficult to categorize."

7

Not all readers want romance in their vampire fiction. Some do prefer things more graphic and a bit closer to the alienated spirit, without getting engulfed in a morality tale. Rice acknowledged that the vampire is certainly the prototypical outsider, but her characters exist more like mainstream people than like the truly disenfranchised of this decade. There is a writer who seems to know that mind-set quite well, and she has published a vampire novel, *Lost Souls*: Poppy Z. Brite.

A native of New Orleans, she is a pretty, dark-haired young woman with a pleasant voice and an accessible personality. She wrote her books as an extension of her own experiences. Some of her vampire characters have little charm, and they certainly embody a sociopathic sensibility. They're more like real bloodsuckers, pests that thrive off life and give nothing back.

Brite started writing *Lost Souls* when she was nineteen, living in Chapel Hill, North Carolina. She was not fascinated with vampires per se, but with Gothic culture, of which she felt part—"the black lace and torn velvet, the affinity with graveyards, the bloodletting." The vampire was an essential icon of that death-enamored culture, so she included it as an image of erotic degeneration.

In *Lost Souls*, a vampire more than four centuries in age tends bar in the French Quarter where a young mortal girl comes in the same night that three wandering vampires—who remind us of some of the more decadent rock bands of the era—decide to pay a call. One of them has sex with her, impregnates her, and leaves her to the fate of mortals who couple with vampires: a violent, bloody death while giving birth to a monster. The resulting creature is a vampire, but appears to be mortal. This girl's child is called Nothing, and he is the archetype of the many "thin children in black" who call themselves Goths and who feel as if they truly are nothing—just society's cast-off trash. "I very much fancied myself as one of them," Brite admits. "When I'd visit my dad, I'd go into the French Quarter and meet the Goths there and they were really nice to me. They were a good part of the inspiration for *Lost Souls*. They introduced me to [the drink] Chartreuse, and took me to my first real Goth clubs."

Nothing falls in love with a rock duo known as the Lost Souls, whose lead singer is Ghost, a highly sensitive young man who knows when evil is near and who feels the world's pain as his own. He wants to rescue Nothing, but knows that he cannot, as Nothing joins his vampire father and learns the ways of his blood. The novel winds down in violence, gore, and despair.

At one point, Brite mentions a group of kids called Deathers. "They called themselves that in New Orleans and in North Carolina at the time. Also in California. I once felt the way I described them feeling. I just wasn't really part of a crowd. I definitely was drawn to the dark and the suicidal and the thinking that death was romantic and that Dylan Thomas was so cool because he drank himself to death. In high school, I was one of the pariahs. I guess they could tell that I was strange, and I felt ugly for years and years." She gets as close to the Goth spirit as any author has.

Brite also edited two anthologies of vampire stories, called *Love in Vein*. "People always ask me when am I going to write about the vampires from *Lost Souls* again, and the answer is never. By the end of the book, they just seemed like these annoying little kid brothers. I felt I'd said all I had to say about vampires in that book. When an editor at HarperCollins asked me to edit *Love in Vein*, I was reluctant at first, but there were so few well-paying fiction markets for horror writers that I decided to go ahead with it. I deliberately asked writers who were not known for writing vampire fiction, and I was amazed at the new twists they were able to put on it. I think that's why most horror writers end up trying a vampire story, because a familiar canvas is a way to show your own individual flourishes more clearly."

In the first of these two books, she introduced it thus: "The vampire is everything we love about sex and the night and the dark-dream side of ourselves: adventure on the edge of pain, the thrill to be had from breaking taboos." The bizarre is something to be sought, explored, even surrendered to. The vampire is the embodied reminder of our darkest erotic truths.

No matter what one's preference in vampire fiction, there's a writer out there who expresses it. There's even a growing subgenre of children's vampire tales, led by best-selling author R. L. Stine. It's a category of fiction whose diversity will only continue to develop, and though some say nothing original can be done anymore, I think there are still plots and characters we haven't yet seen. A vampire for a new age, Lestat called himself. Few anticipated him, and from what I can see of vampire culture, there will be others who may yet surprise us.

CHAPTER SIX

vampiric diversions

I

The character played the most often in film is Count Dracula. At this writing, there have been 133 films featuring him, and nearly 200 vampire films made in this country. Dracula also appears in songs, on stage, and in any number of vampire entertainments. Many people get their idea of the vampire from movies, absorbing information on everything from the image of vampires as creatures of the night to the color of their eyes and the size of their fangs.

According to J. Gordon Melton, who wrote *Vampires on Video*, the first vampire flick was *The Devil's Castle* in 1896. It was only two minutes long.

After that, there were others, but it was the 1922 *Nosferatu* and 1931 *Dracula* that had the greater impact, spawning such offspring as *House of Dracula*, *Son of Dracula*, and *Dracula's Daughter*. There were also spin-offs of L. Sheridan Le Fanu's nineteenth-century tale, "Carmilla." Hammer Studios introduced Christopher Lee as the nefarious count, and others followed, including George Hamilton in the comic *Love at First Bite*. Frank Langella played the part sensuously on stage and in a 1979 film.

Other vampires came along in *The Hunger*, *The Lost Boys*, *Fright Night*,

Martin, and *Near Dark*, but we returned to Stoker again in 1992 with Francis Ford Coppola's rendition of *Dracula*, billed as Stoker's original story (though it wasn't). By 1994, after eighteen years of trying, Anne Rice's *Interview with the Vampire* was finally produced. It starred Brad Pitt and Tom Cruise, a couple of real box office draws. There were also space vampires, sex vampires, zombie vampires, robo vampires, lesbian vampires, black vampires, child vampires, and vampire conspiracies. In whatever venue a vampire could be used, from trailer parks to spas to the Bowery, it was. As Rosemary Ellen Guiley and J. B. Macabre point out in *The Complete Vampire Companion*, however, "The major problem with these vampire films is that the writers and directors fail to seek inspiration in places other than the film industry," which has led to rehashed plots.

I was told by several knowledgeable sources that a "new wave" in vampire films would feature vampire hunters, such as the film and television series *Buffy, the Vampire Slayer*. A California cheerleader, Buffy, is told by her guardian Watcher that she has an undeniable genetic heritage from a long line of vampire hunters. This primes her to destroy the vampires plaguing her community, and prepares her to face the longtime nemesis of her clan, the vampire Lothos. It's a provocative idea to bring serious moral issues into the life of a Valley Girl who thinks in terms of clothes and dates. Yet the television show far outpaced the movie in character portrayal, psychological intrigue, and issues of growing up. This Buffy is a bit more serious. Her Watcher is a befuddled librarian, Rupert Giles, and she has a vampire boyfriend named Angel, who can't quite conquer his vampiric ways. (A telling metaphor?) Yet the vampires she kills are unambiguously bad. How do we know? They're grotesque, just like in the gory action flick *From Dusk Till Dawn*. The vampiric part that exhibits their all-out blood-lust is just hideous—which is yet another Hollywood rehash. Still, Buffy does have a strong following in novels and Internet personas.

Other television shows featuring vampires have inspired entire cultures as well: *Dark Shadows*, *Kindred: The Embraced*, and *Forever Knight* have spin-off novels, online chats, fan clubs, fanzines, and conventions devoted to them. A *Dark Shadows* revival failed, but in my opinion, that's because it did not take into account the vampire's contemporary appeal. It also stuck to outdated story lines that had worked for daytime after-school soaps, rather than bringing a fresh approach to this prime-time rendition.

I saw lots of those movies, and have no doubt formed my own ideas from the repeated patterns devised by Hollywood. Yet I know what scares me and I know what excites me. I'd like to have both in the same film, but unfortunately, many of the vampire movies available have the same tired effects, which are neither scary nor erotic.

So I thought of looking into vampire pornography. Rather than just reading descriptions in some catalog, I decided to rent a video and watch it with a friend, Lori Perkins, who is also my agent and a long-time vampire pal. She has much greater tolerance for schlocky (and gory) vampire films than I do (she can watch all three *Faces of Death* videos in a single afternoon!), so I let her pick. We had such choices as *Muffy the Vampire Layer*, *Dracula Sucks*, and *Dragula*, as well as hundreds of gay vampire films. She just took whatever the video store had, but it was supposedly one of the good ones.

An erotic charge was thick in the air as we made popcorn, opened some vampire wine from Transylvania Imports (always on hand), and verbally anticipated what was to come (so to speak). This was better than asking some video vendor to wax eloquent on the vampire pornography trade. We could be the experts. We knew vampires. We appreciated the erotic arts. I'd even written a companion guide to Anne Rice's "elegant sadomasochism," and the research for that had given me . . . well . . . *experience*. So we were primed and ready.

We settled down in front of my forty-eight-inch television screen, turned the lights low, downed some more blood-red Merlot, and slipped in the video. This was really too exciting. What could be better than combining vampires, sex, and death?

After seeing it, I can think of a few things. I can think of *lots* of things.

Neither one of us can recall the title or much of the action, but basically, these two vampire guys got mortals into their lair and they watched from a distance with bared fangs and bare chests as people had sex. They growled a little. I think the idea was that they were projecting their vampire natures into those hapless mortals, and watching what happens. A comedy of errors, so to speak, in which no one quite knew what was going on, including Lori and me. Of course, there was the obligatory female-with-female scene, and even some guys together, but the acting was poor, the bodies nondescript, the cinematography fuzzy, and the plot nil. We ended up playing it on hyper-speed just to stay entertained—and to get it over with.

Somebody ought to make a good erotic vampire flick for the nineties!

2

Since I actually know a producer who loves vampire tales, I decided to consult with her. Gail Zimmerman has worked for television for more than twenty years, and she did a story on Anne Rice in 1993 for a program called *Day One*. That's how I met her. She invited me to have lunch with her in Manhattan, and I soon discovered that her first stint in television was on *Dark Shadows*, and that she knew vampires in the media pretty well.

"Vampires have certainly become more alluring since Rice," she said. "I suppose they always had the ability to seduce and entice, but now that we know them better, we can understand why they are so appealing. Here are creatures able to be forever beautiful who have all the time in the world to learn and appreciate the arts. They are capable of emotion and sensual pleasures more intense than any human could imagine. And they now bear little resemblance to the mouldering, mindless monsters featured in so much of pre-Rice literature.

"Rice's work has changed film vampires, perhaps mainly because she has redefined what vampires are in general. Coppola called his film *Bram Stoker's Dracula*, but there was more than a little Rice thrown in. I don't remember the Prince of Darkness being so brooding and introspective."

"What do you think of recent vampire films in general?" I asked. "Not the ones everyone sees, but the more artsy ones." I hadn't seen very many, myself.

"There have been some delightful films—the Canadian *Blood and Donuts* comes to mind—but in general, as difficult as the genre is to pull off in print, it's even harder in film. Maybe it's all that night shooting, or maybe it's just hard to pull off an immortal, eternal creature when you're barely thirty, but for whatever reason, thought-provoking vampire films are few and far between."

"What about television?"

"Well, there was Barnabas Collins, of course, the resident brooding vampire of *Dark Shadows*. Though campy, bumbling, and stuck in scripts that made little sense, Barnabas got a lot of it right. He struggled with his vampire nature, but used its power to his advantage. He had regrets—and for very good reason. Over the years, there was plenty of time to develop a character arguably more morally ambiguous than any on TV.

"The show *Forever Knight* was successful, too. That was about Nick, thirteenth-century vampire, who was a modern-day Toronto cop. Guilt-ridden by the sins of his past, he seeks a 'cure' with the help of Natalie, the coroner and keeper of his secret. Natalie, like so many nineties women, is convinced she could change a man whose very nature makes him extremely dangerous. Moreover, as an older vampire points out, it's that very nature that attracted her in the first place. In the final episode, she wants to try a physical engagement. Nick agrees, soon loses control, and kills her. I've heard similar stories, metaphorically speaking, from plenty of my female friends; there's surely some moral lesson here about trying to change a man who hasn't changed in eight hundred years."

I enjoyed Gail's applications. She never fails to keep her perspective, which gave her a good objective base for my next question: "What do you think makes the vampire such a compelling cultural image?"

She'd given a lot of thought to this. "The theme of the monster within resonates with us because we humans have been capable of some very dark deeds. While many of us would like to think our essential nature is good, there's plenty of evidence to the contrary. I've covered many crime stories, and I find that the crimes that are most unsettling to people are not the depraved acts of a crazed psychopath on the loose; rather, they're done by the seemingly normal people who do horrible things. We don't want to believe that people like ourselves are capable of horrific acts. Perhaps it stirs up impulses we work hard to suppress. But the vampire shows us.

"Also, an immortal who lives on human blood is intriguing, in large part because it's a fantasy that raises interesting questions about the human condition. Presuming that none of the 'real' vampires are immortal—and yes, I am willing to say that they're not—I assume that what makes them vampires at all is a predilection to the night and a taste for blood. By actually doing this, with all the clumsy physical elements that it must require, it seems to me they might be destroying the fantasy and the imaginary world that goes along with it. Some things are best left to the imagination, I would think."

3

Blair Murphy, thirty-three, decided to make his own vampire films. He became a producer at the age of twenty-five, when he worked at odd jobs and borrowed money to create his first independent feature. He keeps his head shaved and sports an anchor tattoo on his arm. His production company is Empyre Films.

His parents were coroners and he was raised in a funeral home, so dark themes feel natural to him. "In second grade, when asked to explain what our parents' jobs were, I stated quite innocently, 'My dad paints dead people's lips.' It was my first press quote. They printed it in the town paper." Since then, he has been most interested in themes of sex, death, God, and artistic expression.

"Was it creepy to be raised in a funeral home?" I asked him.

"Nothing was creepy to me about it," he said. "Caskets and bodies are as normal to me as a basketball sitting in the driveway. My father was also big into home movies, so I ended up making movies. And there was no question that my first feature would end up as a vampire feature." Even so, he wasn't thrilled with the vampire films already available, and decided to aim for a more philosophical angle, inspired by Nietzsche's ideas on the *übermensch*.

Jugular Wine features a scholar in search of vampires who goes to Alaska and witnesses the death of a beautiful female vampire who has captivated—and partially transformed—him. He kills another, only to discover she's a scholar who disappeared years earlier. Unfortunately, she had the answers he needs as he feels himself going through disturbing changes.

When the movie came out, Murphy began to meet more people in the Gothic/vampire underground culture. He co-produced a feature documentary film of Dracula '97, but his second independent film, *Black Pearls*, was inspired when his girlfriend left him. "I came home after a particularly bad fight with a young woman I was in love with, to find she'd moved out. I had to do something, so overnight the idea of a new film dawned. I called up all these different devoted artists and crazy people and said, 'If I drive to your home will you do what you do on camera or let me ask you questions on camera?' So I stepped out into the American night, in secret, alone, and drove 55,000 miles in eleven months all over the United States interviewing people.

I went into some very strange homes. I recorded a full-on actual bloodletting ritual, which is the most extreme moment of the film. I followed a lot of the vampire role-playing gamers. I lived in secret next to the Westgate 'House of Death' Gallery on Magazine Street in New Orleans for a very fun, strange year. I went to Cairo, Egypt, and bribed a soldier to let me climb a pyramid. All of this is in the film. I also used a poem by Stan Rice, 'Excess is Ease,' as a sort of artistic battle cry."

Even so, he says, the film is not just about vampires. "I was following many avenues: the Gothic scene, music, magic, vampire authors, makeup artists, and pop funerary culture. I was also inspired by two other works: *Sherman's March*, a road-trip journey film that takes place across the South, and Jack Kerouac's book, *The Subterraneans*."

It was a cathartic experience, a personal statement as much as an exploratory project. Still, he's not sure whether he will do any more vampire films. "I'm only half into vampire culture," he told me. "I'm just as influenced and inspired by the American Beat writers. And to be completely honest, I think this modern pop/Gothic culture is very much from the efforts of the earlier Beat culture, but no one makes the connection."

I asked Murphy to comment further on this angle, since I knew Anne Rice was influenced by her reading of Jack Kerouac and her exposure to Beat poetry. He gave a well-considered response.

"Besides the blood theme of the vampire story, which I see valued as more a metaphor for intimacy, what does this culture actually champion? Exploration, history, desire, experience over taking things as one is told, the forbidden, the occult, questioning absolutes, self-discovery, sexuality, poetry, high-risk education, literature, a self-contained fashion and music community, and finally, an arena where one can go as any kind of outsider and rise without judgment. This is very similar to what the Beats were championing.

"I fully believe this: What I'm doing and what I see others doing, and our sense of exploration and self-examination and the creation process we are summoning, don't really have anything to do with Vlad the Impaler. I'm not just talking about vampire literary culture. I'm talking about what is going on in this period just before the millennium. A lot of these kids have not even read Stoker's book yet. The 'homework' they're doing comes down to finding out what works for their own truths. Because when it comes down to it, Stoker, Vlad

Tepes, Anne Rice—or even the vampire metaphor—are not absolutes any more than are the things these kids are using vampires to escape in the first place. Dracula and Lestat are merely the guideposts and starting points and big boys of the playground. But the true information one is summoning comes down to what works for each individual explorer.

"I went out and rented every documentary possible about vampires out there, and they were about Lugosi walking around with a cape or about criminals that sucked their victims' blood. And yes, all of it was interesting, but what does any of that leave me that I can apply to my own life? Breaking taboos is part of what makes this whole vampire tradition so empowering to the individual. It's part of why it's exciting. I think vampires are popular, in some ways, because it's the image of an isolated individual with his shoulder right up against the wall of his own mortality, questioning God and actually having the permission to explore these things and feel legitimate in one's quest to do so. That gives the modern vampire seeking his place in the universe a very real, fierce appeal to those who live vicariously through it.

"Self-exploration is high-risk, because going into it you may come out the other side changed forever. That's the point of going through your own personal darkness. I have interviewed so many people who say they have been through some sort of sexual abuse as a child. And they end up totally loving these books about a being that may or may not be real that comes in the night and no one believes it exists, and it's sexual and haunting. When kids are feeling cut off from their emotions and dressing like they're dead, I don't believe they're trying to become as dead as possible. All these funerary images people are adorning themselves with are not about reaching an end. I believe it's the opposite. I see this all as merely a starting point. The entire Gothic/vampire/pop funerary culture is actually about rebirth, and what we are seeing is actually a phoenix rising from the grave."

That was an interesting take on the exploratory aspects of vampire culture. But what about the blood, I asked him, particularly for those who believed they needed it to feel powerful or spiritual?

"Personally," said Murphy, "I really could care less about the blood aspect. I mean, I don't drink blood. Do you? Does that make me less of a contributor? Or do I get less enjoyment from the metaphor? Is Anne Rice known for blood-drinking? So why all this press looking to those particular individuals as if they are the leaders of the pack? In a book, descriptions about blood can be very poetic and beautiful, but in documentary footage, it just looks dangerous and psycho."

One thing Murphy noticed a lot in the scene was an emphasis on rules about what to wear, how to think, and whom to read in order to be a "self-styled loner." He felt disgusted with those who claimed they wanted to escape judgments, only to turn and impose them on others.

"The 'unlimited existence' promise of the vampire image is what attracts most of us to play vicariously in its sandbox in the first place," Murphy said. "So why are any of us justified in putting our personal limitations on it once we get there? Some people are promoting this entire lifestyle package. And they may have had such a fucked-up past that as an adult they can only see the world in terms of this us-against-them sort of twisted view. They put up rules as to what is legitimate and what is not."

I'd seen the same phenomenon, and over time had found it much more interesting to talk with people who claimed to be vampires but who weren't part of the club scene, where most of the conformist pressure seemed to reside.

"Where do you think it's all going?" I asked.

"Who knows? I interviewed my friend Alexandro on camera just last month and he wore this wacky cyber-vampire outfit. There were fish-tank tubes running all over it and he put some kind of glow-in-the-dark green gel through them, and he has on these moon-man industrial sunglasses. And his entire speech was about how vampires are exactly the same as Jesus Christ . . . positive, givers, seeking God. That we are meant to drink blood symbolically as one drinks the blood of Christ.

"Personally, I think the entire culture works better in isolated appreciation. You read alone. You consider thoughts of your own death alone. You contemplate your place in the universe alone. Your fears are your own. What your imagination brings to the canvas in the dark is your own. As much effort going on as there is to share, and the fun that happens when people lurk around in their undead costumes and perform at shows—I still think it comes down to a solitary experience."

From my own encounters, I found much that was legitimate in Murphy's perspective, and I often recalled some of his statements as I clarified my personal response to vampire culture.

4

Vampires inspire other types of theatricality as well. There are endless staged performances of *Dracula* in every form, from ballet to Broadway. I looked around for something a little more unique and found it in other types of productions.

In Boulder, Colorado, "Theatre of the Vampires" is a low-flying trapeze act put on by Frequent Flyers Productions. Nancy Smith is the show's creator and artistic director, and she claims to have seen countless vampire films and read over three hundred vampire novels to get inspiration. "We premiered the show in 1990," Smith told me, "to rave reviews and sellout crowds. The audience even came in costume." It's an annual event in Boulder, and Smith plans to take it on the road. She'd love to show it in New Orleans to honor Anne Rice.

It seems that whenever one links theater with vampires, one thinks of Anne Rice's creation of that dark performance troupe in eighteenth-century Paris, but Tony Sokol says this was not, in fact, the original inspiration for his own Vampyr Theatre, or La Commedia del Sangue. Instead, he was inspired from several sources: the concept of the Grand Guignol theater, an old 1971 movie called *Vampire Circus* (in which vampires arrive in town as a dark carnival troupe), details from his interviews with people who claimed to be real vampires, and the poignant work of a young poet named Maria A. Vega.

"I have written some poetry that is vampiric in nature," she told me. "It's sufficient to say that it's written from the lesser-explored side of the psyche and appeals to those who find darkness a safe haven. Tony was looking for vampires with unusual circumstances. I always felt that part of me was inherently vampiric, and it showed in my art."

Tony Sokol is a man of high energy, multifaceted background, and numerous skills and interests. He's a playwright, musician, researcher, and journalist. He seems to be ever in motion, darting from one place to another as he oversees his vampire production. He talks fast and calls himself a "man of many words but few coherent thoughts."

His grandfather was a grave-digger in Brooklyn, and he once lived in a haunted house with a ghost that his sister called George. His great-grandmother owned a copy of the 1903 edition of Bram Stoker's *Dracula*, and his mother was so impressed by it that before he could even read, Sokol bought a paperback copy. His mother read it to him.

Then he added Poe to the mix, and *Yellow Submarine*. His 1997 production was based in part on the Blue Meanies from that film, who "only took no for an answer."

His first production, *The Auction*, occurred in 1992 at the very "uptown" Le Bar Bat in Manhattan. The following year, Sokol was invited onto Joan Rivers's talk show with several guests who were there to discuss otherworldly subjects: horror expert David Skal, vampire musician Vlad, and the lead singer from One of Us. Sokol offered his phone number on the air, and afterward, people of all sorts—vampires, alien abductees, and conspiracy victims—contacted him to tell him their experiences. "Most of them were victims of something," he said, "or had some kind of nastiness in their background."

Sokol, I discovered only after seeing a performance, was the very person I had wanted to contact early in my research when Susan Walsh had disappeared. Because of his connections in the vampire world, she had sought him out. She'd come to the play and had then asked him for material for her article. He'd even read the first draft. They'd become friends, and together had met with other people who were concerned about covert political conspiracies. When I talked with him, Sokol admitted he felt that Walsh had reason to be paranoid, but offered no details. His hope was that she was still alive. I pressed him for more, but he steadfastly refused to divulge anything. Dead end there, except for his experiences with vampire culture. In fact, that interested me more. The search for Susan Walsh was beginning to pale against the search for vampires. I'd nearly forgotten to even ask him about her. I was growing more interested in the tales being told, as Sokol himself was.

To get vampire material, he'd placed an ad in the *Village Voice* and other free papers around New York. I had thought of doing that myself, but had so many contacts from other sources, I never got around to it. He told me he'd received many calls, and about two hundred were from people who lived a vampiric lifestyle. One-fourth of those were vampires, and about four were something he called "less than human or more than human." He did tell me about the risks he took seeking out the "fetish squatters" in a park on the Lower East Side. Reputedly, they were into bondage and S&M—and some of them into vampirism. He thought there were about five vampires among them; and it was Susan Walsh's boyfriend, Christian, who had introduced them both to some of the members of this group. Sokol had gained their trust and listened to their stories, finding within their sense of reality the same kind of rage against society and culture that he felt. He had seen some of the riots sparked by police efforts to rid the park of squatters, and felt that the homeless themselves were less frightening than the law enforcement personnel.

The more he listened to these vampires, the more material he gained for creating his plays. "They had heard about the play and wanted to talk to me, so I met them at twilight in places where there was a very clear exit. I've only had one person come at me, and one person ran away from me because apparently her hunger overcame her while she was talking to me. She ran down the street screaming, 'You're not safe!' These people have never seen the plays, so I don't know what they think. But I've based characters on more than just vampires. I've also interviewed SRA survivors, people with multiple personality syndrome, the AUM Shinrikyo cult, and UFO abductees."

I didn't know who all these groups were, but I was glad to know about his encounters with the squatters, because I had ventured near this park on my own on two occasions, and had not found them. My next approach was going to be at night, but he saved me the trip. They didn't sound like a very enlightening source.

This past year, Vampyr Theatre was based at 45 West 21st Street in Lower Manhattan. The production was called *Just Us Served*, and it began with fog blowing across a dark stage and a young girl being questioned sarcastically by a group of vampires—one male and two females dressed up in leather, corsets, and other Goth accoutrements. They were based on real people that Sokol had interviewed.

We, the audience, sat in rows of chairs that rose up from the stage, and most of the savvy crowd had dressed in black—although there was one couple in their sixties who were dressed as if they had just come from an expensive restaurant on the posh side of town. I wondered if this was where they'd meant to come.

I have to admit, I looked around a few times. Sokol had mentioned that real vampires sometimes attend, and I wanted to know if there were any in my immediate vicinity—particularly behind me. I didn't see any who looked obvious to me.

The plot centered around an FBI agent who was on the trail of the lead male vampire to bring him to justice. The vampires threw together a court in which an ancient vampire served as magistrate ("Your Heinous"). The agent's attempts to bring the vampire to justice were frustrated, and finally he broke down, killed his star witness, and sucked her blood. The overall implication, I felt as I left the theater, was that the government itself is a vampire. The artistic impression was a blurring of the lines between vampires and things we don't normally associate with bloodsuckers, which is what Sokol felt vampire culture is all about.

5

I wasn't sure I agreed. There was plenty of anger in Sokol's play, and a real sense of vampires being society's disenfranchised. I do think that the vampire is an icon of social rebellion, but those portrayed onstage had been coarse and vulgar, politically enraged over prejudice and oppression. I see that side of it, but I tend to appreciate what Blair Murphy had said: that the full effect of the fantasy is best experienced as a solitary pursuit. That's why I enjoyed Wraith's stories, I think, over the more collective and politicized interpretations. And I did hear from him again.

It was several weeks after our last encounter, and I'd nearly given up hope that he'd contact me. He called again late one night and, as if seducing me toward some as-yet-unidentified goal, he launched right into another of his past vampiric conquests. I let him talk without interruption, aware that he was getting bolder and darker in his descriptions. In any other context, this might have been considered an obscene phone call.

"I slink into the bar at midnight, cruising for a boy," he said, so low it was nearly a whisper. "I quickly assess the crowd and then edge into the dark recesses of a corner and wait. I'm a lion that has not eaten for days, and I intend to kill tonight.

"An hour passes and I know the territory is ghost, so I move on. Reaching for the tacky brass doorknob to leave, I'm startled by the entrance of a young, beautiful boy. He smirks at me and asks if I'm leaving. 'Not now,' I reply. We walk together to the bar.

"Moving close to his ear, I whisper, 'You're exactly what I want tonight.' He blushes. To my surprise, he's a novice at this, fresh prey. He's twenty-one and has never had an 'ultimate' experience.

"I charm him into taking me to his house—where he lives with his mother. He has a comfortable room with many soft pillows—

handy props. I sit in his rocking chair and ask him to undress. He's a little uncertain, but it's dark, and he removes his clothing slowly, in a sensual manner—as if he thinks *he's* in charge. But I've chosen him. He's perfect for me—his body tone, erotic style, passion, and sense of adventure. He's clearly eager to commence. So am I.

"I lay down the rules—he is not allowed to see my body until Halloween night. He's disappointed but charmed. I get him off and then make two more dates to prepare him for the ritual. I promise a lot, which excites him and also makes him anxious. I know he thinks I'm mysterious and elusive—and that he likes it. I'm the Latin lover of his dreams, or so he thinks. His eyes are lost when he looks at me. He enjoys being controlled, and I enjoy him needing me in this way. But I don't wish to hurt him. I have to provide a crack through which to slip after Halloween is over. I never keep them after the ritual is finished.

"The night before Halloween, we meet to walk on the beach together. The rancid odor of rotting seaweed arouses me as we talk to the beat of the shifting surf. I have abstained from him for a full week and I explain that I'm giving him tantalizing previews of the following night. He wants me to start now, but I quiet him with a deep kiss. He agrees to wait, though he's disappointed. I tell him what he must do to prepare himself for the ritual.

"He is to thoroughly wash every orifice of his body and then apply baby powder between his legs for softness and stimulation. He is to wear nothing beneath his jeans.

"On Halloween night, I arrive to pick him up for dinner. He's terribly excited, but I make him wait through the entire dinner before I touch him. We go back to his house, where his mother and brother are asleep. By flickering candlelight, we undress each other in his room. His hands shake and I ask him why.

"'I'm too excited,' he whispers.

"'There's no such thing,' I assure him. As I move to kiss him, I puff hot wisps of breath into his mouth, licking, not kissing, his lips. I lick gently, then kiss him deeply. He gets wild and I calm him again, though I'm aroused by his trembling, urgent anticipation. Standing entirely naked, we look at ourselves in the candle-pitched mirror. It's a beautiful moment.

"His mother is a surgical nurse, so he has a scalpel on hand, as I've instructed. I mentally direct him to pick up the knife and, as if practiced, he uses it to slice his left nipple. A small trickle of blood streams down his smooth chest. Before it cools, I lick ahead of the flow, moving my tongue to his breast. He moans softly and kisses my head. I lift my head and let him taste his own blood. He likes it.

"I back away and watch his green eyes searching for me in the darkness. This is a premonition. He will search for me in the night and I will elude him. I reach for his blood and smear it on his chest. He takes my hand and smears it against my own chest. Then we have sex, and afterward lay still together, listening to our breathing as it powers down.

"We sleep and then awaken to repeat this with his right nipple. He falls asleep again, and I leave. He will want me to come back, but he won't find me, and no matter how much I like him, he's gone from me now. This is the darkness of my ritual, the final emptiness."

When a silence ensued that seemed to question whether I was pleased, I asked, "Do you really feel satisfied with all this?"

"Yes, completely. Because of the mystique and the high degree of anticipation. It's vital to the hunt. His youth works for me—the younger they are, the more willing they are to wait and do what they're told. They seek mentors. He was everything I'd hoped. He was intensely responsive to me. He reacted with strong lust to my every touch, glance, innuendo, and caress. What more could you want?"

I asked again if I could meet him. He laughed softly. "Maybe," was all he would say before he hung up the phone.

He was seducing me, and it was working.

CHAPTER SEVEN

new york by night

I

Most people who visit Manhattan know the changing splendors of Rockefeller Center, the majesty of St. Patrick's Cathedral, the glitz of Trump Tower, and the array of expensive shops along Fifth Avenue: Saks, Bergdorf Goodman, FAO Schwartz. Then there's the Plaza, Broadway, the Met, Central Park, and Radio City Music Hall, where the Rockettes still perform. Even the notorious Times Square is cleaning up its act. Or one might visit South Street Seaport to see the renovated East River waterfront or take a trip up to the one hundred tenth floor of the twin buildings known as the World Trade Center, which dwarf the Empire State Building. And there's always the New York Stock Exchange and the United Nations building. Familiar names, all.

To find the offbeat, people hail a cab or jump on the subway and head for SoHo's art galleries or the East and West Village boutiques, where one can find fetish gear, death shops, eyeball rings, and Gothic garb galore. They ignore the ragged homeless and avoid areas where raging crackheads holler at the air.

First-time visitors often are nervous. They've heard about New York's infamous crimes. Guidebooks warn tourists to be watchful, but the criminal element adds its own allure to the city. Those who dare can take guided tours to famous murder sites. First stop: New Amsterdam's first recorded murder in 1638, the result of a brawl. Butcheries, mob hits, grave plundering, and fatal love triangles all contribute to the Big Apple's dark heritage.

Of the clubs that cater to offbeat nightlife, I'd already been to the Tunnel (a dance club converted from a former subway tunnel on Twelfth Avenue), Mother, and the Bank (once a real bank). For the most part, the scene was the same in each place: lots of Goth clothing, Victorian and Edwardian garb, corsets, walking sticks, top hats, black lace, vinyl boots, belly rings, dog collars, black lipstick, androgynously slim bodies, satin vests, blood-red eyes, frilly cravats, and fangs everywhere you look.

I also knew about the Gothic church-turned-club on Sixth Avenue called Limelight, that was open, then closed, then open again. I'd heard of the Cave and the Vault. Vampires also went to restaurants. At night, anyway. Night Poe, the online Nighttimer who taught vampire classes, had told me about an eating establishment in that area, which she called a werewolf theme restaurant. However, she believed it was owned by vampires, who called themselves Lunars "because they're more like mythical werewolves than vampires, but they're real vampires."

2

Few tourists venture into the East Village, where funk and punk rule. Once an area dominated by gangs, brothels, and pool halls, it became a center for organized crime. Now there are clubs for every taste, many of them open until four in the morning.

It was on St. Mark's Place, a mecca of tattoo, leather, silver, body piercing, and exotic clothing shops, that I went to get fitted for a pair of vampire fangs. James Fenimore Cooper had once lived on that street, and the Sundance Kid had roomed nearby before departing with Butch Cassidy for their fatal trip to Bolivia. The first recorded Mafia hit in the city was on St. Mark's and Third. Not far away is Tompkins Square Park—Hippie Central in the sixties; in the eighties, confrontations between the homeless and the police had curtailed much of the drug trade there. Some of its original gentility had been restored, although this is where I'd heard that many mentally ill homeless lived. One such person, Daniel Rakowitz, a schizophrenic afraid of the devil, had killed and dismembered his girlfriend in 1989 and wandered the park bragging about how he had boiled her various parts. This is also where the vampire squatters hung out.

However, my task that day was to get teeth. Father Sebastian, who had run the Long Black Veil at Mother, had insisted that I must have some professionally made fangs, which he would supply himself. I agreed to meet him where he fitted and carved them in the back room of Andromeda, a body-piercing shop. Andromeda sat high off the street. On the stairs were two young males and a female lounging about on a hot afternoon, their bodies sporting a wealth of piercings and tattoos. They let me pass, but I was aware how strange I looked. I had on an ordinary blouse and skirt—at least the skirt was black!—and my hair lacked frizz, spikes, or any other type of the exotic ornamentation I saw all around on the street below. So did my face. I felt utterly conspicuous.

While I waited for Sebastian inside the shop, I was treated to a demonstration of the various sizes of needles used for piercing—one was alarmingly large!—and instructed in how to care for skin violations. The pierced tongue, I was told by a guy whose own silver-laden tongue clicked noisily against his teeth with nearly every word, heals the fastest. Other parts of the body, particularly those that stay moist, take a couple of weeks. One of the girls told me that when she began to wear corsets she had to stop wearing a navel ring because it hurt too much. I just nodded like I understood.

Finally Sebastian arrived, walking in on platform boots that made him six inches taller than his already tall height. He carried a black vinyl corset—his own—that needed repair. With breathless energy, he ushered me into a small room in back where he kept his equipment. He made thousands of sets of fangs every year, he claimed, and offered a variety of shapes. I could have the ordinary fangs fitted to the canine teeth, or a set of upper and lower fangs, or fangs set closer together ("laterals"), or double fangs. These teeth needed no adhesive whatsoever, he insisted, and I found that hard to believe. I'd tried my share of Halloween fangs and had failed to find any that I could wear for more than five minutes.

Sebastian had been trained as a dental technician, so he knew what he was doing with the materials he used. He made a cast of my canines, and in short order had teeth made for me of "approved den-ture material." (Some people opt for gold or silver, or get them permanently implanted. A few go so far as to have their real teeth filed into fangs.)

He told me that the fangmakers in Seattle had started the sort of vampire scene that he wanted to emulate here in New York. In 1993 a couple of fangmakers responded to the requests of the role-players who were part of the White Wolf game, "Vampire: The Masquerade," and its fan club, the Camarilla, which was based in Seattle at the time. Sebastian appreciated the feeling of "family" that the fangmakers created among their clients. "They also achieved a certain evolution of aesthetic beyond any other scene I've known," he said. "I base almost everything I do on what I've heard of them."

As he worked, I asked him if he'd ever run into Susan Walsh. He flashed me a wary look and admitted that he knew people who had known her.

"She interviewed a lot of us around here," he said, and then dropped his voice conspiratorially. "That's still an ongoing case. We're not supposed to talk about it."

"Why not?" I asked, unwilling to let it drop that fast.

"There's just more to it than most people know, and I can't talk about it."

"Do you think she's alive?"

"She is. No one around here was involved. It wasn't the vampires. The police investigated us all. It wasn't us."

"How do you know she's alive?"

"I just can't talk about it. But I know."

I continued to press, but he yielded nothing further, although he too knew Walsh's boyfriend. Christian came and went, he said, and no one had heard from him in some time.

As Sebastian filed down my new fangs, he told me how fulfilling his work was. "When a fangmaker makes fangs," he said, "the client gets a piece of the fangmaker because he sits with that person and he inspires them. He awakens them by talking to them about the perspective of what it's like to be a vampire." His plans were to develop a "coven" in which the leaders of the various sections would be a network of fangmakers across the country.

Then Sebastian was ready. He held up the fangs and showed me how to pop them in. They felt just right. And he was right. They stayed in place without adhesive. I was impressed. These teeth were in there until I worked them off with a bit of force. The points hurt my bottom lip a little, but I figured that was just a matter of getting used to them. So there I was—a vampire!

Or at least I looked like one. At the very least, I looked like a role-player striving for authenticity. I was ready to party.

But first I had to learn the proper care and feeding of these fangs. I was to keep them in a contact lens container with a drop of water, avoid eating with them in or wearing them for more than twelve hours at a time, avoid contact with blood capsules (which stain them pink), leaving them near heat sources, drinking heavy liquors, and biting cats, dogs, people, or small woodland creatures. No problem. "If you bite someone and break their skin," Sebastian warned, "we suggest they get a tetanus shot."

After that, Sebastian invited me to accompany him to a historic former synagogue on Norfolk Street, just below Houston. It had been built during the German Romantic period, the first synagogue in the city. Now it housed the Angel Orensanz Foundation and was to serve as the site of Sebastian's Halloween vampire extravaganza. He planned a banquet, a role-playing room, a theatrical performance, and several popular bands.

As we walked, I asked him about himself. He told me that as a teenager he had become immersed in role-playing games. His parents were having problems and he found solace in his imagination. He spent all of his time and money on game books. He even sneaked away to do it. At the time, it seemed the only thing holding his life together.

"I was always a costume buff and enjoyed bringing my imagination to life," he said. "I wasn't very interested in the tabletop games because they bored me. They seemed very slow and I just read the books to expand my imagination. I got involved in live medieval role-playing and I could totally immerse myself in my fantasy, virtually feeling I was somewhere else. It was perfect, but—with one exception—it lacked the enthusiasm of reality. That's why I approach vampire games and mythology as a realistic aesthetic and not a fantastic experience.

"I never claim to be immortal, drink blood, or turn to ashes during sunlight, although I never could stand garlic. Hey, I love the beach and tanning. I hope to grow old and have grandchildren."

I liked his sense of humor, although it was clear that he'd been through some trauma with his addiction to games. He'd had a breakdown in eighth grade and had to give all his books away. He seemed to have better perspective on it now at the age of twenty-three.

"What's the appeal of the vampire for you?" I asked.

"It's simply an aesthetic fetish, to my mind. I love how we can make it sexual, theatrical, and romantic, and use costuming to look like the real thing. I love how well the dominance-and-submission techniques can be redefined with vampire terminology. I do find the idea of drinking blood to be sexy, but I don't want anyone to drink mine. My body is a temple. That's how I feel about it."

He described himself as a born-again Christian, die-hard Republican vampyre entrepreneur. Christ was a servant, and so, according to him, is he.

"How do you combine the vampire mythology with your spirituality?" I asked him. That part puzzled me.

"Vampirism is a fetish for me," he reasserted, "not my spirituality. I am a very unorthodox Christian. I try to ignore the Catholic approach and relate to my own interpretation of what my personal relationship with Jesus is. This is partially influenced by the Quaker faith of Christians who meditate in silence every Sunday and then debate what their relationship with Jesus is for each individual. In fact, my next line of products, Seraphim, will reflect my religious beliefs mixed with sexual freedom.

"As for politics, I am very liberal on many points, but I do stand for the real issues the Republican Party stands for, such as less government and more individual freedom, and the right to bear arms. Also, I'm a very family-oriented person. Basically, I want to provide the kind of stable family for my kids that was taken away from me when my parents divorced."

Returning to my original question, he said, "Although I'm a Christian, I relate to both existences and feel they're not that far apart. I found out I was a Christian just about the same time I started making fangs back in 1994. But I never really found a way to deal with both issues until August 1997. I realized I always loved my relationship with Jesus and felt it was personal. So many people in my life disliked Christianity for its murder of thousands of pagans. But I realized that was the Church, not Jesus, and the lessons I learned from my time with the Quakers opened my eyes to realize that Christianity is about purifying your soul and looking at a perfect person: Jesus as a role model. So when I'm on my deathbed, I'll realize that I've reached salvation and that I strove as well as I could to live up to what is right according to a set of universal truths."

He mentioned that he'd found a small group of Christians who felt the same way he did about vampires and who planned to pursue the organized practice of an amalgam of the two mythologies. He wasn't sure exactly what they meant to do, but it excited him that others existed who believed as he did.

"Thus, my conflict ended when I realized I had a fetish for the vampire aesthetic and a special spiritual quality. This meant I could make a difference in my own little world and be kind of a Father for the vampire scene here. That's why I'm Father Sebastian. I'm providing something good. People have told me they've had the greatest sex of their lives when they do it with the fangs in. Making the fangs is like a spiritual experience for me because I know I'm enhancing people's lives."

Along with his fangmaking, Sebastian ran a multifaceted enterprise called Sabretooth. Inspired by the worldwide Vampire Connection described in Anne Rice's novels, he had started it with his fang business and had expanded into jewelry, clothing, and vampire events. He also wanted to put out a magazine and he was quite astonished to find that no one had yet trademarked the name "Vampyre" for a publication. He saw it as a guide to the scene, and a way to advertise the array of merchandise available for people to enhance their fantasies. He was also planning several vampire gatherings, such as the Halloween Ball, a Vampyre Valentine's Day Ball, a weekend-long event that he called the Endless Night, and some role-playing games sponsored by House Sabretooth, his client/member social club. He hoped to make the New York vampire scene dominate all others.

"With these concepts," he pointed out, "I've more or less fostered a whole community with its own etiquette, culture, and music. It's taking on its own life. That's what I want to be remembered for, and I'll gain a sort of immortality from the vampire myth. Upon my passing, people will say, 'Father Sebastian started the vampire scene here in New York and sparked the Vampyre Connection around the world.'"

I was impressed with his ambition, but not so sure all the other vampires would want to congregate under his rule. Yet he did have a following.

House Sabretooth was formed to foster a positive relationship between Sabretooth, Inc., and its clients. "I had a vision several years ago," said Sebastian, "and that was to network the vampire scene. My dream is to actually open the clubs and restaurants as what they're like in the Anne Rice novels. Location for location and club for club. Making them reality. If that comes to pass or not, I will never know, but for now I'm happy to network vampire-themed nightclubs such as the Fang Club in LA and Mother in New York."

Membership is offered free to all of those who purchase fangs from the company. House Sabretooth is meant to be similar in organization to a vampire clan. The benefits of joining include a free silver ankh, access to events, discounts on paraphernalia, a place in the "family lineage" of clients, and an astrological chart based on the day the fangs were made.

The first rule of etiquette—given how many definitions of the vampire were circulating out there—was to be quite clear about what they mean by the word: "The vampire is the most powerful legendary figure in human culture. Each and every culture throughout human history has had its own vampire mythology, from ancient China to Europe, from Africa to Central America. Our own culture has its version, as defined by Bram Stoker, Anne Rice, Poppy Z. Brite, and various other writers. It has been incorporated into our lives and has become a cultural fetish."

Sebastian also makes a distinction between *vampire* and *vampyre*. "When saying *vampire*, we refer to the creature of legend who has been represented in myth and literature. When saying *vampyre*, we refer to modern vampire enthusiasts who incorporate vampire mythology into their lifestyle. Such practices include wearing fangs, contacts, and white makeup, going to vampyre clubs, and social interaction.

"Vampyres can either be solitary creatures or they can form Circles. A Circle is a group of friends and/or lovers who have made a commitment to each other. Close-knit Circles rarely have more than three to five members, while looser Circles can have upwards of thirteen members."

Sebastian's group "promotes people who do not claim to be immortal or turn to ash during sunlight. If blood-fetishists, they keep their fetishes safe and between lovers. Bloodletting and blood-fetishes are *very* dangerous practices, and if performed, should be between those who have taken proper precautions for safety and health."

There are also Havens and Domains that have to be kept straight.

"Havens are local gathering places, which are most commonly night-clubs. Here vampyres can escape the 'mundane' life, openly bare fangs, relax, enjoy one another's company, dance, and follow the social dictates of their region. A Domain is a territory that publicly 'belongs' to a certain Regent, House, or Circle."

Then there's the issue of "mundanes"—those people who just don't know what this scene is about. "When we refer to mundanes," said Sebastian, "we mean nonvampires. Within the scene they're called Swans, because swans are romantic and elusive, but if you feed them, they come to you. Black Swans are lovers or close friends who completely accept the vampire lifestyle, while White Swans cause problems. Many times we make fun of mundanes for their lack of mental freedom."

I couldn't keep it all straight, especially with all the terms and definitions involved in becoming a member. Yet I knew that's what people attracted to role-playing loved: the elaborate rituals and secret names and levels of expertise.

"As each culture in human history has had its own version of the vampire myth," Sebastian explained to me, "so does modern western culture. We just have a new angle on it. Instead of fearing it, we embrace it and have made it heroic. Since the myth reflects specific dark aspects of each culture it has touched, the modern western myth represents erotica, untouchable desires, mystery, and things we cannot even think of possessing, such as immortality or people lying at your feet through vampiric powers."

Sebastian has so many plans for expanding his vampire enterprise that his enthusiasm becomes contagious. In fact, before I quite realized it, he'd swept me into it by asking me to edit *Vampyre Magazine*. I was hesitant. I had enough on my plate, but the idea intrigued me—particularly as a good entrée into the vampire scene. I agreed, and we put together a list of people to profile, interview, and review.

3

The next invitation I received was to attend an extravagant private event—a vampire fetish ball. It was to be held in a famous dungeon called the Nutcracker Suite, and I had to wear something Victorian, rubber, vampire, or fetish. I decided on a kicky short black dress with a chain around my waist from which hung a black leather paddle, a tiny knife, and various other suggestive instruments. Around my wrists I wore leather handcuffs with silver studs, and I carried a multiflayed whip for good measure. I added black silk gloves and leather lace-up boots over sheer black stockings. My fangs went into a tiny plastic container, to be installed after dinner. Over this getup I donned a light jacket so I could catch the train without a lot of gawkers talking among themselves about what I was up to. I was just going as a spectator. Or so I thought.

I had tried to get Outlaw to go with me, but he had declined. I had shown the invitation to several friends, which featured the bare buttocks of a young woman bending over, ready to be whipped by a demonic-looking character. The invitation promised seven dominatrixes, five lavishly equipped dungeons, a deprivation chamber, a special duct-taping performance, branding, scarification, mummification, feminization (what could *that* be?), and piercing. Oh, and also bondage and spanking.

My friends laughed and said they could never attend such an outrageous event. But they urged me to go because they wanted to know all the details.

I told a friend, Jana Marcus in San Francisco, of my plight—to go alone at night to a fetish ball in an unfamiliar New York neighborhood. Since she had lived in Manhattan and knew the scene, she didn't think it would be any big deal, but she offered to set me up with D'Shan, a friend of hers in Brooklyn.

So what was the difference between going alone and going with someone I'd never met? Well, he was at least "pedigreed" by a friend's recommendation. D'shan and I talked on the phone and he asked if he could take me to dinner, to La Nouvelle Justine, the fetish theme restaurant that was making news at the time. Well, okay, let's just make it a full fetish evening. Before he hung up the phone, he asked for my neck measurement. That was a first. I gave it to him and wondered what he'd do with it. Not a dog collar, I hoped. It would never go with my dress.

So Friday evening arrived and I got to La Nouvelle Justine on 23rd and Seventh. The suggestive sign outside of a naked woman told me I was in the right place. Justine had been written up in several local papers as a place where one could go for a meal and a thorough humiliation by the wait staff. Sounded fun.

I entered a room with black walls, red lighting, and iron railings all around. It was a small space, crowded with tables. I looked around but saw no one who resembled Jana's description of my date. I expected a black man dressed in some sort of elegant vampire garb. All I knew of him was his first name and that he designed jewelry.

I asked for him, but the host said no one by that name had checked in. Then one of the waiters—wearing tight black pants and a strikingly well developed bare chest—told me that someone had called to say he'd been robbed and would be late. Perhaps that was my date. Well, it *was* New York. That was possible. So I went to the bar to order a drink—I needed one—and to wait. Among the choices were "The Masochist"—a blend of vodka, orange curacao, sambuca, and lemon juice; "The Necrophiliac"—gin, rum, triple sec, and lemon juice; and "The Autophiliac"—light rum, contreau, and cream. I ordered a Merlot.

As I sipped it, I noticed all around the ceiling overhead was a border of black-ink etchings of nudes. Separating the bar from the main dining area were black curtains, through which I could see that some of the booths were made to look like beds, with votive candlelight. Waiters and waitresses ran from table to kitchen sporting tight leather clothing, collars with silver spikes, rubber corsets, or transparent garb that made them appear almost naked. Some of them carried small whips, and the females wore very high spiked heels. Most of them were pierced somewhere on their bodies, and many showed off an array of tattoos.

Smoke had already shrouded the place in a misty haze, and loud punk music made the waiters step smartly as they took orders and served meals. As I watched, a few brave souls purchased extra services, all listed for their dining pleasure in the back of the menu: spankings, "doggy" obedience training, shoe cleaning, foot massage, public humiliation, and verbal abuse. One man was led on his hands and knees in a dog collar across the restaurant, while a woman was placed in handcuffs hanging from the ceiling and smacked with a leather paddle as her friends whistled for more.

My date still hadn't shown, but a troupe of four men sat near me at the bar and told me they were all "doms." They invited me to a full weekend of fetish activities—imagining, I suppose, that I was there because that's what I liked. I declined. And I didn't believe for a minute that four men who all claimed to be dominant would get along as buddies.

Then in came a balding man in his sixties wearing a black T-shirt that said something about the reign of death. He'd been drinking elsewhere, and he pulled out a deck of cards and urged me to pick one. I did, and he laughed and began to babble about some kind of conspiracy that he knew about that we'd all better watch out for. I began to think I should probably leave.

At that moment, D' arrived. At least, the person who could *only* be D'. He was dressed elegantly in an eighteenth-century frock coat. He also carried a silver-headed walking stick. His thick black hair was caught in numerous exquisite braids that fell to his shoulders and down his back.

He had brought with him a necklace sculpture made of interconnecting strands of silver that resembled both a spider's web and the body of a very large spider. From it, on a silver chain, hung the metal replica of a human heart. Not a valentine-type heart. A real one. He apologized profusely for being late and smiled as he presented the necklace to me, showing his vampire teeth. It was not your conventional corsage, but it was a dramatic gesture. I accepted it and put it on.

We were shown to our table by the bare-chested host, and while another male customer was bound to two chains that hung from the ceiling in the center of the room in preparation for a spanking, we looked through the menu. I noticed that, while the food looked fairly normal, one could order a large and expensive chocolate shoe for dessert filled with raspberries and mousse. "La Chaussure Fetiche de Justine."

We ordered, and I asked D' about his fascination with vampires. I already knew that he'd been completely entranced with Anne Rice's second vampire novel, *The Vampire Lestat*. That book had provided some structure for the way he was thinking about things. He had been profiled in Jana's book on Anne Rice fans, *In the Shadow of the Vampire*, and I wanted more details.

"How did the vampire image structure the chaos in your life?" I asked, paraphrasing him. "What was the chaos about?"

He seemed eager to explain. "When I started to put away 'childish things' such as thinking that Santa Claus was a person, I began the process of centering and balancing myself. I then saw how this world has became a contradiction of itself. I looked at the major influences of our lives on this sphere that we call Earth, and the attitude broken down to its essence states that we're all vampires. I just choose to wear this type of outer covering on my body to go ahead and look like a vampire. My thinking is much more centered than most folks in the position of religious guides."

Okay. He was intense. I wasn't sure I really understood. I knew he'd never been a horror fan, but did love vampire movies as a child. He liked the fact that vampires were outsiders, and being a black person in Texas where he grew up, he felt a kinship. He understood the way society projected its fears onto outsiders, and he loved the way vampires like Rice's Gabrielle embraced the darkness. "Her books helped me understand my own feelings," he said. "I used to be very angry when I walked by people and they got scared of me just because I was black. So I thought of myself as a vampire. I now go down the street dressed like this and people are scared, but they have a reason to be. And I feel more powerful, like a wolf. Like I have the vampire's blood in me, so they have a good reason to be afraid."

He did look pretty disturbing with those fangs, and he told me that one day soon, he'd like to have them permanently installed.

After observing a few more S&M role-playing events, we decided it was time to get to the Nutcracker Suite. We went to the address, and taking an elevator to a penthouse suite, we found ourselves walking into a maze of darkened rooms, each of which contained a different type of authentic torture device. I was impressed. This was expensive equipment. I learned that people could rent this place for an exorbitant fee and put a partner or two through their paces. In fact, it was quite a popular place.

I saw a vaulting horse, but I was sure it was not used for gymnastics. I could tell from the straps and cuffs attached to it. It wasn't long before a man led a nude, overweight woman to it and strapped her, facedown, on the implement. He whipped her lightly, teasingly, and then turned her over, working on her legs, breasts, and stomach. She moaned with each quick slap of the leather thongs. A crowd of onlookers gathered around, fascinated, although most of them seemed intimately familiar with these proceedings. I heard several European accents, and also learned that some couples had traveled from other states to be here.

Many of the females present appeared to be someone's "pet."

There were lots of dog collars, corsets, bare bottoms, and breasts among them, but the males were mostly dressed in rubber or leather—particularly chaps. Nothing private was exposed on them. A few had on vampire drag, and everyone seemed to have some type of whip or paddle in his hand or attached to his belt. One woman with a tightly corseted waist told me she had been in training for over a year to get her waist down to twenty-two inches. That meant she had been cinched up as much as possible during that time. I envied the waist, but not at that price.

I got bored fast in this room, so I went searching for action. I noticed that no one was on the table that tilted people onto their heads, but in one chamber I spotted a fully equipped gynecology chair. Yeah, that was a torture instrument, for sure. A woman was being positioned on it and I did not wish to watch.

Another young female, this one thin and clad only in black silk panties, was handcuffed by an older man, who hoisted her arms overhead and fastened her cuffs onto a large hook. He then took a long leather whip to her skin, all up and down her bare legs, while she chirped out surprised little whimpers of pleasured pain. Her skin soon turned a bright red from the lashings. She writhed against her restraints, which was obviously meant to excite the crowd. The man smiled, patted her tenderly, and continued his work.

D' came up beside me to watch.

"What is it with all these females?" I asked. "Why are they the ones getting stripped and tortured?"

"There's a guy in the other room," he told me. I was on my way.

That long-haired man was bare-chested, but wore leather pants. Not very vulnerable, I thought. The woman from Mother who had worn the long black veil was standing in front of him. She had on the hat and veil, and textured stockings with a black, frilled corset. She held two lighted candles from which she dripped wax onto her submissive's hairy chest. He flinched and muttered a bit, but hardly seemed in any pain. Once or twice she reached for a whip from her blond female assistant, whose head was partly shaved, and smacked the man lightly in a rhythmic manner. She also ran a spiked finger ornament over his nipples. Big deal.

Sebastian, who sponsored this event, came in to see how I was enjoying it. I said I was disappointed with the emphasis on tormenting females, and he found that amusing.

In the next room, a young man was getting thoroughly wrapped with tape into immobility. I supposed that this was meant to excite him with his own fears of losing control, but I didn't see the fetish in it. Each to his own, I guess. I'd heard of a man who got aroused only when buried in concrete (that's a trick). But overall, the whole scene seemed more playful than serious, and hardly like the novels that describe pushing someone to the edge with genuine pain until they reached a euphoric, ecstatic state. Maybe that was done in private.

In the hallway, a young woman asked me if I was into blood. Thinking quickly, I said that I was—well, I was writing about it—and she asked if I would drink from her. She was a donor, she said, seeking a vampire. I declined.

These activities were scheduled to go on all night, but I had to catch the last train back home, so I began to head toward the door. Before I got there, the man who had whipped the woman on the vaulting horse stopped me and said, "You're just the kind of woman that my partner and I fantasize about having as a third. Would you join us?"

I was stunned. I had no idea what to say. They'd just complimented me (I think), and I searched for an answer that wouldn't offend them. I quickly mumbled something about the train.

"Just for a few minutes," he said. "Come on. If you're going to write about this, you should experience what it's like." So much for my cover.

Okay. I'd been caught playing Fossey. I had decided to immerse, so now I faced a real test. I'd dodged Diogenes earlier when he'd pressed me about drinking my blood, and now the girl in the hall; but I was really on the spot in this situation. It was time to get involved. I went back into the room with him and he handed me a whip.

It looked a bit harmless and I slapped it a few times against my leg to test it. Not too bad. But just then Sebastian came in and gave me his own whip, which was much more lethal-looking. The man instructed me to use it against his partner's breasts while he worked on her from behind. I looked at her and swallowed hard. This was it.

Quickly he mentioned something about a safe word. I knew what that was: people used nonerotic words like *orange* or *mole* to indicate they'd broken out of the fantasy because the pain was greater than they liked. You couldn't use *no* or *stop*, because those were pretenses to sharpen the edge.

I cringed. I didn't want to whip someone. Yet she was waiting, her naked breasts thrust toward me. At least I was the "top" and she the "bottom." I wouldn't have agreed to it any other way.

So I started. Sebastian's whip had many thongs, like the fringe on a sixties style leather jacket. I slapped them lightly across her large breasts and she closed her eyes and began to moan. The man looked around her body up at me and urged me to go at it a little harder.

Okay. They wanted a dominatrix, I could be a dominatrix. I set my feet and positioned myself to put a little muscle into it, but just as I raised my arm, I caught the eye of someone on the sidelines. Diogenes. He watched me with an amused expression, one eyebrow raised. I should have realized he'd be at this event. I turned away and brought the whip down hard against this masochist's vulnerable skin. She jumped a little, as if surprised. Her partner smiled and nodded for me to continue. I did it again, and then again, gaining confidence and force with each stroke. In fact, it was rather fun. I could get into this.

"Mercy!" she cried, so I hit her harder. She said it again, louder, and I was about to strike when her partner jumped up and grabbed my arm. "She said 'mercy,'" he told me. "That's her safe word!"

"Sorry," I said, and I handed him the whip. "But what kind of safe word is that?"

I turned to leave. He jumped close to me and handed me a piece of paper with their phone number on it and a smiley face, asking me to call and be friends. "Let's do it again," he said. "We'll teach you."

I slipped the paper in my pocket and left.

I walked by another room where a silent crowd had gathered, so I decided to take a quick peek. The light was bright, the atmosphere intense, and everyone's eyes were on a young man in the center of the room. His back was bare and another man was drawing a razor blade across it, opening up shallow gashes. Crimson streams ran freely down his back. I was horrified, but then I realized what it was: scarification. The fetish of cutting. The new skin decor. A way to fire up the excitement by seeing fresh blood. I noticed Diogenes there, watching with a hungry look in his dark eyes.

I knew I'd see this same thing again somewhere along the line, so I ran to catch my train. During the cab ride over, I reviewed everything I'd just seen, and felt a little rattled by that last scenerio. What people will do for the rush. I could only imagine what might go on among those who liked this form of vampire fetish. I wondered how much further I wanted to go in that particular direction. I hadn't really asked myself that question yet, and if I didn't have an answer, I'd surely be caught off guard again.

I made it to the train with a minute to spare, and as I stood waiting for the doors to open up, I slipped the handcuffs off my wrists, first one and then the other. I unbuckled the paddle and the knife from the chain around my waist and dropped them into my purse. Then I noticed a young preppie guy watching all this—the fetish gear, the lace-up boots, the vampire fangs—with an astonished expression. I smiled, winked, and got on the train.

CHAPTER EIGHT

different tastes

I

Susan Walsh didn't leave New York for her vampire investigation, but since Tony Sokol knew vampire-oriented people in Los Angeles, I had every reason to believe she knew of them, too. Yet that's not why I was going to L.A. It was time to shed Malefika and be myself. Anne Rice scholar by day; bloodhound by night. I was to find that this switching of identities would work quite well, depending on the person to whom I was talking. Admittedly, there were times when I guessed wrong and lost access, but mostly, one or the other of my identities tapped a rich vein. And sometimes Dr. Ramsland, the therapist, was even better.

I was invited to speak at a conference in L.A., and it seemed a good opportunity to investigate the vampire community there, Susan Walsh aside. In fact, I had decided to shift my focus from her disappearance to what she'd been doing before she vanished. I'd still keep my ears open to information about her, but the vampires had taken center stage. Anyway, those vampires who'd known Walsh weren't talking. At least, not about her. But they were giving me plenty of provocative details about themselves. It was time to go outside my sphere and find out what Those Who Love the Night were like elsewhere. I knew I still had a date with Diogenes, which was coming up quickly, but I had this to do first.

The year 1997 was the hundredth anniversary of the publication of Bram Stoker's *Dracula*. Scholars gathered in conferences the world over to mark this event. I was going to Dracula '97. On my way, I stopped first in Las Vegas to catch the stage act of Jakarr, a vampire magician.

Anne Rice once called Vegas a vampire's city, and so it is. She had intended to set a scene with Lestat there, but ultimately chose Miami instead. The night I was there, I walked down the fabulously lit main strip of this desert town, where immense casinos lined up one after another in their glittering gowns. It's easy to become completely entranced by this dazzling display. The larger casinos are like small cities, offering all kinds of lures to get you in so they can drain you of your money. On one side are pyramids and massive waterfalls; on another, volcanoes, palaces, and fairy-tale kingdoms. Everywhere you look, someone is advertising an exotic performance, often with half-naked women. Couples line up at the instant wedding chapels, and the clanging sound of the slots never ceases.

I went to see Jakarr's show at the enormous fake castle, Excalibur, which offers a vast arena of Camelot themes in its many theaters, shops, restaurants, and game rooms. The staff walk around the black and red decorated areas in King Arthur garb to create a medieval atmosphere. With four thousand rooms, Excalibur has plenty of action for families, including free stage shows, one of which was Jakarr's.

I watched as he came onstage, dressed in Victorian ruffles and cape, to perform a bit of impressive magic. He used smoke and colored lights for atmosphere, and when he smiled, you could see his fangs. It was not overtly vampiric, just a subtle hint. Afterward I asked him about his act, and he told me that his clothing, long hair, and fangs provide a way to bring his chosen lifestyle into his act. It adds a sinister flavor, but doesn't scare anyone off. And it makes him unique among magicians—who are a dime a dozen in a place like Vegas.

I knew that "Vampire: The Masquerade," one of the most popular role-playing games, was hosted just outside the city on Roadrunner Ranch—in fact, they had seen several thousand players come through at one time or another—and I asked Jakarr about this Blood Moon Social Club, as it was called. He seemed to have only contempt for those who played the role of vampire but were not the real thing. Vegas, he said, is full of them; they're like the town itself, which has no substance behind its glittering allure. Role-players dominate the vampire scene, he insisted, and there's not much that he can do about it, save retreat to his own abode. Jakarr's place is set up like a large coffin, and he tends to keep to himself.

Las Vegas yielded nothing more except vampiric slot machines, so I drove across the desert to Los Angeles.

2

The City of Angels was a provocative setting in many ways for this international conference. Most people know it for Disneyland, Hollywood, the Simpson and Menendez trials, violent gangs, plastic surgeons behind every bush, and the highest per capita number of manifestations of deception and phoniness in the country. In fact, it's a far more complex place. In his novel, *Sole Survivor*, Newport Beach resident Dean Koontz describes it thus: "The most glamorous, tackiest, most elegant, seediest, most clever, dumbest, most beautiful, ugliest, forward-looking, retro-thinking, altruistic, self-absorbed, deal-savvy, politically ignorant, artistic-minded, criminal-loving, meaning-obsessed, money-grubbing, laid-back, frantic city on the planet."

And so it is, with its stylish clubs and amusements parks. But that's not all you can get here, if darkness is your preference—and I don't mean the smog-overcast skies. There's a sizable Goth community with plenty of businesses that cater to any and every fetish.

There's Necromance, a boutique for people who like dead things. You can purchase a full human skeleton or just a skull; a bat preserved in formaldehyde; all sorts of coffin-shaped objects, including jewelry; torture instruments; and things made from bone and teeth. Along the same lines is Skeletons in the Closet: the L.A. Coroner Gift Shop, where you can get a toe-tag key chain or a hearse-shaped coin bank. If you're not a collector, then take the Hollywood Death Tour and see the places where homicides, suicides, and idiot deaths involving the rich and famous took place. Want something quiet? Get a map to the celebrity grave sites. In Beverly Hills, several people involved in the vampire scene have opened a boutique called the Dark Gift (clever name) not far from the the Fang Club.

Catrina Coffin, a blood-drinking vampire who sleeps in a coffin and drives a hearse, runs the Los Angeles Hearse Society. She's also the founder. "I started running into other people with hearses," she said. "We put the thing together and I was voted president. We've been together about six years now. We have picnics in cemeteries, meetings at mortuaries, and monthly Gothic parties." She lives with forty-three pets, including snakes, frogs, toads, and lizards, and says she's been a vampire since she was a child. "I've been drinking blood as far back as I can remember." She does a lot of talk shows and documentaries on the subject, and has changed her practices in recent years. "I have donors, and nowadays I use a medical scalpel. I've known my donors for a long time. You can't just meet someone on the street and take their blood. There's no such thing as a blood condom, so I have to know what I'm doing." She's the real thing, she says, and has no patience for pretense and vampire wannabees.

Also located in L.A. is the Secret Order of the Undead (SOUND), a.k.a. the Bat Pack, run by Pandora, the "Auntie Mame of the Undead." This is a vampire and Gothic interest group, associated with the Vampire Haven, which promotes themes of darkness. Since 1988 they have kept an archive on dark historical characters such as Jack the Ripper, Vlad Tepes, and Mary Reilly. "We were founded to preserve macabre history," Pandora explained. Her own name derives from the name of a pub in White Chapel, near where Red Jack did his deeds, and from a haunted ship, the HMS *Pandora*. SOUND puts out a newsletter, *The Red Ink Pages*, and stages original theatrical works. One of their members runs the Jennifer Welling's Extreme Scenes casting agency, where she can supply film directors with any manner of freak or supernatural creature. She's managed to get some members from the group onto the television show *Buffy, the Vampire Slayer* and into the movie *Revenant*. Some are former members of the Undead Poet Society, and a few belong to the League of Vampiric Bards. They promote discussion groups and sponsor poetry readings and lectures on macabre subjects.

Pandora herself has been heavily involved in the vampire scene for the past decade. "I used to drink blood," she told me, "and then I got sick, so I got into psychic vampirism." A theater major now working on a master's degree in drama, she has studied Egyptology and mother-goddess worship. Often her group can be found at one of the vampire clubs in the Los Angeles area.

3

One of her close friends is Nicolas Strathloch. To my surprise, he was a longtime member of the Temple of the Vampire, based in Lacy, Washington. I'd heard of them when I'd first begun my observations of vampire culture ten years ago. Apparently, they had read my article for *Psychology Today*, "Hunger for the Marvelous: The Sudden, Curious Allure of the Vampire," and they wrote me a letter hinting that, while I was on the right track, I did not "really" know what a vampire is; *they* were the guardians of that secret. One member, G. Clinton Smith, insisted that vampires do not drink blood; instead, they take the life force from their prey "much as one would milk a cow." There's mutual benefit, not wanton destruction. Those who equate blood with the life force are relying on primitive errors more attuned to human psychopaths.

Smith described vampirism as an ancient religion that encourages spiritual evolution, and mentioned that the Temple of the Vampire is a federally registered church.

I wrote back requesting more information. He answered my letter after a month's delay because my questions required consultation with "another." He wasn't clear about who or what this "other" was. They don't seek members, he told me; members seek them. And such people are rewarded through mature efforts to belong. He did congratulate me on my work to date and said that I was "very close" to understanding.

Almost two years later, I received a packet of papers and a letter assuring me that Lucius Martel of the priesthood of Ur had been authorized to correct any misinformation I might have. The packet informed me about how to purchase a vampire ring, a vampire ritual mirror, a vampire medallion for whatever level of membership I purchased, and a price list for an array of books and pamphlets, including *The Vampire Bible*. This bible contained fundamental magical lore drawn from the ageless oral tradition of the *Shurpu Kishpu*, a book of sorcery. It would teach me the secrets of vampirism to draw on the life force of my victims, and to perform the ancient rites of the calling of the Undead Gods. I would also get to find out about the approaching apocalypse and the Final Harvest. Annual dues were $100. For that you got a newsletter and a sense that you were part of an organization that was "watching you." In fact, they let me know that, member or not, they were aware of my activities regarding vampires.

That was a little spooky, but I had no intention of pursuing it at the time. Over the course of the years that followed, I heard from others that the Temple personnel refused all interviews; but then I found their Web site.

According to the information posted there, the Temple of the Vampire is an international church, registered since December 1989. They maintain absolute confidentiality about their membership, but tolerate no criminal activity of any form. They view themselves as predators, exalt the ego and the rational mind, and believe that magic is real. The Family is reserved for those born to the Blood, who feel the Call of the Night. They are different from the norm, and they glory in that difference. The Temple's mission is to locate those who do not yet know their heritage and to train them to prepare for the Final Harvest. There's a different bible for each of the five stages of learning, from initiate to the Vampire Adept—which requires a recognition of the Dragon Within. They have a creed, a way to call on the Undead Gods, a list of vampiric methods, a chapter on dreaming, and a description of the approaching apocalypse. I did notice that the contents page of their bible has this quote: "Within lies fact and fancy, truth and metaphor. Discriminate with care."

I gave some thought to contacting them, but wasn't sure I'd get much more than I'd already learned. Then I met Nicolas Strathloch. He sits on the council of the original northwest group, but lives in Beverly Hills and acts as the regional director there. I was interested, first, in dispensing with rumors, so I asked a few direct questions.

"The Temple is often presented as if there's no real organization behind it," I said, "and it's just a scam to get money for publications and medallions." I was thinking mainly of the people interviewed in Jeff Guinn and Andy Grieser's book pointing out the amount of money solicited and the fact that member activities seemed to include aggressive recruitment tactics.

Nicolas seemed unruffled. "It's far from that," he assured me. "We have members in seventeen countries around the world. We have many different clutches. We're primarily an umbrella organization that brings together smaller groups."

"Are you in any way associated with the Temple of Set?" This was another organized vampiric group that reputedly had satanic overtones.

"We have no relationship to them," Nicolas said. "Many people say we're satanic, but we don't practice that. However, as outlined by Anton Lavey in *The Satanic Bible*, it's more of a social Darwinist philosophy, the survival of the fittest. That's about as close as we get to the Satanic Order."

I'd read one of their principles: "I acknowledge the Powers of Darkness to be hidden natural laws," so I could see why people got confused. The overall point of the religion seemed to be to make the most of life, here and now. "What inspired you to get involved with the Temple?" I asked.

"I've been associated with it since its founding. For me, it carries on tradition. My family has been involved in this sort of thing for many generations. We were part of the Order of the Dragon, so it's a way to be able to pass on our teachings, to help people to better themselves. We have a year's training period that is very strict. If applicants don't pass through with flying colors, then usually we'll point them in another direction, perhaps one of the other pagan religions."

"So this is a sort of pagan religion, then?" I knew there was some overlap between paganism and vampire culture.

"Yes," he said. "We worship the ancient Sumerian vampire dragon goddess, Tiamat, and trace our priesthood to the ancient city of Ur. I'm one of the inner circle, which is what we call the Master Adepti. We set ourselves apart from the human world."

"How often do you do the rituals?"

"I do rituals on a daily basis, but blood rituals usually only during the full moon and new moon, and it's strictly from donors. I take it from my life partner and we've been doing that for some time. We don't publicly acknowledge that the Temple practices blood rituals. It's a matter of personal taste. Publicly, we do look down on it aesthetically. We're primarily psychic vampires. We feed off the life force of other persons, drawing energy from their auras. We don't teach the mechanics because that's primarily instinctual. The mission of the Temple is to seek out what we call the Lost Children of the Blood. We believe that somewhere in the genetic codes, we actually go back to the time of the *Annunaki* in ancient Sumeria. It means 'Those Who From the Heavens Came.' They're the Nephilim, the angelic forces that took human form. That is what we are."

"You can tell this genetically?" I asked. "By drinking blood?"

"The blood is one of the ways it can be done. Or it can be that you have natural psychic abilities that are beyond the norm. Sometimes people have feelings of alienation, always feeling that there's something meant for them. It tends to manifest itself in a quest. Those are the ones we seek out and gradually let them know that we do exist. We don't take everyone. We figure for about every ten thousand requests, we take about one hundred. Out of those hundred, maybe five or six will complete the whole training."

Still, I was curious about motivations. "If you get to the inner circle," I asked, "what's left to strive for?"

"Immortality," Nicolas responded. "You never stop learning. I got involved because it was a way to help me understand why I was different. It was a way to reconcile things within myself. I died when I was five years old. I drowned. They pronounced me clinically dead for over twenty minutes. When I regained consciousness, I could tell what people were thinking, what they were feeling. I had the ability to see things that people couldn't see, primarily the *Bwca*, which is similar to the Irish *Beansidhe*. My people are from Wales, and when my grandmother knew I could see it, she said, 'That's it. You're the next one.' My grandfather was the head of the Great Dragon Lodge. I joined the order at age twelve, which was a blood ritual. And as soon as I took the blood, it opened my eyes to really see that I was part of something that had been carried on for so many generations."

"So how shall I present your organization? What's the essence?"

"Really, we are vampires. Technically we're *Annunaki*, or another word is *Akhkharu*, which means 'Those Who Travel the Night.' Primarily we're scholars and magicians. To perform our magic and understand the dimensional travels that we work in—we work with out-of-body-projection, astral vampirism, and moving into the higher levels of the astral plane. We try to help you understand that in order to sustain the life of the astral body and to give you power to work the rituals, you have to take energy from other human beings. Like the mythological vampire, we need to feed in order to stay alive."

4

There are many Goth clubs in Los Angeles, such as Stigmata, Helter Skelter, and Coven 13, but those clubs technically devoted to vampires are Vampiricus and the Fang Club. Vampiricus has relocated to

Long Beach and features the cemetery "prop art" of Robin Graves. Among other events, they host Vampire Mad Tea Parties and are open every Monday night.

Jack Dean, thirty-one, owns and operates the Fang Club at 9575 West Pico Boulevard in Beverly Hills. At six feet two and one hundred sixty-five pounds with a shaved head, he's an impressive figure. He has scars on the back of his head from an accident that changed his life. Part Cherokee, he has olive skin and hazel eyes.

The Fang Club is "the only place where people can meet Vampyres and live to tell about it." It meets on Sunday nights—"a direct irony," says Jack, "in that Sunday is the traditional day of Christian worship." Decorated with candelabras, skulls, a Celtic cross, gargoyles, and ghoulish art—such as a life-size painting of Vlad Tepes—it has a dance floor, a bar serving vampire wine, and dark booths set up for mysterious liaisons. It also has an upstairs lounge for VIPs, like leaders of the various "Masquerade" clans. The club is devoted to the vampire scene, but "we accept the Gothically inclined as well. The Goths are derivatives of the punk scene. They carry rebellion a step further. They dress in black and want to look like death, whereas the vampire movement is all about period and historical attire. It's not a rebellion, but a step back to a nicer time." In addition to Sunday nights, they have special events like a Halloween Party and a Victorian Masquerade Ball.

The Fang Club opened on February 2, 1997, to coincide with Candlemas, a pagan holiday. Jack has competition from Coven 13, a nearby Goth club, but when they're not running, he counts as many as four hundred people at his club.

The building looks like an old New Orleans mansion, which made it quite a find. "I was looking for a place to put my club," said Jack, excited by how it all came together, "and I called the Dragonfly in Hollywood. An acquaintance worked there, and she answered the phone and told me about this club called Orsini's. She told me to ask for Igor. He invited me to come down and take a look. It was perfect! So here's Igor in a place that looks like a haunted New Orleans mansion. You couldn't have written it better. It has excellent ambiance."

"Why did you want to do a vampire club?" I asked.

"Because I'm a vampire." As simple as that. I asked him to explain.

"I actually died in a motorcycle accident on January 28, 1993. I was on my way to work and a car knocked me into a parked Cadillac. My helmet came off and I flew through the air and hit the pavement at forty miles an hour. I broke my leg and my jaw and eight teeth. I had a subdermal hematoma and died on the way to the hospital and a few times after that in the hospital, when they were trying to revive me. A big chunk of my leg was torn off by the Cadillac bumper and most of my blood went out through that wound. The rest went to my head. When your brain gets injured, it wants all the oxygen from the blood. There was no blood left in my body to sustain life. There were just pockets of air. So they pumped massive quantities of blood back into me and were able to revive me and I could sustain life again. By the mythical definition of a vampire, I died and was brought back to life with other people's blood."

"But it wasn't magical blood," I pointed out. "It wasn't blood that makes you immortal."

"I don't think I'm immortal."

"Do you drink blood, then?"

"I have, but that's another part of the story. When I came out of the hospital, I was a completely different person than when I went in. I was in a serious coma for eleven days. I was brain injured and I was in the hospital for six months. I went in as this blond rock 'n' roller with long hair. When I came out, I immediately dyed my hair purple and went through the whole underground Gothic scene, trying to find myself in the vampire world."

"And did you?"

"Kind of. I was doing massive amounts of research on the occult and satanism, and vampirism. I came out of the hospital fifteen times more intelligent. I read as much as I could find on all of this. I went from a guy for whom the most important thing in life was partying to a guy for whom the most important thing was information. I found the truths and falseness of the whole thing, and found my place. I'm happy with the way I am now."

I was curious about this. "What's true in that world?"

"Because of what happened to me, I think there are higher powers and things that aren't explained. People who don't believe in those kinds of things are full of themselves. The falsity of it is the idea that they're immortal or can turn into a bat and fly—that kind of stuff."

"So after all that, do you think there's a purpose to your life?"

"Yeah, I do. I think the reason I came back was to build my knowledge to build an empire. A legacy. I have to make a mark. Each day, I feel like I have something I need to do. I feel satisfied, but not content. I'm driven."

I wanted to know about other aspects of his new existence, so I asked him, "When you were drinking blood, did you have donors?"

"Yes," he responded. "I was trying it to see if there was any power to it. I investigated the whole thing thoroughly. Once or twice a week, I'd find a girl who would let me have her blood."

"Do you think you got any power from becoming a vampire?"

"Yeah, I can feel things now. Maybe it's because I'm more sober than I used to be, or maybe I got it from my rebirth, but I have intuition about events now. The Fang Club came from a dream. I followed it and here it is."

"Okay," I said, "I know you've opened a Fang Club in New York. Do you notice differences between L.A. and Manhattan?"

"Yes, there are differences. The music is a bit different. Here we're more interested in the ambient style—more the softer, mellower music, whereas in New York it seems like a harder, more Industrial mix."

"Is there anything that bothers you about the vampire scene?"

"These people drinking blood and doing harm. I know that sounds hypocritical because I've tried it, but I realize the error of my ways. They need to see what the real interest behind it is, the spirituality. Everyone else is flying toward the future as fast as they can, and we're stepping off here to enjoy ourselves in a more classical and romantic environment for a while. That's what this is all about. It's fun to be dressed up and elegant and chivalrous to one another. We step back to a better time."

"So society itself is a vampire? Is that what you mean? To stop its effects, you become vampires?"

He laughed. "I like the way that sounds. Society is a vampire. Yes, that's what it is, and we become vampires to stop the effects."

"But don't you see a lot of drugs? It's not all romance. Kids in other places try to enhance their experience."

"You see drugs," Jack admitted, "but not in large amounts. Ecstasy and cocaine, mostly, because they want to be up all night, as creatures of the night. Pot is not a drug of choice, and a lot of people choose not to drink, either, although there's certainly alcohol."

"How about the fetish scene? Do you see an overlap in L.A.?"

"We do have that here, but it's more among the Gothic crowd."

This really did sound different from Manhattan. "Do vampire enthusiasts get together in other ways," I wanted to know, "or is the club the social center?"

"A lot of them role-play. We have tea parties, and there are also vampiric bards who do poetry readings at local coffee shops. A friend of ours owns Dark's Art Parlor, an art gallery for alternative expression. Vampires hang out there when they have art openings. Some of us belong to the Hearse Society. One guy has a hearse that's lit up around the bottom so when you park it, it's purple-lit underneath. They come to the club and park their hearse in front. It's a great effect."

"How long do you think this whole thing is going to last?" I asked, referring to the vampire phenomenon.

He wasn't sure, but gave me his own estimate. "It's at or near its peak, I think. It will never go away, but it might decline a bit. I'm guessing, worldwide, we have to be close to a couple hundred thousand in number, if not larger. And that's not counting the role-players."

"So what's the essence of the vampire experience for you?"

Jack's answer was quick and right to the point. "Calling myself a vampire and separating myself from the mainstream of society makes me feel more powerful. I'm above it all. When I dress the part, when I put in my fangs and get into costume, I feel powerful."

5

"Dracula '97 was an international conference that drew scholars together with Goths, commercial writers with academics, role-players and vendors with vampyres. It was tirelessly organized by Elizabeth Miller, Jeanne Youngson, and J. Gordon Melton, all well known in their respective fields. Not only was it the hundredth anniversary of *Dracula*, but also the one hundred fiftieth anniversary of Stoker's birthday, and two hundred years since the birth of Mary Shelley, creator of the Frankenstein tale. Seventy-five years earlier was the opening of the silent film *Nosferatu*.

Jeanne Keyes Youngson runs the Count Dracula Fan Club out of Manhattan and has been in business since 1965. She makes frequent trips to Romania, oversees the Bram Stoker Memorial Association, and wrote *The Further Perils of Dracula*, *The Bizarre World of Vampires*, and

Private Files of a Vampirologist. She also has a vampire museum and a research library for Dracular subjects, and she's always a delight to talk with. I looked forward to seeing her.

Elizabeth Miller is a professor of English at Memorial University of Newfoundland in Canada, specializing in nineteenth-century British Gothic fiction, particularly *Dracula.* Her book is called *Reflections on Dracula.* In 1995 she was awarded the honorary title, "Baroness of the House of Dracula," at the World Dracula Congress in Romania. Currently she is president of the Canadian chapter of the Transylvanian Society of Dracula. She is a warmhearted, open person who takes her work seriously, but has no qualms about dressing in her fabulous custom-made, silk-lined vampire cloak and mingling with Goths.

J. Gordon Melton is known for his impressively detailed *The Vampire Book: The Encyclopedia of the Undead.* He followed this with another comprehensive guide called *Vampires on Video.* He's an expert on religions, and has been fascinated with vampires since he was a teenager. He has an extensive collection of books and comic books on vampires, and knows all the important people connected to the field of vampirology. He spotted the errors introduced into our cultural beliefs about vampires by early researchers, and set about to correct the misunderstandings. He is founder and president of the American chapter of the Transylvanian Society of Dracula. A gracious host, he seemed to be everywhere at once that weekend.

Dracula '97 was held near Santa Monica, at the LAX Westin Hotel. When I first walked into the lobby, a large sign emblazoned with "Dracula" hung just over the doorway of a shop that sold Disney and Winnie-the-Pooh characters. The juxtaposition seemed oddly appropriate.

I looked forward to seeing others with whom I was acquainted, such as folklorist Norine Dresser and author Chelsea Quinn Yarbro. I hoped to meet a few people I didn't know, but whose work I admired. Anne Rice was not attending, but many other vampire novelists would make an appearance.

Right away I ran into Raymond McNally, Dracula scholar extraordinaire. He and I had appeared together on television once, and had corresponded a few times. He teaches at Boston College. This gentlemanly, white-haired scholar has a real heart for the image of the vampire in our culture. He read horror stories as a child and graduated to horror movies. What drove him toward serious research on Dracula was the 1931 movie. He was watching it one day and realized that the settings were real. He figured that if Stoker took such pains to include that information, there must be some historical basis for the blood-thirsty count.

He and a colleague, Radu Florescu, researched the fifteenth-century ruler Vlad Tepes to see how closely he resembled the vampire in Bram Stoker's novel. They went to Romania in 1969, and in 1972 published *In Search of Dracula*. In 1989 they published the results of two decades of research in *Dracula: Prince of Many Faces*; and in 1994, after discovering Bram Stoker's notes and diaries in Philadelphia, completely revised *In Search of Dracula*.

"The main difference between the two versions," he told me, "is that in the new edition we demonstrate our discovery that the historical Vlad did drink human blood and could thus be classified clinically as a living vampire. When he used to dine amid his impaled victims, he had their blood gathered in bowls on his table, and then he would take bread, dip it in the blood, and slurp it down."

Many people in vampire culture name themselves Vlad after this man, and they have McNally and Florescu to thank for the information.

Among other conference attendees were the special guests of honor, television's vampire hostess Elvira, and writer Fred Saberhagen, author of *The Dracula Tape*, with Gahan Wilson as the toastmaster. Also Leonard Wolf, another long-standing scholar of *Dracula*. In 1972 he published *A Dream of Dracula: In Search of the Living Dead*, and followed this with *The Annotated Dracula*. Then there was David Skal, who wrote the encyclopedic *V Is for Vampire*, and a definitive guide to the various films and stage plays of *Dracula*.

The program was a provocative mix of work on Count Dracula and modern-day vampires. There were rigorous articles like "Marx and the Vampire" and popular topics such as "The Vampire as Hero." I was to give the address on Sunday to wind up the "Salute to Anne Rice," and my other paper was "Voluptuous Captivity: Evolution of the Vampire Erotic." I was teamed up with my longtime friend, Richard Noll, who used *Dracula* to examine nineteenth-century psychiatric techniques. Evening programs included *Dark Shadows* stars, continuous movies, and a costume ball.

During a book signing, I met Barbara Leigh, the first Vampirella, and she was as beautiful as ever and truly delightful. All kinds of men, young and old, asked if they could take her picture. She told me the story of how politics had forced her out of her role as the model for the comic book character, and how she hoped to one day write a book on it.

In that same room were dealers selling jewelry, costumes, books, and other vampire-related paraphernalia. So many people were walking around in elaborate period costume that I felt I needed to look into purchasing a truly vampiric outfit for the ball that evening.

On Saturday afternoon, I met Tim Powers, the funny fellow who penned *The Stress of Her Regard*, and vampire novelist Nancy Holder. We made a fine team as we sat together at the ball and spun a vampire wine–inspired commentary on the parade of costumes lining up to enter the ballroom. My own—bought hastily that afternoon—was a form-fitting black velvet Morticia-like dress, cut low in the laced-up front, with a slit up the back and tight sleeves with frilly lace cuffs. I also wore my fangs. It was amusing to us to watch elderly European scholars mix with teenage Goths, each eyeing the other, and in the end, accepting that they all shared a fascination with vampires (though I'm not sure the older generation appreciated the loud rock bands).

6

I was pleased to renew my acquaintance, face-to-face, with Richard Noll at this conference. He was one of the people I most wanted to talk with about vampire culture. He's a clinical psychologist with experience in psychiatric settings, and he wrote two books that cover cases of vampirism from a clinical perspective. In his first one, *Bizarre Diseases of the Mind*, among such disorders as multiple personality, possession, necrophilia, and the impostor syndrome, he lists vampirism. He describes the powerful fascination of blood, and then offers a case from 1872, in which Vincenz Verzeni had killed several females and drunk their blood. He got at the blood of his victims by tearing off hunks of flesh with his teeth. As a boy, he had enjoyed decapitating chickens and watching the blood shoot out. Noll also noted other more famous cases, like George Haigh, whose vampirism had religious associations. Noll summed up clinical vampirism as a compulsion to drink blood, and noted that some pivotal event seemed inevitably to be involved with its development.

There are people who still think that anyone who drinks blood as part of modern vampire culture has this pathology, so I was interested in asking Noll more about this. His second book, *Vampires, Werewolves and Demons: Twentieth-Century Reports in the Psychiatric Literature*, devotes an entire section to vampires, with articles by mental health experts who relate their encounters with vampiric manifestations in their clients.

Noll even invented a new disorder, "Renfield's syndrome," in response to those patients who echoed the fictional Renfield's sentiments that the ingestion of blood was necessary to sustain his own life. The characteristics of this syndrome include a pivotal event that makes the ingestion of blood exciting; the progression from autovampirism to the drinking of the blood of living beings; a compulsion for drinking blood; and the viewing of blood as mystical or empowering.

"After reviewing the clinical literature on blood-drinking and the ethnographic literature on things like cannibalism," Noll explained, "I began to see certain patterns. What was interesting in the psychiatric literature on clinical vampirism was that there seemed to be a certain rough parallel in patterns of the syndrome, and that these patterns roughly matched Bram Stoker's description of the clinical case of Renfield in the novel *Dracula*. The gradation from nonhuman to human blood-drinking seemed to be the common link between fiction, folklore, and psychiatry. I therefore suggested referring to clinical vampirism as Renfield's syndrome. It's actually a syndrome that cuts across numerous diagnostic categories and should not be confused with consensual sort of blood-drinking."

We set aside some time one afternoon to talk. Tall with Germanic features and dark blond hair, Richard Noll is always ready for an intense discussion—that's probably why I like him. We sat together in one of the hotel lobby lounge areas as I prepared to put him on the spot.

But before we got started, a young man walked over and interrupted us. He told us that he's a blood donor for vampires and that he sells his blood at a cost of five dollars for a pinprick taste, or fifty dollars for a liter. A vampire whore. He got his first taste of blood at the age of fifteen, from a girlfriend. He drinks it still, he said, about once a week, but won't pay for it. We soon gave him the exit signal and got down to talking.

"You've mentioned that one of your motivations for seeking out unusual cases is 'the thrill of the hunt,'" I said. "Have you ever encountered a case that made you wish you didn't have such a curiosity?"

"Actually, I did have a case of a not very verbal man who liked to eat his own flesh. We constantly had to put mittens on him because he would eat away the upper layers of the skin on his hands—and sometimes his arms—to expose the muscle tissue below. We wondered how long a human being could survive if he just ate a little meaty bit of his own flesh each day. The only other cases that made me wish I didn't have that curiosity were those of murderers and rapists, invariably the repeat offenders. Vampirism would only be a secondary aspect of their killing. I never met anyone who killed solely for blood."

"Do you still think that it's some pivotal event in a person's life that leads to clinical vampirism?" I thought he might have changed his mind with more experience, but he hadn't.

"For the extreme cases of pathological clinical vampirism, I'd say so, yes. My opinion hasn't changed on that. Especially if the blood-drinking behavior has a long-standing erotic component to it."

"Okay, but in my observations of the subculture, developing a vampire identity is not so much a syndrome as a fetish or a status symbol. Would that still be considered clinical vampirism?"

"I'm not out to diagnose the Goths!" he said with some amusement. "Some Goths who engage in that behavior may indeed have a compulsion that may have childhood roots, but most probably don't. Blood-fetishism? Maybe. Actually, it's more like a secret handshake that the Shriners have, or as you put it, a symbol of social status or initiation. There's no need to pathologize the Goth or the vampire subculture. It's not the same thing as true clinical vampirism."

"Then what would be your perspective on the increasing numbers of people who indulge in blood-drinking as part of a ritual or cult in order to identify themselves as vampires?" I asked.

"From a medical point of view, it's a terribly risky thing. But from a social or psychological point of view, as long as the blood is given freely out of an act of will on the donor's part, I have no problem with it. Violence and coercion as a method of extracting blood is something I oppose."

"Then just how prevalent would you say actual clinical vampirism is?"

He shrugged. "There's no hard evidence that clinical vampirism is prevalent to any great degree in North America or anywhere else. The media attention given to anecdotal evidence has inflated our perception that clinical vampirism is a widespread phenomenon. Consensual blood-drinking among those youth subcultures that identify themselves as vampires is probably more prevalent."

"What do you think people get from viewing themselves as vampires?"

"Acceptance by a peer group. A feeling of personal power that may have been lacking previously, since vampires are such icons of immortality and power, especially Anne Rice's Lestat. He's a fusion of all our fantasies of immortality, and in our postmodern culture, of divinity. He's not only immortal in the spiritual sense, but also a rock star and a media celebrity. The opposite was true in *Dracula*. True, Dracula was immortal, but his stigmata of degeneracy were highlighted: He represented decay, spiritual and cultural degeneration, and unredeemed, meaningless death. When one thinks of Dracula, one is always reminded of the scents of offal and necrotic human flesh. No vampire subculture sprang up after *Dracula* was published in 1897 the way that a Goth or vampire culture has arisen with the popularity of Anne Rice's novels. Today the icon of the vampire has little to do with death and decay, but instead is associated with perpetual regeneration and cinematic immortality. Being a vampire is like being a movie star or a media celebrity. I believe the standard black clothing, fangs, makeup, and droll facial expressions of today's vampires invite the same sort of excitement and scrutiny that media stars receive when they're in public. This sort of attention from others can be powerfully reinforcing as a validation, of sorts, of one's newfound sense of personal power after adopting the vampire persona."

I found that an interesting distinction. "What about role-playing?" I asked. "Some people say that it's dangerous to be so intensely involved in a vampire mind-set. What do you think?"

"I find it quite imaginative, actually. But look, there will always be people who go too far. There will always be some people who are troubled prior to engaging in role-playing, and the role-playing may only worsen their difficulties. But I suspect for some people the opposite will be true as well. In other words, this form of play can be beneficial. Let's take our culture's institution of psychotherapy as an example. Psychotherapy is largely role-playing. We all know, or are trained to adopt, the appropriate personas when we're either a therapist or patient. Generally, the role-playing game we call psychotherapy is framed as positive, healing, and acceptable. Not so with other role-playing games—and the dress-up role-playing that goes on in the vampire subculture is a good example. But long-term studies of psychotherapy have found that in all modalities of psychotherapy, some people actually get worse. Why shouldn't we expect some people to come away from their vampire role-playing in worse shape than when they started the game? But there will be many others, of course, who get something out of it. And I think there obviously must be something beneficial for vampire role-players, otherwise it would not attract so many young people."

I agreed with Noll on these things. Thus far, I'd seen no cause for alarm over people engaging in vampiric identities or role-playing. Of course, that was before I was confronted with something more serious, which proved to be an exception, but still reason to be careful about my assessment.

CHAPTER NINE

the vampyre
mystique

I

Very quickly at the conference, I met Madame Elisandrya, an experienced professional dominatrix whom Jana Marcus had profiled in her
book *In the Shadow of the Vampire,* and who seemed to have an interesting
life in the vampire fetish scene. She introduced herself to me with
great flourish, dressed elaborately in a colorful, flowing outfit.

It's not unusual to find vampire fans among those who adopt the
dominance-and-submission lifestyle. In fact, one of Anne Rice's contributions to vampire fiction was a refined clarity on the way those
relationships between vampire and victim—and even vampire to
vampire—were charged with the eroticism of power struggles. She
drew her knowledge from published erotica and adapted it to vampire
psychology. Many vampire fans have read Rice's Roquelaure series as
well—and she herself recognizes how close in theme her "elegant
sadomasochism" is to her vampire tales. Through her masochistic
characters she shows just how much power they actually have in the
D/S scenario. People like Madame are quick to affirm that Rice knows
whereof she speaks.

Madame has her own bevy of slaves (if they cook, I want one), a professional dungeon, and a slave training academy. She walks into a room with a great deal of confidence and determination. She's a large woman with an exotic face and a quick, easy laugh. She immediately draws all attention to herself, whether she's dressed for fantasy or not. I found her to be one of the most impressively alive personalities at the conference.

She explained to me that she was introduced to what vampires are by her grandmother, who taught her about the sacrificial use of blood. An exchange of blood, to her mind, is the most intimate form of communication between two (or more) people. It implies a high degree of trust. Currently she's writing a book that combines her fantasies with autobiographical elements, called *Memoire of a Mad Vampire*. She likes the image of the vampire because it's a creature that always seduces another into submission, and she uses that mystique in her own scenarios.

"I exploit vampire imagery," she said, "but not with what is seen so often, such as using fangs. I use the quieter innuendoes and the dark seductiveness that always awakens sweet prey. I use my dark side to entice and taunt them. It's the vampire within myself that makes the effect."

"What sets you apart as a vampire dominatrix?" I asked. "How are you different from dominatrixes who just insert a pair of fangs for effect?"

"Once my charges place their trust in my hands," she responded, "it's up to me to reflect my inner dominance in the most comfortable way for myself, so it's always with a dark edge. That reflection is most usually seen and felt as a darkly passionate controller, one who takes little to entice once intrigued. My physical appearance changes subtly. I've been told I appear heated, predatory.

"I haven't adapted my vampiric depths from what I've seen or heard, but from what I have felt deeply within. I feel myself most clearly when my darker attitudes emerge. That usually happens when I sense fear of any kind. I want nothing more than to edge closer to that fear, taunting it for my personal amusement, until it falls into my hands, fully vulnerable.

"There is nothing, in my opinion, more deeply moving than an emotionally confident person now weakened by my obvious desire of them. Rather like a deer trapped in the headlights of my otherwise calm demeanor.

"Fangs and all the other trappings are unnecessary when I prey on my charges. They merely serve to turn the obvious into something very nearly ridiculous. I have the heart of a vampire. I could devour my charges with my intensity, and often do emotionally. That is far more deadly to encounter than a pair of plastic fangs or any of the usual vampire trappings.

"I think, overall, that I shock and surprise those that are otherwise unaware of my deeper side, because I can seem rather normal and reserved most of the time. But if they get close enough, and lean in just right, I will show them what lurks quite naturally beneath my human exterior. Something as subtle as a simple touch on the hand usually gets the point across with no mistake. That's when the fun begins. I do try to keep it humorous at times, if only to make it less . . . intense."

That night in L.A., it was her intent after the masquerade ball to have a party in her room. When we went up, I noticed that her retinue consisted mostly of females. (Later, at the ball in New Orleans, she led one female and several male slaves on chains attached to collars around their necks and became the talk of the party.) I enjoyed being around her energy, but the conference had exhausted me, so I didn't stay for the all-night festivities.

Madame is from the coastal town of Santa Cruz, at the northern end of Monterey Bay. She told me it was known as the vampire capital of the world, having "the highest percentage per capita of witches, pagans, and vampires." The nearby mountains are even nicknamed the Little Carpathians.

The Santa Cruz boardwalk sports an amusement park and a surf museum, and the town has a diverse art community. On Friday nights, role-playing games abound—in fact, one of the largest games in the region. This has been Madame's home for the past five years. She came here from New Orleans, where she was involved in the pagan and vampire community as well.

I asked her whether she invites vampires into her home.

"I invite a lot of people into my home," she said. "Some who perceive themselves as vampires, and some who wish they really could be. There's really nothing unique about that, though, since I don't believe in the flying bat theory. But the shape-shifting is true enough, and I appreciate those with the energy to be who they truly are." I wasn't sure what she meant by that, but I was to find out soon.

Madame, with Jana Marcus, started a monthly vampire fetish party in one of the Santa Cruz clubs, the Blue Lagoon. Called the Tower, this special night debuted on April 24, 1998, advertising itself as a "FetishLeatherLatexPVCLaceVelvetGothicVampirePirateBondage" gathering. It includes a full dungeon setup, Gothic dancers on stage, and theme drinks such as the Vampire's Kiss. Nearly four hundred people attended on opening night, greeted by Mistress Eva Destruction. They expect this party to be very popular for some time to come.

Santa Cruz is close to San Francisco, where Madame and her circle frequent the clubs. Think San Francisco, and think the Golden Gate Bridge, Fisherman's Wharf, Alcatraz, steep hills, morning fog, the Castro district, Haight-Ashbury, Chinatown, Ghirardelli Square, cable cars, the 49ers, and Lombard, "the world's crookedest street." In a city that flaunts its fetish and gay presence, one can find nearly any kind of entertainment, including Danielle Willis, who performs an erotic vampire act at the New Century Theater. Willis contributed a story to Poppy Z. Brite's vampire anthology, *Love in Vein*, which featured a vampire held captive in a medieval freak show that provides perverse sexual outlets to peasants. Willis is also portrayed in *True Blood*, Charles Gatewood and David Aaron Clark's book of blood-fetish and vampire photography. Readers who look through it must have a strong stomach for razors, hooks, hypodermic needles, pierced skin, blood-encrusted teeth, ritual scarification, and bloody garments. Of course, the cover is pretty straightforward: a woman wrapped in barbed wire with needles in her forehead, blood running from her nose, and piercings through her neck. You know what you're getting, and some people like that. Gatewood, photographer and cultural anthropologist, explained this world to me in a compelling manner, but I agree with Rice's Armand, who claims that real vampires are a lot more fastidious than these portrayals of blood drenchings suggest. I didn't see the appeal of bathing in blood or decorating my skin in this manner.

Madame's experience in the San Francisco vampire scene has been relatively deep. She's made many observations. "People here are more emotional vampires than actual blood-fetishists," she said. "Of course, the scare of disease keeps a lot in perspective. But those that have the affinity for vampirism do gather together in clubs and private groups to share the experience with like-minded aficionados. Unfortunately, most see it as a nineties trend, which has gotten slightly out of hand. Anyone who can afford the fangs or play the street game can get involved, but those who truly appreciate the darker, more serious aspects, do so consistently."

"At which clubs do people tend to gather?" I asked. I knew about a few. The San Francisco Goth clubs are listed online in an index called the Black Pages, and among them are Roderick's Chamber, the Crypt, Backflash, the Death Guild, and the Catacombs. The shops include Gargoyle, the Bone Room, and Blackened Angels.

"There are clubs, yes," Madame replied, "and the street games for vampires. But the vampires tend to float about in many arenas, never focusing on one place for long. Usually when a place becomes over-popular, the consistent vampires in the San Francisco scene will find a clearer space in which to gather."

"Is there anything about the scene there that distinguishes it from that in other cities?"

"Not in my experience, no. This is just as attractive a city to the vampires as any other city. Just as dreary, just as underground. It's all in the way that people see themselves. Some feel that as vampire afi-cionados, they would be more comfortable in a city like New Orleans, and some prefer the warmth of San Diego. San Francisco isn't a breed-ing ground, but anyone who has walked through Golden Gate Park at dusk, when the fog rolls in slow and gloomy, will see it's a fine habitat for vampires seeking solace."

2

Jana Marcus, who lives in the area, introduced me to Conan, a young man she had also profiled. In his interview with her, he had described how he'd gained a sense of the power of a vampire's appearance by going in Victorian vampire drag to a club known as Bondage-a-Go-Go. A San Francisco native, he had participated in the Goth/vampire scene for about four years. He makes supernatural-oriented merchan-dise like vampire fangs and a cat's (or werewolf's) glove with silver claws, and has seen the vampire scene associated with this club first-hand.

"I started out by going to a Goth club in Berkeley called House of Usher," he said. "It was a nice little club. My friends and I went together, and that's why I started making dental-acrylic fangs. I looked around and realized, hey, here's this wide-open market close to where I live that I really ought to be tapping. Then we explored some of the more Industrial clubs in San Francisco and then found Bondage-a-Go-Go."

Held on Wednesday nights at the Trocadero, it offers an introductory peek at the fetish world. "Hawk is the one who runs the play area," Conan explained. "It started out as just a VIP party, I think, by the Janus Society. Hawk monitored things and then they asked him to do it on a regular basis."

"What's it like?" I asked.

"It's what I would call a hybrid club. It's a dance club with this fetish area roped off in a lounge upstairs. There's a little bit of equipment and a bar with eyebolts screwed into it suspended from chains from the ceiling so that people can be hooked up to it. A group of regulars would play while the curious would watch these half-naked people being abused. I like the environment because it gives people who have never been exposed to the scene the chance to experience it a little. They can see that it's not all freaks and violent psychopaths. It's just people having a good time."

"So are you a vampire, then?" I asked him. "Or just having a good time?"

"I don't think of myself as a vampire," Conan admitted. "I like to be dressed up. I like to be pretty. I like allowing that part of myself to emerge that I wouldn't normally let out. It's made me a more open person and I feel better about myself. And I like being everyone's best fantasy. It's mostly theater. The costuming works on me physically. My vampire look had a level of elegance to it that appealed to a lot of people who wouldn't necessarily have approached anyone else. I tended to get novices who were just curious who wanted to try things with me because I seemed safe. People told me they were fascinated with my reserved demeanor. I didn't work the ropes like other people did, and it came across that I was very selective. I was just shy, that's all. And I like to be a little more sensual than just raw leather."

"Did you ever meet people who claimed to be real vampires there?"

"Every once in a while, I had the impression I was being disdained by those who believed they were real. But I don't think the environment was really Goth enough for the hard-core types to show up. Lots of people in the scene were into blood-play. And I'd make teeth for people who actually wanted to use them to bite someone. Those are the people who immerse themselves to the point where the lines get blurred. Personally, I prefer the romance of it and it's a wonderful way to meet people. That's how I met my fiancée."

3

In the cities, the clubs seem to be one of the more popular venues for vampires to meet. Many of them have regular Goth nights, and in every major city in this country, there are large gatherings to celebrate some event or holiday. A lot of people I met were preparing well ahead of time for Halloween.

According to Buffy's mentor, Rupert Giles, Halloween is considered "dead night." Vampires stay home while mortals go running around pretending to be them. I don't know about that, but the club scene for vampires comes alive that night in spectacular and engaging displays. Besides the Fang Club and Vampiricus in Los Angeles, and the clubs mentioned above in San Francisco, there are numerous other parties and party places, among them DraculaFest in Chicago, Blood Lust and the Sanctuary Vampire Sex Bar in Toronto, Anne Rice's bash in New Orleans, and Darkangel's Theatre des Vampyre aux Goth in Salem, Massachusetts. Salem also puts on an annual Vampires and Victims Ball in the Town Hall. Events include a costume judging contest and a coffin raffle. "Victims will be flogged til midnight," the 1997 flyer promised.

I received tickets for this on which was printed a poem that began, "It writhes, it writhes! with moral pangs/the mimes become its food." Tracy Devine (a.k.a. Mistress Tracy) told me this ball was a benefit for a wildlife organization called New England Alive. They—the Eternal Sisters of Damnation—actually auctioned off "slaves." They hoped I could come and purchase one. Well, I did need a cook, but I had other obligations.

I elected to stay in New York for Sabretooth's Vampire Ball at the Angel Orensanz Foundation building that Sebastian had shown me months before. He was going to have merchants and bands, a belly dancer, and dance music, but he'd had to drop the idea of a banquet.

I dressed the part with a long black gypsy wig, fangs, black velvet gloves, velvet lace-up boots that Anne Rice inspired me to buy, a black velvet dress, and a bright red velvet hooded opera cloak with gold chains. Sebastian had insisted that I needed a corset, and he had a variety of them to show me, but I'd declined. I like to breathe. I rubbed white makeup into my skin and used thick black eyeliner and crimson lipstick. I wasn't sure anyone would even know me. (They didn't.)

For the most part, the party was just a series of rock bands, with people in costume standing around watching. Vampires as rock musicians is a natural. Rice's character Lestat realized that, and in *The Vampire Lestat* created his band, Satan's Night Out, complete with CDs, music videos, and his own autobiography as an accompaniment. Even before that, musicians inspired by Rice's stories had recorded songs like Sting's vampiric lament, "Moon Over Bourbon Street." In Chicago, Vlad's Dark Theater was one of the early bands to exploit the image with his Industrial/Egyptian/Metal, and now many rock groups around the world either present themselves as vampires or sing vampiric lyrics. There's the band Lestat, and the Savage Garden from Australia, both inspired by Rice. Like her vampire novels, the latter group points out, there's beauty in their music, but also savagery. There's Bauhaus singing about Bela Lugosi, Helster's Nosferatu, and Goth favorite, Sisters of Mercy. Blair Murphy told me about the Voluptuous Horror of Karen Black, whose act was inspired by the Hammer Studios vampire films. Gore, viscerality, sex, and morbidity form the predominant themes, exploited as far as possible for shock value and over-the-top imagery.

A long time ago I had listened to the seventies band Black Sabbath. I remember the clandestine thrill my friends and I got as we sat in darkened rooms, urged ourselves into altered states, and with the music's constant repetition felt as if we were getting close to the devil. I suppose that's how young people feel today when they imbibe reckless lyrics of hatred, death, and blood. These bands almost demand black clothing, dripping candles, and a knife within easy reach—just in case the melancholy overburdens. By 1990 Gothic groups were making the circuits, becoming almost commonplace. Bands such as Christian Death, Marilyn Manson, Voltaire, Alucarda, and Type O Negative keep the darker emotions aroused and the mythic symbolism fluid.

I can't say I'm a big fan of the Industrial sound, which seems to pervade the clubs I've attended. Seems too much like a screamed resignation to larger forces. I prefer the more subtle notes of the ghostly Celts, which have their own vampiric aura. But I appreciate the temper and restless intensity that the blending of vampires and rock music brings to the scene. I like to watch the vibrations of rage and sensuality roll through the singers as they shout their epithets and rouse the audience to peak feelings of pain and longing. If the intensity reaches the right pitch, it seems to be implied, one might even catapult straight into the supernatural, with its promise of heightened sensation and extraordinary power. At the very least, those who indulge could defy en masse any and all social conventions that stripped them of youth or self-referential enlightenment.

As I looked around that night, I noticed some dancing of the pagan variety, but not much other movement. I was close enough to see one young man nose behind his date's left ear and rub his rather longish fangs against her tender skin. Hoping they wouldn't notice me, I took a few steps closer and thought I saw his tongue quickly lick at a small wound. She hadn't stepped away or cried out, but it did look like he'd actually bitten her. Then he drew her close against his body, his face still buried in her hair, and that's all I could see without being obvious.

I knew this went on. I'd heard people describe to me how they got high and drank from each other on these Dark Nights Out, but I believed it to be fairly infrequent. I hadn't expected to see it so blatantly.

The party was an interesting production, and the cutest outfit was on a member of Sebastian's staff: Cleo was a fallen angel with black wings and a barbed wire halo. But there were many varieties of vampires, and most of them dispensed with the black capes in favor of Victorian or Edwardian garb. Sebastian had startling red cat's eye lenses, long fangs, and a top hat, which were quite effective.

Several males sported elaborate jewelry that extended their fingers into long silver claws, and at one club event, I met the man behind this fashion. His name was Axel, and his card dubbed him "The World's Most Dangerous Jeweler." He'd been making art since the sixties, inspired originally by Salvadore Dali. Not only did he make the silver pieces, but he also used his own blood in his surreal paintings— like his depiction of a bat with breasts—though he did not consider himself a true part of the vampire scene. He disdained collective movements.

"People want a bit of the artist," he told me. "What could be more intimate and personal than a piece using my own blood? It's an introverted art form, using myself and giving of myself. When you buy my art, you're truly getting a piece of me. And it's unique. No one else who paints with blood will have the same DNA." He plans to do a book of instructions on jewelry-making and how to paint safely with your own blood.

I had hoped to meet Vlad at one of these events. He was another vampire magician, and he had sent me some of his material. He even had a vampire doll modeled after his look, but negotiations between him and Sabretooth had fallen through. His form of magic exploits occult symbolism, with an emphasis on the romantic, seductive side of the vampire. "My act is primarily what is considered 'closeup,'" he had explained to me, "which is magic performed in an intimate setting for small groups. That way, everyone has an intense experience. I never tell them I am a vampire. It's subtle."

What I most enjoy about the vampire club scene is that it seems to draw people together who otherwise feel isolated with their darker preoccupations. And people of all types who participate in some way in the Dark Side feel welcome, not just vampires. The club scene is a microcosm of the diversity that I was finding all over the country. Goths, psychics, pagans, role-players, witches, Real Vampyres, fetish vamps, wizards, werewolves (I was told), and those of another mindset that was not actually vampiric, but had some association: They called themselves "shifters." They were there, I knew, mingling with all the rest.

Madame had mentioned such people, and someone in a vampire chat room had directed a shifter to me. It made sense, since some people view vampires as shape-shifters, and Dracula himself was presented as a creature who could change from human form to animal.

4

When he introduced himself to me as Shifter, I first asked him to explain what he meant by shape-shifting.

"It's the transformation of a human being into another species," he said. "Often called lycanthropy, it's not actually the same. The ability is either natural or brought forth through ritual. It's a link to my past life, and my spirit guide is a male black bear which roamed for six years in the forest northeast of the Maine/New Brunswick border."

He went on to explain that one could shift physically, like a werewolf, spiritually the way shamans do, or mentally, which is what he does.

"Mental shifting" he told me, "involves the complete or near-complete removal of human identity from the mind, replacing it with the animal."

I asked for details of a personal experience, and he soon sent an e-mail that contained the following account: "In 1986, shortly before my fifteenth birthday, I encountered a black bear in the forest above my aunt's farm. The bear approached me and I strangely felt no fear. When she was within about seven to eight feet of me she stopped and checked the air, then walked slowly 180 degrees in an arc around me till she could continue past me. I nearly fainted. Since then I have had regular encounters with black bears. My first actual 'shift' came in 1994 during a cool spring night. It started as an odd tingling in my spine, then a loss of color vision. Next I felt myself getting 'pushed' away. It was as if I was sitting at the back of a bus, and looking at life through the windshield far in front of me. I tend to try and get to a wooded setting before anything happens, as the bear tends to panic quite violently in a closed-in area.

"Most times, I can feel it pushing my conscious mind to the background. It reminds me of being on a train, when you're half-asleep, and the scenery is moving by your eyes in a surreal sort of way. A few that I fight off last for only a few minute. Some episodes, so far as I can tell, have lasted for about twenty to thirty minutes."

"Would you say that people who think of themselves as vampires are participating in some form of mental or spiritual shifting similar to what you're describing?" I wrote back.

He did think so. "I fully believe many vampires may in fact be shifters or *also* be shifters. I know a fellow who is a psychic vampire. He will not feed off of my aura, his reason being, 'I can feel something in your aura that is not supposed to be there.' This statement is what led me to really pursue the discovery of shifting."

He couldn't emphasize enough that it was very dangerous for people to try this who fail to understand the forces to which they are opening themselves. "For this reason many shifters refuse to admit the ability, or to talk to people who do not share in it already."

A few months later, he contacted me again and told me of another experience he'd had with shifting. Through meditation and training in mental control, he'd managed to retain more consciousness during a shift and could thus remember the details better. He recalled running, picking up a scent, and killing a small animal.

"I later noticed two very large scrapes on my face, one on an arm, and three puncture wounds on my hand. That led me to muse that some aspect of physical shifting perhaps crosses over into spiritual shifting. I came to, covered in blood, with a dead raccoon in front of me."

Shifter is the kind of person that Dr. George described who has the ability to indulge so strongly in fantasy that it becomes quite real. Some people confuse this with dissociative identity disorder, but Shifter claimed to be well adjusted and living a normal life. The vivid details of what he calls his recollections are what I believe many people are seeking when they take on vampire identities in a manner so intense that they believe they see the world as a vampire sees it. I understood why they might feel at home in the society of vampires.

5

Another person I met at one of these vampire gatherings was Viola Johnson, author of *Dhampir: Child of the Blood*. She talked freely about her "vampire children," and offered a very different understanding of the vampire's function than many I've met. In *Dhampir*, she collected together the letters she wrote to her vampire daughter, a young woman who became a vampire at a conference in Toronto in 1995. Through the letters, Viola teaches this "Cub" about what to expect from the effects of the "mara," or vampire virus, in her system.

Vi is a plump, sparkling, African-American woman with dark hair clipped close to her head. Her daughter, whom I also met, is a thin, blond Caucasian who likes to dress as a male from an earlier era, with cravat and brocade topcoat. She's just produced a documentary about vampirism and tuberculosis in New England. They were initially introduced to each other by a mutual friend, also a vampire. Both were warm and welcoming as they told me about themselves.

Viola is a member of a vampire clan that she calls the Children of Lilith, part of the secret order of the Illuminati. She wrote her book in order to pass on the sacred traditions to her kith and kin. She dedicates it to her sire, Abba, who is forty-one years older than she, and was once a well-known medium who taught her about metaphysics.

"My Maker was a man named Allen, but I have always called him

Abba, which means 'father.' He and my mother worked together. Mom encouraged me to ask questions of him. By the time I was fifteen, I knew that there were many more things in the world than just what my school books told me. One of them was the fact that my mother's friend was a vampyre. [Viola uses *vampyre* instead of *vampire* because the former seems more familiar.]

"I decided to ask questions the day I saw him feeding from a friend. It looked like he was kissing a cut, until I noticed an unusual amount of blood around his mouth. He made it all seem perfectly normal."

Eventually he transformed her. "I was sitting with a group of Abba's friends and we were discussing the power of blood in tribunal and religious ceremonies. Afterward, Abba cut an area just below his wrist to feed one of his friends. I asked if he would feed me, also. He asked if I was sure I was ready. I said yes. He asked again and I said yes again. I was seventeen. He had waited, as is the law among the Illuminati, until I was old enough to give my consent. He hugged me and kissed me and then held out his arm and I started to suck on it like my life depended on it. It felt like the blood was flowing forever. When I finally stopped drinking, I felt suddenly quite sleepy. I fell asleep with my head on his lap. When I woke an hour later, I started stuffing anything into my mouth I could put in there. The only thing that stopped that first hunger was more blood."

Viola in turn brought two others into the fold, and surrounded herself with a trusted feeding circle—the only ones from whom she would take blood. She has a husband and wife—both female—and a variety of other relationships that form her vampire family. She also has three other blood siblings, but does not know them all.

"To those of us in the Children of Lilith," said Viola, "children are the most precious gift we are given. It is they who fully give us immortality because they carry on our line. We look for someone who is morally strong and who will abide by the laws that govern us. We seek someone who loves and cherishes knowledge. Someone who loves and respects life, and who is strong enough to hold fast against their own desires when things get turbulent. We don't make offspring indiscriminately. I have to see that my children are fully equipped to go into the world with this 'virus' in their system."

This daughter, Cub, wrote an Introduction to her mother's book in which she described herself as being drawn to acting and to the leather scene. The weekend she became a vampire, she did not really believe it was anything more than a game, but she claimed she developed a genuine biological need for blood and had to feed right away.

One of the more interesting aspects of vampirism that Viola discusses is the difference between genders. She says that the female vampires differ from the males in that they nurture life. "Our males would feast and let their food fall prey to the arms of death. I have no desire for the tasty morsels that give me life to lose their life force. Food nurtures and is nurtured in return." She urges Cub to be careful not to take without also giving something.

"I believe that the differences between male and female vampyres," she says, "are just an offshoot of the differences between males and females in general. Some are biological; some are cultural. My Maker says that far more females make children than males. Women are less wasteful, generally, and more patient in teaching the young what they need to learn. Men as a whole don't have the inclination to nurture. They just take and go on."

According to Viola, vampires can go into the sun, but should shield themselves from direct exposure; they cast a reflection; their digestive system is complex and delicate; they have heightened senses; they are not undead; they are vulnerable to disease; they must be invited before entering someone's home; and they are enlightened. "Part of what makes the vampyre unique and sensual," she explains, "is the acknowledgment and acceptance of our animal nature. We live hand in hand with the beast within us, and that animalistic force is at the base of much of human sexuality. We are predators. That's the nature of the animal. It's just that some of us have been taught how to understand, balance, and—on occasion—cage the beast that is part of us." She estimates that there are about 350,000 blood-drinkers in this country. She runs vampire workshops several times a year for various leather and fetish conferences, and finds that some people who attend have a "genetic quirk" that makes them feel they are vampires.

I asked whether she takes blood from anyone who asks her to.

She denied this. "I don't take blood from 99.9 percent of the people who offer it to me, although I nibble on hundreds of people a year. I have run a very strange 'Kissing Booth' for charity. I get to bite, which salves my need to chew and have flesh in the mouth, and the charity benefits from the money—all without taking blood. We vampyres form feeding circles. For me, feeding is a very intimate act. I feed from a select group of seven or eight people, and they are carefully screened."

"In retrospect," I said, "are you glad you made the decision to become a vampire?"

"I'm delighted and proud to be me, with all that that entails. I know no other life, so I have no idea what kind of person I would otherwise be. Only once was I ever so ashamed that I wished that I were anyone else but who I was. About three years ago in Portland, my family did a workshop on vampyres for the National Leather Association. There were about eighty people in a room made for twenty-five. After the introductions and a brief spell of history, we realized that many of the people in the audience had experiences that they wished to share.

"Well, the Seattle-Portland area has a rather large clutch of vampyres in the area, and what came out during the workshop were horror stories about this group. We heard story after story about all of the horrific things that had been done to many innocent people, and how many more had taken their lives rather than deal with the aftermath of vampyric behavior. All I could do was listen and offer comfort. On that day I would have given the world to be anything but who I was."

I was also curious about the greater vampire realm, in her experience. "Is there a vampire network?" I asked her.

"Yes and no. Most vampyres are hidden. They're paranoid that someone might try to kill them. It's difficult, but not impossible to find others. One of the reasons for publishing my book was to try to contact other Illuminati and collect their stories. I believe that the knowledge of our existence is the most important thing that I can tell the world. It's lonely out there when no one can understand what a vampyre may be going through. Not many friends are sympathetic when they see that you view them like a rare piece of roast beef, because you're hungry to the point of blood-lust. I think it's important that people know that we might be anyone. We don't all wear black. We don't have to sleep in coffins. We can go out in the daylight, and we're unique individuals with a rich tradition."

"What is your own experience of drinking blood?"

"It's something I must do to satisfy the hunger. Sometimes I can be playful. Sometimes I will react to the sexual or erotic submissions and needs of my vessels. It can be quite thrilling to hold the body of a beautiful man or woman in my arms, knowing that they are usually having an erotic experience. But I don't know if that is what you are talking about. I'm always mindful and respectful of the intimacies of receiving lifeblood, for it is the most precious of all gifts, but for the most part it is a biological function, like any other. I don't think about the sensations themselves unless I am with my most intimate partner.

"Feeding my children or another of my kind, however, is a very peaceful feeling. I can feel the blood flow out of me and into them as they suck. Our heartbeats synchronize, become one, if you will. For the time of feeding we are one being, existing side by side. Part of me now exists in them, and that is a sensation beyond thrilling."

6

Blood kinship, blood ties. There are more types of vampire families than the nurturing image that Viola presents. I discovered that when I finally went to meet Diogenes. I'd put him off a bit, canceling and rescheduling several times, in part to meet others in the scene, and in part because he made me really nervous. Yet he was still willing to show me what it was like to drink blood from a human, and I soon discovered that I wasn't ready for the total vampire scene—not this aspect of it, anyway.

People have always had an attraction for blood. The blood is the life, and for some it has a magical, spiritual element. In some cultures, warriors used to drink the blood of their enemies to gain their vitality. Countess Elizabeth Bathory in the sixteenth century thought bathing in it would keep her young. When Dillinger, the notorious criminial, was shot down in the streets, people dipped their handkerchiefs in the blood that pooled from his body and merchants sold what they claimed was his blood in tiny vials. Catholics believe that the Communion wine transubstantiates into the blood of Christ, blood accompanies birth, and a blood donation can save a life. It is a sacred substance.

Diogenes, it turns out, was quite enamored of blood. I'd seen evidence of that at the fetish ball. I met him at the appointed spot and he quickly took me to a dingy, sparsely furnished studio apartment where several people—one male and two females—were engaged in a blood-fetish ritual. For some, this is vampirism at its most exquisite, while others think it has nothing to do with real vampires.

I smelled burning incense and saw a small glass container filled with dark liquid being heated on a stove. Several hypodermic needles lay on the counter nearby. One of the women, a blonde who had streaked her long hair with ribbons of crimson, sat on a bed, leaning forward with a towel over her breasts. There was a scar on her shoulder that looked like a brand. Her back was bare, and the other woman had drawn several lines across it with a surgical blade. Blood ran in streams from these cuts toward a towel that was fast turning from white to red. The artist was following a design that looked something like a tree, and she had the brightest light in the darkened room shining directly on it. A candle stood by for heating her knife.

The male, tall and lanky, with numerous face and nose piercings, and a colorful tattoo that started in his throat and went down somewhere into his black shirt, stood transfixed. He didn't even turn his head when we walked in—he just bounced it slightly to the beat of drum music that came softly over two speakers across the room. His brown hair was tied back away from his face and I caught a glimpse of a fang against his bottom lip.

"Breathe out with the cut," the skin artist told the girl.

Diogenes closed the door behind me. I nearly gagged on the smell of fresh blood and alcohol in the room. The incense didn't cover it.

I knew about the alternative forms of body decoration—raised scars (keloids), hot or cold brands, ink rubbings, and burns, from fine to heavy, depending on the type of tool used. I don't even want to talk about braiding, which involves strips of skin to make a rather extravagant keloid. For some it's a rite of passage or a means to greater spiritual insight; for others it's about gaining pleasure through pain—and their scar is a sort of trophy. Blood-sports, S&M-style. And some people just like it for aesthetic reasons, although psychologists generally consider cutting a form of self-mutilation.

It looked like the cutter had vinegar there to rub into the cuts to irritate them and raise the lines. That's what it smelled like. I couldn't imagine the pain of having that rubbed into the wounds.

Diogenes invited me to have a seat nearby. He introduced the cutter as "Ophelia," the entranced male as "Rod," and the blonde as "DiDi." She nodded toward me, but looked pretty stoned. "It's the endorphins," she said, as if reading my mind. "It's a rush. You might think this hurts, but it really doesn't. It's incredible."

I looked at Diogenes and saw him watching me for some reaction. To be honest, I found the whole thing rather repulsive, but I was determined to stay. For the moment, anyway.

"Want a design?" he asked.

"No," I said. "That's not why I'm here."

He wiped one of his fingers across DiDi's back and held it up, covered in crimson. With a smile, he put it into his mouth. Then he picked a yellow rose, just blooming, from a nearby vase, drew it through her blood, and offered it to me, stained at the edges. A drop of blood splatted onto the floor.

I shook my head.

"We're all safe here," Ophelia assured me. "We've all been tested. We only do this with each other."

"She's a donor," Diogenes said to Ophelia. "I think she wants it taken, not given."

Ophelia gave him a look that said, *Then why did you bring her?*

"She wants to see what it's like," he explained. Ophelia nodded absently, intent on her work. DiDi whimpered a little, but held still. Blood ran in bright red rivulets down her back, catching the light.

I didn't want to see any more. I didn't have to. I was growing ill, and from the look of things, this was going to take some time and was probably going to get more extreme. I tried to think of a way out.

Blair Murphy, the film director, was right. It's less about blood than about fantasy, and this was some tribal ritual, not vampirism. Even if they all sat around afterward and licked DiDi's back with fangs in (which I've seen photos of with others), that wasn't about being a vampire, but only a blood-fetishist. I was beginning to learn my prejudices a little better.

After a few minutes, Diogenes went into the bathroom and I seized the opportunity. "Look, I'm going to leave," I said. "This isn't what I was looking for. Just tell Diogenes I'll come some other time."

Rod glanced up, but said nothing, so I left and went out into the night. I'd see Diogenes again, since we both went to Manhattan events, but I wouldn't ask him for anything else. Even if he'd intended to show me what it was like to drink from DiDi, I knew now I wasn't interested. Nor would it add anything to what I was trying to understand. It's one thing to *imagine* a vampire sinking his teeth erotically into a tender neck; it's another to see someone who thinks he's a vampire with his mouth full of real human blood. I didn't have to be there to know about this rather explicit part of vampire culture. They can do it all they want, but for me, no thanks.

CHAPTER TEN

in the heartland

I

Chicago is famous for its strong winds, jazz festivals, museums, universities, ribs, pizza, and underworld figures. But there is more to this city than meets the tourist's eye. Big cities, with their congested streets, busy sidewalks, and glass towers, attract the power-hungry, the fortune hunters, and the just plain curious. They also attract people trying to get lost in the crowd, who want to disappear. Those trekking Michigan Avenue—the Magnificent Mile—never see one of the city's more intriguing attractions: vampires.

I met a vampire from Chicago who reported largely secret meetings and activities, and who claimed that the vampire's beauty—a powerful aspect of this community—is really a curse. He should know. With his greenish eyes, fine features, and long dark hair, he could have passed for a girl. He was thin, too, which made him even more androgynous. Since he insisted that a true vampire keeps to the shadows, I named him Shadow. We sat together in his sparsely furnished studio apartment just outside Chicago and I asked him to tell me about this curse.

"Beauty foisted upon unsuspecting individuals lifts them to levels outside the average," he explained. "Beautiful people are at the mercy of our culture. External beauty is rewarded at every turn, granting an unbelievable amount of power to its holder. This is a license to manipulate people—to vamp off them. Only those without conscience fail to see it as a curse. They simply use what they've got to get what they want, and walk away with the prize, no matter who they might hurt. Anything I've wanted, I've been given. Any person I desired was mine. The temptation to wield this power—and to increase it—is strong."

"But you don't *have* to exercise it," I suggested. He looked down and I noticed how long and thick his lashes were. Yeah, right, don't use that.

"We get enamored of it," he said. "And we can't accept aging. We can't accept our power diminishing. So that makes beauty corrosive to the soul. Beauty itself is a vampire. It can make a person desperate and utterly narcissistic."

"Do you regret it?" I asked him, very much in doubt that he did. "Do you wish you'd been born with a different face?"

"No . . . and yes," he claimed. "I've been seriously affected by my activities as a vampire. I recognize now what I suspected earlier in my life: I believe that my vampirism and my narcissism are joined in my personality. Narcissism for me involves primarily the need to be adored. I've grown up expecting to be admired and placed on a pedestal—needing it!"

He stopped for a moment and seemed just then to look like something Raphael might have painted. He tried to rephrase. "Here's where the vampire enters my life: Vampires are powerful beings who are the objects of lust and craving, venerated for their beauty and youth, for their immortal charm. As a child I possessed beauty and intelligence, as well as wit and charm. I quickly learned how to harness and utilize these assets in order to experience the rush of being adored. This led to my fascination with vampire characters. It was natural for me to identify with vampiric figures on and off television because they represented the way in which I viewed my own life. I was drawn to the vampiric lifestyle because I was accustomed to power and adoration. This fed into my ego and eventually led into exchanging blood between friends, drinking blood from an open wound, and seeking the supernatural power that I believed was available through blood. It was during this time of experimentation that I began to appreciate the power of psychic vampirism, the ability to manipulate people and circumstances. I saw the advantages of using people to accomplish my goals. I used to get discounts on toys and other products through psychic vampirism. In short, my vampire life became the ultimate expression of my narcissistic personality. I learned to feed both my ego and my libido through it. I was in complete denial of my self, seeking only to satisfy and maintain the hunger to which I was accustomed."

"You make it sound so empty," I observed. "I mean, narcissists need constant attention to preserve any sense of self. Without the mirror provided by others, they lose substance."

"Vampires are always searching for what they think they don't possess," Shadow said. "They try to acquire the traits that they feel are necessary for their own lives, but often they already possess these traits or abilities. A lot of the vampires in my acquaintance are blind to their own talents, seeking victims who exhibit what they think they need but don't realize they already have. They're down on themselves, without eyes to see their own value. They hunt to artificially inflate themselves, but overdose because they're taking in what they inherently stock."

He was deeply involved, he said, in a secretive vampire community there in Chicago, but he would not pinpoint its location precisely. As he described to me some of the things they were doing, I understood why.

Originally I'd asked him to get me entrance into this group and he'd come back with their answer: I was an outsider, not one of them. He was forbidden to bring me.

"Maybe they'd be more open if you told them about the books I've written on Rice," I'd suggested.

"I did that, too," Shadow had said. "And they were impressed. They wanted to know if they could drink your blood."

I had decided to just go with Shadow's account.

According to him, vampires require privacy to carry out their rituals, and there is no better place to be a vampire than in Chicago. The underground vampire community there is not as well known as those in New York and Los Angeles. Even Florida has more public coverage of vampire activity. So how is it that the third-largest city in America has overlooked the vampires within its midst? Because they conceal themselves deliberately.

"Unlike many other communities," Shadow said, "the Chicago vampire scene is a secret organization dedicated to stealth. There is no public demonstration on the streets during Halloween, at least not by the 'real' vampires. Any vampire activity during this time of year is hosted by the would-be vampires, the 'pretenders.' Real vampires hold them in contempt, but appreciate the fact that their presence serves as a diversion from their own operations.

"The vampires in Chicago are some of the most dangerous in the nation. There's a very real element of destruction among them. The underground community boasts more than one thousand members living and working in the city limits, with a few smaller 'houses' in the surrounding suburbs. They're highly organized and dedicated individuals who have pledged their allegiance to the consumption of blood in order to acquire the energy of another soul. This energy is believed by many vampires to provide a youthful beauty and strength that will sustain a mortal immortality.

"Each house has a set territory in which to prowl, a 'turf.' These houses are something like the famed Chicago Mafia, an organized army of dedicated soldiers trained to feed off the lives of others.

"I went to a vampire cult in Chicago's Halsted district. Most of the vampires there are beautiful, powerful, and seductively dangerous. They share my own prowess for predation. I found them when I was cruising in Side Tracks, a bar there, and spotted another of my kind. He was six feet tall, a natural blond with Cherokee bone structure. He wore solid black—a long-sleeved silk shirt with jeans. His lips were red, as if he'd been standing in a cold wind for hours. I played demure, ignoring him on purpose, and sat in the corner sipping brandy. I wanted him to hunt me. After an hour of flirting with it, I got up and walked past him. He followed me and in a dark corner, he reached up behind my right ear and gently bit and licked my neck. So hot! We decided to go stalking together. It was a strange sensation—to cruise with another so like me in precision. We found ourselves distracted by each other—the vamp vamps the vamp. Ha!" Shadow's green eyes lit up as he said this, and he smiled.

"Then he invited me to his place, which turned out to be a coven. The rooms in this two-story town house were decorated in deep, rich hues and fabrics. There were nine others there, male and female, sitting around in various poses, listening to music, staring at candles, or talking quietly. My vampire took me upstairs and I felt others following behind. We then proceeded to have a vampire orgy, with biting and sucking and licking everywhere. No one cared what gender anyone was. We just got into the total sensation of it.

"Over wine afterwards, I was invited to join them. I gave them no definite answer. That's always best. As it turned out, I was the 'catch' for the night. Their ritual dictates that one or two go out cruising and bring their prey back for the rest."

"What is a coven house like?" I asked.

He thought for a moment, and then said, "There's one house in particular, the house of Abel, that is central to the community. I call him Abel because the name means 'exhalation, vapor, mist.' The idea is something vain and empty, as was he. Abel is a leader among the vampires, possessing a practiced charm. His house is an opulent sanctuary for his flock, with approximately ten living with him. The carpet is a thick royal purple with matching drapes that cover bone-colored French windows. His furniture is cherry wood, Early American style. There are very few lights in Abel's home, and what light there is comes from the indirect glow of the electric candles positioned near the vaulted ceilings. This creates a cathedral effect not unlike a church, an interesting contrast between two houses that worship the same thing: the spirit.

"The house is deliciously creepy. There's a subtle scent of damp stone wandering through it, a fragrance rising from the basement crypts where Abel sleeps. They live like vampires, lying asleep in their underground coffins by day, and stalking the streets of Chicago by night.

"In this vibrant city, Abel is a quiet king who saunters the pavement in search of new blood. He dreams of becoming a god, a ruler with his own kingdom—a cult consisting of hundreds of vampire children bred to carry out his plans."

"Did you visit others?" I asked.

"I did. Another place was a plushly decorated apartment in a remodeled basement in an older section of town. A massive space, with ten rooms, each painted with its own separate hue. There was a ceremony room, and I was there to see four young males and two females initiated. All were in their early twenties. They were stripped naked and tied to poles arranged in a circle, facing one another. The coven surrounded them in a circle on the outside, while the leader stood in the center of the initiates' circle. He said a long prayer for the proceedings, some of it in another language. Then five vampires entered the initiates' circle with sharpened knives and slit each of the naked bodies in four separate locations: a slice on each breast and a slice on each inner thigh. More prayers were offered while this was being done."

"Prayers?"

"Coven prayers, which are usually offered to the spirit vampire to which the coven has access. Vows are taken to reaffirm and reestablish the blood-oath, that life is the blood and that energy comes from that red life. As for killing others to renew that oath, it is a witch-like crossover.

"The initiates bled freely and their fluid was collected in silver bowls placed beneath them. After ceremonial cleansing by fire, the blood was consumed by some of the members, each drinking another's life. Then the Giver was brought in."

"The Giver?" I asked. "This really does sound pagan."

"He was a young man with his wrists cut open a bit. He offered each of the initiates a drink from his veins. Then they were cut down and taken to a separate room for engaging in any activity of their choosing. The fulfillment of long-term fantasies was strongly encouraged. If they had seen someone in the group they wanted, they selected that person to accompany them."

"Don't they worry about diseases?"

"No, they never do. I've never seen a vampire who did, anyway, not a true vampire. Most with whom I've been associated feel immune, or else they just don't care. If they die from it, they feel it is their fate as vampires."

"Okay, then go on. The ceremony."

"This ceremony took about two hours, and afterward I retired to a room that had been set up for me. It was furnished with a bed and dresser, a nightstand and a full-length mirror. The carpet was a deep shade of crimson, very thick. The only light was a dim torchére in one corner of the room. This room was for sleeping only. Abel told me that there were rooms reserved for darker activities than I had witnessed, where 'things happen.' I suspect that illegal activities are conducted in some of the rooms. I think that the annual blood-hunts culminate somewhere in a lower level."

"Culminate? You think they kill people?"

Shadow was noncommittal on this point. "The taking of a life for the renewal of a coven—it's said that such things happen all across the country. It's so secret and the murders are so infrequent and well planned that vampires such as these are hard to catch or convict. It's called a Sacred Death, and I've never taken part, though I've been invited to."

"Would you?"

He looked at me and then shrugged. "I don't know. I don't think so."

"Are there are other kinds of killings besides the Sacred Death?"

"Traitors. It's a lifetime contract, once you're part of the coven, and outcasts are hunted down. Sometimes there's just thrill-killing."

"Just how did you become part of this group?" I asked him. I was beginning to worry a little on his behalf. "Did you find them or did they find you?"

"Both, actually. I was in a club and met some young men who invited me to their place. We established that night the kindred vampire spirit among us, and began to openly diagram our intentions with whomever we had selected as prey. We already knew one another as vampires: eye contact, gestures, content of conversation."

"What kinds of gestures?"

"Well, for example, one vampire 'pulsed' me when we first met. He shook my hand with his forefinger pressed against the inside of my wrist. I acknowledged what it meant."

"And so you became part of their coven? Or what?"

"No. I'm a loner. I never really went back after that one night. But I did cruise with them sometimes, especially Abel. I learned from him about a vampire circuit, a group that goes from city to city to teach or organize other vampires. I don't know much about it. Wasn't interested, really. But he was part of that. He said it was comprised of twelve covens of twelve members each, although the Chicago underground itself is burgeoning with vampire groups everywhere. There were twenty different groups under Abel's command, he said. But there are many others with their own distinct tastes and practices. The thrill for them is based entirely on their invisibility—that no one really knows what they are."

"If you felt the kind of affinity you describe, why did you never return to the cult?"

"It was *because* of the affinity that I didn't go back. I sensed that I could lose myself. At the time, I was afraid of what that could mean."

"Can you tell me about one of the times you hunted with Abel?"

Shadow was quiet for a moment, as if searching for the best story—or for the one that would provide the best disguise—and then said, "It was a rainy night. We met for a drink and the conversation eased into blood and sex. He assured me that the night ahead was going to be fun. We finished our drinks and went up the quiet streets to a club. The walls enclosing the alley were moist and hazy in a thick fog. We went to a bar called . . . no, never mind." He smiled. "Can't reveal that. When we went in, Abel immediately took control of the room. A man in his forties came down the steps and stopped upon seeing us. He nodded and then climbed the stairs and disappeared. We got some drinks and ascended the wooden staircase into an upper room. It was scented with mulberry candles, which lined the walls. About twenty people stood around, watching us. Some were seated, others were leaning on white columns separating the bar from the parlor. I learned later that they were all vampires.

"In a few minutes, a twenty-one-year-old male with dirty-blond hair was led naked into the center of the room. They made him lie down on two black pillars, facing the ceiling. He did so willingly. Then a hooded figure entered the room, and with him the stench of a cemetery, as if he'd pulled his cloak out of a grave. He hovered over the boy with a pitcher full of something and lowered it onto the boy's chest. He said something that was too mumbled for me to hear but sounded like Latin, then lifted the pitcher and poured its contents onto the boy. It was thick and dark and smelled like fresh blood, so I assumed that's what it was. I learned later that it was the mingled blood of all the people in the room—except me. The hooded man basted the boy with this blood and then stepped back to form a circle with the others. A beautiful chant ensued, followed by each person present—and they were mostly male—licking the blood off the boy's body while he writhed in pleasure and fear. The last person to lick cleansed him thoroughly and then swiftly sank a pair of sharpened eyeteeth into his neck and pierced the skin. He drank for a full minute before releasing the initiate to the Hooded One.

"He motioned for the boy to rise, at which time each member planted on his mouth a Holy Kiss and then embraced him. Some of the vampires whispered in his ear, and I'd kill to know what they said. I suspect it was some sort of sexual invitation. The Initiate was then prepared for ceremonial cleansing. Some of the male members masturbated, shooting sperm onto him that he was to rub into his skin. Then the Hooded One lifted his cloak, revealing his thighs, and slit his skin below the groin, offering it to the Initiate to drink. The boy went to his knees and licked at the sacred wound. The rite was completed. In the eyes of that group, he was a vampire now, committed to psychic exploitation. All that remained was for him to know the full joys of being the seducer rather than the seduced."

"Did you participate in all this, too?"

"Yes. Abel took my hand and led me to the boy. I stared into his eyes, looking past his conscious fears and desires. I was searching for his soul, for his vapor heartbeat, hidden beneath the veneer. Then I found the spot on his soul that would release his deepest longings, his secret passions. What he most wanted was humiliation, so I moved into position and began to piss on him, over his face and into his mouth. At the same time, two of the other vampires pricked his skin and began to imbibe the full power of his passion."

I cringed. That was not my idea of someone's "deepest longing."

Shadow smiled. "Do you want more detail? It gets even more kinky."

I shook my head. It didn't take much imagination to know where it was going. I'd heard the ritual of passage and that was what I was after.

"When it was all over," Shadow said, "the boy went out with the Hooded One, for more teaching, I suppose, and I left with Abel to go hunt."

I confess that Shadow's story seemed rather over-the-top, with all its rituals and secrecy, but he appeared to be quite sincere about it. As I listened, he seemed at times to contradict himself or not to have his story altogether straight. I wondered if he was just a particularly vivid fantasizer and had made it all up, whether he simply didn't care if the details were right as long as he delivered the essence, or whether he'd told me certain things that weren't true in some attempt to shield the others. The person of Abel, particularly, seemed a bit incoherent, and this may be because he didn't exist. It might also be that, if he did exist, he'd told Shadow contradictory things about himself or Shadow was telling them to me this way to protect him. He'd said he could manipulate with his beauty, and I felt willing to give him the benefit of the doubt, probably for that very reason.

What interested me about his story, if it was true, was the mix of male and female and the apparent genderlessness of the vampire experience. They seemed to have been affected by Anne Rice's notion that male and female did not really count once one was a vampire. And sexuality was obviously a very strong aspect of becoming a blood predator amoung this group.

2

Another resident of the Chicago area, where a stained glass window of the Little Bucharest restaurant features Vlad Tepes, is Martin Riccardo. He lives in Berwyn. Key to vampire culture, his expertise spans two decades. Riccardo, with support from his wife Denise, has kept track of vampire doings all over the country since 1977 via his Vampire Studies center. He once edited *The Journal of Vampirism*, and has written several books: *Vampires Unearthed* (a bibliography), *The Lure of the Vampire* (a collection of essays), and *Liquid Dreams of Vampires*. There are more projects in the works as well, since he believes that "there's always a new angle to be found on this subject." Once a behavioral hypnotist, he also wrote a book about meditative states.

He knows most of the vampire connections around the country—maybe all of them—and he is well aware of the more overt members of the Chicago community. He told me about Jule Ghoul, who runs *The Vampire Archives*, a monthly newsletter for vampire fandom; and Vlad, the vampire rock musician who used to frequent talk shows and who has drawn the attention of more than one journalist. Vlad leads the group Dark Theater, whose first album was *Matters of Life and Death*, and he once claimed to be an indirect descendant of Vlad the Impaler via some illicit liaison. At the time, he believed that the soul passes from body to body and that his own soul was first born in 1431: he's his own grandfather, so to speak. He also claimed to drink blood once a week to renew the core self. I had seen him in concert and he certainly looked vampiric with his pale skin, long black hair, and dramatic eye makeup that intensified already intense eyes. I sensed a great deal of anger in his music, but Riccardo insisted that he was a fun and colorful character. He appears prominently in Carol Page's book *Bloodlust* and Guinn and Grieser's *Something in the Blood*, although he views himself more as a blood-drinker than a vampire. Riccardo says that Vlad is too unique to categorize.

With his huge collection of books, magazines, newsletters, and correspondence on (and from) vampires, Riccardo has been featured on numerous programs such as *Sightings*, and in newspapers and magazines seeking to define, connect with, or understand why people want to be vampires. He gives lectures and writes articles on vampirism, and sometimes hosts fan forums for discussion in the greater Chicago area. He's also founder of the Ghost Research Society. Through his training in hypnotism, he discovered that with practices such as past-life regression, there was no way to distinguish between fantasy and reality, and he quickly learned how much overlap there can be between subconscious images and what people believe is actual. It's not that hard for people to believe they're vampires if their imaginations allow it. That realization even inspired one of his books, *Liquid Dreams of Vampires*.

Martin and Denise Riccardo are down-to-earth people, completely unpretentious and sincerely interested in the stories that Goths, vampires, victims, and other participants in this culture bring to their door. Riccardo is tall, sports a mustache, and keeps his brown hair neat and short. Denise has long brown hair, wears glasses, and has a friendly smile. Both are tolerant, accessible Midwesterners who embrace people of all types and make them feel right at home. This is probably why they have acquired such an extensive file on individuals involved in vampire culture.

"I think when you're sympathetic, interested, and not patronizing," says Riccardo, "they feel comfortable talking about their lives. Like anyone, they like attention, and if they feel you believe them, they're willing to talk about things that might disturb or even shock someone who cannot entertain the possibilities."

People tell Riccardo about lovers who were cold as death and had no heartbeats; vampire dream-teachers; telepathic creatures attempting to lure them into an altered state of existence; anemic-looking foreigners who shun the sun; bite marks that reappear with recurring vampire dreams; and sudden blood-cravings after a vampire encounter. Riccardo even met two young women who claimed to suffer from a vampire entity engaged through a Ouija board. He knows a man who investigates vampire-related ghost activity, and has heard from a couple who claim to be channeling the spirit of the fifteenth-century Vlad Tepes. Although he is skeptical about reports of someone being a member of the living dead, he gives credence to psychic vampirism. He is even credited with coining the term "astral vampirism," for the practice of sending out one's spirit to drain someone of blood or life energy.

Over the years, he's noticed a trend: "These days there are more and more people who know they're mortal and call themselves vampires. Often they're attracted to the typical trappings: the black clothing, the fangs, and some have even slept in coffins. There are those who look normal, of course, but because some of these people do drink blood, they tend to identify with whatever the prominent image of blood-drinking does—and that means wearing black, using fangs, and shunning bright sunlight."

In his latest book, *Liquid Dreams*, Riccardo studies the subconscious power of the vampire image through dreams, fantasies, and vampiric experiences. "Vampires are the stuff that dreams are made of," he says. The vampire is "one of the great mythic images in the modern world." Therefore, he felt that the best way to explore the power of the vampire image as a healthy fantasy release in the nineties was to look at a range of real dreams and fantasies about vampires. It was a project that lasted six years and drew hundreds of responses from all over the country.

"One thing stood out," he reports. "I found that the majority of accounts portrayed the vampire as a desirable romantic figure, not the real horror of the vampire generated hundreds of years ago in Eastern Europe. Some of those who wrote to me wanted to be swept off their feet with an overwhelming passion. They wanted to be seduced by a beautiful creature who desired them with aching hunger. Even being bitten is described in ecstatic terms, like 'a pain that felt real good.' A lot of people envisioned scenes of being transformed by drinking a vampire's blood—which is interesting, since that isn't common to the lore. A significant number of accounts depict the vampire as having hypnotic powers. To my mind, these vampire encounters seemed to be permissible expressions for sexual desires that might not be socially acceptable."

Riccardo's conclusion is that the attraction for the vampire image could not be reduced to any single element. Different people relate to different facets of the vampire's energy, appearance, or behavior. "It's an all-purpose fantasy outlet for secret desires and repressed passions." He agrees with Joseph Campbell that "myths are the dreams of the world," and his book is a valuable contribution to the body of vampire literature.

3

There's a strong musical subculture in the Chicago area with a Gothic orientation. Riccardo told me that one Goth night is every Tuesday at a club called NEO, at 2350 North Clark Street. The disc jockey there is a woman named Carrie Monster. Another Goth night takes place at Smart Bar at 3730 North Clark, with a DJ known as Scary Lady. She operates American Gothic Productions, which is involved in many Gothic music events in the Chicago area.

Riccardo also referred me to the former wife of the rock musician Vlad, who once had been a member of his band. Her name is Lynda Licina and she is now a "subcultural diva," writing a vampire column called "She Poison" for a Chicago-based gay and lesbian publication, *Nightlines Weekly*. Previously she was the editor and design person for Screem Jams, the company that she ran with Vlad, which produced the publication *Screem in the Dark*, and sponsored Vampire Circus and other vampire events in the Chicago area. (A vampire circus is a full night of simultaneous appearances by rock bands, psychics, magicians, fangmakers, tarot readers, artistic sideshows, a coffin raffle, and Renfield, the yo-yo spinning vampiric clown at whom "you'll laugh so hard you'll bleed." A three-ring event, so to speak.)

Lynda has gained a following for her witty observations about the culture at large, gay or straight, Goth, vampire, or other. Some of her topics include the gay obsessive-compulsive poltergeist in her apartment, the Web site that assists in calculating your personal mortality so you can plan your exit, and "Things I'm comfortable not knowing," e.g., "what garlic breath smells like" or "what's up with men and gerbils." Now she's producing a gay- and lesbian-oriented vampire magazine called *Fugue*, because she believes this to be a very large, untapped, and hungry market.

I decided to contact her to find out more.

Lynda was born in 1956 in Chicago, but moved to the suburbs when she was three. "Growing up in the 'burbs was a challenge," she told me. "I have always been different. In the sixties and seventies, when most people were into the Allman Brothers, Fleetwood Mac, and Carole King, I was the glitter-glam queen into T-Rex, Gary Glitter, David Bowie, the New York Dolls, and anyone else whose performance included glitter, rhinestones, or sequins. I began wearing solid black as a seventh grader! I was always aware that things were a bit way over the edge with me, be it wardrobe, attitude, ideas, or drug habits. I've done it all. It bores me now. I suppose I needed to experience all I did then to realize now that drugs are so *not* a part of the creative life." At one point in her life, she was a race-car driver, and her first marriage while still living in the suburbs was brief.

"I thought I'd learned from that," she said. "*Wrong!* During my first marriage I really began to seriously get into vampires. This is also when I began to wonder about my sexuality. I was very attracted to a female friend of mine, and it seemed to be a bit more than just an attraction. I, of course, denied it all to myself, and continued to live with men."

"How did you meet Vlad?" I asked.

"I was living with a man named Stephen for two years, and then entered ... Vlad. I hung out with a regular group of friends at a Chicago club called Exit, a very famous punk club in Chicago's history as well as my home away from home. One evening, two of my friends, Stephen and Ceil, were with me at Exit, dancing as usual. Well, the dance floor is encased in a 'thunderdome'-type cage, as well as being a few levels below the regular floor. Vlad was at Exit that night promoting the first effort from the Dark Theater, a three-song cassette. I was dancing with Ceil and Stephen on the floor and he apparently circled and saw me there. He has proclaimed he felt an instant love for me, and decided right then and there I was his female counterpart and that we would be married. I don't know how long he watched me, but at one point, he leaped, cape and all, over the metal cage surrounding the dance floor, shimmied in between Ceil and I, and handed me a cassette saying, 'This is for you. I know you have a boyfriend but I just want you to have this.' Inside, as I later discovered, he had written his phone number.

"I was more than intrigued by this man with fangs, a cape, and a command of the language to make any poet jealous. What charm and charisma! Later during the evening, we talked alone and he told me that Carol Page was interviewing him for a book ... and he was a vampire. I left Exit that night knowing that Stephen and I were doomed.

"I let it go for a while. Then one day, using the pretense that I had forgotten the title of Page's book, I called the number he gave me. He answered and we made plans to meet again to 'talk' at a Killing Joke concert. The rest, as they say, is history.

"This was September 22, and on December 1 of that year, we were married. We got married in a cemetery—the hearse, the clothes, the whole thing. I went on talk shows with him and they tried to make me look like an idiot. I was presented as his monogamous donor, but I never claimed to drink his blood. I said that I drank his blood one time only, which was on our wedding day. We stayed married for six years.

"I became the keyboard player in his band for three years and the editor and layout/design person for *Screem in the Dark*. I ended with issue thirteen after Vlad and I divorced. I also was designer for all of the Screem Jams screen-printed garments and other printed material.

"Vlad and I remain 'distantly friendly,' but my life has changed dramatically, as I have admitted my questioned lesbianism. I exist in a new community with a new set of rules and opportunities. I retain my day job as a graphic artist for a screen printing company, but have become somewhat of a quasi-celebrity in the Chicago gay world, as this community had not been confronted before with a so-called lesbian vampire. I am She-Cago's Child of the Night. I'm also part of a few performance-spoken word groups in the city and continue the vampire theme throughout my many projects.

"In an attempt to bring the gay and straight world together via vampires, for Halloween I designed the display window at the Gerber/Hart Library in Chicago, the Midwest's largest gay and lesbian library and archives. I put together a 'One Hundred Years of Dracula' exhibit, including as many gay-themed images as I could. I have gotten raves from everyone down to the Republican board of directors of the library to the effect that this is the best window the Gerber/Hart has displayed in the history of their existence."

She's a busy lady, but Lynda had time to send her latest columns. They were all rather humorous, and I picked the following as a sample because it touches on some of the same things I've noticed about Goth (not to be confused with vampire) culture. She gave me permission to publish her original uncut version:

In response to the voluminous (seven) amount of mail I've received inquiring "How can I become a spooky goth chick/dude?" (They're interchangeable of course, the more androgynous you are, the less reconstruction you'll have to do.) Hereafter follows the "Goth makeover checklist in one dark hour or less" wherein I, celebrated VampGirl of She-cago, help YOU turn your dreary existence into an even drearier existence! These tips are designed for those who want to temporarily play "dress-up," as any permanent change would be followed by a few weeks of therapy to regain some semblance of reality.

Now that you have been disclaimed . . . onward . . .

The first basic rule of gothdom: Become Visibly Depressed. (BVD—hah!) Remember, the entire weight of the world is on YOUR shoulders and it's YOUR fault! No smiling from here on out. Practice clinical depression in your spare time, it must be perfected. The second goth standard would be to forget how to spell and start using words like etheareal, melloncollie, despare and deth. Spell them wrong ov course.

Now for the "look." You gay boys are pretty close. Girls, pay attention. . . .

Make-up and hair: Spooky is the key word here. Try your best to look dead. If you can starve yourself, that's always a plus. Otherwise, white base followed by black eyeliner, black lipstick, black blush. Hair? First, dye (this word occurs regularly) it black, shave random parts, arrange and spray other random parts. If most of it covers your face, all the better. Let long hair hang free—in front of at least one eye. Ignore depth perception.

Clothing/Accessories: Anything black, lacy or velvety and flowing. Could be drapes or a tablecloth. Could be a few yards of lace from a Minnesota Fabrics remnant bin. A safe rule of thumb—lace for summer, velvet for winter. Capes are always good. Boys . . . become a drag (and I mean DRAG in every sense of the word) queen, short skirt, black fishnets and a body hugging, stretchy lace shirt. Girls . . . a long flowing black dress is basic, I'd love to see cleavage—but that's me. Accessories are what counts after all and can include everything from a rosary necklace to dead flowers to a coffin.

Choose carefully. A coffin will probably need a hearse, or a car at the very least. Just try getting on public transportation with a coffin; it's awkward and they'll probably charge you full fare. Other ways to accessorize include tattoos and piercings. You'll want to be "different" so try piercing some body part that is exclusively you—perhaps an eye (not the one the hair hangs in front of) or vital internal organ. Tattoos should be plentiful. Accessorize as much as possible; minimalist is NOT part of the goth vocabulary. I don't even think they have a vocabulary, but just in case . . . minimalist, not there.

Music/Dancing: a goth's favorite pastime is dancing, or what they consider "dancing." Mostly you will sway a lot and position your hands to resemble Karate moves. That is the body part that does most of the dancing—hands. Doesn't matter the tempo, it's the same movement, nothing fancy schmancy to learn! Most of the music is dirgey and repetitive D minor crap.

Tune it out and get to swaying and Kung Fu fighting— you'll be an expert dancer in no time! And while we're on the music subject, go buy some OLD Sisters of Mercy CD's. This was the definitive music at one time. They're no longer relevant since Mr. "I am not goth" singer Andrew Eldrich has "reinvented himself" into a yellow-haired industrial (yes, I am only in my 20's) punk. Ouch. Right. Then try some Siouxsie or a Cleopatra compilation. (You MUST ditch the 70's disco (guys) and Indigo Girls/kd/Melissa (you know who you are).

At this point, you should be able to look in the mirror and become very very scared. The few final goth codes of etiquette include becoming poverty stricken. You do not need money for any reason, remember that. Purchase some fangs, every good goth needs a pair, and change your name (while in the persona) to Christian or Lucretia, or something equally "romantic."

Voila! You are now on the path to becoming seriously disturbed—in one easy lesson! Don't thank me, it's my job. I look forward to seeing all you lovely cleavaged and velvet laced goth girls out there in the dark. I'm getting the vapors already. . . .

In quick review sweeties, to become a member of the undead, you must first pass the "GOTH" test. Sharpen your No. 2 pencils, study hard. And NO SMILING!

Okay. That's the way to be perfectly Goth. But I did meet some people—not Goths—who were smiling big, because they'd met their vampire lover.

CHAPTER ELEVEN
blood ties

I

"I first met 'Scot' at a rock club in Florida. I was dancing and I felt this need to turn my head. I did, and there he was, in black velvet and a poet's shirt . . . Gorgeous!! He was dreamy, with full, black curly hair, about shoulder length . . . piercing, intense blue eyes . . . and just as graceful as they come. I walked up to him and commented on his wonderful taste in clothing. He smiled and I saw the fangs. I fell in complete lust at that moment. Scot had that air of self-confidence and cockiness that always attracts women. It seemed that we both frequented this club quite often, so we began to play this little game. We'd flirt with each other continuously. One night I came up behind him and yanked his hair back and heard him gasp as my tongue traced his jugular and just nipped at him enough to give him a warning, and then thrust his head forward as I walked away. At times he'd just show up at the edge of the dance floor in the shadows, watching me intently and as soon as I'd noticed him, he'd disappear. Or he'd pop up out of the blue and gently lean down and bite my neck with his fangs, just to make me jump, and then walk away as though nothing had happened. We played this game for months. Then one night, I ran into Scot, and, god, did he look good. I grabbed him and just threw him back on the table and kissed him. Scot has that animalistic quality that brings out the aggressiveness in women. It's all in his presence, his commanding aura . . . his eyes . . . He reminds me of the way the mystical vampire arouses that lust instinct in women. So he almost broke one of his fangs, but the sex at his place later was primal, with a lot of biting. It was a crazed session that just seemed completely natural."

2

Whether role-playing, having spontaneous encounters, or working on it long-term, many people in the vampire community seek the kind of romance described above (under strict conditions of anonymity). Gay, straight, or bi, the image of the seductive, confident, and alluring being who possesses power and mystery inspires endless fantasies.

Online, I found a site for recording vampire weddings. "NiteTrain and Catrina," "Cochease and Vampiria," "Osyras and Nala." Some offered photos on their private sites. A "special note" on the site claimed that there had been thirteen vampire marriages recorded there as of September 1997. One woman told me how she'd met her vampire lover online shortly after her husband died, and got married fairly quickly. (Hmm. Did this vampire know of her before her husband died?) On the downside, three-fourths of the couples who'd gotten married had sadly recorded the failure of their fantasy on the vampire divorce site.

Yet those who succeed have a shared connection in dark desires that might otherwise have remained secret within each individual. One woman, "Blu," told me that her involvement with vampire culture had affected her life in a magical way. "Take a chance meeting . . . an online meeting, of two seemingly unimportant names in some random chat room of AOL. I was seeking refuge from a painful night alone on an abandoned Christmas eve, he seeking shelter from a shattered heart. There's a spark, and an immediate chemistry. The conversation traverses nearly five hours . . . nonstop. And there's a tie there, something underlying in the conversation . . . hints at darker, more intimate things. But he's polite . . . and doesn't step over boundaries. So the correspondence continues. He's a musician trained in the art of classical piano . . . long liquid fingers over ivory keys. He sends a WAV file . . . a piece of a Chopin waltz, and then a nocturne. He enchants, he intoxicates with flowery words."

Beginning his letters with such greetings as "My darling princess of the night," or "My precious moonchild," the vampire lover sends romantic sentiments. Only two days after their first online communication, he says, "I have been thinking continuously of you since our first encounter . . . I suspect you are a rare and wonderful creature. I like things that have to do with darkness. Must be the vampire in me. Like sitting in a dark movie theater snuggled up to you . . . or staring deeply into your eyes so that I may drink of your soul."

He assures her that each day he comes home to the treat of finding her letters waiting on his computer. He reads each word, and reads them again, astonished that the two of them share so many of the same interests. He speaks of spicy food and then assures her with, "I do love sweet things, too, like the scent of your lovely neck, the taste of your lips . . . I dare not continue!" He signs this note, "Your vampire." In other letters, he speaks of how he thinks of her, dreams of her— including erotic dreams—and wants to be with her. He asks her to do a special New Year's Eve ritual that will draw them together in spirit. The same goes for other holidays on which they cannot be together.

"Finally," said Blu, "I ask what his obsession with dark vampiric things are and he tells me. He was going back to school for another degree and one night he was at a smoky little bar. He ordered dinner, had a drink, and felt someone watching him. It was, in his words, 'an exotic woman.' She seemed to inquire with her eyes. He waved her over . . . she sat . . . the food came, it got cold, he never touched it. They had conversations without talking. He paid the bill, they left together, arm in arm, down the street until they got to someplace dark. She pushed him against a wall. He remembers feeling the brick against his back. She kissed his neck, nibbled . . . and then he felt pain . . . but it was short-lived. His mind swam. She suddenly backed away and turned to leave. Startled, he asked if he would see her again, but she only smiled and replied, 'Maybe.' She disappeared into the night. He never did see her again.

"He says there were no marks on his neck. He doesn't like to admit that anything really happened. But what he will say is that his life changed that night. He found himself obsessed with the beauty of the night, of classically Gothic things, of deep romanticism. He jokes about being 'half-vampire.'

"Our conversations continued via e-mail and private rooms for over a year. I swear we read each other's mind. There are countless times we type in the same sentences ... same thoughts, springing from out of the blue. And one night, at the same time, this one thought seeped into our shared consciousness. I remember the conversation so clearly. It was a thought, a desire, that neither of us had ever had before that night. It was a birth of an obsession. We had talked about being together in intimate ways and I suddenly said, 'What I really want ... is for you to complete the circle'... And he knew what I was talking about. He finished my sentence. There is no delicate way to put this ... and I can imagine anyone reading this will think us quite mad. Between us, there's a terrific, obsessive desire to be totally emerged in each other, so intimate that souls connect and real consciousness is lost. The connection is in blood ... and in a shared heartbeat ... in a moment of passion, as I take him into me, he takes me into him, completing an interconnected circle."

Gradually they revealed secrets to each other that caused each the pain of anticipating instant rejection. There were difficult times, temporary conflicts, relieved embraces (symbolized online with {{Blu}}).

"Finally we met last June for a glorious day together," Blu told me. "It was our first meeting after almost three years of correspondence. We have not, yet, spent an entire evening together ... and that is what we look forward to the most. At night something happens, moods change, eyes widen, and there's that vampiric urge that pressures both of us. I will think of him, and suddenly he's on the phone, or on my computer, sharing sighs and tormenting pangs of wanting to be together. Sometimes this urge is almost unbearable ... the desire to feel that exquisite pain, to lick crimson stains from his lips ...

"And so we continue on. I have since made him read Anne Rice's books. He is her new biggest fan. He finds understanding and kinship in her words. And I just want to say, there are people ... seemingly 'normal' people out there who hide this dark obsession. It's funny, he's a physician and I'm a computer analyst. Wouldn't our coworkers just die if they knew where our true passions lay?"

3

A man named Dave, who signed "Draugr" (the Norwegian vampire) after his name, contacted me to tell me about a relationship he has with someone who willingly lets him take her blood—and has been doing so for five years. He had persuaded a dentist to give him vampire teeth and had spent a lot of time compiling lore about vampires in Norwegian folk legend. His mother had studied the occult, and his fascination with vampires and werewolves reaches back to his child-hood. He has worked as a network engineer and has also acted on stage.

"I have been involved with the vampire/blood-fetish lifestyle for many, many years," he said. "In fact, all my life, I would argue, as I've always had a blood-fetish. One of my first and boldest statements was expressed about six years ago, when I had my canines elongated. This was less an expression of the vampiric, to be honest, and more the product of vanity. I had always desired them that way, and though they do add an enjoyable spice to my fetishist expression, I generally used other methods to insure my victims' comfort."

"How old were you when you started?" I asked.

"I never had the boldness to initiate my blood-fetish aggressively until seventeen, when I started carrying around razor blades in a tiny pouch. They often invoked conversation when I would 'accidentally' let them be seen. Then when I looked in their eyes, I'd know if they were willing. Usually, once I explained what the razors were for, if the individuals were interested, they'd offer.

"I used to play with blood, and since you're going for the real story here, I feel I must explain that I had a rather Trollish obsession with it. My mother said I used to wipe it on the walls, suck on my own wounds, trade with friends. Whenever we were getting into little acci-dents we would make trades, then never speak of it. By eighteen, I constantly had razors on my person, My favorites ran about $1.50 at the local convenience or grocery store, and came in a little plastic box, with a nifty slide compartment in the side to put the used razors in."

I was curious about his teeth. "How did you have your canines elongated? And how do people react?"

"At a dentist. I saved up my funds, and he begged me not to do it. My roomie at the time told me I'd hate them, but I still love them. When I can afford to I am getting a tiny pair on the bottom set of teeth, so that they are perfect. People react wonderfully. This is defi-nitely the age when accentuation of the primal spirit—of the devil within, if you will—is embraced. I am constantly asked at nightclubs, 'Will you bite me?' It's amusing, to say the least. So that you know, I never break the skin without permission; I'm not a monster. Some people freak out, but it's never been a problem at jobs. They usually think it's a birth defect."

"How often do you indulge in your blood-thirst?"

"I used to do it four or five times a week. When I was eighteen, I went to the free clinic every two weeks to get my blood tested. I've been indulging infrequently now, as I've a fiancée. For both of our safety's sake she is my only donor."

"You don't seem to have worried in your early days about getting any infections from the blood of others. Did you take any precautions, as you seem to now?"

"Then I didn't worry, didn't feel I had to.... Perhaps youthful naiveté, but people just flocked to me and I usually just had a feeling. I remember that some friends of mine called the AIDs hot line, asking if it was possible to get infected by ingesting blood. The operator paused a bit, then said, 'Why on earth would you want to do that?!' She put them on hold and came back, stating that unless you had cuts in your mouth or receding gums it shouldn't technically be a problem, that stomach acid kills the virus. So bolstered in a fine rationalization of our lifestyles, we fed quite a bit for a few weeks."

Dave's fiancée told me her side of the experience, and what it meant to her. "I became involved in giving blood through Dave. I do not remember having any qualms about doing so, but I may not be remembering clearly. I say this because I have a complex about having my blood taken from me. When I have had to have my blood taken for any medical purposes, I have had very severe hang-ups about doing so. Even with those samples where they take only a drop from your fingertip, I have been very uncomfortable with the idea of any-one else having my blood. It always seemed to be a kind of spiritual theft. After all, at times it was the only thing I had left that I could call my own. If I did have any fears with Dave, I quickly got over them. It could be because of the trust that I have always had for him. We are now at a point where quite often I will offer him blood just because I feel like having him feed off me.

"Giving blood is a very special thing to me. As far as I can recall, I have not had any others drink my blood. I feel that sharing my blood with Dave is a kind of bonding. He does not drink as much as he did when we were together before, and in a way, I miss the 'old days.' When Dave first started drinking my blood, I would actually get a kind of high off it. I was anemic at the time, and have heard that this is a common effect. Currently I still do get a high off of feeding him, but it isn't at all the same. I feel elated, and so close to him. It is sometimes a sexual thing, mixed either with lovemaking or foreplay—quite the aphrodisiac. At other times, we simply decide that it is time to have another cut put into my skin. Lately he has had a thing for carving delicate hearts on my shoulder blade. To my disappointment—but not his—no recent cuts have scarred. We always use clean, sharp razors for this in order to avoid infection. There have been times when none have been available, and it is torturous to wait. Therefore, we are quite often seen at the grocer's stocking up on razors."

4

From engagement to marriage, I was invited to attend a vampire/pagan wedding in Florida. While I wasn't able to make it to the ceremony itself, I decided to meet the lucky couple beforehand while they were in the planning stages. I flew first to Orlando, because I'd heard there was a fairly sizable vampire community there—mostly very young—and I wanted to check it out in person. I'd been told that there was a network of club personnel who monitored the Goth/vampire scene and sometimes offered special vampire nights. The police supposedly kept a close watch because there were drugs readily available, and many kids among the Raver crowds were too young to drink legally. Even so, there were some seven or eight clubs that vampires liked to frequent.

As I was about to arrive, I was informed that all vampire activities had been suspended. No meetings held, no covert blood exchanges, and no attendance at any of the clubs. They were cautious about 'sting' operations among the police. "If any vampires are out, they will not stalk, kill, or participate in any way with any activities." It was a citywide mandate to remain elusive and invisible.

I thought this was hilarious. Since when does a committee dictate what a vampire will do? It seemed completely incongruous with my idea of the vampire.

Anyway, I went to one of the larger clubs, the Firestone, because with a capacity of one thousand people, it seemed likely that vampires would hang out around the edges. I'd heard about other clubs, but was told that one was closed and another was so small, I wasn't bound to find a lot of action. The Firestone was huge, with several tiers of balconies from which to watch the dance floor. Most of the males wore muscle shirts or no shirts at all, while females dressed in skimpy or tight clothing. Fog machines and cigarette smoke gave a surreal coating to the place, and music blasted in a loud beat, repeated from one song to the next without pause. Red and black posters of writhing, naked bodies reminded dancers what they might be there for, although I was told that some of those dancers were undercover cops. The atmosphere was wet with heat and excitement, as if everyone expected to make that chance encounter that would change their lives. Messages were flashed around the room from eye to eye in quick but knowledgeable code.

There was a "quiet room," set apart from the deafening music, but filled with cigarette smoke (among other types, I'm sure). I went in there and walked around outside to find people willing to talk about their experiences. One young redhead was nineteen (he said, but I didn't believe him) and he came there for the music. Sometimes he took a stimulant to allow himself to melt into the scene. It made him feel, he said, as if he had no boundaries, no limits, and no prejudices. "It's good," he murmured. "Everything's fine."

Ecstasy, or E or X, seemed to be the drug of choice down there. I was offered a hit several times, but I declined. Ecstasy had been around for a long time, and when legal, had been used by an extensive network of psychotherapists to help their clients feel relaxed and open. The folklore says it was once used by the military as a truth drug, but there is no evidence for that. Also known as MDMA or Adam, it became widely used in the mid-eighties. It wasn't until the early nineties that young people adopted it as the dance drug of choice. It was officially banned in 1985, but that didn't stop it from being prevalent at warehouse parties and clubs.

Known as a psychedelic amphetamine, it had the odd effect of being simultaneously stimulating and relaxing, and also provided a sense of empathy. Movement was more fluid, and people report feeling like a child again, before self-consciousness set in. There were also reports of a greater sense of tolerance, nondefensiveness, and belonging. It was a feeling akin to being in love, and relationships were often started while on the drug. (There were also reports of dry mouth, paranoia, depression, exhaustion, and a general sense of malaise when coming off the drug.) Many people mention that their spirituality has

OF DRACUL

OPPOSITE PAGE BOTTOM: Jesse and
Mike Hazel. bonding with blood.

THIS PAGE LEFT: Vampyr Theatre.
(CREDIT: TINA COLOMBO)

OPPOSITE PAGE CENTER: Caught in the
act at the Vampyre Valentine's
Day Ball at The Bank.
(CREDIT: VITTORIO SARTOR)

BACKGROUND: Lynda Licina's
window display at Chicago's
Gerber/Hart Library.
(CREDIT: LYNDA LICINA)

Vampyre
MAGAZINE

La Nouvelle Justine

LEFT: Myke Hideous, of the Empire Hideous, in a blood-drenched performance. He'd just removed a dozen needles from his scalp. (CREDIT: VITTORIO SARTOR)

BOTTOM RIGHT: Catrina Coffin asleep in her coffin.

TOP RIGHT: Outside of The Bank on the night of the Vampyre Valentine's Day Ball. (CREDIT: VITTORIO SARTOR)

BOTTOM LEFT: Le Comte Dracula in Paris, decorated for a Goth/vampire gathering.

deepened as a result of taking Ecstasy, and that they feel more attuned to nature. Some kids claimed to be psychic while on the drug, but none could demonstrate this ability. Overall, everything just feels right. No wonder they think, "It's all good."

Someone who urged me to try it told me this about his experience: "I felt that I was being absorbed into the music, and I got strange visual images flashing through my head. I saw graphs and charts in technicolor, surreal landscapes, and flashes of the Virgin Mary. I could feel the crowd without actually looking at them. I could perceive the souls of people nearby, and I felt the utmost compassion for them all. The harder I danced, the more intense it all became until I felt like I was about to explode. I felt powerful, like I was releasing extraordinary amounts of energy. I sensed a unity all around me, permeating everything. I realized this is what drives are made of and drives are all that matter. The will to power—I worshiped it! I wanted to reproduce, to ravage, to command! My consciousness was opened up. My mind was glowing and my thoughts were so lucid. For the first time in my life, I really felt in touch with myself."

Okay, well, it didn't seem all that different from speed or mescaline or LSD. Maybe a little less intense, even, but still too *fluid* for my purposes. I was there to watch and to analyze the scene, not to fall in love with everyone. I know the feeling of having an absolutely brilliant insight while high on some drug, only to see how mundane or incoherent it is the next day. I declined to experiment. I already had experience with altered states, and I could understand how one might feel more like a vampire if one's senses and feelings of power are heightened. And I could see, with all this empathy thick in the air, how the concept of the vampire might evolve into a being that is more closely bonded with victims and other vampires. But I felt some trepidation for those kids who seemed to live only for the drug, as if their own day-to-day lives just weren't enough. Those were the kids who often went over the edge in search of ever greater highs.

Another guy—a Disney-loving nerd wearing eight-inch platform shoes—told me in a slurred voice that he adored "studs, couples, women, and men with their shirts off." Well, that about covered everyone there. He drank blood from pinpricks, he said with a giggle, and came to the club because it was easy to get blood there, especially from girls.

A transvestite transgender vampire had told someone who

revealed it to me that s/he vamped off straight men in local bars, drinking everything s/he could get. S/he transformed into something different with each new encounter and became their fantasy.

A girl who looked fifteen told me she had been approached by several people that night who asked if they could drink her blood. A young man who went out dancing four times a week said he had gone home with a guy who looked just like him, and after sex had said, "I want to taste your blood and I want you to drink mine."

"And did you?" I asked.

"Sure. It was an experience. He thought blood would enrich his life and be some sort of salvation. He made an incision on his own wrist and pressed it to my mouth. Then he wanted me to bite the inside of my lip so he could taste my blood."

I learned about vampire identification signals, like the handshake described to me by Shadow in Chicago. "But many times," a young brunette told me, "it's a simple process of eye and mouth reactions. A vampire will say a word or flash her eyes during a key moment in conversation. Or you can simply ask. But you can usually tell by the way they flirt. And some of them just ask for blood. If they lick you behind the ear, you know you've got a vampire."

I stayed at the club for a while, but found the whole thing a bit less vampiric than I had anticipated, with all the heated dancing, disco lights, and club music. I guess I just like my vampires to stay in the shadows.

I do find it interesting that there's a vampire community so near to Disney World, but it makes ironic sense: vampires as the shadow side of the great symbol of normal life and family fun—and vice versa. It seems you can't have one without the other.

What I learned about Orlando's vampires is that, like the Florida youth culture at large, they like to ingest drugs to give their all-night clubbing experience an extra kick, they're bold and promiscuous in their practices, and they emphasize body perfection and sex. More specific to the vampires is that many of them gather in places along the ocean an hour away to engage in rituals, often under the moon. No one wanted to go on record with a name, but they were willing to talk in confidence. I don't know how many participate, but I was assured it's sizable. I would have spent more time among them, but I had an appointment in South Beach.

5

Before I met Jesse and Michael, I had already heard Jesse's story about developing a desire for blood. Her screen name was Dementia, after the girlfriend of the Adams Family's Uncle Fester.

"I was adopted at a very young age," she had written to me, "and from what I understand, I was never truly liked by my adopted family. When I turned eighteen, I moved to Miami to meet my biological maternal family, although my mother had passed away. I was living with my aunt, and had begun to read books by Anne Rice. By this time I had already adopted the night habits of a 'vampire,' such as keeping late hours and dressing in black. I was watching MTV in the living room one afternoon and somehow I cut my finger, and the blood began to flow. By instinct, I stuck my finger in my mouth. That's when my aunt walked in. Seeing me all in black, sunglasses during the day, with a bloody finger in my mouth, she went nuts. She started saying I thought I was a vampire and told me to get out. So I guess you could say my aunt 'awakened' me to the possibility.

"There's always been a supernatural influence in my life and I'll tell you why. My biological father is of Caribbean descent. They're very spiritual and deal very deeply with nature, and their bloodline seems to have a sensitivity to these things."

When I asked Jesse about other influences on her life as a blood-drinker, she told me she'd had a few potent experiences with witchcraft. "I suppose I slowly had a growing fascination with the underworld and the occult, but never really had met anyone who I could entrust this with. I think it all surfaced one night at the age of twenty. I was at the club, Washington Square, on South Beach, and I was working there with one of the singers of a band. I was going to a technical school at the time for music business, and one of the people I knew from the school had attracted me for some reason—something deep, dark, and sinister, and I couldn't pinpoint it. He was a 'player,' so to speak, and normally I wasn't attracted to that type, so I was surprised when he and I ended up back at my place. We slept together that night (simply slept) and the next morning he woke up lying on my chest and he smirked and asked me, 'Do you like blood?' I suppose the look in my eyes gave my answer away because the next thing I knew he somehow brought up blood into his mouth effortlessly—almost like it flowed. I never seemed to figure out exactly how he did it. And it dripped onto my chest. I was, to say the least, enthralled.

"He'd done it on a couple other occasions, and then it all came to a head one night when we were at his place. His room was bathed in black light and the bed was set up almost as an altar. So we're going at it, and he flipped me on my back and held my hands above my head and just sat, looking at me. He told me to close my eyes and open my mouth. I did, and next thing I knew I had my first taste of blood. He hovered over my mouth and just dripped it into me. I can't describe it, Katherine, it was simply orgasmic . . . just the intimacy of it.

"So that was the beginning. Usually when I've done it, it's been primarily sexual, and I pretty much perfected my technique as I got older. I don't understand how people like to be bitten. Another boyfriend enjoyed biting me and that was just too painful. I mean, human teeth aren't made for puncturing.

"I just lived off the high I got. Not a physical high, I guess, more of a psychological and mental high, but comparable to an orgasm. I found myself becoming more and more involved with parts of the scene. Like I said, I've always liked the black dress, and was always a late-night person, but I became involved more and more, partially because of Anne, and from going to Renaissance Festivals, where these types of people seem to congregate. I fell in love with the Gothic era and with Renaissance/Victorian lifestyles."

I asked Jesse what she thought was the vampire's allure.

"I believe it's a number of things. Many people would do anything for that sort of emotional detachment from their surroundings, to be able to escape the pain of everyday living . . . and the night itself is just so glorious. The typical nine to five is a hustle and bustle, hurry and wait, tie and jacket kind of world; whereas the night is dark, and the harsh, bright edges of daylight all become dim, blurry, and merged into a sub-reality where people can be whoever they want to be, without authority looking over their shoulder telling them what to do. I think the idea of draining the life force of another human being gives a sense of power, a sense that is overwhelmingly erotic, that is so intimate. Being a vampire would give people a chance to break out of the mold they've been cast into, and to make their own set of rules. It would give them a sense of being truly free."

Her fiancé, Michael, did not share her blood experiences, so I asked how she met him.

"I'm an exotic dancer and have been for about six years. We met one night when he came into the club I was working in for his friend's bachelor party. I seemed to stand out, as he told me later. I 'had an aura.' He couldn't describe it. Something had drawn him to me, much like I was drawn to Derek years before. He became more entranced once he got a taste of my 'dark' background. As a dancer, of course, I embellished a bit (I later confided this to him), but it turns out he was basically a straightlaced, apple pie kinda guy—usually the type who have the deepest intrigue with the 'other side.' Once we began dating I told him about my 'fetish,' and he genuinely was open-minded and actually quite interested in the whole subject. After we had become intimately close, I told him of my desire to share such a thing with him. He was very eager."

They decided to hold off on this ritual until the wedding, although they worried about how to do such a thing in front of friends and family without upsetting people. They were still wondering about that when I met them.

Michael and Jesse arrived at my hotel at South Beach and we went out for dinner to a local Italian restaurant. South Beach is the southern strip of Miami Beach famous for art deco hotels, beautiful bodies, Caribbean restaurants, and the steps of the mansion where the designer Versace was gunned down. It comprises Ocean Avenue, Collins, and Washington. Anne Rice set the opening scene of *The Tale of the Body Thief* here, and Lestat had a room in the Park Central Hotel. He tracked the "Backstreet Strangler" up Collins Avenue, and killed an elderly woman. It was the first place I ever saw one of those creepy palmetto bugs.

Clubs abound on Ocean and Washington, and for those who dress in black, the clubs of choice are the Kitchen over the causeway, and the Groove Jet on Sundays when "the Church" is open. That's a weekly party for "gravers"—Goth kids in period costume. "The most fun you can have without actually being dead," said one review.

Jesse has curly red hair and an eager, lively manner. Her words came fast and her eyes were always sparkling. Michael, good-looking and clean-cut, was a little more subdued, but cordial. I wasn't sure how forthcoming he would be, since it was my experience that those mates of blood-drinkers who have no real appreciation for the life only tolerate it at best. But that was not the case with Michael. He was a Porsche mechanic with a great love for nature and fishing. He told me that his life before Jesse had been routine and safe, and that meeting her had allowed him to express himself in many ways that had been rather exciting. "I can be myself with her," he said. He wasn't afraid of things he doesn't know, he assured me, and he believed that marrying her would be an adventure.

In fact, they were both enthused about getting into Renaissance costume for this sacred event. Michael would wear black pirate pants and shirt with a burgundy and emerald cape, and Jesse had picked out a green emerald dress with long sleeves. Her hair was long and over it she would wear a chain-mail headpiece with emerald jewels. She would wind baby's breath on ribbons to fall away from the headpiece. The invitations would be hand-lettered calligraphy, with a pen-and-ink illustration of a castle and an explanation of the ritual of handfasting that they had planned. They expected about seventy-five people—who were all to dress in period clothing—and thought their honeymoon might be postponed until the Anne Rice ball in New Orleans the following October.

"So where are you registered?" I asked them. "Lord and Taylor?" That sounded a bit medieval. They laughed. They'd never even given it any thought.

"Well, I'm not sure I'd know what to get for such an unusual wedding," I said. (I ended up giving them a floating candle in a druidic-looking tree, and a Day of the Dead wedding couple in a coffin labeled "Eternal Love.")

They described to me the ritual of handfasting, saying that it was an ancient Celtic wedding ritual that sanctified the union of two people before witnesses in a way that that raises energy into the universe. They didn't wish to just have a traditional wedding, and not even a traditional pagan wedding, so the blood exchange made it unique. They wondered out loud just how they ought to do the bloodletting that would seal their spirits together, and just how public it should be. "I believe the taking of someone's blood bonds you to that person," Jesse explained, "much as in the biblical belief that when you have sex with a person the same occurs. So I've always been selective about who I've shared blood with. The bloodletting Michael and I will partake in at the wedding, and each bloodletting thereafter, is a revival of who we are, and what we stand for, and our commitment from each to be part of the other. Like we said, it's the ultimate intimacy, the ultimate bond."

So on February 7, 1998, they joined their left hands with a braided ribbon around the wrist—tying the knot, so to speak—in front of about fifty guests, and said a wedding prayer and their sacred vows. Afterward, they invited the guests to enjoy the Renaissance Festival all around them, and prepared for a private ceremony with just the wedding party. This was the bloodletting. Jesse had bought a gargoyle chalice for this part, since Michael loved gargoyles, and they used a lancet to open the skin.

Nothing came.

It was unusually cold for southern Florida in February, around fifty degrees, so they had some trouble getting even a few drops. They tried again. Nothing.

"It was hilarious," said Jesse. It took about ten minutes, but finally they managed to squeeze out a little blood each, and exchanged it as part of their vows.

So all those looking for vampire lovers, take heart. They're out there. After seeing how close these couples were, I gave some thought to finding one of my own. I could place a personals ad, "Desperately seeking vampire," and see if I get any bites.

CHAPTER TWELVE

i'm okay,
you're a vampire

I

At the first vampire club I went to, I met a young girl—she looked sixteen, but I'm sure she was older, since we were in a nightclub that checked IDs. (Of course, she could have had a false ID.) She wore black eye shadow, a tight red satin corset, black velvet gloves, and a tight microskirt over black lace stockings and lace-up leather boots. Her breath smelled of cigarettes with a faint hint of marijuana. She did not have fangs and when I asked why, she confessed, "I'm here to find a vampire."

"To find one?"

"Yes. I want to be a donor. I want to give myself to someone and let him drink from me."

This seemed to me the equivalent of unsafe sex—maybe worse, since she could be putting herself into the hands of someone who could really harm her, even kill her. She seemed so eager.

"Why do you want to have someone cut or bite you?" I pressed.

"It's not about that," she insisted, her eyes dreamy enough to give the impression she was taking something, possibly Ecstasy. "I had this experience once and I want it again."

"You were bit by a vampire?"

"I was *taken*. It scared me, but then it turned into something else. I've never felt anything like it since." She leaned her head back and closed her eyes. "He had these large, dark eyes that seemed to know me. Knew everything I'd been through, how bad I felt, how I wanted to just escape it all. I saw him at a rock concert and when I got close, I heard him humming. Deep in his chest. He kept humming as he watched me and it felt like he was drawing me forth. He tapped his fingers against his leg as if giving a beat to my life story. I sat down by him and I could feel how warm he was, but it gave me a chill. He smiled slightly, but not so much that it broke the mood. He was communing with all the misery I felt just being alive. He felt it, too, and knew how to use his body to make it all into poetry. I felt as if he'd memorized my diary and it was okay, all of it. He accepted it and loved me for it. He was calling to me to give in."

"Did you?"

"Yes. After the concert, I went with him. We walked together for a while without saying anything. He held my hand and sometimes he looked at me. Then he took me behind a building and asked if he could drink my blood. I was scared. I didn't know what to say. He took out a little razor and said it wouldn't hurt, not really. He lifted my arm and I let him unbutton the cuff of my blouse. I felt completely powerless to stop him, but I didn't really want to. He pushed it back to expose my wrist and used the razor to just nick it. I started to bleed and he looked at me with a smile. I just melted into those eyes and offered it to him. His lips were hot against my skin and I felt this strange pressure, but then I felt good. Peaceful even. Like someone really loved me—really *wanted* me. And I want to feel like that again."

"What did he do then?"

"Nothing. He took me back to the concert and left. I never saw him again, although I wrote stories about him and dreamed about him for weeks. I wish I could find him again, but it doesn't matter, really. I just want someone. I want a vampire."

I couldn't say anything to that. She didn't elaborate, but it seemed that she had shouldered a lot of pain and was seeking relief. The romance of submission to someone who paid such unique attention to her was clearly a powerful lure.

2

Some people present themselves as vampires merely to bewitch some vulnerable person. One young woman described to me a man who told her he could make her a vampire, but first she had to have sex with him three times so he could decide if she was worthy. In search of immortality, she complied, and he locked her in his apartment and continued to use her for sex until he tired of her and let her go. At no time did he even pretend to fulfill his end of the bargain.

In some ways, the idea of a vampire date rape seems incongruous, since the vampire is, more or less, supposed to be an unconscionable seducer. I was somewhat amused when I heard about a young man who knowingly went out with a person who said he was a vampire, but protested when his date took advantage. They were both wearing fangs, he got drunk, and the vampire bit him and sucked his blood. He's thinking about suing. Excuse me? Since when does a vampire get sued for sexual trespass?

On the other hand, there certainly can be totally unsuspecting and unwilling victims. One vampire told me what he'd done in secret: "The mind of a wolf," he said, "never remains in the shadows for too long. Any normal student goes to parties, no? Some friends invited me to this large gathering. I met a girl and she was all too willing as I took her away from the others. She shouldn't have followed me, really. So we went to a quiet area of the house. Don't mistake me. I didn't want to drink from her, no. Just play with her as any drunk guy would. We had sex, but she was already passing out. That's when I thought of doing what I had always wanted to do. I just took a beer bottle, broke it, and cut the side of her waist down to her inner thighs. A well-hidden cut in an intimate place. It was slight, just enough to taste her. I left that night looking back to a hundred students lying everywhere, drunk, stoned, trashed . . . and for myself, full."

3

Victims are not just exploited for sex or blood, but for psychic energy as well—at least, according to them. I received a frantic note from a woman who claimed that her best friend had become a psychic vampire—and didn't even know it. She felt tired around him at all times and he was disrupting her life. She had heard there were rituals or exorcisms one could do, and she wondered if I could suggest any.

I asked her for details and it turned out she'd been reading a book about psychic vampires. The whole situation struck me more as a case of suggestibility than a real vampire.

It seems easy enough in the age of blood-borne diseases to take on the persona of a vampire by claiming that one feeds off the life force—energy, not blood. I must have encountered ten psychic vampires to every one blood-drinker—at least! But I find that there's a great deal of confusion on the subject, and more than a little role-playing.

Is psychic vampirism real or just mental manipulation? To answer that, it's important first to make a distinction between psychic and psychological vampirism. The first is about a genuine energy drain that could ostensibly be physically measured with the right equipment (but it's very hard to prove). The second, which I call covert vampirism, is about the draining of emotional resources by someone with a serious personality disorder. It's more of a vampiric metaphor, but tends to be what many people mean when they talk about psychic vampirism. This kind of person has left a clear mark on the metaphors that pervade and inspire vampire culture.

To my mind, covert vampirism, an orchestrated eroding of the ego, is far more prevalent than psychic vampirism. It's often the key factor in what has become known as codependent relationships, and those who identify themselves as real vampires will exploit these methods to make a more powerful impression. Yet the expression of it by *anyone* is equally insidious.

The movie *Blue Sky*, starring Jessica Lange as Carly Marshall and Tommy Lee Jones as her husband, is about the kind of person whose repetitive mood swings have a vampiric effect. Carly's husband is a patient man who works in the military to detect dangerous levels of radiation after bomb tests. While he tries to do his job, he must also keep track of his erratic wife, who constantly changes her hair color to look like various movie stars, throws childish fits, makes up fantastic stories, manipulates men with her body, and thrives off of attention. She recklessly puts her husband's career at risk, and then makes a deal that forces him into a mental hospital under such heavy sedation that he becomes a zombie while his career falls to pieces around him. When she finally helps him to get back on his feet (only because she desperately needs him), she's ready to start her manic phases again, come what may.

Carly Marshall is the kind of person that attracts people. She's spirited, free, eroticized, electric, energetic, and beautiful. People put up with a lot from her and men are magnetized by her. Even her husband, who knows all too well her depressing cycles, finds her charming and sexy. She drains him again and again and nearly destroys him, yet he stays with her. Most of us know someone like this, and we've experienced this vampire's charms, as well as the inevitable destruction that follows from their needs, lies, manipulation, and demanding moods. They tease, provoke, and exploit high drama to create an impact. Their desire to feel larger than life seduces you. No one is safe with such people, but the allure is strong to be in their company. And it's that allure that blinds you to the dangers.

The problem is that these covert vampires are not empathic. They have no feeling for how they damage you. They focus only on their own needs. They are impulsive, adept at illusion, able to exploit vulnerability, and are often driven by a rage that boils just below the surface. If they don't get what they're after, watch out!

They feed off confidence, ego, self-image, values, and whatever else constitutes your sense of self. The stronger you are, the more interested they are in your resources. This is because their inner world is empty, lonely, and indistinct. They take for themselves but can never be filled. They have no bank account of the soul, so to speak. They can't recall kindnesses done, compliments, assurances. They have little to sustain them in troubled times if no one is there to keep telling them they are okay. Often they live episodically, in the moment, always in conflict between feeling entitled and feeling unworthy. Their environment becomes a theater for playing out various scenarios with no reference to truth.

They have an endless supply of victims who willingly feed them in order to stay close to the electricity. They inspire in others a desire to take care of them, pay their way, open doors, and deliver a multitude of resources. They have a knack for discerning how to exploit or wound someone in such a way as to keep them connected and giving. They can hone in on the exact triggers needed to drain others of hope, confidence, values, and security.

I know these vampires well. I've had several such experiences. Paul was probably the most potentially harmful. I noticed him across the room at a conference where I was speaking. He nodded at everything I said and afterward insisted that he needed to speak with me. He was in his fifties, but his face was unlined and beautifully sculpted. His manner was calm and assured. I told him to look for me at the party later that night.

After getting my fill of hors d'oeuvres and wine, the thought occurred to me that I should see if the guy was there. Some five hundred people were spread out in several large rooms, so we could easily miss each other. To my surprise, I turned and there he was. He said that the thought to find me had just occurred to him, too. It seemed a surprising synchronicity, so we found a private place to sit and talk.

The conversation became intimate and even secretive as we swapped stories about having gone through terrible health ordeals that were eerily similar. He told me that he had been healed in a vision and had developed psychic powers that had made him something of a shaman. He was now an ordained minister and a certified counselor, much in demand. The one thing he wanted to do now was to get published as a writer, because he felt he had an amazing story to tell.

We kept in touch and he sent me his manuscript, asking for suggestions and hinting that I could make connections for him so he wouldn't have to jump through the hoops that other beginning writers endured. Whenever I resisted helping him shortcut his way to fame and fortune, he got irritated, but quickly smoothed it over and started again. It got to be a pattern. Then one day in his home I came across a letter he'd written to an editor at a large publishing house. In it he claimed a number of publication credentials that he did not have, and pressured the man to send him a response in short order. I was perturbed that he would resort to such lies.

Then Paul got sick and I went to help. He didn't want me to come, and I soon discovered why. It seemed that he'd told people that I had gotten him a contract for a book for which he was getting an advance of sixty thousand dollars. He'd also told people I was leaving my husband for him. I was stunned. I didn't understand. And then I met a woman, "Anna," who had been a longtime friend—and ultimately his victim.

Anna told me she had become psychic as a child and had developed finely attuned mental powers. When she met Paul, he recognized her gift and asked her to teach him. Being a lonely female, she succumbed to his charm and believed he wanted to be with her romantically—a notion he fed for as long as he needed to until he got what he wanted. She helped him to move quickly through the process of ordination in her Church, although, since she spoke out in his behalf, he did not actually go through the steps. She was convinced that he was uniquely gifted and did not need to do all that was required. Then, once he had the certificate in hand, he told her to leave him alone. She was terribly hurt. He became abusive and spread stories about her to discredit her and to raise himself in power among her own clients. They began to come to him. He usurped Anna's livelihood and damaged her self-esteem and sense of security. After this experience, she felt she could no longer trust her own instincts—which was terrible damage indeed.

When Paul died not long afterward, I learned that his entire life had been created from deception for the purpose of manipulation. He had no college degree and no certification for counseling. His ministerial degree was a sham. He had claimed to be certified in hypnosis, and that too was false. He'd never had the same illness as me, the way he'd claimed when he met me. Some people thought he was married, some thought he was published, some thought he was a professional business consultant, some a healer. I began to understand what he'd had in mind for me—to build an emotional bond and then use my resources to get published—but he had died before achieving it.

I was truly crushed. I had believed we were close, the best of friends, and that I had value to him as a person. Clearly, I did not. I felt utterly drained of energy and motivation. I'd spent a lot of time and money to attend to his needs as he was dying—and I'd just been used. In all my work with the subject of vampires, I'd never even detected it in Paul, and that's why it worked for him so well.

More precisely, this is how the covert vampire operated:

1: He perceived what would impress me or win my attention.
2: He fabricated a story for himself similar to mine to make me feel we'd known each other for a long time.
3: He mirrored the traumas of my life to show how attuned with me he was.
4: He made me feel special by repeating my name during our initial conversation, or at opportune moments, referring to my status.

5: He gave me compelling reasons to want to get closer to
    him.

6: He made me feel that he needed my help.

7: He presented himself in a way that seemed to offer
    something that was missing in my life.

8: He was ready to lie in whatever way necessary to continue
    to draw me in.

9: He lied to other people about me in order to strengthen
    his fantasy in their eyes—and his.

10: He got into position to seem a friend in need, when all the
    while he had targeted me as someone who could advance
    him and whom he'd discard when he achieved his goals.

11: He had devised alternate plans when his goals were
    frustrated so he could approach me again with renewed
    energy, to wear me down until he had taken whatever I
    could give.

12: He had developed the confidence of success through
    undetected and repeated exploitation of others.

13: He had no conscience about the immorality of deception,
    exploitation, and betrayal. To him these seemed natural
    tools.

He was more than just manipulative. He was a taker. I had
immersed myself in this relationship, believed in our bond, trusted his
words. Had it gone further, I'd have been depleted, my resources
exploited. Even worse, like Anna, my self-respect would have been
diminished, if not damaged irreparably. Paul had nearly eroded the
structure of what was meaningful to my life: truth, integrity, and
trust.

Covert vampires do *not* give back. What matters is to feed. They
cannot offer real romance, real pleasure, real friendship, or real intimacy, but only the illusion of those things. They let you believe whatever you need to believe and facilitate whatever illusion you desire, in
order to reap the richest resources from your heightened expectations. Thus, they don't *seem* vampiric. They build you up, like the old
witch feeding Hansel, to make their own meal all the more enticing.
Covert vampires feed you in order to feed *off* you. When they encourage you to achieve, to reach a higher order of spirituality, to increase
your health and energy, it is secretly for their benefit. And you only

realize what they're doing when you're left empty.

But they are not psychic vampires. They deplete emotionally, but do not suck genuine physical energy. There are several books on this subject, but they all tend to confuse vampiric manipulation like Paul's with psychic vampirism. The most practical one is *Vampires: Emotional Predators Who Want to Suck the Life Out of You* by Daniel and Kathleen Rhodes. They offer some interesting material, but since they disagree on whether such vampires are actually siphoning out real energy or just seeming to do so, the confusion remains intact. In their analysis, a vampire is someone who assaults or injures you emotionally, but tries to make you take the blame. They keep you psychologically off balance, and do so repeatedly. Their target prey are unsuspecting people who are emotionally generous.

What's tricky about covert vampires is that they don't want anyone to realize what they're up to. In other words, they won't just tell you they're vampires, like so many psychic vampires I've met. They may not even see themselves as vampires. And they resort to methods for which a psychic vampire would have no need. They often bring in a third party to deflect attention and use what's known as projective entrapment: The vampire may want to hurt a person against whom he feels inferior (which makes him feel even more empty), so he identifies someone else whom he can put into motion to accomplish his goal. If he can diminish the other person without losing access to that person's resources, he gains in two ways. For example, an institutionalized patient who wants to hurt her doctor may manipulate him into giving her special favors, invoking against him the anger of the nurses who must care for her. She gets the favors *and* thrives off his humiliation, and he's only upset at the nurses, not her.

4

Now, what about psychic vampirism?

It seems to go back to the idea of medieval hauntings of sexual entities, better known as incubi or succubi. These creatures "came in the night" to have some kind of sexual congress with their victims— not all of whom minded. And Greek lamiai were spiritual entities of a vampiric variety. So psychic vampirism is nothing new. It's just become increasingly prevalent in this nineties subculture, and even a bit fashionable. Susan Walsh's boyfriend, Christian, reportedly is a type of psychic vampire, and he believed she'd been mentally victimized by manipulators whom he labeled in print as the negative sort of psychic vampire. In the article I'd read of his, he offers evidence for psychic vampirism in experiences like a "contact high," the energy created in an erotic encounter, and the group chemistry on a dance floor. Yet it's not always energy used well, he says. He goes on to talk about parents, businesses, and social institutions as being parasitic and therefore psychic vampires. Thus, he, too, confuses metaphor with the drain of actual physical energy. A psychic vampire may also practice covert vampirism, but to my mind, they are two distinct entities.

Dan Simmons wrote one of the most comprehensive and impressive novels on the idea of psychic vampirism. In *Carrion Comfort*, he features a group of vampires who possess the ability to subconsciously provoke people into acts of violence and then feed off the energy inspired by the subsequent deaths. They make a game of it, seeing who among them has done the most impressive vamping, and when they tire of that, the stakes go higher.

Even Bela Lugosi claims to have experienced something that sounds like psychic vampirism. He once described a time when he was a young actor in Hungary and he fell in love with a woman with pale skin and pointed teeth. He went weak in the knees around her, feeling drained, sick, and dizzy, but he became immediately infatuated. Only leaving the country, he insisted, broke her spell over him.

I've met a number of people who claimed to be psychic vampires. Yet put to the test, they have all manner of excuses why it doesn't appear to be working. I did challenge people to try it on me—I wanted to feel what it was like to have my life force drained. "Go ahead," I'd say, "do it. I'm ready." Inevitably, they declined, saying they didn't want to or I was too aware, or was one of the rare immune ones. Some said they had to have a special bond with their prey, or be in the right mood. Whatever.

Do I dismiss this form of vampirism as an easy out, a way to avoid any real risk? I'm tempted to, but I asked a very grounded clinical psychologist, Barbara Kirwin, whether she'd ever run into this sort of thing in her practice, which includes clients with an affinity for the dark side.

She had, indeed. "I had a young man as a client. Things would happen in the room when that kid was at a level of malevolent rage that bordered on poltergeist activity. Things would pop, machines would go on by themselves. I would be convinced that there was so much disgruntled, rage-filled energy emanating from him that electronic equipment picked it up, and invariably after those sessions, I'd wind up with some kind of physiological breakdown. Sore throat, laryngitis, or something like that. We actually did what I would call 'entity work.' I would tell him to conceptualize the murderous rage he had as an entity, as a possession, and not part of him. As something he had to fight against and externalize. And it worked."

I was willing to grant it some credibility, but still wanted a demonstration or some kind of proof.

I was put in touch online with Lori, who said she was a psychic vampire and had done a lot of thinking about what such a creature is, so I asked her to tell me about her experiences.

"I'm not really sure how I became a psychic vampire," she said. "I just started noticing one day that I was feeding off of energy. Then I started seeing what all I could do with the energy, mainly change it into energy that my body could use."

"What is it like?" I asked.

"I'm able to see things that most can't, and feel things that people would lock me up for years for mentioning. When I feed, it's heaven, or the closest I think I'll ever come to understanding it."

Since she said she'd pondered the subject, I asked her, "How does one become a psychic vampire?"

"I believe that it's hereditary," she responded. "There's a certain gene that controls everything that has to do with psychics. I first started noticing what I did when I woke up from sleeping on the bus I rode to school. It may seem odd to you, but I noticed that whenever I did something, which I now know is feeding, I'd get a high feeling, as if I had a drink. From there I started playing with things that created energy, electricity mainly. Then I said, well, if I can do this with electricity, then why not people?"

When I asked what kinds of energies she thinks there are, she sent an essay that she'd written. The information was compiled from the combination of her own experience, what some of her friends had to say, and what she had read on other Web pages. The following is an excerpt:

"Psychic Vampires are just one of the many types of vampires. Although they aren't well known, they are the most numerous of the vampire species. In order for someone to fully understand a psychic vampire they must first understand the different energy classifications."

Lori listed the three types as "Non-living, Living, and Magickal."

Non-living energy was like electricity or a car engine, and the psychic vampire tended to feed so much, he or she destroyed the source. Living energy involved physical, mental, emotional, and life sources. "Life energy," she explained, "is the energy that human beings use to stay alive, similar to what is also called the soul of a person. A soul is energy and therefore I refer to it as life energy." The third type, Magickal energy, is raised from magic spells or rituals.

"The main question [for the vampire]," said Lori, "is how to feed and yet not destroy something totally or make a person very ill. One way to keep from doing damage is to switch what you feed from often, never feed from one thing more than once if you can keep from it. If it's Non-living, just pick something that's not yours and isn't owned by anyone that you know of. Remember to switch constantly. Another way is to make sure that when you feed, you feed thoroughly. This will keep you from feeding so many times and feeding subconsciously—if you're hungry you'll be feeding just a little bit from everything you come into contact with. The last way is to find some means of being able to stop feeding."

Lori says she is currently trying to find a cure for psychic vampirism, or a means of controlling when a vampire feeds, so that they can go for long periods without feeding or can prevent their subconscious from feeding on their behalf.

As I said, this was an exchange of notes online. I'd have been very interested in meeting her, or someone like her who's deeply involved in this lifestyle, to get an actual demonstration. I'd love to see a vampire blow out a car engine. That would impress me.

5

Not everyone who gets "bitten" has such a pleasant aftertaste as the young girl I met in the bar who was looking for Mr. Goodvampire. One thirty-two-year-old man named Michael believed that he was actually being turned into a vampire from an eerie encounter he'd had. He had met a woman through an IRC channel online that catered to vampires. She was so interesting that he decided to meet her offline. He was surprised at how strong she was when she went to hug him. That night he was overcome with lust and they slept together.

"I'm not proud of that," he admitted. "During the course of the evening, I bit her. I don't know why. It just seemed like the thing to do. She started to bleed, which alarmed me, but she only smiled and I felt driven to lick at her wound." He felt this was all quite uncharacteristic of him.

He stayed for a few days and one day she bit him, but didn't take any blood. Then he felt a strange compulsion to be with her, and he said that when he touched her he felt as if electricity was passing through his body. Some nights he would wake to find her standing over him. Other times when he sat with her, he'd feel sleepy or pass out altogether.

As they got to know each other, she told him that she was into magic and admitted that she was a psychic vampire. He wasn't sure what that was, but when he got home, he read a book about it and believed that he was now under her spell. He experienced mood swings, and felt a strong hunger for blood. Someone he knew who was into Wicca told him he was being turned into a vampire. He felt confused and afraid.

"It all happened after I lost my fiancée," he told me. "It was a very difficult time for me. I had just gotten done watching *Forever Knight*, and I logged on to my computer. I went onto the IRC and typed 'Vampire.' Lo and behold, there the channel was. Everyone was so kind, and I made many friends. One day someone invited me to 'VampireHall.' Over the course of time, I grew close to this woman, let's call her 'Magess.'"

She told him she was having trouble with a former boyfriend and was afraid of him. That's when Michael decided to go meet her, and he ended up staying several weeks. Magess refused to let him ever take her picture and she insisted that he remove the silver cross he always wore around his neck, which he did.

"I don't know why," he said, "but it went okay for a while. Still, I noticed presences, I guess you'd call them, and she kept wanting me to touch her tarot cards and wands. We were talking marriage, and I went home to get some money together. She had given me a strange necklace that was a pewter dragon's claw clutching a teal crystal and said never take it off. She said her essence was in there and she'd blessed the necklace, and had used it during all her spell-casting. Now, this will sound weird, but sometimes that necklace felt hot, sometimes it would throb, and sometimes it would feel like it was pressing against me. One night I got up to get a drink of water, and I swear I saw her all in black walking up the hall to my room. I sent back her necklace and then noticed presences that felt intensely evil."

Michael consulted a Wiccan who gave him some incense to burn and who urged him not to give in to his hunger to "feed," lest he transform into a psychic vampire. She urged him to say the Lord's Prayer whenever he felt the hunger come upon him.

But his nemesis would not leave him alone. "She said she wanted my soul, that she would bond me to her body and soul forever."

He told me he was afraid and asked me whether I thought he was being turned into a vampire. He had a gnawing hunger that seemed insatiable, and the place where she bit him often throbbed and hurt. He had dreams about the woman and felt that she was nearby.

I asked him to tell me some of his dreams, and the influence of role-playing was evident in the language and images. He admitted that he'd role-played on the IRC channels with her and that she'd called him her knight. He also hadn't been with a woman in quite a long time and was fairly vulnerable to a "damsel in distress" who wanted a man to rescue her.

What I said to him was this: "I've heard of others who have had a similar experience to yours. In fact, I believe there's a person in the book *Vampires Among Us* who talks about it. To some extent, the power this woman has over you is psychological. She has made suggestions and possibly used hypnosis to get you to think and feel certain ways. And the more you do, the more aware you are of what has happened, and that usually magnifies the fear and the sense of doom. You can certainly resist becoming a vampire if you want to. Do you? If not, then you'll start to view people as prey. You'll fall into patterns of manipulation and exploitation—and you'll feel more and more empty, with a deep need to fill up by taking from others."

About his concerns over the bite, I said, "If you feel the bite when you are aware of her, that's a sort of trance-induction. The power of suggestion is very strong, but she can only bind you to her if it's something you secretly want. Look into yourself. Does this experience excite you in any way? Are you enticed? She can't hurt you unless you make yourself vulnerable to her, such as wishing she would be with you or take from you. You may feel her trying to get into your mind. This, again, comes from suggestion. But you have power over it. You can shut it out. Whenever you feel this hunger, or feel afraid of her, start counting. Get your mind onto something else. If she feels your strength, she'll move on to weaker prey."

I heard from him several times over the next six months and he admitted that her influence was weakening. At one point, she even asked for forgiveness, but he did his best just to avoid her. And there was no reason to believe he would ever become a vampire from this experience, psychic or otherwise.

6

There is a person who serves as a consultant in cases of psychic vampirism. He goes by the name Konstantinos and he's written *Vampires: The Occult Truth*. In it, he makes a distinction between intentional and unintentional psychic vampires.

He points out that psychic energy has been known by different names, among them orgone energy, Odic Force, Chi, and Buoplasma. All living things seem to generate some form of it. Psychic vampires, then, can be found among those who cannot generate enough of this life force for themselves, such as the old and ill, and dead things bound to the earth. He goes on to explain the mechanics of how it works, including the notion of astral vampirism and osmosis. "The principle at work is that the aura or astral body of a psychic vampire develops to accommodate feeding . . . and can be programmed to perform certain functions on its own." He believes that this energy drain tends to take place at night while the victim is sleeping.

He discusses the various mechanisms used by psychic vampires— touch, close proximity, eye contact. He offers accounts of his personal experience with psychic vampirism, and then provides modes of defense. Among these are purification and astral-body reprogramming. Just as a vampire can refine his aura to attack and feed, any of us can do the same thing for our own protection.

Since I'm pretty much a skeptic when it comes to the high percentage of people in the vampire community who claim to be psychic vampires, I contacted Konstantinos to ask a few questions. He has very long dark hair and dark eyes, and looks appropriately mystical. First, I wanted to know his background. He told me he was born on Long Island and had developed an interest in the occult at the age of eight.

"My grandmother used to watch my sister and me when my parents both had to work," he said. "She would tell the most wonderful stories of folklore from the Old Country—Greece—and I didn't believe that it was all made up. So I began a lifelong interest in the occult. I've been a practicing magician for more than a decade."

Vampires, he admitted, appealed to him on many levels. "There was the whole idea of immortality, and the alluring prowess. I always found it interesting that the world was full of vampires, and each culture had its own take on what a vampire was. Yet much as I enjoy horror in all its forms, I don't believe that the fictional vampires are factual. In my book, I try to make the distinctions between what people once believed, and what people spend money on today to temporarily accept onscreen or in printed form."

"What is the most bizarre thing that you have experienced in your occult investigations?" I asked.

"Narrowing it down just to vampirism, the most bizarre thing I saw was the first time I witnessed a psychic vampire actually feeding. Right there in front of me was a woman using tentacles of subtle, normally invisible etheric matter to draw energy away from others."

"You could actually see that?"

"Yes. It's what led to me write that book."

"Would you say this phenomenon has increased in recent years?"

"If you look at the folklore, you see that it's always been here, since the days of the Sumerians. I can't say it's necessarily any more prevalent in populated areas than it was in the past. It's just not possible to know how many attacks were happening hundreds of years ago compared to today. I've seen a lot in the present time, though, and I help victims on a regular basis."

"How many psychic vampires do you estimate to be part of our population?"

"That's a toughy. If you take into account unintentional psychic vampires, or people who don't know they're draining others, I'd say you've got quite a lot on your hands. As for the ones doing it on purpose, there are significantly fewer of them. Only a handful of groups practice it in this country, and the solo vampires can't be all that numerous."

"Do you think everyone who claims to be a psychic vampire really is?" That was my prejudice showing, but since I had an expert, I took advantage.

"No," he replied. "I've seen more than a few fakes—but I've seen the real ones, too, which helps me discern the pretenders."

"What about victims? Could some of these people just be exaggerating their experience?"

"That can happen," he acknowledged, "which is part of the reason I never used to tell all the symptoms of attack. I didn't want to suggest anything to someone who might just have had an upset stomach from eating before going to sleep. And stories do often get better in the retelling—a person threatened with a pocketknife on the subway might be relating a tale of a machete-wielding madman by the time he or she gets home. However, it is possible to figure out which experiences are authentic by comparing certain facts with known occult laws. Just like a forensic pathologist can determine a cause of death, a magician can use certain techniques to investigate a case of supernatural attack. Yes, people fake paranormal experiences, but there are many real ones out there.

"The whole I-want-to-be-like-Dracula syndrome has something to do with those who pretend to be psychic vampires themselves. When I was on the Ricki Lake show, the basic point I had to make to the 'vampires' was this: Let's examine motives. When did you first get your craving for blood or energy? Was it after you became a fan of vampire fiction?"

I saw his point. Suggestibility again. "Do you find yourself being drawn often into consulting positions regarding cases of vampirism?"

"I receive an overwhelming number of letters every week from all around the world. Unfortunately, I can't personally help everyone who needs my assistance. People who read the self-protection steps in my book will be able to help themselves."

7

If you're seeking to create the impression of power and connection to an occult influence, psychic vampirism seems to be the way to go. However, in some cases, this can take a more complicated form. I talked with a young woman diagnosed with dissociative identity disorder, also known as multiple personality, who said that several of her personalities are vampires. She's just over five feet tall, has shoulder-length, straight black hair, and dark brown eyes. She is not sure how many personalities are actually in her "system," but the one who spoke with me—I'll call her Acacia after a tree that symbolizes immortality—thought there might be a great many that she didn't yet know. Acacia is "out" most of the time, but she knows other personalities who serve functions such as processing pain, enduring verbal abuse, expressing overt sexuality, and presenting a "good girl" persona. Some of them inflict abuse on the body, others are nurturing.

Sexual abuse, coupled with a traumatic family life, inspired splitting into alternate personalities for her as a means of surviving. "My first conscious awareness of a split," Acacia explained with some difficulty, "was at the age of six, but I now have an understanding that it was occurring even before that. When I was six, I stayed after school because I didn't want to go home, and a substitute teacher raped me there. Six personalities were born at that time."

I asked Acacia about her vampire personality and she told me that at one point, she believed her vampiric feelings were merely her imaginings, but then realized they were being acted out. "I'm hesitant to talk about Alex," she said in reference to the vampire, "because she means a great deal to me emotionally, physically, and mentally. Speaking about her is awkward and discomforting. Alexandra appeared when another alter of mine was brutally raped when we were thirteen years old. The vampire came as a response to the brutality and to take the body home and literally lick the wounds clean. She came as immortality at a time when it seemed the only good option was a quickly ended mortality. Alex has done many things over the years, such as feeding physically and mentally off of people and animals. She can keep me in check, and I have no real control over her. Alex is five foot eleven. She has hair that is white and her eyes are white with a slight blue tint and black irises that never contract or expand. She is slender and speaks with a British accent. Her skin is like the color of porcelain but gets rosy after feeding."

Acacia had said that Alex indulges in psychic vampirism, and I asked her to explain.

"She performs psychic vampirism in a 'give and take' manner," she said. "While she may take, she gives, too. She uses the victim as a filter of sorts, pumping in bad energy through the victim's emotional sieves and ending up as good energy that she takes. It also holds true of sexual energy. While she may take sexual energy, she gives as much . . . to be filtered and purified and used at the next sexual 'feed.' The amount of times she can feed off of someone is determined by the strength of the victim . . . or if she gets bored.

"She seems to be a very intelligent vampire and only does things that she knows she can get away with. My understanding is that there are numerous vampires that manifest themselves in many different ways. Because I am not co-conscious with them, I don't know how often they manifest themselves in the body."

One of the ways she has experienced their manifestations is when one of the personalities becomes self-abusive, such as making deep cuts. "Alex comes out to clean up the messes, sucking the wounds until they clot. The body is not much of a bleeder and Alex usually goes away screaming because we shouldn't be doing this to the body or to her—meaning that cutting the body and her only getting a taste pisses her off."

Developing a vampiric personality, psychic or otherwise, is an interesting way for the psyche to defend against being a victim. Acacia had suffered in many ways, and here she'd located strength, connection, and a way to acquire resources for any further attacks.

8

Speaking of victims, one of my messages from Wraith had been a brief but poignant e-mail about what can happen when a "victim" gets too emotionally involved in the vampiric scenario. It was titled "Sean: My first blood lover," and was about another predatory encounter.

"Sean stood naked on the balcony facing the water. As the breeze tossed his boyish blond curls, he whispered, 'Take me. I want you to.' He lifted his green eyes to meet mine, and then moved toward me until he was so close we were sharing the same breath. We embraced, kissing gently. Then he whispered again, 'Take me, please.'

"I knew what he wanted. He'd been asking me for the past three months to drink his blood. I had refused because he was so young and I didn't wish to douse his light. But he had everything planned that night. He had rented a suite, ordered my favorite wine, and was playing my favorite music, Rachmaninoff's Rhapsody on Paganini. The setting was perfect, lacking nothing.

"I desired him more than I had any other, but also loved him more than any other and so couldn't bear to drink from him. Not him. I could not experience his beating heart but for a moment. I knew that drinking his blood would seal us in some inescapable way. He knelt down and laid himself flat on the carpet, his neck fully exposed as he turned his head away. I paused long enough to study his determination, and then knelt beside him and went for his throat and bit into him. He jumped a little, but then held still. I had penetrated his skin, more quickly than I'd anticipated. Clamping my mouth around the tender, moist wound, I began to suck at his blood. He writhed in pleasure beneath me, shaking in a seizure of ecstasy. Our lives were now one life, one heart.

"I lifted my head to kiss him but he pushed me back to the wound. 'Take more of me,' he begged. 'Take it all.' I was in a frenzy, feeding from one so willing to give, so needy. I hoisted my body against his, aligning our forms perfectly. This excited him to orgasm, sealing us in passion. He christened our unity, mind and soul.

"Unfortunately, he got addicted to me. I had to leave him. He was just one of many more to come, but he was so distraught over losing me that he tried to poison himself by drinking two bottles of straight whiskey over a two-hour period. He thought he'd have heart failure. But they found him in time and pumped his stomach."

As usual, this e-mail address, too, failed to work when I tried to contact Wraith again, so it was still my lot to wait on him. I wondered if he might be a psychic vampire of a different sort, feeding and then feeding *off* my sharpening curiosity. I was soon to find out.

CHAPTER THIRTEEN

let the games begin

We fight monsters; this is what we do. They show up, they scare
us, I beat 'em up, and they go away.

—BUFFY TO RUPERT

I

Vampire role-playing games (RPG) are everywhere these days, from
online chat rooms to card games to live action (LARP). Much as the Real
Vampyres claim to separate themselves from this aspect of vampire culture, there's no doubt that the role-players who enter an alternate world
through fantasy make up a large percentage of it. Without them, there
may not be the growing market for period clothing, vampire fangs,
dark-themed jewelry, and other vampire paraphernalia. (I've heard
there's a booming coffin business as well.) Demand is high among role-
players for an authentic appearance, and the Real Vamps are benefiting.

As I mentioned before, when I surfed around online, I found a
great many chat rooms called such things as "Vampire Castle" or
"Vampire Diner." It looked like the participants were having fun. It's a

great way to exercise the imagination and to meet like-minded people with whom one can create exotic scenarios.

Some of the games are based on characters and plots from novels, such as the Anne Rice chat rooms. Others are structured by an outside company, such as the advanced version of "Dungeons and Dragons" that features Ravenloft; but White Wolf leads the pack. I was aware of many types of vampire games, both online and offline— board games, cyber games, and murder mystery dinner parties—but since I participated in the White Wolf scenario, I chose to concentrate on that.

Many thousands of players around the world enjoy "Vampire: The Masquerade" and its variations. Created by Mark Rein-Hagen and published in 1991, the game's first incarnation was a tabletop card game. With the help of the Internet for passing the word and forming a players' community, the game took off. In many ways, it was a big improvement over the popular "Dungeons and Dragons" games from the previous decade, which relied largely on players explicitly stating their intentions and actions, and on the toss of the dice. "Vampire" emphasized the art of storytelling, and its later refinements made it even more sophisticated. For tabletop play, the dice dictate players' movements, but the LARP form that evolved relies on hand signals, which keeps action moving.

The game's basic idea, influenced by various vampire mythologies and quite strongly by Anne Rice, is that all major events in human history are caused by the manipulations of vampires, a.k.a. the Kindred, who are descended from the biblical brother-slayer Cain (spelled "Caine" in the game). Supposedly, God had cursed him with a blood-thirst. The older Kindred generations are more powerful, and some of these ancient ones don't hesitate to let young vampires know it. In fact, there is pressure to stop procreating new generations. Each clan strives for power, prominence, and influence as it coexists uneasily with all the others, and double-crossing abounds. There's also a personal element, as players get to know themselves through the traits, abilities, and weaknesses they choose to make up their characters. Because of the near-annihilation of the race during the Inquisition, the vampires have since then done their thing in secret from the mortal world, calling it the Masquerade, and they have certain rules that all vampire clans must follow in the World of Darkness. Each city has its own set of hierarchies, feuds, and dramatic events that require immediate action. Sometimes this is coordinated with what is happening in other parts of the country or the world. There is some interaction with intelligent mortals, but much of the action centers on intrigue within the clans.

The Kindred formed a society called the Camarilla, made up of seven clans (plus an outcast category). Each was formed by lineage and personality traits or aesthetic preferences, such as the artistic Toreadors or the sophisticated Ventrue's leadership abilities. For example, if you prefer to play a tricksterlike entity, you might choose the Malkavians, who are insane but insightful. If you're more reserved and solemn, you might prefer a Gangrel persona. (Supplements that followed the core game book reveal that there are actually thirteen true clans, which provides even more choices.)

People become part of a clan by being "embraced" into it. Characters select traits and powers, and can gain further powers by adopting a few handicaps as well. Character development can be so detailed that it becomes like shedding one's identity and stepping into another world altogether. As to who wins and who loses, according to the book, "It is a game in which you are likely to lose, for it is difficult to do anything to slow your character's inexorable slide into chaos." The idea is to just get involved and benefit to the max from the unfolding drama.

White Wolf went on to create other games that expanded the range of supernatural creatures involved, such as "Wraith: The Oblivion," "Werewolf: The Apocalypse," "Mage: The Ascension," and "Changeling: The Dreaming." But the vampire game proved by far the biggest-selling item. A second core rule book with its own supplements was *Vampire: The Dark Ages*. There were spin-off books, such as Robert Weinberg's *Red Death* trilogy, and a Fox network television show, *Kindred: The Embraced*. In 1993 White Wolf created the Mind's Eye Theatre, an improvisational live-action fantasy that made for greater immersion in the characters.

I spoke with Greg Fountain, the director of games marketing at White Wolf, to get more details. I first asked how many participants they had.

"It would be virtually impossible to tell," he said. "There are over 250,000 core books out there, and each of the fifty supplements can range into the hundreds of thousands of copies. Sometimes many people play off one book. We do have a fan club, which has over three thousand members."

The fan club he means is the Camarilla, White Wolf's official LARP group, which has gone through many incarnations since its founding in 1992. Its world headquarters is in Salt Lake City, Utah, and it spans five continents. It encourages social activities, such as parties, community blood drives (not for drinking), and convention events, as well as gaming.

The Camarilla uses a chapter structure to allow its members to tailor their participation to their own preferences. According to information on the Camarilla Web site, "Members write for our quarterly fanzine, *Requiem*, help each other develop Web pages, work on costuming, write poetry and fiction, discuss their interests, and improve their role-playing, storytelling, and leadership skills."

New members start with characters created with White Wolf's Mind's Eye Theatre materials. Characters advance through the accumulation of "experience points." Members can also earn the privilege of playing more complex characters through service to the club. The rewards are based on degree of participation and organizational support.

Chapters are independent and self-governing, and groups of chapters can form Domains by electing a Domain Coordinator. The Domains have a Storyteller who weaves the Chapter Storylines into a larger chronicle. Domains and independent chapters are supported by one of the eight Regional Coordinators in the country.

The Camarilla also offers correspondence courses covering leadership, storytelling, and acting. No one under the age of eighteen may join unless their parent or guardian is a participating member.

"They have developed something of an official continuity," said Fountain, "that deviates from our official play style of Mind's Eye Theatre products. So now the job of getting everyone on the same sheet is being coordinated. It's going to benefit both organizations greatly."

"What's in the future?" I asked.

"Well, for 'Vampire' specifically, LARP continues to expand, and we'll have a video game soon. We're going to release a new version of 'Vampire' that will include all thirteen of the clans, update certain cultural references, and add developments in the mythologies. We're going to put out a special limited edition with a beautiful binding.

"We've also opened Asian frontiers with 'Kindred of the East.' It's an entirely different creature, based in Asian mythology. They're not even embraced. They have a really bad karmic debt and they have to fulfill it. They have to balance the yin and yang aspects of their energy. They have powers that have never yet been seen in the game.

"We're convinced the vampire phenomenon will continue its popularity for some time to come. At the very least, those fans who are enjoying this game will continue to enjoy it. There is a saturation of vampires in the culture at large, but we'll all see what the turn of the millennium will bring."

Some people stick to playing the game during specified times, such as every Thursday night at Ricochet's bar. Others like to carry their identity around as a secret. They may take a screen name online that reflects it, such as the Rice characters, or may simply go in and out of chat rooms "in character."

As I went into these online rooms, I noticed how people aligned themselves with some specific aspect of the vampire mythology. Most were vampires, but some liked to be mortals who had a secret bond with vampires. I talked to a few male role-players who wanted females to take submissive roles so they could be their "sires," i.e., boss them around; and there seemed to be plenty of girls willing to be "children" or "thralls." So much for equality of the sexes. Yet there were some people who actually preferred the role of the vampire hunter.

"I and my guild will eventually rid the world of you all!" warned one such player, and another, a fourteen-year-old, could feel his powers as a hunter "beginning to explode." Offline, a young woman in New Jersey sent letters to the various vampire organizations with the following request: "I am writing to you searching for information on vampires. The reason I am on this search is because I am a slayer. I am not a hoax as you might first think, but am a true slayer of the undead." Vampires have told me this makes them nervous. Some idiot, they fear, who takes the role too seriously might locate them and stick a wooden stake through their heart!

Yet taking this role is all part of the act, a way to associate with the overall scenario while standing apart in a unique way. One of the key players in the *Dracula* tale is Professor Van Helsing, the vampire expert who leads the hunt for the nefarious Count. The modern-day Van Helsing is Buffy, and she plays no small part in the interest among teenagers of becoming vampire hunters. Even the film *Blade*, with its gritty urban appeal and avenging Day-walker, has contributed to the hunter's mystique. In many past cultures, it took a person with special powers to hunt for vampires, and to know what to do with them once found. In his encyclopedia, *The Vampire Book*, J. Gordon Melton tells us about the *dhampir*, the physical (but mortal) son of a vampire, who supposedly could detect these creatures and destroy them. Film buffs are also aware of the 1985 Japanese animation, *Vampire D*, about a powerful vampire bounty hunter. Identification with these characters offers a way into the vampire arena without being vampire or victim.

Some players use the White Wolf materials in unofficial ways, such as the Black Rose Web site, created by Lillith and Darryle Toney. They offer a directory for online game sites and LARP organizations, and help to prepare new players for the scene. Greg Fountain says that other clubs may use the logos, but the sites are subject to approval and must become part of the "Dark Spiral," which means they provide a link back to the White Wolf home page.

Serious players like Stacy Kirk take this even further by not only playing within White Wolf's parameters, but developing new creatures not yet known in the World of Darkness. She calls them the "Antiveninne," a lab-created race with a type of blood that temporarily restores humanity to vampires. The blood has other potencies as well, such as healing and heightening desire. She has worked out all the powers with a point system that fits into the White Wolf scheme, and has many complex details about their physical makeup and appearance. Her hope—like that of other role-players whose imagination spawns original details—is that White Wolf will take notice and give her idea a shot.

2

There are large LARP organizations, such as the Blood Moon Social Club in Las Vegas and the street games every Friday night in Santa Cruz. I even met a small group of guys who travel from one city to the next to play the game in an organized circuit.

In New York, an extension of Sabretooth is the Syn Factory/New York by Night. It's based on White Wolf's World of Darkness, including both "Vampire" and "Wraith." They hold events monthly in locations such as Mother and the Cloisters. A member of One World By Night, an international network of orchestrated chronicles, the Syn Factory has a common exchange of characters between three other places: Chicago, Westchester County in New York State, and northern Virginia.

According to background fictional information on the Web site, New York is a disputed city between the Camarilla and the Sabbat. There is an unsteady truce to divide the place into territories. The Camarilla takes Manhattan, Riverdale, Westchester, the airports, and Long Island. The Sabbat, an inhumane bunch, dominates the outer boroughs and most of Newark, New Jersey. The feud provokes dark deals and plots over territory, calling on powers of all sorts to threaten and resolve disputes.

Johnny, an enthusiastic thirtyish man sporting a long ponytail, is the Master Storyteller, and he explained the setup to me: "Syn Factory is a semi-theatrical improv experience organized to cater to enthusiasts of the growing LARP social scene. Organized by individuals willing to tell stories about the existence of supernatural creatures within a role-playing format, most of the groups employ the Gothic/punk alternate reality setting created by White Wolf. Their easy-to-learn set of rules allows players to set aside the table, the papers, the charts, and the dice in favor of employing costumes, makeup, and theatrical talents, to spend an evening at a rented site actually playing the parts of their created vampires, werewolves, ghosts, mummies, and all the other monsters and madmen that struggle to keep their supernatural activities outside of humankind's notice. Syn Factory concentrates on the vampires and the ghosts of the New York City domain."

"How did you get involved?" I asked.

"It came about ten years after I had retired from refereeing conventional games like 'Dungeons and Dragons.' I wanted to get into show business, writing, acting in, and directing movies. I decided to write my first script, which involved vampires. One of the materials I bought for the sake of perspective study was the game book for White Wolf's 'Vampire' game. That led to my notice of the first-edition box set for the Mind's Eye Theatre interpretation. A group called Brainstorm Productions ran a LARP in Queens Village, and I chose to play a Russian vampire of the Ventrue clan. I got raves from the other players. That led to running a LARP of my own."

"Is it the vampire or the clan structure that appeals to you most?"

"Definitely the vampire, but the clan structure was well constructed, especially in the fact that it used popularized vampire archetypes as its basis."

"What motivates you to get so deeply involved and spend so much time on it?" I asked, since Johnny seemed to represent more serious players. "Do you get paid?"

"Not a dime. I wouldn't want to get paid for the opportunity to give people a chance to escape the horrors and the concerns of our reality . . . and the issues we wish we could make a difference with, but ultimately can't . . . for the space of at least a single evening. We're all entitled to that."

"How many people do you have in your chapter?"

"We have over fifty characters on the database. However, we'd be lucky to top twenty-five players who actually attend."

"Is there anything you want people not now involved to understand about the game?" I asked him. I knew the whole thing sometimes got a bad rap.

"For one thing," he responded, "don't read into the incidents that shows like *Sixty Minutes* and *Jenny Jones* like to exploit about LARPs and role-playing games. They present them as endangering the lives of players or their families and friends by compelling them to commit real crimes based on the subject matter their characters are dealing with. None of us are real vampires or killers. We do not drink real blood and if it looks like we are, that blood's gonna have a mint flavor . . . which is to say it's totally fake. We don't inspire participants to kill or otherwise break the law. What I aim to do as a Storyteller is to entertain, enlighten, and illuminate through the fun our participants share in our monthly sessions."

In view of some of the negative press, one thing I wanted to know: "Are you ever approached by people wanting to get involved who are just the wrong types?"

"Yes, there are players who want to get involved for the same reasons the average game player wants to play a game of football—because they want to compete. I'm trying to promote stories rooted in human emotion and unlikely alliances, to foster hope that there might be a chance at coexistence—and then the role-playing game equivalent of Mike Tyson wants to kick some ass because he's got this nasty character designed to do just that. The background [that potential participants fill in] is the most important part of a character sheet. If it tells me that he's done nothing short of beating the crap out of five Nosferatus and ten werewolves for no reason (worst-case scenario) or because he thought they violated a Camarilla tradition, that gets me scared. He's there strictly to turn a LARP into an episode of *American Gladiators*."

An example of an invitation that Johnny sends out, along with an extensive update of the story line, is the following: "You are cordially invited to join the kindred of New York City in a grand Ball being arranged by his royal highness, the eminent and influential Prince Lawrence Ocus. The festivities shall begin at 9:00 on October 31, 1997 A.D. and costumes are encouraged in recognition of Halloween, itself a tribute to our sect's undisputed recognition of the tradition of the Masquerade. His Majesty has taken the liberty of inviting many of his mortal associates and his friends around the world to a conventional celebration of the fictional vampire genre *Dracula* and novelist Anne Rice have inspired over the past few decades. These festivities shall proceed on the upper level of the Angel Orensanz Foundation, and those kindred who choose to celebrate amongst them do so at their own risk and are bound . . . under penalty of final death . . . to following the Masquerade's tenets. You and the rest of the kindred shall join His Majesty below the Foundation's surface revelry . . . which, as some of you are aware, was the former haven of a notorious Sabbat pack called 'Ezekiel's Own,' which had relocated to Los Angeles in the wake of former Prince Gabrielle Octavia's recapture of New York. We shall be spending a portion of the evening in remembrance of Gabrielle and her struggles to keep our beloved domain free of the violence born of the Sabbat."

3

I decided to get involved in Syn Factory's game, so Johnny walked me through the process of developing my character. I had little time to read all the White Wolf materials and knew this could adversely affect my experience. The other players would be far ahead of me, and like the first day of an aerobics class, I knew it would feel clumsy.

First I had to choose a clan—to pick one appropriate to the temperament of my character. Johnny thought Toreador, since I'm a writer, but I wanted to be a Ventrue. I had liked Julien in the television show *Kindred: The Embraced*, and appreciated the Ventrue qualities: They're the blue bloods, sophisticated and genteel. They're elegant and they remember their moral roots. They also control powerful mortals and bring a certain refinement to the vampire experience.

Johnny didn't care for the name I selected, so he gave me Gabrielle

Weyland—which combined Anne Rice (Lestat's mother) with Suzy McKee Charnas's *Vampire Tapestry*.

Next I had to pick physical, social, and mental attributes from a list of possibilities. I chose "survivor" for my "nature," and added a rapport with animals, detective skills, leadership skills, knowledge of ancient mysteries, and the ability to manipulate. From the list of "influences," I zeroed in on the media, the occult, and the university. I also wanted to be commanding, to be able to erase memories, and to project feelings of terror onto others with my "dread gaze."

That felt powerful, but there was more. I knew for sure I wouldn't remember all of these. I needed a "beast trait," so I chose lust. Then I had to come up with lots of historical facts for background, such as information about my sire and how I've coped with my "unlife." That was harder because it was more personal. (What we spin out of our own imagination says a lot about ourselves.) I devised a few things from what I'd heard from my Real Vampyre contacts.

Finally I had it all finished and Johnny put it together in a Character Record. He presented this to me at the club where all the other players were gathered. He had informed me that, for clothing, they adhere to the Gothic/punk sensibility, which basically meant wear black. There were about a dozen players that night, and they all seemed to know who they were and what to do. I didn't, but I figured I could watch them and learn. Wrong! The action took place so fast, and the plot was not only complicated, but also called on knowledge of previous gatherings that I had not attended. I could see how this could be energizing if I knew what I was doing, but I had a difficult time following it all.

As the Storyteller, Johnny ran around all night, upstairs and down in the various darkened rooms directing people with information that they needed to make the game progress. He had little time to advise me. I did get my fortune read by a tarot reader, and the end result was gaining traits or powers that I was supposed to add to what I already had. I could use them if some conflict arose, and probably win, but I was never put to the test (much to my relief).

I noticed that people resolved disputes with scissors/paper/rock hand signals, which replaced rolling the dice. Apparently, the character sheets also resolve disputes by comparing powers and weaknesses, but I never saw that done. The players were scattered all over the building, and I'm sure they were familiar with which powers are stronger, just as skilled poker players know the best hand. I spotted one person I knew, but his "character" didn't recognize mine, so he would not greet me. That was a little jarring, but it showed me how seriously the players took their roles. There was a lot of energy in the room, and secretive exchanges about a hidden bomb. I could only hope it wasn't hidden on me.

By the end of three hours, everyone gathered together and talked about what they got out of the game and where the "situation" stood. Johnny listened for things he could use to create the next complex scenario.

I asked people about their experiences and they agreed that the game had been satisfying. "I get to be a different person," said one young man, "to escape my daily situation and just have fun." A girl in a black jumpsuit who looked fifteen, but had to be older to play, said she liked the feeling of belonging to the group, of knowing the others and pretending with them to be in a different world. A few people were there from Virginia, coming into Syn Factory as part of the game circuit. They thought it had been worth the long drive. They were going next to Ohio, I think, which meant taking an entire weekend for the game. I was amazed that they devoted so much time to it, but they'd probably feel the same about how much time I devote to my work. I'd often been called by vampires during the night to "come and party," and they couldn't understand that I wanted to write.

I walked away feeling mystified but a little more aware of this segment of vampire culture. I'd been an actress in summer stock theater, and it was fun, but I'd learned quickly that it wasn't how I wanted to spend my time, so I was not ready to sign on for regular participation. Yet these games go on all over the country and around the world. They are certainly fulfilling to the many thousands of people who participate in them. Had they been around when I was much younger, I might have been as fully involved as the people I met from the Syn Factory.

4

And speaking of those who identify with vampires, I finally received another call from Wraith—it had been a couple of months—and this one shifted things a bit my way. It also gave me a better sense of what it was that some people seek when adopting the role of a creature like the vampire.

He had another conquest to describe to me. He'd made an actual appointment with someone who wanted to drink his blood. He wasn't so sure about doing that, he said, but he'd met the guy anyway. He figured he could always say no and walk away.

"We went to a couple of clubs for drinks and conversation," he told me. "I thought it would be a good time to prepare for the evening. Jeff was very excited about the night. He was anxious to get started. I told him it wouldn't be long. After a few drinks and a little dancing, we ended up on the back porch of a mutual friend, who was clearly asleep in front of his TV.

"Jeff asked if he could have some of my blood instead of me drinking his. He wanted to suck it from the back of my thigh, explaining that he believed the greatest power in the blood was found near the loin. So, I made a small incision with the scalpel I'd brought and he licked and sucked gently. I was turned around, almost sitting on his face. All of this was done in the dark, save the little flickering strobe of the TV inside."

"So what does that mean?" I asked. "You're usually the taker. What's it like to be in that position?"

"I don't prefer it," Wraith said. "It doesn't mean anything, really."

"But he's not like prey that you discard. That was intimate. Or will he now discard you?"

"I don't think so. I don't really know what will happen now." He seemed almost uninterested in the whole experience.

"Why didn't you take his blood like you usually do?"

"It just wasn't right that night. I'm invested in the ritual and I keep it secret. My vampire nature requires my silence—to reveal it jeopardizes its potential. I hadn't really told him anything. He still doesn't know. It's just something he wanted to do. Lots of males are into blood around here. So I said nothing."

"You're revealing your vampire nature to me," I pointed out.

"I'm confessing it, yes, for my own reasons. It's not the same as revealing it to them. What I've been seeking is a limit experience, and confession is part of that."

"What's a limit experience?"

I'd heard of it before, associated with Foucault. I didn't know if he'd read this philosopher, but terms like that get passed around among college kids. A limit experience in Foucault's sense happens by pushing mind and body to the breaking point, supposedly to erase boundaries between the conscious and subconscious, or life and death. It's a shattering type of painful pleasure. Foucault thought of it as the lifelong preparation for suicide.

"A limit experience," Wraith explained, "is a tear piercing the concrete psyche, a rip in the fabric of conventional experience. It is a series of unrestrained moments moving at unidentifiable speeds through unidentified terrain. When my mind and body collaborate to transport the whole of me into an uncharted dimension of sensations, I experience breakaway euphoria. A limit experience is a break with reality as we know it, a split from the way things are. I'm empty. I need more. I need to fill myself."

"What does this have to do with being a vampire?"

"My vampire experience transgresses conventional lines of intimacy. The very idea of combining sex with blood consumption is a limit experience. Drinking blood transports the mind into a state of euphoria—at least my mind. I always look for ways to make mine and the other person's experience one of transcending some sort of boundary—even that of the vampire."

"Well, then," I said, "how about doing a limit experience with me?"

He was silent. Then he said, "What do you mean?"

"I mean, meet me. Confess this stuff, eye to eye. That should expand your experience a bit. You've never done that before, have you?"

"No."

"Then . . . ?"

He was silent. I thought he might hang up. But then he said, "I'll think about it. I'll call you."

With that he was gone. But I had gained some ground. He was considering it now, and I'd suggested that there was something in it for him. Something he claimed he wanted. The question was, which of us had taken the bait?

The image of Susan Walsh flashed into my head. Hunting vampires was risky business. I made a note of that.

CHAPTER FOURTEEN

vampires
intercontinental

I

While Wraith pondered what he was going to do, I decided to take another trip. I'd heard that vampire culture was international, so it seemed that I ought to go abroad. From what I could see on the Internet, I had a lot of choices. England, Germany, Australia, Japan, Spain, Brazil. Where to go? It wasn't easy to decide. I didn't know where the scene was most popular or most unique, and the reports I'd received from various sources were incomplete and contradictory.

So I did what any rational person would do: I laid out a world map on the floor of my apartment and spun an empty bottle of vampire wine. I watched with bated breath as it turned round and round, hoping I wouldn't land someplace like Antarctica in winter. I was determined to go wherever the bottle led. Africa, New Zealand, Canada.

It slowed in its rotation and then came to a halt.

Ha! Paris, France.

Well, okay, if I really must.

The last time I went to Paris was to take photographs for *The Vampire Companion: The Official Guide to Anne Rice's Vampire Chronicles.* It's such a perfect setting, with its art museums, winding streets, cemeteries, and Gothic architecture for the Theater of the Vampires. There's the famous Paris Opera House, where Gaston Leroux set *The Phantom of the Opera,* and the Latin Quarter where writers such as Sartre, Camus, Baudelaire, Hemingway, and Wilde hung out. Also, the historical sites of bloody violence, such as the Hotel de Ville and the Bastille (now gone). And, of course, that great Gothic cathedral, the Notre Dame.

So on to Paris, where Rice had set her infamous *Theatre des Vampyres* on the Boulevard du Temple, and where Louis and Claudia had found Armand. It was also where Armand and his band had lived beneath the decrepit Les Infants cemetery, the Body Thief had contacted Lestat, and Louis had learned that the truth of his existence was as he had feared: There were no answers to life's most pressing questions.

Just before I left, I was contacted by a young woman named Marianne Bergès, who lived in Paris and who was writing a master's thesis on Anne Rice. She couldn't believe I was coming there, and she volunteered to be my guide. I accepted. Marianne was bubbly, childlike, and pretty, and we immediately engaged in the most intense conversations as we planned my Paris adventure.

She was part of a role-playing group, and she told me that four or five of her friends would sit around a table in her apartment and participate in virtual scenarios, acting as vampires or other supernatural creatures for as long as eight hours at a time. "Being a vampire or a nephilim [an entity that enters the bodies of humans]," she said, "gives us a new perspective on the human condition."

It surprised me when she said that few women participate in such games, and she and her friend Jessica (an assertive, intelligent young brunette with an appreciation for Dostoevsky) garnered suspicion and disapproval for their involvement. Role-playing there was typically a male sport—though it was barely tolerated even for them—and girls who played must have other problems.

Marianne wanted to introduce me to Yohan Meheu, the Master Storyteller of their group, so we agreed that the appropriate place would be the famous Pere Lachaise Cemetery on what turned out to be a cold, overcast afternoon.

Yohan met us at the subway entrance, and I was struck by how perfectly he captured the persona of a Parisian vampire. He was tall and thin, with longish dark hair that he tied back away from his face. He wore a long black coat, as any vampire would. His lips were sensual and his blue/gray eyes were set deep in his handsome face, which looked pensive and just a bit guarded—as if he had a few entertaining secrets to hide. And, yes, he had that lovely French accent. I could almost have believed I was meeting Louis de Pointe du Lac.

Even better, as we entered and walked through the cemetery, he wanted to talk about fascinating subjects. I learned from him and Marianne things about the cemetery that no average tourist would ever find out:

With the thousands of executions during the French Revolution of 1789, there was an immediate problem of where to bury them all. They were stacked up in small churchyards, but the stench and contagion forced the politicians to recognize that they needed to look outside Paris for a solution. Napoleon purchased a park named Pere Lachaise, but Parisians thought it too far to go to bury their dead. Napoleon tried to make it more enticing by moving the remains of famous people long dead, such as Moliere. Still, it didn't work. So the writer Honore de Balzac began to "bury" his characters in Pere Lachaise when they "died." That sent readers out to see the place, and finally made it a popular resting ground. Now in this outdoor museum of sculptures we find the graves of celebrities such as Sarah Bernhardt, Oscar Wilde, Marcel Proust—and of course, Jim Morrison. (His grave is small, unadorned, and rather mundane in contrast to the rich artistry all around.)

Marianne pointed out that there were secret doorways into some tunnels beneath the cemetery that go all the way back to the heart of Paris. Some also just reach a dead end. She had heard that people have parties down below, so we went into several tombs with open doors or broken floors to see if we could find one of the passageways—or maybe just a few bones.

Marianne and Yohan explained to me their experience of playing the virtual reality games with vampire characters. Yohan had been involved in role-playing games for several years, and he was taken with "The Masquerade" because it was set in the present time, it was dark, and it was thrilling to play such powerful creatures. He met Marianne in a class and invited her into his game. She'd been involved in another scenario in which the Storyteller reserved most of the power for those who had played a long time, and "young vampires" like herself didn't have much fun. Both of them preferred to play the game with a small group of people they knew.

"When I play," said Marianne, "it helps me understand what human beings are and what I am, and all the possibilities and opportunities I have. When I play vampires, I envy humans, even though I'm dismissing them as just food."

They understood, given the strong virtual imagery of the games, that there were some risks in role-playing and that parents were frightened, but they insisted the danger was minimal. "If we see that one of our friends is having problems and the game is getting dangerous, we just stop," said Marianne. "It's just a game. You have to be stable to do it. Just like some people don't have enough imagination to play, some have too much. They can't get out of it."

As we walked along the roadway between rows of tall mausoleums and carved marble, Yohan asked me if we had a word in our country for "cataphile."

"What is it?" I asked.

"A person who's addicted to the catacombs."

Addicted to the catacombs—those underground tunnels full of skulls, bones, and strange poetry. That sounded almost vampiric. Certainly Goth. I wanted to know more. It turned out that Yohan had a friend who was a cataphile, who went into the catacombs nearly every weekend for parties with other cataphiles, or just to spend the night.

Running mostly beneath Paris's Left Bank, the catacombs are vast tangles of tunnels originally built by the Romans. Altogether they are about two hundred miles long. In the late eighteenth century they were used to store millions of skeletons from disused graveyards to make room for more bodies, and during World War II they became the secret headquarters for the French Resistance. In the 1830s the bones were arranged into patterns and the catacombs were opened to tourists. Some passages are covered with human bones, and only a small part of the system is officially open to public access. Obviously, from what Yohan was saying, there are those who disregard the rules in order to partake of the darkness, isolation, and silence deep underground—just as there are those who prefer to inhabit the deepest pockets of the psyche.

"Well, we don't have any catacombs in our country," I told Yohan, "so I don't think we have a word for it, but I'd love to know more about them."

He explained that he had gone down with a group of about eight other people, including his girlfriend, Jeanne. I asked him to tell me about it, so with tombstones on every side, and under increasingly dim skies, Yohan described his adventure. (Readers: Imagine this being told to you by Rice's Louis, in a French accent.)

"We went at midnight into the Cata, as the cataphiles call it, at the Porte d'Orléans in the south," he told me. That was not the official entry, I knew, so that meant it had been something of a clandestine tour. "We went from there to St. Michel near the Seine and then we came back. Jeanne and I spent seven hours under Paris. First we had to go down on an ancient railroad called the 'small belt'—*la petite ceinture*, in French. It's just a hole in the ground. People gathered around the hole, with the only light coming only from candles all around. We put our lamps on, and crawled into the hole. In the tunnels there is room enough for one person at a time. It goes from two meters to eighty centimeters in height, and you always have to watch out. You can wound yourself on the ceiling, because the height always varies, but you also have to check if there is water on the ground.

"We saw two parties going on in small rooms. It's just like any other party: a lot of alcohol, marijuana, and music. The point is that you won't be disturbed by your neighbors. And that's the allure. The rules of the surface no longer exist there. There are many different people, but they all share the same need to have a break from the surface world; here, they can do whatever they want, spend the whole night doing nothing, sleep there, smoke grass . . . they have a feeling of freedom. They become their own master, and there is no one to forbid anything."

"So these people just really love it down there, then?" I asked. It sounded enticing.

"That's what my friend says. Jeanne saw it as a challenge for them, for it is rather physical and absolutely forbidden. These people gather under the earth at night to talk about what the world should be. Most of them know each other. Jeanne says they are a town beneath the town—a micro-society with its own rules and codes. It's all about gathering in a forbidden place, smoking forbidden grass, and dreaming about a utopian world."

We never did find a secret passage in the cemetery tombs of Pere Lachaise, but it was an afternoon well spent.

Marianne and her friends were also going to get me to the Dracula Exposition, at which I was speaking that weekend. (Okay, so I didn't really spin the bottle.) Sandrine Armirail had introduced her-self to me at Dracula '97 in Los Angeles and had told me she was plan-ning this vampire convention. I'd said, "Just tell me when. I'll be there."

I think it surprised her, but she was glad to have me on the pro-gram. My biography of Rice had been translated into French, and many people knew of *The Vampire Companion.* Marianne got the exhaust-ing job of being my interpreter. There were about two hundred people who attended the conference overall, and it gave me the chance to learn more about Sandrine, who was deeply involved with the vam-pire community.

"I've always been interested in everything about what we call *fan-tastique,*" Sandrine told me. "I think that my attraction to vampires came from a more general attraction to predators. There was a time when I was fond of sharks. I wanted to dive with them, to touch them, to feel their power beside me. I was also fond of dragons, and that may be how I came to the role-playing games. I think I had the same attraction to vampires. They are predators, the dark side of humankind, a part of us that we don't want to show in public, but who are deeply inside of us; they awaken the predator inside of us and make us feel stronger."

She had watched vampire movies, but her real interest developed with Anne Rice's novels. She wanted to share this with others. "One day I read a classified ad where a Belgium girl was looking for 'every-thing about vampires,' so I answered her. It was the beginning of a friendship. We started to have the idea of making a magazine about vampires because in France there was nothing. We phoned other fans of vampires, I met French authors and scholars, and we created *Vampire Dark News.* The first issue was in October 1995. In 1996 I created Vampire Story, a society, and now we have more than two hundred members. We organize parties and meetings, like movie outings and the Dracula Convention."

I knew of another vampire organization in France, the *Cercle d'Etudes Vampiriques* (Circle for Vampiric Studies), founded in 1989 and run by Lea Silhol. This society "is dedicated to studies of the vampire myth in all its forms." They have compiled a comprehensive archive and provide a local loan library and Web site for people to ask ques-tions, find pen pals, or offer further information. They also publish a quarterly journal, *Requiem,* and they sponsored a Dracula festival and exposition in the south of France during 1997. They desire to "twin" with other vampire associations around the world to integrate and organize resources.

"Our main difference from other vampire societies in France," says Silhol, "is the scholarly aspect. It's not an easy thing to focus on vampirism in France because of the bad reputation of the Gothic subculture and numerous incidents of bad behavior in cemeteries. People often think that vampire fans are somewhat crazy, but our members are chiefly readers of fiction and cinema fans. We don't believe real vampires exist."

I met many such vampire fans at Sandrine's exposition, which featured films, posters, vampire paraphernalia, books, and speakers. Dracula scholar Jean Marigny, who wrote *Vampires: Restless Creatures of the Night*, introduced me, and after my speech I talked with many people who were interested in further promoting the vampire image. One couple told me their plans for developing a vampire exposition that could travel around the world. I'd heard that an exposition was about to be set up by Catia Lattanzi in Milan, Italy, and also taken on the road. I also met the president of the French Camarilla, a club for participants in "The Masquerade." His name was Vincent Audigier and he was twenty-four years old.

The club, he told me, has about three hundred members in France and Germany, and another three hundred fifty in Belgium. With some friends, he created the first chapter in Versailles. Then Vincent became a regional coordinator and soon became national president. He also organized an international Camarilla council. He is in touch with people who play this game in the UK, Belgium, Germany, Australia, Japan, Italy, Holland, and the States; and has met many people interested in vampires all over Europe. They all use the same set of rules. Being in the Camarilla made Vincent aware of the large Goth community in France as well. "In essence, we are two different groups with some connections. We listen to the same music and like the same type of books and movies."

As there is no specific Goth club, the Camarilla often organizes Goth-type gatherings, such as parties, concerts, and fashion shows. They promote history, culture, and Gothic-style art. Vincent's own interest in vampires began five years ago, mainly from reading Anne Rice. Then he got involved in "The Masquerade," though he had played other RPGs since he was eleven. "As my involvement in

Camarilla was growing, my knowledge of this subculture increased. In France, the Camarilla is viewed as one of the biggest associations of this subculture."

I asked for more information on the Goth scene itself, and he told me, "It was a small, exclusive group, but in the past year it has become more fashionable to be a Goth. The biggest parties are in Paris, and they can gather five hundred to seven hundred people."

I told Vincent that in the States, there is some overlap between Goths and people interested in vampires, but there's also a gap.

"We have a gap, too," he said. "Not in the dress style. All Goths have a vampire look and are generally more than a simple vampire fan. In mentality, yes, you have an important gap. The vampire is just a part of what interests Goths. Generally, in France, Goths are concerned about fashion and music."

After the convention, there was a private dinner party at a very special place. At Number 3, Rue Erard, in the neighborhood of Victor Hugo's house and former site of the Bastille, is the Goth club known as Le Comte Dracula. The walls are richly decorated with a mural of a Romanian castle, fake bats hang from the ceiling, and there is no doubt that one has entered an establishment where vampires and those who love darkness feel welcome. People came to the dinner dressed in vampire drag, and it proved to be a rather festive atmosphere in the darkest of traditions.

Georges Horhat, a Romanian refugee who was born in Transylvania, is the owner, and he presides over the place with panache—speaking English with an Eastern European accent. He'd once thought about becoming a priest, but opened a vampire bar instead. Two evenings a month, he hosts Gothic events there, and he even has his own brand of vampire wine.

For us, he cooked a wonderful meal of authentic foods from the time of Vlad Dracul: veal with Romanian spices, a special sort of vegetable, and apple strudel. At one point in the evening, he dressed in a vampire mask and cape to camp it up.

I was at a table with Marianne and her friends Manu, Jessica, Fred, Yohan, and Jeanne. Manu, who hopes to study serial killers as a profession, had tried to apply long black sculpted nails to his fingers, but could manage them only on one hand. Even at that, he had a difficult time eating. Yohan, who with his longish dark hair, soulful eyes, and slender frame already looked like a vampire, had applied makeup to enhance that impression. Fred, with curly black hair and a quiet demeanor, had put dark smudges under his eyes and wore a "bloody" torn shirt to look as if he'd been attacked, while the young women were decked out in black elegance, their dresses to the floor. As one might expect in the world's couture capital, they knew how to be stylish.

"The vampire is considered a romantic figure here," they assured me. They did not understand why people wanted vampires to be brutal or animalistic. To them it was fun and provided an opportunity to dress up in ways they would not ordinarily do. Not in fangs and capes, but in evening gowns. I found it interesting to observe that they liked playing out a very feminine role while still being vampires, whereas many young women I'd met in the States (who were not "thralls") adopted a more aggressive outlook. They liked the romance, too, when they imagined a vampire taking them, but in the vampire's role (aside from the nurturing types), they had no trouble with the hard-edged predatory angle. It made me think about the way culture itself influences the specific manifestation of a subculture, even when that subculture defies national boundaries.

That evening ended my visit to the vampire community in Paris, although I'd been told to look for a vampire tea room not far from a fetish clothing shop. "You can tell it's vampire friendly," said the informant, "because there will be a tiny drop of blood painted onto the window. Of course, when too many people discover that, the vampires move on, and the blood drop disappears."

I didn't find the place, which only means I'll have to return.

2

Another international vampire-related organization is One World By Night. According to their description on the Internet, they are a group of live-action role-players independent of White Wolf and the Camarilla, and they're interested in taking things "into the next level." Their diverse "chronicles" are located in various cities around the world, and complicated plotlines weave the community together. The site lists numerous American cities as participating locations, as well as cities in Brazil, Holland, New Zealand, Australia, Canada, and Spain.

Then there's the Australian Vampire Information Association, which "acts as a resource center for anyone involved in the fascinating world of vampire reality." What they offer will "enable vampires to be better vampires, give vampirologists the opportunity to put forward their own theories," and other additional services.

I also got in touch with Intervamp, run by Rob Brautigam from Holland, who told me about his own interest in vampires.

"I've been into vampires for over thirty years," he said. "As a teenager I spent my summers in Bosnia and traveled quite a bit through Bulgaria, Romania, and Greece. I can't help feeling that my interest in vampires is connected with my love for the Balkan region and its people. My grandmother was half Czech, so I like to think I have a tiny drop of Slavic blood in my veins.

"My main interest is in nonfictional vampires—the traditional European vampire. After that comes vampire beliefs in other countries. Then anything that has to do with vampires. I'm talking about unexplained phenomena and manifestations of draining of a parasitic nature. I am talking about haunted graves and corpses that do not decay, not about people acting out fantasies."

"Are there others there who like vampires?"

"Over here in Holland there used to be no interest at all in vampires, so I was leading a pretty isolated existence."

He had managed to locate a girl from Delft who liked Dracula, a guy in another town who had turned his house into an amateur Dracula museum, a children's writer, and "a couple of vampires from The Hague." That was his assessment of the vampire scene around him.

"Another ten years of isolation," he said. "Then, around 1989, someone gave me a card with the U.S. address of the Anne Rice Vampire Lestat Fan Club, so I thought I'd give it another try. Through them I discovered other clubs and newsletters. It was fantastic to get in touch with others who shared my interest. In 1990 I put out a newsletter. I pompously christened it *International Vampire*. The first edition was about fifty copies, which I sent to all the important vampire people that I had heard about. Much to my surprise, most of them liked it. So after that, I put some material on the Internet.

"Looking back, I think starting *International Vampire* has been the best move in my life. Before, I was nobody. Then I suddenly became 'our country's one and only vampirologist.'"

3

Rob also brought my attention to a book by Mick Mercer called *Hex Files: The Goth Bible*. Mercer had spent four years compiling an exhaustive source for locating the Goth, vampire, pagan, and fetish scene in many different countries. It contains illustrations and contact addresses for over two thousand merchants, bands, magazines, individuals, and societies in such countries as Australia, South Africa, France, Germany, Greece, Spain, Italy, Scandinavia, Poland, Britain, and the U.S.—among many others.

Mercer is from England, one of the countries with the most to offer to the Goth/vampire community. I had been to England and Scotland a few years earlier in search of ghosts, witches, and Taltos for my guidebook to Anne Rice's *Witching Hour* series. One of my favorite places was Whitby, where Bram Stoker wrote *Dracula*. It's on the northeastern coast of England. I had driven across the Yorkshire moors on an overcast day and taken a room in a guest house that overlooked the cemetery by the haunted Whitby Abbey that Stoker had viewed in 1890 as he had concocted his Gothic tale. I was even told that the room I was staying in was the *very* room that Stoker had rented, but I'm not so sure about that. Close enough, anyway.

Whitby held a Vamps and Tramps centenary in June 1997. This is also the site of one branch of England's Dracula Society, run by Bernard Davies in London, while Ireland has the Bram Stoker Society. Whitby offers "The Dracula Experience," an exposition of wax figures from the novel, and an annual ball for vampire fans.

London also has many sites from *Dracula*, including the Highgate Cemetery in a northern suburb. In the late sixties, strange incidents in the 160-year-old cemetery were reported that gave rise to rumors of vampires. David Skal points out that scholars believe this was the place Bram Stoker chose to bury Lucy Westenra after Dracula transformed her. David Farrant, along with Kev and Crissie Demant, have started the Highgate Vampire Society. They publish a magazine, and in the first issue ran an informative article linking the Highgate entity with the ghost of Jack the Ripper. Kev and Chrissie also put out *VAT* magazine—Vampires Against Tories.

There is a large Goth community in London, due to the musical influence. England boasts a huge variety of fanzines and rock bands related to the Goth/pagan/vampire/fetish scene.

Originally, *Gothic* referred to the dark romantic literature of the late eighteenth century, which evolved from a desire to explore the inner self and to defy conventional mores. Gothic authors brought attention to the forces within that cannot be contained—chaos, intensity, disorder. However, people today who identify themselves as Goth are part of a community that arose from England's punk scene in the 1980s.

A group called the Bromley Contingent wanted to get beyond the nihilism expressed in punk and to look more internally. Other bands, such as Bauhaus, the Sisters of Mercy, the Cult, the Cure, and Siouxsie and the Banshees, were doing the same. London's Bat Club gave them exposure. This movement in music and fashion (black or white hair, exotic eyeliner, silver jewelry, and romantic clothing—usually black) flourished and was picked up around Europe and in the States. The Goth look was rumored to come from the lyrics of a song by the English group, the Smiths, that said, in short, they wear black to express how they feel inside.

The movement tends to draw sensitive, alienated kids who seek mystery, magic, and a distraction from the dullness of mundane life, and who resonate to death images. They often have an artistic bent and tend to be introverted. Drugs are ingested primarily for creativity and spirituality—for looking into the abyss. Many respond to the image of a vampire as the ultimate Gothic icon, but many do not, and not all vampires adopt the Goth look.

Goth peaked and declined in England, but fanzines, bands, Web sites, and even Gothic dating services keep it alive and well (so to speak) in the States. There's even a humorous Goth skit with several variations on *Saturday Night Live*.

4

In Germany I found Alex Janke, "armchair adventurer and part-time gentleman," who runs a vampire Internet site. "It started as a site about vampire books and films," he informed me, "with reviews and thoughts about books I've recently read. I also started a vampire LARP group here in Marburg, and so my Web site got a new look."

I asked him about the vampire scene over there.

"Here in Germany," he said, "there is a very strong fandom for horror pulp literature that goes back about twenty-five years. There are different titles published every week. For example, *Vampira*, which is a series about a female vampire battling evil forces. The series is very erotic, and one can say it has broken new ground for erotic vampire literature. Of course, Anne Rice has some influence here. Each of her books is a major success. Also a phenomenon is a children's book series called *Der Kleine Vampir* by Angela Sommer-Bodenburg.

"Germany is also one of the strongholds for Gothic music, especially for the new romantic side. In the nineties there was a boom of Gothic music dealing with vampire themes. One of the most successful was Mozart. He published a CD called *Gedanken eines Vampirs* (Thoughts of a Vampire), and the music ranged from thoughts of Nietzsche to strong erotic lyrics."

Mozart actually sent me his CD, *Umbra et Imago*, and he told me that his band was very unique. "Our leitmotif," he explained, "is romanticism and the philosophy of the vampire, with a clear tendency toward eroticism, and especially sadomasochistic games. The creativity lies within these elements, which for us are interconnected, exuding a fascination which inspires us to ever more escapades."

"Those who want to take it a bit further," said Janke, "either role-play or believe they are vampires themselves. In the RPG scene there was this boom for vampires only last year. Almost every city now has its group, so if you want you can live in different cities every night as your character. Most LARP stories are political, but all have in common a strong historic background. If you want to play vampire in Germany, you bring your history book! An interesting fact about the role-playing vampire society is that they don't want players who believe they *are* vampires. Those persons are blocked in almost every case.

"Role-playing has a bad reputation so we try to keep it as normal as possible. The headline 'Role-player Bites Policeman' isn't good publicity. We have problems with the Church and the *Sektenbeauftragten* of the police, which is a person who watches the different religious cults.

"A friend of mine has been in the U.S. and told me that the playing style is quite different. The American LARP is more for one evening with a small plot and everybody comes as they are. Here we have an ongoing story, basically simulating the vampire society that goes through the whole week. Costuming is an important part of the game. We try to simulate everything as accurately as possible."

Some of the German groups mentioned that they travel a European circuit, which told me that interest in Gothic music was high all over. I also looked into the vampire scene in Spain, Japan, and Brazil, and heard about some activities in Mexico City. It seemed there was no end to the appeal of the vampire, even as far away as South Africa.

I'll get to these countries the next time around. But having listened to people from other cultures, I had a new perspective on the scene here, and it was time to interview some professionals. I wanted to have some grounding, just in case I managed to convince Wraith to meet me.

CHAPTER FIFTEEN

the disarticulated soul

Generation X is a state of mind of our times. We're changing the values. To the Boomers, smoking is accepted, but we're fazing it out. For us, sexual freedom is important and repression a sin. We see things for what they are and make changes for the better. We're helping society to evolve.

—FATHER SEBASTIAN

I

The New Age singer Sarah McLachlin has a song called "Building a Mystery" about a young man who takes great pains to develop a dark persona. He adopts the trappings of occult mysticism, lives by night, feeds off fear, and searches endlessly for ghosts. He works very hard at creating this enigmatic impression, even in the most intimate of embraces.

He's not as isolated as he may think.

I have discovered a revived interest in the 1948 existential classic *The Stranger*, among people who resonate to the vampire image. Written by the French Algerian Albert Camus, the story is about a man, Meursault, who feels alienated in the world. He cares about nothing, feels nothing, takes whatever he's given, and even mindlessly commits a murder for which he feels no remorse. He'll accommodate others only if the demands aren't great. He feels indifferent to his own life. The institutions of family and Church mean nothing to him, and he cannot even tell the woman with whom he is having sex that he cares about her. She's interchangeable with anyone else. His mother dies and in retrospect he cannot recall which day she passed away. He simply does not abide by the emotional rules of "normal" society. He is truly a stranger. Only his impending execution awakens him to life's meaning.

It disturbs me that college-age people resonate to Meursault. So many young people today seem to feel the same: aimless, unattached, unmotivated, restless, unsatisfied. I've taught philosophy for fifteen years, and in the past five I've heard a shocking number of comments like the following:

"I was around fourteen or fifteen when death began to dominate my thoughts. I forced myself to feel what an absence of feeling would be like."

"I believed that my life was nothing but suffering and I accepted that there was nothing I could do to relieve it. I thought this suffering may be eternal. I lost hope that my situation would ever improve."

"Last year, a close friend jumped to his death from the roof of his dorm. The year before, a classmate swallowed pills and slit his wrist. He survived, but his mind is gone. Not long ago, another friend's sister and her buddy lay down together on the railroad tracks to wait for the train to blow them into pieces. One of my relatives with AIDS asked for help to die; an acquaintance smothered herself and three years later, her husband killed himself. At age sixteen, no stranger to death, I contemplated taking a bottle of pills and ending it, too."

"I have no sense of direction. All I feel anymore is despair."

"My peers and I were raised in an affluent suburb with a well-respected high school. Our parents were college educated. The vast majority of us went to college. Why did so many of us come back suicidal, with eating disorders, or with substance abuse problems?"

"I enjoy the comfort that sadness gives me."

Hearing the deeper stories behind these comments is even more shocking. It's no wonder the vampire has such appeal for these young people. It offers power, death, and heightened experience all wrapped in a single package. Vampires are sexy and possess finesse—even without any sense of purpose. They're the perfect role model for those who experience pervasive postmodern uncertainty. There's defiance in their immortal charm that has tremendous appeal for people who feel blown by almost any wind.

Like gods, vampires bleed the human soul to make themselves more intensely alive, more fully present. Even in their monstrousness, they have a radiance erotically reminiscent of a supreme being. There's a quickening in the vampire's embrace, a new vision—if only fleetingly before annihilation.

And in recent years, they've been stretched to become even more. I've noticed significant changes in the way the vampire is embraced and presented among this group. Initially I was surprised when I learned that a vampire need not be immortal—and often isn't. They can go out during the day, eat food, dress any way they please, get diseases; and some even have a nurturing side. As I learned more about "twenty-something" vampires, it seemed to me that they exploited the metaphor's malleability to make it meet their needs rather than simply accommodating the age-old traditions.

Elton John's song about Marilyn Monroe (and later Princess Diana) captures the impression of someone who feels insubstantial and unprotected, a "candle in the wind." Increasingly more young people experience themselves as fragile and flickering, impermanent, without direction, unformed. Some live on the edge to feel the abundance of anxious emotion. Yet they embrace something one day and have no use for it the next, because they feel no constant sense of self, no predictability. Life is experienced in fragmentary episodes. Without a substantial image with which to identify, they're unsure who they are or which values really matter.

I've talked to many people about their fascination with vampires, and most of those who actually identify with vampires seem to be between the ages of about fifteen and thirty, although they can be younger or older. One of the more poignant expressions of generational malaise that connects with the vampire came from Clint Catalyst, age twenty-six. His photo appears in Charles Gatewood's *True Blood* as an androgynous, baby-faced young man with long black hair and a single silver pipe curl on each side. He's a writer and performance artist deeply involved in the San Francisco fetish scene. In short, he cuts himself for others to see, and indulges in the blood-sports arena. Although I didn't quite appreciate my experiences with Diogenes, Clint gave me a better understanding of the motivations:

"My involvement with blood-play came from my childhood. I was molested as a child by neighborhood boys, and the more I came into being, the more I began to pilot my own set of procedures. I was definitely attracted to blood because I didn't really feel at home in my own skin. I felt like I was wearing other people's fingerprints, and so bloodletting helped me reclaim my body. I marked an expanse of flesh with a razor blade in my parents' bathroom, and that enactment became something I later did publicly.

"Searching for answers, I was drawn to the vampire. Blood is salient for the nineties. Love it or loathe it, one must react and reacting is feeling alive. Blood can't be ignored. Blood is what binds them. I feel like I'm wandering between two worlds, between misguided passions and safe territories. The dynamic that I need for my life I get from penetrating my flesh. All of the emotional and intellectual energies of my soul are translated into that instant when I'm being cut. I'm being literally split open."

He went on to say that this set him apart from his peers.

"I'm lumped with the 'twenty-nothings,' and it's become terrifyingly fashionable to be apathetic, so to me, the vampire is going for the jugular, for raw feeling. It represents the *inhuman* when in this day and age to be human means going to the mall and watching TV and living a credit-card existence. *Feeling* is what's risky now. Being cut represents that."

I asked him how he actually views the vampire, and he said, "In these times, when sex is as casual as a handshake, I find no real intimacy. So the role of the vampire is a demand for connection with the body and spirit. It's anathema to polite society, power books, sterile office cubicles, safety nets. It's a terrifying display of the truth of the need for feeling. The vampire is about the search for something genuine in an era when almost anything can be faked."

2

Many of the vampirologists I talked to said that they've repeatedly heard stories from participants in vampire culture that involve childhood trauma or abuse. The vampire appears to be a means of self-reinvention for those who wish to cut themselves off from a family or culture that they disown, and to rediscover themselves purely as individuals.

"A rogue is an outsider who enjoys being outside," one Goth-type vampire said. "I savor being alone, and being an outsider sanctions this feeling. If you step inside, people try to keep you in by changing you into them. You can't be yourself. So, okay, to be alone is to suffer, but we make it poetic." Through the vampire, they believe they can become something greater, with a sort of self-induced, permanently altered consciousness.

The vampire seems to possess a certain omniscience about the very things that we feel are shrouded in secrecy: power, sexual seduction, and control. They have an eloquence of mind and motion, existing on a plane apart, and those who associate with them as specialists, hunters, victims, lovers, or companions view themselves on this same plane, set apart and superior, partaking of the omniscience and power. They're beyond the reach of the banal, which seeks alternatively to suck the life out of them.

There is no "profile" of a person attracted to vampires. I've met many, and no two are alike. Some are paranoid, some trusting; some are creative, some happy to work within an established framework; some view themselves as outsiders, some have no such affiliation; some smile, some don't; some are borderline mentally ill, some are healthy; some like to present themselves as dangerous, others as nurturing and harmless; some thrive on the image that they love or need blood; others find this disgusting.

In short, the vampire fills a need for characters larger than life who dare to do what we cannot do ourselves. They provide a frame in which we can act out our fears, desires, and needs. It's a way to venture to the edge, to look into the abyss, to test ourselves.

3

I spoke with Dr. Barbara Kirwin, a psychologist who has clinical experience with young people attracted to Goth and vampire imagery. Kirwin has written *The Mad, the Bad, and the Innocent* about criminals and the legal system. She understands from firsthand experience with sociopaths the interplay of good and evil in the human soul.

Kirwin views vampire culture as primarily harmless, and even at times as a helpful way to deal with difficult developmental issues. She feels that most kids attracted to the Goth scene, death imagery, or vampires are involved for reasons that they will eventually resolve. Many are bright, imaginative, and equipped with the resources they need to be functional adults.

Kirwin is a competent, attractive woman with reddish-brown hair, dark eyes, and a professional demeanor. She holds her own in any debate and has served as a media advisor. I asked her what she makes of the pervasive attraction to vampires in recent years.

"It *can* signal extreme pathology," she admitted, "or it can signal a transcendent kind of phenomena. That is, it may be about something superior to the average, and you can't just make a knee-jerk reaction. You really have to look at it in the context of the individual. Of the adolescents that I see who are involved in Goth and vampire stuff, I find they generally are the bright kids who are not making it in the banal, materialistic culture of privilege, and who are also disinclined to jump into the typical adolescent sex and alcohol scene. So their sense of vampirism raises them to a loftier plane. Their parents come in very alarmed, but personally I see it as a viable defense and I work within it."

"A lot of the media simply dismiss them as deviant," I pointed out, "and leave it at that."

She found this attitude to be too shallow. "I make a distinction between deviating from the norm and real pathological deviance. Some of our best and brightest are movers and shakers who have to deviate from the norm. That's how growth occurs. There's something fundamentally very depressing and *oppressing* going on with young people right now. Baby Boomer parents seem to have a psychic vampire style that consumes their children's youth. These kids are wearing the same fashions their parents wore twenty years ago, they listen to similar music, and there's just nothing that's theirs anymore. So I don't get put off when I see kids dress in odd ways because I think that they're at least exploring something that's shut off to a lot of these mainstream kids."

"I do see your point," I said. Her comments reminded me of what Dr. McCully, the psychiatrist who'd written about autovampirism, had said to me: Don't look at the vampire's manifestation to understand it, but the ground from which it arises. Boomers as vampires. "I guess some parents can be rather vampiric," I commented.

"They can be," Kirwin agreed. "The Baby Boomer generation are sucking the youth out of their own children so they themselves can keep forever young."

"And the kids really feel that."

"Of course they feel it, but they can't articulate it, so they act it out. As parents, we've become so invasive that we've taken over their world. And I've seen parents who are the very meaning of succubus."

I almost didn't want to ask, since I'm among those Boomers, but I said, "What else do you see?"

"Another thing that's gone on with this generation that I don't think we can discount is that traditional rites of passage that have to do with sexual encounters are now life-threatening. So they have to find some other way to connect with one another that isn't as dangerous as the real world. They engage in role-playing as a major outlet."

I thought she had a very good point here. There is a great deal of sexual and romantic imagery in the role-playing scene, and lots of overlap between fetish and vampire culture.

"And I see the longing," Kirwin continued, "the erotic, the spiritual quest that's part of vampirism, the eternalization of things, the total surrender. I think it appeals to young people right now because we're in an era that doesn't nurture or protect the emotions of children well. Parents are preoccupied; they're otherwise engaged. And one of the things that goes on in vampire lore is the total absorption that the master has with the enslaved. Once you make that surrender of will, you're engulfed and protected. There's someone always there for you. And I think these kids are pretty abandoned, so they respond readily to that experience."

4

Before going any further, I will say that most young people relegated to the category known as Generation X or twenty-nothings dislike the dubious distinction and believe it's just a Baby Boomer's need for categories that compels such schematizations. They may be right. Certainly, not everyone within the defined set of parameters shares the traits attributed to them. However, in my experience, there are grounds to call at least a subgroup of the generation in question GenXers, in the way it's been defined. So with that in mind, I talked to a couple of young men who struggle to understand the spiritual ramifications of being members of a group that speaks so much of darkness and alienation.

Jud Wilhite and Mark Spivey both have master's degrees in theology, and Wilhite is currently working on a doctoral dissertation that specifically addresses the spiritual climate of people his age. An earnest young man from Texas who balances a great many responsibilities, he is in his mid-twenties. Spivey, from Florida, is older, although his dark hair and eyes, and his trim physique, make him look younger than his age. He has done extensive work with the GenX fascination with vampires. He feels the burden of what Generation X means because he, too, has experienced the sense of floundering and intangible identity that often characterizes it.

"First of all," I asked Wilhite, "just who is this generation?"

"I don't know that a static definition of GenX is possible," he said. "I can only offer a definition that has grown and changed for me over time, but which is suitable for my work with this age group. In 1991 Douglas Coupland published a novel entitled *Generation X* that described three twenty-somethings who left, as he put it, 'the merry-go-round of status, money, and social climbing that so often frames modern existence' to search for purpose in life. The *X* defined not a chronological age, but a way of looking at the world. After some heavy doses of media exploitation, the term Generation X became one caricature among many that negatively referred to those born in America between 1961 and 1981. A *Time* article from the previous year, entitled 'Proceeding with Caution,' started the hype by painting a pessimistic picture. Since then, media coverage has abounded with negative generalizations."

"What were some of them?" I asked him.

"The best way to answer is to go to the initial article. In 1990 *Time* said that people in their twenties possess only a hazy sense of their own self but a monumental preoccupation with all the problems they inherit from preceding generations. Their indecision creates a kind of ominous fog around them. They're also described as being afraid of risk and rapid change. The emerging picture painted a generation of white middle class whiners still suffering from their parents' divorce, who feed on an endless array of cable channels, and who eat and sleep their way into oblivion."

"So what does unite you all as a generation, then?"

"I think it's clusters of loosely connected pop culture memories and referents."

"Such as?"

"Television, music, movies, from *The Breakfast Club* to Atari to Heavy Metal. In many ways MTV was a sound track for the generation. MTV's coming of age involved superstars of Generation X's younger years: Michael Jackson, Billy Idol, Madonna, and older icons like the Bee Gees. Those shared referents give us a common set of assumptions that are often mediated by pop culture, and we have a sense of maturing in a time characterized by such things as AIDS, ecological disturbance, and massive debt. For instance, one grows up watching *The Brady Bunch* and gets a certain perspective of what family life should be, despite the fact that the majority of younger adults were latchkey kids whose families were in shambles. Thus, many are cautious about marriage and family, and have given up on the TV dream. Another assumption is a lack of trust in leaders coupled with the disappearance of heroes.

"It's important to see Generation X as a broad way of viewing the world. It sets up what I've seen called an 'ironic distance from one's own existence.' This distance emerges in certain forms of music, movies, literature, and an overall sense of angst. The distance is filled with a disillusionment at life coupled with a sense of homelessness. In its essence—and this is a point the media has often missed—it's a longing for something real, something substantial, which cannot be found in selling out for money or climbing the corporate ladder."

"Okay," I said, "but why do they feel distant from their existence? What do they have to feel angst about? Most would say, they're a rather privileged bunch."

Wilhite acknowledged this, but was ready with a defense. "The psychological and physical trauma of growing up amidst a breakdown of political leadership, a disturbing dissolution of family structures, and a chaotic education with no clear objectives has taken its toll. What results is a fractured self. And just as GenX grew up and entered the job market, the U.S. shifted from being the world's largest creditor to the world's largest debtor nation. The concern for financial stability

is reflected in the growing belief that the best has passed; only drudg-
ery and decay are to come."

5

That's when I turned to Mark Spivey, who has explored the affinity
between the modern vampire image and these GenX concerns, for
clues as to what accounts for the emptiness many claim in their spiritual lives. His findings revealed that the vampire proved to be a powerful icon, almost a hero, and he labored to identify the reasons for the
attachment of spiritual or religious experience to the vampire
mythology.

"What got you interested in this connection?" I asked him.

"While talking with friends one night," he said, "I was surprised
when one of them compared himself to a character in a book he was
reading. 'This vampire is so much like me,' he said. 'His life is just like
mine—fucking miserable. He's as confused and bored as I am, man.'
He was reading *Interview with the Vampire*. 'Louis and I are blood brothers,'
he went on. 'His way of looking at life is so dreary, sort of like a fallen
god forced to accept his black fate.' Other friends of mine had echoed
those same sentiments.

"It seems to me that many of us identify with the vampire image.
In large part, this came about from the way Rice refined the idea of the
vampire. When she published her book in the seventies, people were
seeking alternate forms of spirituality. They'd lost touch with traditional values and craved a more immediate and intense experience.
Now in the nineties, that same hunger for meaning still makes the
angst of her vampires relevant."

"What do you mean by that?" I asked. "Relevant in what way?"

"Many GenXers see themselves in Rice's characters because they
feel a similar malaise, an uneasy despair that persistently seeks release.
Characters such as Louis portray a dark sense of despondency that
feels authentic. He's the epitome of malaise. He has his 'Dark
Moment,' which Rice describes as a sensation of dread that comes
from doubting absolute values; it's the stark recognition of ultimate
chaos. That's like contemporary society. As Jud just said, we can't trust
politicians and there are no clear values or outstanding role models.
The Church tries to give moral instruction, but we see religious lead-

ers caught in hypocrisy. Even our parents seem caught up in dysfunctional relationships, and they can't offer solutions to our most pressing questions. We have nowhere to turn.

"Thus, some of us experience life as outsiders, and a percentage react to the Dark Moment by gravitating toward an image of rebellion and power: the vampire. There's a general sense of being cursed to live on the margins of society."

I knew what he meant. In Rice's novels, many characters express this dreadful uncertainty. Louis has trouble deciding what he is. He cries out, "I don't know whether I come from the devil or not! . . . I am to live to the end of the world, and I don't even know what I am!" He complains that Lestat left him "somewhere between life and death" and he wishes to be released from his monstrous existence. He mourns, "It would be sweet to die. Yes, die. I really wish to die."

Spivey continued with his argument: "The advent of postmodernism heralded the official dissolution of absolute truth within the religious community. Essentially, we believe what we want to believe. If one does not like the idea of hell, then one simply refuses to believe that hell exists. If a particular law or commandment is annoying, then it's eradicated from the personal spiritual life of the believer. It is not uncommon to hear the phrase, 'That may be true for you, but it isn't true for me.'

"That phrase permeates the spiritual atmosphere in Generation X. They accept no absolutes, and as such, the vampire lifestyle is not only acceptable, it is preferable to the 'dead liturgy' of traditional spirituality. To be spiritual in the postmodern age is to be whatever one wants to be. It is to find spiritual experience in existential exploits—and vampirism is a premiere exploit for spiritually starved GenXers. In fact, vampires offer a more legitimate form of spirituality for GenXers. It feels like a genuine religious experience. In the absence of other, now dead, traditional religions—the vampire assumes the position of priest, prophet, and pacifier."

"So are you claiming that the vampire supplies something that's missing among people this age?"

"For some, yes. What's missing is an awareness of substantive truths that are meaningful to life experience. They're hungry for a sense of the divine, and without a clear sense of direction, they search for the marvelous among the undead—and surprisingly, they often find it."

"Okay, then," I said, "since you did an extensive study, describe for me the general traits of those who have a strong interest in vampires."

"The general traits of the segment in question include listlessness, malaise, confusion, feelings of abandonment, loneliness, attention deficits, lack of healthy self-esteem, desire for control or power over their otherwise powerless circumstances, hopelessness, and the need to 'be somebody.' This is a general profile. There are pockets of GenXers that exhibit these traits profoundly. I feel the majority of Generation X who admire the vampire as an antihero are expressing their desire for recognition and power."

"But why do such an involved study of this theme?"

He shrugged, turning his dark eyes on me. I wondered how much he, too, identified with vampires.

"It was as much personal as professional," he admitted. "Personal, because I'm interested in vampires myself, seeing my own life in terms of a vampiric existence. In a professional capacity, I'm interested in how humans see themselves in culture, especially cultural icons and/or mythology. I wanted to understand who else in my generation might see themselves as vampires."

"How did you go about gathering data?"

"I used hundreds of personal interviews, along with official questionnaires distributed in college classrooms. I knew some people connected with the vampire underground, so I asked them a lot of questions. I searched through relevant books, but relied mostly on my own research and my intuition. It was a very personal project that appealed to a surprising mass of peers. I was astonished."

"What aspects of the vampire itself offer something to meet the needs you've described?"

"GenXers are desperately out of control and lack power for their lives and futures—in their minds at least. The vampire represents the power, the control over circumstances and the sensuality that elude them. Most GenXers seem uninterested in living forever, scratching the immortality issue out of the picture; but then, some of Rice's vampires also dread living forever in that they must contend with their boredom. The vampire existence, as depicted, is a very real description of the typical GenX lifestyle: dark, mysterious outcasts who subsist on society's blood, feeding when and where they can to survive—and survive they will at all costs. When the magic is drained from life, the spiritual vortex begins to swirl. Vampires become the junk-food spirituality for the hungry.

"And perhaps the biggest and most overlooked element of vampire life striking close to home for GenXers is the sense of community that binds them all together. Vampires in Rice's novels, at least, are unified—and for the unhappy GenXer, there must be company in misery."

"Is there anything positive about this association?" I asked. It didn't sound like it thus far. But he had an answer to that.

"I think vampires offer a heightened sense of self-esteem, even though it can be overinflated. Vampires give some kids self-confidence. They also lend credence to being sad, to being outcast, to being misunderstood. Vampires, current models, are not the horrid creatures of the past. They're conscientious, often intelligent, and they are philosophers who have something to say about the way the world ought to work. This is a positive outlet for many GenXers who are genuine thinkers. Of course, all of this energy can, and sometimes does, find its way to harm."

"Like what?"

"The absurd extremes to which many go to identify with a community, such as the cults that kill cats or drink the blood of neighborhood children. Also, adopting the ways of a vampire with the limitations of mortality is a most difficult project—and can lend to depression when they can't achieve it."

Since Spivey had ministerial experience and had counseled people in spiritual contexts, I asked him, "What would you advise parents to do if they were worried about their child's obsession with the vampire image?"

"Seek to understand what kind of vampire your child adores. Don't dismiss; immerse yourself into the culture and understand the how and why of the phenomenon for your child. Blatant denial and negative reactions will exacerbate your problem and estrange your child. Get into the vampire of your child's choice and use the image to have a dialogue that will keep them balanced in the real world."

Easier said than done, I suppose. "Do you see the trend changing in any way? Any predictions?"

"I think the vampire is growing as a myth, even moving into a lifestyle as credible as the beatniks, gypsies, and gay communities. I believe the future will see vampire communes protected by laws enacted to preserve freedom of religious expression—because being a vampire is a religious experience. It's a soul movement and it will develop in our postmodern culture with all the ease of any other movement. Vampires will have their day."

6

I'd heard this sort of thing from people of the age that Spivey had described. Vincent, for example. He called me in the middle of the night to tell his story.

When Vincent was twenty-one, he got involved with a couple of women who, during sexual play, asked if they could tie him to the bed. He consented, and while they lavished him with caresses, he closed his eyes. Then he felt a sharp scraping sensation on each arm that he could not identify. He opened his eyes and saw them both sucking his blood from small cuts in his arms. He was alarmed at first, but then found he liked it. "It's a better rush than anything you can take," he told me. "You feel like you could die if they didn't stop."

They did this with him a couple of times before he tried drinking blood himself. Then they all began to dress up as vampires, painting their fingernails black and wearing fake fangs and vampiric clothing.

The blood-sport soon developed into risky behavior with an S&M edge to it. "I felt safe with my group," said Vincent. "We were taking risks, but it got more dangerous when we took it outside the group and invited others in."

Eventually he felt it had gone too far, and he stopped. Looking back, he realizes that it had given him something when his life was at an all-time low, but that, ultimately, the whole experience was rather unproductive, even "demented," and he was glad he'd escaped it. He believed, given his sense of malaise, that things could have gone too far.

Vincent is like so many people looking for a buzz, trying to make life feel like *more*. His is not an isolated case, and a few who take it further than he did do get into trouble. What are we to believe about this phenomenon? Just attribute it to postmodern malaise, the price we pay for our limited vision?

I listened to Kirwin, Wilhite, and Spivey, among others, and wondered what the burgeoning of vampire culture in recent years said about us—all of us. As McCully had said, look at the larger picture. It's not just about those who participate but also about those who view them with aversion, amusement, or disdain. We can analyze the vampire subculture all we want for its "shadow" elements—and I have done my share of that. But I also believe that subcultures in general absorb and express something about the culture at large. Creatures from the shadows always show us what we don't wish to see, and the vampire is especially well suited to mirror our self-deceptions. To dismiss people who identify with vampires as evil, out-cast, or demented is just a way to shield ourselves from seeing more ugly truths.

Kirwin's analysis of the Boomers vamping off their kids raises the issue but doesn't take it far enough. As a culture, we participate in collective bad faith. We shun or denounce kids who dress as vampires even as we covertly encourage large-scale social vampirism. We often protect, and even institutionalize, the very thing that we claim to decry, and while we say vampirism is evil, we support corporations and politicians that plunder us. Take whatever you need, is the unspoken philosophy, value people only insofar as they are useful. Protect yourself and survive, no matter what it takes. Others are merely numbers.

Middle class success literally depends on vamping off others, but we conceal this secret behind a facade of order, respectability, and family values. We strip the environment, cut corners on health to promote profit, and harbor internal prejudices that dehumanize whole groups. We strive for domination, tolerate political scams, and remain indifferent to the strip mining of our well-being by those who have the power to impoverish us. We secretly cherish those in power and submit to their domination.

Participants in the more overt vampire culture articulate what we wish to keep silent. They are a sharp-edged figure to our diffuse background; we see them more clearly than we see ourselves, so we label them and shove them into the category of "deviant" to try to separate them from the herd like wounded cattle. They are Other, not part of us. But like it or not, we're their context. As long as we sanction forms of vampirism in our business practices, politics, and institutions, but *pretend* through our ideals that we don't, we will have a youth culture willing to act out the vampire role, fueled by the turmoil of our own contradictions.

The vampire is a transgressor who can make us forget what it is he has transgressed. He brings random closure to life, but injects his victims with ambrosial sensation to make them forgive and embrace their termination. We honor the vampire's rebelliousness, his individuality, his disconnection from mundanity. We eroticize his egoism, fetishize his impetus to destroy us. We love the thing that exploits us. We act to contain and destroy him, but then we want another to replace him. The vampire is our collective Limit Experience, our means by which to move beyond restrictive boundaries that suffocate life. We want to feel his power, so we authorize his slide into the very heart of our endeavors.

In short, we say we reject violence and exploitation, yet we covertly accommodate it: Our contemporary value system has a built-in slippage effect so we can use whatever moral context we need to suit our purposes. Thus, we develop a blind eye to some forms of vampirism so that we can, in all good conscience, claim to be a benevolent society. We don't wish to know this truth about ourselves, but younger generations who see it detest the lies and use dramatic extremes to show us what we do.

And I was about to get the most shocking example of this that I had yet encountered. Wraith called and told me to come and meet him.

CHAPTER SIXTEEN

interview with a vampire

I

Wraith had instructed me to go to a city fairly far from where I lived. I had to fly there and rent a car. He'd asked me to meet him at a Goth club to which he provided directions, and had given me a time and date.

When I got there, it was crowded. As was typical of such places, young people were dressed in black velvet, leather, lace, and fishnet. Scattered among them were Ravers, there for the music. In open view, people passed substances around for ingestion to heighten their experience that night. I didn't think it would be a good place to talk, but maybe Wraith just wanted to get a look at me before he decided to approach me. I wouldn't know him in such a place. He could be anyone there. So I sat at the bar, ordered a Merlot (no vampire wine here), and looked over the various people who *might* be him.

I had just about settled on a young man dressed in black with thick brown hair to his shoulders, who had eyed me a couple of times. But then I noticed a guy several seats away, watching me. He had black hair, cut short, dark brown eyes, the faint shadow of a beard, and an easy smile. He was dressed in loose-fitting jeans, stomper boots, and a plain white T-shirt. There was not a trace of Goth in his demeanor or apparel. He seemed out of place. In fact, he could be anybody—your next door neighbor, your express delivery man, your boyfriend. Yes, yours.

Had to be him. When he smiled directly at me, I knew it was Wraith. At last, after all those mysterious calls and exotic descriptions, I was seeing him face-to-face.

I noticed there were no protruding fangs, no sharpened canines. His smile was like anyone's. Normal.

He got up and walked over to me. I figured him to be around six feet and he was of average build. I watched him the whole time to show that I wasn't afraid . . . or else to make myself *feel* bold. He held out his hand and—no lie—it was cold to the touch. Nice effect. Probably from an ice cold beer bottle. And it was definitely his sexy voice. He gave me a name which I was certain was not his real name, and said he wouldn't talk there. He wanted me to meet him elsewhere. He told me a time an hour hence and offered a new set of directions.

That was frustrating. I was ready to get started and now I had to drive to yet another unfamiliar place. And worse, it seemed dangerous to go somewhere away from the crowd.

"This doesn't seem like such a good idea," I said.

He shrugged. "You want my story?" Obviously, it mattered little to him. He hadn't put himself out in any way and he seemed uninterested in publicity.

I debated whether it could be worth whatever risk I might be taking and decided that, thus far, he had trusted me with what he claimed were his secrets. He certainly had reason to be cautious and to request that this meeting be on his terms. I thought about *The Mole People*, recalling Jennifer Toth's courage in Manhattan's dangerous underground. If she could do that, I could do this. I decided to go ahead and meet Wraith wherever he wanted. Besides, I'd grown less disturbed by the things I had heard thus far. I understood more about the culture of vampirism than I had before, and did not believe that this man wanted anything more than an audience. Not publicity, but a listener.

"Okay," I said. "I'll be there." He smiled and left.

To kill time, I went inside and watched the dancing for a while. I didn't see him, so I figured he was on his way to prepare for my arrival. I pondered calling a friend to give her the address, but she was many miles away in New Jersey. Besides, she'd just get upset. She'd been upset enough over every stage of this book that she'd had a charm—a tiny cross—specially blessed for me in Brazil. I was wearing it at that very moment on one of my earrings.

Finally I had to decide: either go for it or just forget it.

I couldn't help but recall my pervasive childhood fear that every person had within him a beast that would emerge at some point when we were alone together. I had believed that my sister, who shared a room with me, would stab me with a knife, and most nights through-out my childhood I had lain awake until I was sure she was asleep. Now I was getting apprehensive about being alone with this man whom I hardly knew, who claimed to have even darker secrets than he had yet told me, and who drank people's blood and viewed them as prey. Those thoughts did nothing to reassure me, though I'd already talked with many types of blood-drinkers. Still, most of them did not view themselves as predators, as Wraith did. He had told me that, if I did not understand the soul of a predator, I would not really under-stand the vampire. I had to remember that.

Finally I went out to my rental car, a green Escort, and got in.

The address was not in the city. It looked like it was in a fairly iso-lated place. I thought about Susan Walsh and her treks into the dan-gerous places of lower Manhattan. For some reason, the fact that she hadn't been located, and that the vampires had not yet been officially cleared, became more significant in that moment. I wondered if she'd felt like this as she went forth to interview people she didn't really know who did nefarious things. Had she been scared? Had second thoughts? Had she ever just *not* gone to an appointment? I was doing what she'd been doing, more surely now than at any other time in my investigation. Except that I didn't know what she might have done were she in my shoes.

I was faced with a dilemma. I'd paid a lot to get here. I'd spent time and effort to make this meeting happen. I'd *wanted* it to happen. If I didn't go, I'd be kicking myself later. And yet if I got killed, what differ-ence would any of that make? I couldn't think why this guy was luring me out into the countryside. It really bothered me. Taking a deep breath, I got in and drove. If the place looked really bad, I could always drive quickly away.

It soon became apparent that I was right in thinking that Wraith had directed me to an isolated area. I left the city behind and eventually turned off the highway onto a dirt road that entered what looked like some type of park or preserved forest area. I drove a couple of miles, checking the directions several times, and was about to stop and turn around when I saw a car parked in a clearing. There were lights, but they were widespread and dim. A man in a white T-shirt stood against the car.

It was him. *Wraith.*

2

I pulled up and got out of my car, but kept the door open in case it looked like I should just leave. "What are we doing out here?" I asked.

"This is a significant setting," he said. "I want you to see it. Besides, it's quiet out here, and private. I can make sure there's no one with you."

I ignored that, and protested, "I don't know if this will work. I need better light. I mean, I want to get your story right. I need to record it or write it down somehow."

He shook his head. "I don't want you to record anything. You can take notes, but I'm not going to have any proof of what I'm going to tell you."

"If I don't record it, I could get it wrong."

He thought about this. Then he made the condition that I had to destroy the tapes after I was done.

"I can promise that easily enough. But why would you trust me?"

"I think you'll want to destroy them after I've told you what I'm going to tell you. But I'll accept your word. If you say it, I think you'll do it."

I nodded. "Okay. But I'll have the transcripts."

"That's not the same. For all anyone knows, you could have made them up yourself."

I conceded this point and got out the recorder. No reason to argue, but I wondered why he was so concerned.

I admit, I was afraid. I thought about how the reporter had felt in Rice's *Interview with the Vampire.* He'd been a bit incredulous at first, and then increasingly vigilant, growing aware of the potential danger to himself of having a *real* vampire confess his bloodlust—and feeling trapped. Of course, he'd been in a closed room with Louis, while I was out in the open, but then, I didn't know this area and the vampire standing in front of me did.

Well, this was it. This was the real thing. An interview with a vampire . . . or so he claimed.

But it wouldn't be like that story, the one in which the vampire Louis described how he'd had to kill to prove his worth, and then had killed repeatedly to survive. Not likely.

"How shall we begin?" he asked.

Hmm, I thought. Wasn't that the way Louis had started the story of *his* life? I hoped I wasn't just getting a role-player with a particularly vivid, if derivative, imagination. I'd come a long way for this meeting.

I pulled out a tablet and a pen to note any questions I might have along the way, and turned on the recorder. "Okay, then," I said. "You've told me some of your vampire experiences. How did it all begin?"

"Just so you know," he said, "I have never shared this experience with anyone who is not Other, a kindred blood ritualist. We keep things secret. I've seen people go on talk shows and say they are vampires, but it's pathetic in a way. No real vampire would go near lights and cameras, exposing himself to skeptics of that sort, or seeking publicity. They avoid detection of every sort. The only way to infiltrate real vampire covens is to do something like John Howard Griffin, who injected something into his skin to become black and to immerse himself in the culture. Or like God taking on the guise of man. That's the only way to really know. And mostly, they don't want anyone to know their world."

"So why tell me, then?"

"I'm rogue among them. I would have been expelled long ago, but for their need of me, so this is for you. I want to tell you. I want you to understand."

"Understand what a vampire really is?"

"Yes. At the very least."

At the very least? What else was there? "Okay. I'm listening."

I settled against my car, but he pushed away from his—a black foreign-made vehicle—and walked a few paces. A cool breeze chilled me as I waited. I heard some night birds chattering nearby, and the faint sound of traffic on the road I'd left to come here. I also heard running water and guessed we were near a river or large stream. A duck quacked and another answered.

"It started with an incident in my childhood," he finally said. "With Jared. I didn't know it at the time, but looking back, that's obviously where my life changed."

"And who was Jared?"

He shrugged slightly. "He came to me when I was five years old. I remember it with perfect clarity. I was trailing the edge of a river where I always played—this river in fact." He gestured away from us, behind him. "I was playing with a stick I had sharpened into a sword and I heard someone call my name. I answered, but he just kept saying my name. I walked over to where the voice seemed to come from and asked, 'Who is it?'

"He said, 'My name is Jared and I want to be your friend.' I wanted more details, but all he would say was that he was my new friend and now my life would get better. I accepted that. He seemed friendly enough. He immediately started teaching me things, like how to win at checkers and how to control the thoughts of my peers. He told me that he was very old and wise, and that I should trust him."

"Like a ghost or something? Lots of kids—"

"Jared was beautiful. To my mind, the perfect male: He had strength, charm, confidence, knowledge, and he was pretty. I did not actually see him until later, but I had an image of him burned into my mind. He seemed to know everything about me, even before I knew it myself. He soon became my best friend, and he influenced my thinking and my actions, and sometimes even selected books for me to read. One choice was *Murders in the Rue Morgue* by Edgar Allan Poe. He had a sharp eye for what intrigued me."

"Did he actually talk with you? Like an imaginary playmate?" I asked. I wanted to get clear on who exactly this Jared was. Or *what* he was.

"He spoke . . . mentally. I know you'll dismiss me as half-crazy or psychotic when I say that. Hearing voices." He pivoted around on one foot and came back to lean on his car and face me, his arms folded over his chest. "I did warn you, by the way. I said you'd think I was mad."

"You said *you* thought it. I haven't made any judgments."

Wraith nodded, his eyes narrowed. Then he continued. "Jared wasn't just an imaginary friend. He *came* to me. I didn't seek him out or wish for him or conjure him up to keep me company. I had no such desire. I was perfectly fine all by myself."

"But how was he related to your interest in blood?"

"What I did not know then was that Jared was a vampire. Or a vampire spirit. I learned that years later. Allegedly, Jared had been born in Copenhagen in 1762 and had spent his life feeding on the innocent. He was bisexual, but preferred the scent of a woman. He drank the blood of his conquests, during and after sex. In 1793 he got himself stabbed by a jealous husband. He was caught, but didn't resist getting murdered. He wanted to die in order fully to access the spirit world. He was a wild personality, a risk-taker. He helped me do things I wouldn't have done on my own. He's an instigator. He died just the way he wanted to—violently, caught in an act of passion."

Wraith stopped and looked at me. I didn't respond. I'm sure he believed I had decided to dismiss him, because he then said, "I don't like reality—what you would call reality. I'm puzzled and angered by much of what I know as reality. I prefer a masterpiece of contrived fantasy, if that's how you decide to view this—and maybe you'll be more comfortable if you do. Life is more real to me in my mind than it is in the world, even though I concede the existence of objective life. It's simply not as real as what exists in my mind. I have spent countless hours in cemeteries wondering if the dead are upset at their deaths, worried about their past lives, if they're cold or lonely where they are. As an adolescent, I was the object of scorn and ridicule in school. I used to lie in my bed, dreaming and crying inside. I sometimes cut my wrist and sucked at my own blood, comforting myself with myself. I didn't think anyone else could comfort me."

I nodded. I understood that. "What gave you the idea to do that? Why would you think it would be comforting to drink your own blood?"

"I don't know where I got the idea. It just seemed right to me. I 'knew' it would comfort me . . . somehow. I just knew. I felt isolated and alone, all by myself in my soul and there was no one who could really understand me. It was more than just adolescent ennui—I was different and I knew it. And knowing that I was gay added to my feeling alone. I knew my own blood was who I really was and that if I could reingest it, I could revitalize myself. So, I would lie in bed and use a razor or a straight pin, and open a wound and suck on it—often for up to thirty minutes. I never sucked too much because the wounds were limited in scope—so there was never a danger of serious blood loss."

3

"So what happened to Jared?" I asked. "Is he still around?" I shivered as I said this and glanced quickly over my shoulder.

"No," said Wraith. "He left me when Christian came. He said I didn't need him anymore. I don't know whether Christian chased him away or if Jared had other business elsewhere, but he left me. Christian completely usurped Jared's position in my life."

Christian. He'd mentioned that name before, but had refused to offer any information. Given where we were, I doubted that this Christian had anything to do with the Christian who'd known Susan Walsh.

"Okay, then," I said, "are you going to tell me about him now? You've been hinting about him. I think you want to tell me. Just who was he?"

He smiled in a secretive way, as if Christian was out there in the woods, egging him on from some invisible perch. Another chill ran down my back at the image. This really was spooky out here.

"Let me tell you first what I think for me was the Archimedean Point of my early vampiric experience," Wraith said. "Before Christian arrived. You need to know that."

"I thought you already told me that one."

"You mean Terry? No, this one is different. Terry was important, yes, but Eric really made this whole thing take hold."

"How old were you?"

"I was around thirteen. Eric was my friend, and we'd gotten chemistry sets for Christmas, with microscopes and lab equipment. We wanted to dissect real human body parts, but we couldn't get them, until one day Eric called and told me he had something to show me.

"When I got there, Eric opened the box carefully, making sure not to spill the precious contents. Inside were the remains of a human hand. It shocked me and I asked him where he'd gotten it. He told me the hand had belonged to a sixteen-year-old male who'd lost it in an accident that morning near Eric's home. He'd witnessed it from his tree fort and had dashed down to call 911. Then he hopped on his bike to arrive first on the scene.

"The boy was unconscious. Eric checked his carotid to see if he was still alive—and he was. He also checked for signs of external bleeding, but the victim had only bruises and minor lacerations. Eric figured he would probably live. Then he noticed that the boy's right hand was missing.

"Thinking quickly, he removed his belt to apply a tourniquet, but was surprised to find that the wound had been cauterized by the hot metal that severed the member. 'It was amazing, just amazing,' he told me. 'The hand was completely severed by a piece of searing metal, but the artery and capillaries were perfectly sealed.'

"My first thought was: What an irony that the very person who saved this boy's life has taken his hand. I asked him, 'How could you take his hand, Eric? I mean . . . you called 911 and everything . . . why did you take his hand?' He said, 'They wouldn't be able to reconnect it anyway, not for sure, and I wanted it as my reward for saving his life.'

"It's true that the odds of successfully reattaching a human hand under these conditions were slim. This happened in the mid-seventies, and while medical technology was advancing, successful member reattachments had not yet become routine procedures. Indeed, it was possible that surgeons might have been able to save the hand, if they had found it in time—but they didn't. Eric felt justified in removing it from the scene.

"We'd dissected frogs and other creatures and were already proficient in anatomical structure. We had read that you could send away for human cadaver parts, but they were too expensive. Finding the hand was a gift from the gods, and Eric was not about to give it up.

"We spent the better part of the day dissecting the hand, peeling away the flesh to expose the tendons and fibrils. It was beautiful and I was thrilled to be close to it. The hand became erotic for me. One night I even had a dream that the hand came to life and began masturbating me in the dark. I was both repulsed and intrigued. I think I was entranced by the hand because it had once belonged to what I imagined to be a beautiful boy, though Eric would not confirm the boy's good looks.

"The hand became an impetus for our shared thirst for blood. We had already tasted our own, so now it was time to start tasting our family and friends. We collected blood samples under the guise of conducting lab experiments. We kept our secret lab set up in the tree fort under lock and key. The hand we kept in the box, preserved in a strong solution of formaldehyde. So, it was easy to convince our family and friends to give us blood samples for our work. They thought they were encouraging young scientists.

"The truth is that they were feeding young vampires. We actually fought over the first few samples, trying to decide who would taste whom. I thought it was only fair that I taste my own family while he taste his, but Eric wanted to taste my family. He said he wanted 'strange' blood, not his own kind. I laughed at his logic, but privately I agreed. Blood should be strange. It was here that I began to develop what I had first tasted in Terry: a lust for *other* blood. I had been trying to comprehend why I loved Terry's blood so much more than my own, and now I was beginning to understand the power of it. The term *Other* would one day become synonymous for me with *Vampire*.

"So then Eric and I began to collect samples from strangers, convincing them that it was for a school project. I was more skilled at deception than Eric, mostly because I possessed more natural charm. It wasn't that Eric was without his ways. He just didn't have a quick mind. While he was brilliant, he was awkward. I was quicker, always able to tap my resources for an immediate reaction. I was smooth and very resourceful.

"Eric and I were best friends until he moved away. We did not keep in touch. We'd vowed in the fort, over blood, that we would never speak of our lives together and that if we ever saw the other in public, we would not acknowledge it openly. We had a secret blink that we would use.

"But he moved to New York. I know he still drinks blood because a mutual friend hunts with him. He says, 'The streets of New York are ripe with desperate hearts whose blood is charged with frustrated energy.' Eric always moved toward the desperate. Maybe that's why he liked me."

"So you never heard from him again?"

"No. And losing Eric was hard for me, but it would not be long until one came into my life who surpassed him. This one provided the coronation ceremony for my dark life."

"Christian?"

"Yes, Christian. I'll tell you first how I met him."

4

"I was seventeen, out cruising the boardwalk one Friday night. I had just come out of the water, so I had on baggies and a black T-shirt. I stepped into a local pub for a drink. They knew I was too young, but they let it ride. Gulping down a toxic Cuba Libre, I turned to study a figure I had noticed upon entering. He stood in the shadows, sipping his drink. He was dressed completely in black and he wore sunglasses. The only thing that stood out was his large silver belt buckle. There was something powerful about him and it made me feel aroused. He seemed to be staring at me. Then he started to talk to me, though his lips never moved. I could hear him in my head. He called me over.

"Instead, I asked the bartender for another drink and concentrated on it while I listened to what this guy near the wall was saying to me. We talked across the room without anyone else hearing it. Just us. It was fucking amazing! I couldn't even see his face, but I felt I knew him. Finally I walked over to where he was hiding. He was tall and looked like a male model. His blond hair hung straight to his shoulders and his face was carved ivory. I found out later he'd been born in Sweden. I also found out later that he had sapphire blue eyes.

"'What took you so long?' he whispered. He paused and then added, 'I've been waiting for you forever.'

"I liked that. 'Well, here I is,' I told him. I recognized something dark in him. I think we knew each other's madness. We saw in each other's eyes our mutual destiny."

I made a move to interrupt, but Wraith held up his hand. He wanted to go on in his own way.

"Christian grinned like he knew where Jimmy Hoffa was buried, and I felt demon-possessed, like he had stepped right inside of me. He told me his name. I almost gave him the false name I use to cruise, but then decided to tell him who I really was. I sensed he would know if I lied. Then we talked and drank for hours after that, leading each other through our lives. We stayed together for the next seven years. I had no idea then that I would become his captive.

"We cruised together and called the boys we targeted our 'kills.' Just like a couple of vampires. Together we seemed indomitable. It wasn't long before we were tag-teaming our kills, agreeing silently on someone and bringing him back to Christian's place for a toss. Eventually I moved in with him."

Wraith looked pensive, deep in memory, and then he asked, "Have you ever met someone so like you that you climbed inside them and became one person? This was our life, one life together. We were lovers, but we were also much, much more. We were so attuned to each other's harmonics that we thought for each other and regularly anticipated each other. How I loved him! And we were inseparable.

"Yet within a month, I knew he was crazy. Many of the things he said and did were incongruent, like a manic-depressive. But he was spontaneous, exciting! Every breath he breathed had energy. He provided the opportunity for me to live my fantasies and fulfill my passions. I'd inspire him with ideas and he took me into action. I wrote the plays and he showed me how best to perform them. It was darkness calling to darkness. We empowered the potential that each of us had with substance and life.

"One night, after we had fed off two boys, we were making love and we wanted more of each other. We had crawled so far into each other that it was like having a single, shared heartbeat. We wanted to share blood, gain a permanent connection that transcended mere touch, so we drank from each other's carotids. That moment is frozen in my mind, sealed in heat. We had such a mind-body connection. We felt immortal, flowing into each other. We knew that even death could not keep us apart. Nothing could."

"Was that the first time you'd had his blood?" I asked.

"No. It was just the most intense to that point. It was within the first month of our relationship—partnership, really—that Christian led me out onto the porch for a talk. It was late, around eleven P.M., and we were getting ready to go out. He said, 'I have to tell you something.'

"Before he said his next sentence, I knew what it was. 'You're a vampire,' I said. 'You're a vampire.'

"He fixed his eyes on mine, staring long and hard at me, and finally he said, 'Yes, I have swallowed the blood of the Other.'

"'The Other? Who's the Other?' I asked him.

"But he wouldn't answer me. Instead, he said, 'Your blood cries out for mine and this is what drew us together. This is why we felt so familiar to each other the night we met. Our blood searched for that moment, the time when it would again become one.' He went on to say that he believed that in some previous time, we were joined and then got separated. I didn't know what to say, but it sounded right. We were never out of step with each other. We functioned as one mind. I had never experienced anything so close, so ultimate, so intimate before. Christian was the missing piece in my life.

"I read about vampires who say the blood is the life. This is the truth of my youth, the blood was the life for me. I believed there was no hope for me without blood, without vampirism. And we enjoyed bringing our victims to the brink, making them fall for us and then tasting the sweetness of their destruction. I'd take every drop of the fire in a boy. What a horrible thing to do, and yet I did it as easily as others breathe the air.

"Christian told me that in time I would meet this 'Other,' whoever it was, but at that moment, he intended to answer my cry. I was dizzy, inebriated with the mystery of his words and his voice. I watched as he cut his brachium, just inside his right bicep, and pressed the wound to my lips, urging me to drink the blood. It was hot and streamed quickly into my mouth. I kept swallowing, trying to keep pace. My face heated up, my ears flushed. I felt myself grow more excited. I can still remember looking at the lake and feeling the wind blowing through the trees while he did it. It was so romantic.

"Suddenly he pulled away, and holding his finger against the slit, began to kiss me deeply, to taste his own blood in my mouth. Then he broke away and said, 'Now you and I will be alike. My blood in me will reunite with my blood in you.' I felt stunned by this, by the sensation that *he* was *me*. He was my equal in every way. He was everything I was, but more of it. From that moment, I was a prisoner of my alter ego.

"After that, Christian set out to teach me and improve my vampire skills, honing my seductive abilities, as well as my ability to deceive. His greatest interest, outside of vampirism, was Egyptian kings, Egyptian blood-rites, and such things as that, and it was a power he sought to reinvent in us.

"Christian told me he could use his mind telepathically. He told me stories of his childhood trances, and he could telepathically make me feel him inside me. He first demonstrated this in a club in Tampa. He started to . . . rather . . . I began to hear him from across the room, while he was talking to two other people. I couldn't believe I was hearing his thoughts, so I looked at him and said in my mind, 'Look over at me if you are talking to me.' And he did! I was thrilled. I'd found a new toy to play with. We did this often, but I don't have the power—I don't think—even though he said I did.

"Me and Christian moved like this—as one creature, one mind, determined to fill our hunger. From the moment he saw me, Christian wanted to crawl inside me and become me. He hated who he was. He was never satisfied with what he saw in the mirror, although he was as beautiful as a model. I couldn't understand it, because there were things I didn't like about myself and I wanted to be *him*—to have his perfect form. So we emulated each other's habits, down to brushing our teeth in the same pattern. We synchronized our minds, fusing them into one fluid motion.

"He didn't work, but he always had money. Always. I'd ask him where he got his cash, but he'd always say, 'Don't worry about such things.' But I did worry. Sometimes he'd disappear for weeks at a time and never tell me where he'd been. I feared that he had some nefarious connections that could be dangerous. There were lots of opportunities to get into the drug trade where we lived, to get involved with organized crime, things like that. And as it turned out, my fear was justified."

This time I succeeded in interrupting him. I wanted to stay on track, but I made a note to return to this if Wraith didn't do it on his own. "Just what did Christian love so much about blood?" I asked.

He took a deep breath before he said, "He believed that within the blood was hidden the secrets of raw existence. He thought the spiritual element of blood hides the secrets of different lives. Tapping into the blood through various methods will permit a soul to transfer its existence to one of these different lives. He had studied alchemy and methods that used blood as a means of transport. Early on, he'd decided for himself upon a suicide that involved a ritualistic blood-drenching that would release his body energy into an open void so he could freely choose any of the worlds he encountered. That's what he wanted. He thought it was romantic. Christian and I had often discussed suicide and blood-pacts. He wanted me to do it with him, but I wouldn't commit. Sometimes I believe he was never really human, that maybe he was an evil spirit who came to love me—the bad in me—in his own peculiar way. I thought he wanted to destroy me, and I think . . ."

"What?"

Wraith shook his head. "Nothing. It's not important. But I introduced him to other ideas about blood. He would sit for hours with me and ask questions about the ancient blood-rites that I knew about from Egyptian, Mayan, American Indian, and Mafioso cultures."

"Like what? Tell me what you told Christian."

"Well, for example, young Apache males are important to the power of the tribe, but there are times when the youths don't take this burden seriously. One secret ritual to 'correct' this defect is the infusion into his heart of a warrior's blood. A warrior takes it upon himself to transfer some of his strength, and depending on the young buck's type of insecurity, he might cut from his loins, thereby sharing both his courage and the potency of his semen. Or he might puncture his wrist or breast—even his neck—to make the young boy drink from his strength.

"Blood contains the spirit of their religion. Many cultures have similar beliefs. One member can imbibe the essence of a more powerful member through the blood. By harnessing the power of two or more people, you can transcend your singularity and perform certain magic rituals. And then some of the Old Ones, the ancient spiritualists, taught that killing your physical body after drinking the blood of a warrior would transport you into a parallel life cycle. You would become the spirit warrior. You will assume his spiritual place and occupy his being as he lives. This is what intrigued Christian. It's what he wanted to be. He was relentless about hearing these tales and would sometimes wake me in the night to get more details of how it was done. He wasn't satisfied with the here-and-now. Neither was I. So we fed each other's imaginations and desires for transcendence to a more powerful and meaningful existence.

"And, of course, added to that is the magic of semen. It's a way into the soul of another male, as intimate as you can possibly get. It's deeply personal. And its chemical composition is much like that of blood. Semen has a creamy, delicate flavor when mixed with blood; it becomes a salty brew that drives the mind to the edge of fantasy. Gay males need to fill millions of empty chambers in our hearts, so we imbibe each other's deepest treasure. It's a raw fulfillment of mutual hunger, an attempt to assume each other's life energy. It's perpetually frustrating, because you can't really get what you need, not totally. We're too depleted, but we're also addicted, and can't alter our endless cycles.

"Christian came to believe that he could purify his blood and his soul by ingesting the blood of people he considered to be better than himself. He thought he was bad and he wanted to rid himself of his own blood. He wanted redemption. For this he needed only to drink from the naïve. He needed the blood of others to keep himself cleansed, and he was forever preparing for what he called 'the reckoning.' For him, this was the time when he would transcend his soul's current status."

"So he drank from you, then—from the one he wanted to be?"

Wraith nodded. "Christian drank from me, yes, but I took more from him because he believed his blood was purer than mine through his more frequent feedings from others, and he wanted me to know the ecstasy of his life. We drank from each other, almost always during sex. Once he used a straight razor to slit his tongue and allowed the blood to trickle into my mouth. It was so hot!"

It didn't sound hot to me, but I didn't say so. "So it was always an ecstatic experience, then?"

"There was suffering in it, to be sure. He was so elusive, so unpredictable at times. It hurt me, but I couldn't change him, so I just lost myself in the pain of it."

"You stayed in a painful relationship?" I asked. The question gave me the opportunity to switch the tape to the other side.

"Pain has infected my entire life," said Wraith. "The emotional pain of being with Christian was just more of the same. Having the persistent pain of ambivalence, the indecisiveness of a roller-coaster relationship was to lose myself in it, to *become* the pain. I've learned to identify the nature of my life with pain. I was dismantled and dissolved in the emotional suffering that came with Christian's presence. He was my private torturer. He killed me every day, but lovingly. He was sadistic even in his affection, and I needed him so much that I tolerated everything. I gave him what he needed, and he gave me life, pleasure, thrill. For a while, it seemed a good trade-off."

5

"Okay, then," I said, "what did you two do as actual vampires?"

"A few months after our blood-bond, Christian introduced me to Michael, his mentor. We arrived at his home on the river around ten in the evening and we were greeted by a doorman whose tails were perfectly pressed. He escorted us to a library in the house's east wing and served us fired cognac. While we sipped, we scanned the shelves for works of antiquity. Soon Michael eased into the room. He offered his hand, and Christian kissed it. I stared into his eyes to try to discern his secrets. He sat with us for a few minutes, talking about the joys of darkness and the anticipation of the night. Then Christian said, 'Michael, I've brought my friend to join the Others.'

"Michael's eyes flashed to mine and we locked in quiet heat. He said, 'Yes, he's quite gifted. You're wise to bring him.' He held his gaze on me and continued, 'He's already one of us. He is the reemergence of Jared.'

"I looked at him and asked, 'How do you know?'

"He smiled and said, 'Did you expect us not to know you, Jared?'

"I didn't understand what he meant. Jared was my spirit companion. I was disturbed by what Michael was saying, but I wanted to know more.

"'All of your life you've felt him, haven't you?' Michael said. 'He has always been inside you. He is a vampire from the eighteenth century, a prominent member of the Others in Europe, and the founding father of us all. He was our guide. But he left us.'

"I was mesmerized. I was about to ask where Jared had gone, and suddenly I knew: suicide. That's how I found out about it.

"'Yes,' Michael said. 'The answer is already yours. He bled himself into the spirit world, where he became a psychic vampire, feeding on the life energies of those he chooses. You're one of those to whom Jared has come.'

"Now, Christian was loving this, absolutely loving it. He was always saying that I was special, and that I didn't know my own power. But I wanted to drop to my knees and pray for salvation. I hadn't known that Jared was a vampire. I had thought that connecting the vampire to my being gay was my own invention. Now I was hearing that Jared has been with me all my life and has been partly, if not wholly, responsible.

"Michael stretched out his hands to me and bid me come to him. He could see that I was upset. I stood and walked over. He got up and embraced me warmly, pulling my face to his neck and stroking my hair. 'You're home now,' he assured me. 'Everything will become clear.' He brushed the tears from my face, wiping my lashes with his fingers. He offered me another warm brandy.

"I was in a spiritual stupor. It seemed like ghosts were flying around my head. I remember staring into Michael's eyes for what seemed like forever. Then he broke the spell, excusing himself to go make preparations. When he was gone, Christian grabbed my hand and said, 'I knew you were special! I knew you'd become my counselor.'

"Michael returned and announced that everything was ready.

Christian joined him and they walk ahead of me through a corridor. The brick walls were cold to the touch and I knew we were going underground, under Michael's house. I could smell river water as we descended deeper. Every twenty feet, there were small electric candles on the walls that cast shadows as giant, evil specters of the night. We approached a black iron gate and I heard chanting on the other side. I wondered what was going to happen to me.

"Michael opened the gate and showed us into a circular underground solarium, a sort of garden filled with varieties of roses. The smell was intensely erotic, a sweet but subtle fragrance. Then the chanting stopped and the roses began to move. It was only then that I saw that they were people in red-hooded robes, all coming toward me."

"You mean like a whole group of vampires?"

"Precisely."

CHAPTER SEVENTEEN

the vampire
underground

I

Wraith was beginning to sound like Shadow in Chicago and Nicolas in Los Angeles. I'd even heard something similar in New York when Sebastian had called breathlessly one day to say, "I just met some people. They live out in the country and say they have contact with the real thing. Vampires! It's like role-players—a group of people doing what we do in 'The Masquerade,' only they're *not playing roles*. They really are vampires and they can bring us over. They're talking to me about it."

Clearly he was both nervous and excited at the prospect, but what seemed to fire him up most was the mystery and the feeling of a deeper "layer" of the vampire world somewhere below those he knew that promised an even greater edge—and possibly all the secrets and gifts that came with being a vampire.

This was it! The threshold, the limit experience.

The notion of a secret underground flourishes in all folklore. The underworld is where criminals carry on their worst deeds without remorse. We have Dante's descent into the Inferno and Orpheus into

Hades. It's where western culture posits hell to be—the place where evil and madness are nurtured, the womb that can trap us and reabsorb us into the mother's body, where darkness shrouds license and lawlessness. Some people who enter never return. It's where we flush the waste from our bodies. Where we don't know what happens and can only guess. The idea of going into a cave that goes downward inspires visceral anxiety, and a psychoanalyst might say that we fear our own subconscious because it can show us the monsters that we really are.

But it can also be a place, as Victor Hugo said, where "the secret evolutions of souls" can occur. It's where the disenfranchised may find a haven and resistance movements can work toward freedom and reform. It's quiet, dark, and removed from the mainstream of life. Those who wish to face the fear of encountering whatever emerges may view the underworld as a place of quest and purification. The "underground man" is the ultimate dissident of modern society.

Underground is where secret societies meet. The allure is that of an exclusive community that requires initiation and is dedicated to some focused purpose that grants identity and community to its members. Special signals, passwords, jargon, chants, doctrines, clothing, names, and rituals give members a sense of elevated knowledge— a fortress that keeps outsiders out. Generally, there is an overriding mythology that gives members the feeling that they possess a truth because they have worked hard to get it or are a natural part of an elite group. They have a sense of purpose that sets them apart from the mundane world. Where others are blind, they see, and this grants a feeling of privilege. They now hold secrets that others seek. They've been embraced by something much larger than themselves and they shall be given whatever they need to become part of it.

The most exciting secrets are those that risk losing one's mind to possess, because presumably, if one gets that close to the edge and survives intact, one will be unalterably changed, transformed, enlightened, no longer part of the status quo. The treasure is at hand, whatever it is—the Holy Grail.

I frequently encountered the idea in my research that there are Elders or some elite ruling group that conveys special status on a chosen few. A young woman from the Midwest readily told me how she had met a vampire who drew her into a new life of sexual ecstasy and blood-thirst. She became a vampire and she claimed to meet with others who empathize with her. Her story was elaborate and full of romantic trappings, many of them typical of fictional vampire stories: She was old, she said, but looked very young; she used sexual allure to draw her victims; her vampire Maker was a beautiful young man with porcelain skin. She willingly answered any and all questions, but when I asked if I could include it in the book, she said she had to ask the "others." Soon she informed me that the "others" had advised her not to allow her story to be used in this way. She had also promised to direct me to the vampire underground in Paris, which she knew about, but when pressed, declined because "others" had told her not to assist me. My guess is that she didn't really know anything about Paris.

I heard from others that there had been a disturbance in the vampire network a couple of years ago when a young man began to "crash" some online chats to inform people of what a real vampire was and to try to get them all to comply with his own beliefs. He claimed to have secret knowledge and to be involved with a true vampire coven. He said he was a member of the Temple of Set, a philosophic-religious organization in California based on the Egyptian principles of *Xeper*, which means self-creation or self-improvement. In this Order, great emphasis is placed on the value of the individual. Members move through initiations, or "levels of progress," as indicated by the color of a medallion, with gold being the highest level. According to their credo, they "believe in the existence of a being named Set, once called a god by ancient Egyptians." They like to dress in costume (black robes or ancient Egyptian), act out psychodramas, share their knowledge via secret documents and symbolism, explore telepathy and divination; and they are deeply committed to improving their lives.

Whether or not this "vampire" was actually a member of the organization, he apparently exploited it as part of his own presentation. At some point, he grew belligerent and he began sending threats online and through the mail. He also made a few phone calls to try to get acknowledgment of his own special status from anyone interested in vampires. He said he had lists of names of people who were secretly vampires and could make it public. In his desire to be a sort of Kurtz from Conrad's *Heart of Darkness* and to give a widespread impression of his ancient wisdom and power, he drained much of the fun from vampire clubs.

The problem with all of this emphasis on secret power and special knowledge lies in the ambiguity of fantasy. If someone wants me to believe there are mysterious "others" who block entrance into the deeper realms, they can always retreat into that without having to prove a thing. They may be speaking the truth, and I just can't have access, or they may be seeking to convince me to buy whatever they say and not ask for information that would be difficult to deliver—such as a name or address in Paris. They want to appear to be "in the know," but too much probing blows their facade. A ruling group that demands secrecy is an easy out.

Similarly in Chicago, when Shadow told me the story of Abel, I asked if I could attend such a ceremony, and he returned with the answer that I was not "one of them," so I was not allowed to watch—unless I paid a price that he probably figured I was unwilling to pay. (I wonder what would have happened had I accepted the terms!) There were hints that much went on "beneath the surface" of the orgies into which Shadow had been invited, and they were of a "darker" nature. They were reserved for those of stronger spirit (and stomach) who had what it took to be wholly committed. Without revealing any details, Shadow gave me the impression that this was where human sacrifice went on and rituals that provided an interface between the group and . . . who knows what?

Even as he described it, I'd been skeptical, but to have challenged him would have been to lose a good source. He never claimed to have witnessed anything like a vampire murder, or to have ever gone "down below," so there had seemed no point in asking him how much of it was true. Yet the more exposure I had to the younger members of vampire culture, the more the aura of something magical awaiting them was present in their hopes and aspirations. I couldn't help thinking that the role-playing games that relied on clans and magic and hierarchies had something to do with that.

I also heard that there was a vampire connection among homeless people in various cities, such as New York, Miami, and New Orleans. New Yorkers called them "fetish squatters," and they were reputed to attack people who came into their territory. Susan Walsh had been interviewing these people just before she'd disappeared. Although no connection was every found between them and her, the fact that they thrive in places where most of us would never venture gives them enough of a dangerous aura for a mythology to develop: they know things about being a vampire, and they may know how to contact real vampires somewhere *underground*.

The common detail among stories about the "real thing" is that it is to be found in some seemingly inaccessible place, difficult to get to and perhaps entered only through some type of initiation or sacrifice. "They" allow you to belong only if you identify with and protect them, and allow yourself to surrender to their requirements. You have to be ready to face the most demanding, enlarging, frightening, and transforming aspects of vampire existence—to grant "them" total mastery.

This is the point at which many would say that vampirism evolves into satanic worship: that if indeed there is a secret order, an underground arena for worship and ritual, an experience so secret that only initiates are allowed the details, then it must be evil. Too often people dismiss darkness at its most dense as something to be avoided at all costs because it can only strip us of our enlightened minds, our humanity, and turn us into primal creatures. Or some such thing.

Personally, I was intrigued with the similarities between Toth's adventures in *The Mole People* and the vampire subculture that Wraith and others seemed to be describing, in which it was always whispered that there was something more to be had if only one ventured further into the depths—or out into the country, down the stairs, or wherever one had to go to take the next dangerous step. I suppose that I, too, feel the lure to find Those Who Know. I did love the idea of Lestat's search for Marius in Rice's *The Vampire Lestat*, because the promise was there that a great mystery would be revealed, and the enlightenment would bring life-enrichment, or more. And I had appreciated Toth's risks to learn about a strange world below. Yet, no matter how deeply she went, there was also something just beyond.

Toth ventured into the tunnels beneath New York City, and according to her research, there are some seven levels (a rather mythological number). People live on their own or in groups, and even down there, hierarchies form. She often put herself in harm's way to get the story. For example, she encountered a man who lived under Grand Central Station who called himself the Dark Angel. He exploited the discomfort of the difficult surroundings to taunt Toth with her fascination for the darkness, and told her (with rage in his voice) that part of him was within her. What she was after down there was bad. "Everything down here is pure evil," he said, and to emphasize that, he hissed, spit, and screamed. His setup—a blanket laid across a stack of flattened boxes—was known to other tunnel people as Satan's Den. He acted as if he *knew* something she didn't.

As Toth got to know the tunnel people better, she heard stories about those people who lived at the very deepest levels and who had not seen the light of day for many years. One man's toes, she was told, had grown together from walking barefoot on the stone floors. Those were the true "mole people." They were spooky, because while human, they'd evolved into something that most people did not associate with being human. Even the underground homeless viewed them as a mystery, built stories around them, and sometimes demonized them and believed them to be cannibals. The mole people lived where the rats were the largest, where no one else wanted to venture. Even the police didn't bother them because their lairs were so far underground that the walkie-talkies that could summon help failed to work. Stories about them had become part of underground mythology: You know they're there, people told Toth, because you can "feel the eyes."

The point of drawing this parallel is that humanity loves mystery. No matter what our economic circumstances, state of imagination, or degree of rational intelligence, we still develop mythologies of some other creature, power, or force linked to us but not of us. In part, we love the stimulation of fear that this inspires, but we also like to push ourselves toward possibilities that expand us beyond known boundaries. Are there real vampires out there—the creatures of folklore that can "embrace" us, transform us, and grant us forbidden knowledge and eternal life? Is there a secret sect that has the power and omniscience to be aware of select individuals and bestow upon them a special status that will change them forever?

I was about to learn of one.

2

Because of what I'd already heard among vampires about cults and rituals, I felt less inclined to accept the veracity of Wraith's story at this point, but he seemed not to notice any difference in the quality of my interest.

"The group stopped," he went on, "gathering around me as they sang praises to the night. Their hymn honored the lion and the vulture, both of which partake of flesh and blood. Then they sang of the vampire's ways. Christian took his place near the center fountain, while the others bowed and whispered, 'Jared . . . Jared . . . '

"I looked at Michael and asked what he wanted from me. He said, 'I want to complete your journey. I want to disperse the power of the vampire Jared from your soul.'

"'But then you'll have him to yourself,' I objected. 'You want Jared to come out of me and go into you, don't you?'

"Michael only nodded. 'Will you let him go? Will you give Jared to us?'

"I wasn't sure what to say. I didn't like the idea of Jared leaving me, but I wasn't sure I wanted him to stay. Finally I said, 'I'll allow him to choose whatever host he desires.'

"Michael commended me on having the wisdom of Jared in this decision, and commanded the ceremony to commence. There were several dozen others in the garden—it seemed like a hundred. They had come out under the full moon's influence to try to win Jared. Each hoped that Jared would choose him and give him the Light of Intentions.

"Michael produced a blade from his pocket and asked me to extend my right arm. My shirt had already been removed. The others chanted while Michael and I locked eyes and I granted permission for him to cut me. He placed pressure on the blade, halfway between my wrist and elbow. I felt blood seeping out, which was invigorating. It seemed like energy was being channeled through this wound onto the golden plate beneath. Each fresh droplet seemed to represent a century of wisdom and experience.

"The vampires looked on, some eagerly licking their lips. They wanted to consume me, to take Jared into themselves. Christian seemed to be in some kind of trance as he watched. He stared, looking past me to some place he'd never taken me.

"Then Michael cut into his own right arm and turned it to allow his blood to mix with mine on the plate. The plate filled to the edge and then two vampires bound our wounds. Christian stepped forward, lifted the plate, and passed it carefully over a flame to purify it. The flame was in the fountain, in the center of the water, which flowed over three tiers. Then Christian took the plate to a black marble table and poured the blood into two crystal glasses.

"Michael drank first, no doubt hoping to imbibe me and Jared. I followed him, gulping down the taste of Michael and myself mingled together. Then we both closed our eyes, waiting for the Quickening.

"Almost immediately, Michael opened his eyes and said, 'Jared has made his choice. He wants to stay with our new brother. Embrace your new master.'

"This alarmed me, because I didn't want to lead this group. But they began to file past me, kissing my hand or licking at my wound through the bandage. One guy even bit me! I watched as Jared reclaimed his coven. Then Michael motioned for all to sit while my carnal desires were fed. A red-robed figure approached and stood before me. He lifted his eyes, and it was like looking at my own in the mirror. The vampire pulled back his hood to reveal himself and I gasped. He looked exactly like me, down to the freckle on his right cheek. He dropped his robe, revealing his slender body, and leaned into me with great care and gentleness. He licked at my mouth and throat and kissed my face tenderly, as though I might melt at the blast of his heat. He pressed himself against me.

"'Come into me, Jared,' the boy whispered. Christian walked over and began to kiss us both. 'I love you forever,' he said to me. 'One day I'll replace Jared as the guardian of your soul. Until then, teach me all you know.'

"When the ritual was over, the vampires quietly disappeared into the night. Michael gave us the keys to his house. He offered us every-thing and anything. He said to me, 'You are powerful and to be feared. You have surpassed me. I bow before Jared.'

"Christian showed me a secret exit out of the garden. From that day, I assumed a higher power in the coven, and it was the beginning of a long and fascinating adventure into the dark underworld of vampires."

"But wait," I interrupted. "How could you have so much insight when you were just being introduced? Are you saying you suddenly just started channeling the wisdom of this vampire—you knew stuff you didn't know before about the lifestyle? I've never heard of practi-tioners immediately taking to a novice, even if they believed he housed some great spirit. There must be more you're not telling me. There must have been some proving of yourself."

He was quiet for a moment, as if just realizing that I wasn't some idiot who would swallow anything he said. I sensed he was calculating what to say next.

"Okay," he admitted, "the fact is that I was already known to this coven and to Michael. We misled Christian."

This was an interesting shift. Was it the truth? "How?" I asked. "I thought your minds were melded as one."

"Well . . . the truth is, I had met the group a little more than a year before meeting Christian. Michael didn't like it when Christian attached himself to me. When he had met me initially, he'd seen Jared in me and had wanted to take me under his wing. He didn't tell any of this to Christian after Christian came in. I felt guilty about leaving him out of our secret. Michael and I played him for the fool. It breaks my heart that I did that to my lover. But he wasn't wise enough to see it. I met Michael shortly after Christian bled into me on the porch. He thought I could make things happen for him and help him to become what he wanted to be."

He obviously hadn't heard his own contradiction about when he'd actually met Michael. I didn't say anything. "And why do you think the group itself wanted you so badly?"

"They needed my wisdom."

"At seventeen?"

"Most of them were young, too, but they said they needed my keen insight into blood-spirit matters. They saw my talent for reaching in to people and pulling them out. This, along with my natural leadership ability, made me valuable to them. And they wanted Jared."

I had to admit, I was beginning to feel as if *I* was the one being played for a fool. It was all a bit too fantastic—and inconsistent. This young man knew how to dance around any question or objection. He was quick, but not always convincing. Yet some of his story rang true—enough of it to give him the benefit of the doubt. Even if he *was* suffering from some kind of personality disorder, this was a good story—and it did show the strong impression that vampire mythology can have on the imagination. I felt a little safer.

"How old was Michael?" I asked.

"He was somewhere around the age of thirty, I think. It was never asked of him. He looked thirty, anyway."

"How did he acquire such a house? What was his business?"

"His house was his family's house, given to him due to the death of someone in the family. Michael, from all accounts, did not work. He did what he wanted all the time."

"How did he find all these boys to be in the cult?"

"I don't know. I assumed he played the city clubs and backwoods coven-cults and lured them into his opulent life. He was sort of a madam for vampires. They came from all over to be part of his group."

I must have looked skeptical, because he switched to a more philosophical mode, as if to find a better way to persuade me.

"Have you ever read Nietzsche's *Ecce Homo*? Ever wondered what it means to become one's own true self? I like how Nietzsche puts it: 'The riddle that man must solve, he can only solve in being what he is and not something else, in the immutable.' I have a quest to become what I am. The self is not a given. It's a creative process of *becoming*. It's not discovered, but assembled. Nietzsche says that there's one unique path that no one can walk but yourself. Don't ask where it leads; just take it. As I've told you already, I've thought throughout the course of my life that becoming *me* means going mad."

3

"Yes, you've said that," I told him. I wanted to steer him away from that particular topic, and I was interested in his sudden move to deflect me with intellectualisms. Nietzsche was almost a prophet to some of these people, as if he'd given license to do and be anything—which he hadn't. "So what about Nietzsche?" I asked.

"I agree with Nietzsche that man needs what is most evil in him to become what is best in him. The secret for harvesting from existence its greatest gift is to live dangerously." He paused to let this idea have its effect. "And what if one's genius is madness? Should he still pursue it?"

He looked at me as if I had an answer—*should* have an answer. I had always thought that looking into the eyes of madness would be obvious, that I'd know for sure whether the person was "all there." It had not occurred to me that someone who was demented might look and act completely sane. Completely. Wraith was relaxed, affecting, even beautiful. I shifted against my car, not knowing how to respond. The darkness just beyond the lights overhead seemed increasingly more oppressive. Wraith smiled as if he guessed at my thoughts.

"Think of it," he continued. "Dahmer believed he was an artist. Wasn't he just becoming himself when he tortured and killed those boys? How could he do anything other than play out his hand? And if the game is madness, how can he be responsible or pronounced guilty for merely becoming what he is? Doesn't his integrity of *becoming* demand that he continue doing what he's doing?" His dark eyes seemed sincere. "Nietzsche's desire to find his own higher necessity was a quest for ultimate personal truth. I think his task was conceived in the womb of his own somatic distress. He was besieged with stomach ailments, poor eyesight, migraines, central nervous system disorders, and emotional trauma. I believe he felt lost. Accordingly, he turned his considerable wit toward the task of discovering a higher purpose that gave him a sense of himself. Noting that most people live aimless lives and 'drift about in borrowed manners,' he sought utility with his individuality. He wanted to eradicate those elements in his life that were not really him."

"I know these arguments," I said. "They're usually the sophistries of college students who want to trip up the professor."

Wraith shrugged. "Maybe. But the question makes sense. You have to think about it if you feel you're *on* the right path, but it's not a path that seems sane or normal. Nietzsche's *amor fati*—'embrace your fate'—is my call to rise to the occasion of *me*, whatever it means, no matter how difficult or dark the path."

"What does that mean for your vampirism, then?" I really didn't want to talk about insanity. Not out there alone with him. We could do that by e-mail some time. Vampirism just seemed like a safer topic because I'd been talking with people about it for months. It was ground I knew, particularly if we stuck to specifics. "How do you actually go about doing it? I mean, what's the actual practice of it? How do you drink blood?"

"Do you mean how do *I* do it? Or any of us?"

I shrugged to say it didn't matter; I was curious about this in general.

"To cut the skin," he said, "some use pushpins that they slip between their fingers. Some use sharp knives or scalpels. I have used the needle sticks with which physicians prick for blood tests. Razors are best, because they are exquisitely sharp, and I've already told you how I've used them. The victim never feels it. To enhance the pleasure, you have to keep the pain quick. I've even heard of using shark's teeth for this, or custom-made fangs. Some boys I know use squares of sharpened paper to inflict a paper cut. Under the influence of the moment, the victims can't feel it, especially if they've had drugs or alcohol.

"I find my prey in malls, grocery stores, bars, alleys, movie theaters, the beach, and once in an old graveyard. Frat houses and college dorms are notorious hangouts for vampires like me—great hunting grounds for boys already experimenting with new experiences and contrived initiation rites. But it's harder these days to get a really challenging 'kill.' GenXers are bored with life, mostly, and too easy. They have few hang-ups about sex, so they don't have the inner conflicts and complications that fuel really hot encounters. If I can get them to think it will be different, or at least temporarily exciting, they might put themselves into it."

"How do you do this sort of thing safely?" I asked. "I mean, you can't exactly use a condom. Do you just rely on the other person telling you he's clean?"

"There is no real safe way to ingest blood orally. I take precautions: no flossing prior to the ritual, no mouth sores, cuts. I immediately swallow it to decontaminate it. Many carry some illness without knowing it, so I don't trust what they say."

"But it amazes me that the other boy would just let it happen—let himself be tied up, cut, fed from—it amazes me how far people will go for the ultimate sensation."

"Males are always looking for a new angle, just a little more pleasure. Some of them actually enjoy the razor's cut, a slight pinch on their aroused flesh, and the sucking makes it even hotter. I believe it's impossible to avoid a soul connection. One body cannot touch another without attachments. This may be from some female element in me. I view women as starting the sex act in the mind and then moving toward detailed, stimulating foreplay."

"And what does vampirism actually mean to you? What's the big picture for your life?"

"For many years," said Wraith, "I lived a life of secrecy, loving hard and then disconnecting so no one would discover what I was. Like a vampire who slips up beside you, takes you in unparalleled passion, and then vanishes into the night. This maneuver kept my world intact, but it forced me to live falsely to everyone. Of course, others understand vampirism differently. I think Anne Rice, who has influenced many, has snatches of brilliance, glimpses of genuine vampirism, but her vampires seem to be representations of her own demons. She seems unable to get their balance quite right. They're too surreal. It's the familiarity that breeds contempt that truly terrifies me.

"Familiarity is what a human being sees of himself in a real vampire. The uncanny element that Freud described is what I mean—so familiar, so disgusting, but so *us*. This makes what's horrible in our lives just another day's look at the familiar—and it begins to romance us. I've never seen a writer of vampire stories really capture this well.

"My intuition about vampires is that there is an empty place in the heart, a black hole that vampires are trying to fill with the 'stuff' of others, to drain them in order to irrigate the heart's desert sands.

"I think the deepest truth of human life is despair. I was conceived in despair. I was immediately aware of my difference, the inescapable Other rooted deep within, and I've make repeated attempts to be rid of it. I'm determined to be accepted, but intuitively know I never will be, so I've learned to define myself in patterns of despair, like the vampire. Genuine vampirism is a desperate cauldron bubbling with sweet blood."

Okay, he'd done it again. He'd turned the conversation back to his potential for madness, so I asked him, "Have you ever been to therapy?"

He seemed annoyed by this question. "I've talked to a therapist. He wanted to hypnotize me."

"And what happened? Did you tell him about the blood-drinking?"

"I told him a little. Nothing to satisfy him or truly reveal anything."

"Did you go into a trance?"

"Yes, but I was still in control over what I said to him. He claimed that my mind was too focused and 'extraneously controlled' for him to access my inner being. I was mostly toying with him, playing with his interest in me. He wanted to try it again, but I refused."

"I know how to do it. What if I were to put you under?"

"No way. It's bullshit and it's unreliable. Never again, not by anyone."

4

We'd come to an impasse. I sensed that I'd irritated him, but I wanted to keep going along this track. "Don't you think there's something self-destructive in what you do?" I knew this sounded judgmental, but I wanted to ask it anyway. "Could it be about self-hatred?"

Wraith didn't react much. He didn't seem to mind the question. "I have a self-destructive streak, I admit. I tend to walk too close to the edge, peering down the cliff into the uncertainty below. I tend to sabotage myself. I also have a black, mean streak that sometimes feels like

I'm possessed. It accompanies me on the hunt. I 'kill' my prey by extinguishing their power. I absorb it into my own. I kill their spirit, in effect, through coerced submission. I conquer them so completely that they are not content to just offer themselves to me, they *beg* me to take them.

"In this way, I'm a cold-blooded killer, relentless in my pursuit of total domination. It's an ugly part of me and I have tried to eradicate it, but so far every attempt has failed. The role seems to be stitched into the fabric of my cells. The only time I'm submissive is when I pretend to be submissive in order to dominate."

"Do you think you could ever take it too far?" I asked. "Could your desire to dominate start to control you to the point where you'd really hurt someone?" Okay, this was personal, I admit. But it was also an appropriate question at this point. He'd mentioned a mean streak. I wanted to see just *how* mean.

"I have always feared that I could easily kill, if I chose to," he said, without changing his expression. "I sense a subtext in myself that could easily come forth, because death in every form fascinates me, especially violent deaths like suicide, tortures, or murder. I seem able to move between two poles on the continuum of violence.

"I am living my birthright, Katherine. I used to feel guilty over my manipulations, but I accept them now. I'm the Other in culture—a member of an increasingly political group of outsiders. Ritual secrecy in my vampirism follows gay protocols established in my youth. Since my life has always seemed like a vampire's life, I use that imagery. The 'prey' must be inexperienced, fresh to the touch. They usually have a volatile desire from hours of anticipatory fantasy. When driven to the edge, it erupts like lava spewing forth from the earth's fissures."

"Is the secrecy of it part of the eroticism?" I asked.

"Yes, very much so. Knowing things about myself that others don't know is sexy. It feels powerful. Clandestine. Like a conspiracy with myself. And it's a code for survival. Being gay and being a vampire are similar—you don't trust personal information with many people. Our lot is silent souls and furtive nods, suffering, and the intense desire to be known by just one person who can understand."

"But Christian understood you, didn't he? Did you ever deceive him?"

"I lied to him all the time—as he did to me. I *knew* what he was doing, and who he was doing it with. I *knew* the kinds of people with whom he was aligning himself. We never spoke of deception or lies to each other. We just assumed that we both knew what we knew and acted accordingly. It was a game. He agreed that deception was an effective method of survival and enjoyed perfecting it. He wanted this . . . and other things . . . from me.

"Christian was distrustful of outsiders, but his primary motivation for our isolation was our privacy. We were drunk on a mutual stupor, intensified through secret gestures. He thought of people as weak, pathetic creatures crawling around, their rusty hearts ready to bleed. He was more brutal than me. My heart was controlled by a restless soul, and he would say that he was exploiting the natural insanity buried there. He'd get me into the most extreme exercises in terror."

"For example, what would he do to coerce you?"

Wraith thought a moment, which gave me the opportunity to again change the tape. Then he looked up. "One January evening we hurried along the boardwalk to reach our evening's hunting grounds. The 'Game Room,' as we called it, was the best place to find young blood. The boys were mostly homeless, runaways and street punks. Some were orphans, miles from their guardians, maybe even on the prowl themselves. Most just wanted a buck for a bite or a bang.

"We met Adam there. He was a beautiful boy, possessing white-blond hair. The skin on his face was golden and silky smooth, as though he were made of tanned banana leaves. We actually called him the 'Banana Boy.' He liked us, mainly because we always gave him money. We hung out with Adam all the time, both of us hypnotized by his lusty brown eyes—eyes that pleaded for affection.

"That night we convinced Adam to tag along on a road trip. Drinking stolen Old Grandad's, we made our way to a place near here. Adam never saw it coming—the shovel, that is, from behind, where Christian struck him on the head. He fell to the ground hard, slamming into the dirt like a baby bird falling from its nest."

"What?" I was astonished. "You two hit him?"

"Christian did. He had told me once that he always loved it when birds fell out of the nest. He took out his knife and cut a hole in the back of Adam's blue cords, got down and raped him."

I was incredulous. "Just raped him? While you stood there?"

"Yes. And I knew what he wanted next. He wanted me to do the same. I didn't want to, so he said he'd do something terrible to Adam if

I didn't. Still, I refused, so he cut a branch from an ironwood nearby, and whittling the end, went to screw it into Adam's rectum. I screamed for him to stop, and he offered me a deal. If I would fuck Adam, he would let him live. So I did. I didn't have any choice. He used to say I was weak. That I cared too much to do this thing right, and he wanted to cure me of it.

"Then he flipped Adam over and hoisted him over his shoulder. Walking to an oak tree, he tied Adam's hands and legs to the trunk and cut his clothes off. Adam's head hung low, eyes rolling back in his head, and then he started to come back to us. This was just what Christian wanted—a conscious victim.

"He pulled his knife through layers of soft flesh, slicing into Adam's forearms and thighs. The thin red fluid hurried out of his flesh, as if trying to escape the scene. It was as though the blood knew what was about to happen. Christian started to lick the flowing red from Adam's thighs.

"But he couldn't restrain himself. He wanted a piece of this boy to bring back to our place. He sliced into Adam's calf and removed a sliver of his muscle, carefully excising it from his leg. Adam screamed so hard he passed out. There wasn't much blood. And Christian cauterized the wound with his lighter. Wrapping the hot flesh around his nose, he breathed in the odors. I was worried about Adam developing an infection, so I cut him down and carried him to the car. Christian said something like, 'Let's just dump him and find another to kill— he'll live and he won't dare come around the Game Room anymore.' But I needed to be sure he was all right. At our place, I bathed and cared for Adam while Christian walked out. He was all right. He woke up and left as fast as he could."

I was silent, trying to absorb what I'd just heard, more than a little horrified. Wraith had made Christian seem so mesmerizing, only to now reveal this pathetically ugly side. Finally I asked, "When Christian did something like this, weren't you afraid of him?"

"Yes, very afraid. But I knew I was safe. And, besides . . ."

"What?"

"A part of me . . . felt at home."

"At home. This stuff appealed to you?"

He nodded. "It did, in a way. You have to try to understand. That's why I'm telling this to you. Because I think you *can* understand. There was a certain beauty in his madness. A wild, exciting freedom. In many ways, despite what he did, it was intoxicating. I hate what he did, but I loved that he could do it."

"How many times did he do something like this?"

Wraith shrugged. "I don't know. Fifteen or twenty, maybe."

"Fifteen or twenty! And you didn't think there was something wrong with him?"

"I knew there was. I knew it very soon after moving in with him. But whatever was wrong with him was wrong with me, too. We were a team."

"But you didn't initiate that thing with Adam. You didn't even want to do it. He made you. Were you just afraid to leave him?"

"I was very frightened to leave him and he knew it."

Wraith had already mentioned that he'd become a captive. Now I knew what he meant—sort of. "Did you get angry with him? Did you try to confront him when he no longer had leverage against you with some victim?"

"I was angry, but with him *and* me. I was angry with myself because I *did* enjoy it, and angry with him for exposing me to it."

"And you think there was beauty in it? Isn't that what you just said?"

"I can't clearly elaborate on the quality of the energy involved. Maybe, if I tell you about another time, you'll see what I mean."

I didn't want to hear about another one, but he launched into it.

"We were riding in the car and we had a boy with us who was drunk. Christian opened the door while I was driving and held the boy out the door and ground his face against the pavement. I didn't know what he was doing. I thought the boy was vomiting, but Christian was actually . . . well, what he said was that he was toning up his skin or something like that."

"My God! And what happened?"

"Christian pulled him back in and I thought he was dead. I asked Christian if he'd killed him. But he was just drunk, passed out. I think we left him wherever we were going. I imagine he woke up and had no idea what'd happened to him."

"And that was exciting to you?" I wondered if I were really talking to someone with any rational sense. The spirit of Jared, Eric and his hand, the bizarre coven, and now this. And he seemed determined to convince me that something so horrific could inspire great pleasure.

"It was the fact that he could just think up something like that and then do it. He was so free. He was fully present to what he wanted. That's what a vampire is. Fully present to his own hunger and his own survival, no matter how vulnerable the victim. That's why the vampire is so powerful to us. He has complete license. He *can* be seductive and charming, but he can also just be aggressive."

"And you think Christian embodied the vampire."

"He did. He knew the vampire's soul better than anyone I'd ever met . . . or have met since."

"He seems so full of hate. What was good about him? Was there anything?"

"I don't know, as I look back. He had a schizoid character. There were times he wasn't that way. There were days when he was kind and thoughtful. I'd even see him help people, like carrying some elderly man's groceries to his car for him. I'd be amazed."

"Is it possible, then, that there were times when he wished he wasn't like this? Maybe it was some awful compulsion?"

"When he'd do something nice, I used to think, 'This is his Wally and Beaver side. This is the boy he used to be somewhere in his past.' I've never known what changed him. I used to think that he just woke up one night and shifted into his second self. That the evil in him just turned itself on. I thought he was possessed. I said that to him once and he laughed and said, 'Yeah, maybe I am. And so what if I am?'"

"And yet you stayed."

"I can't say it enough. There was an *excitement* about being with him, a thrill, a constant mystery and unpredictability. There was much to gain. And really, you can get used to anything, to abuse, to misery. You get to love your pain. I've always been drawn to it, anyway. I'm subconsciously tuned in to things that can hurt me. And there was a certain kind of glory to his maniacal life. He thought he was magical, even romantic. That's what drew me to him. I thought he was a genius of madness. There were so many hundreds of moments of nuance and clarity. I could see it. I have a hard time conveying it, but I think if you'd have been there with me, you'd have seen it, too. The way he thought, the way he tied ideas together. It was all very appealing, even when I was appalled. But I could see it as a poet sees it—there was no right or wrong to it, there was just the brilliant pattern and expression. Christian's life was the picture of my own inner verse—the things that drew me. What he figured was, what's there not to appreciate?"

I didn't know what to say. This was an eloquent appeal to accept something that was just *wrong*. Yet out there in the dark, listening to this charismatic, excited young man, it seemed easy to lose one's moral center. I needed to shove something at him, anything, to keep him from convincing me of the amorality of poetry. "The truth is," I said, "the person with the deepest wound, the greatest degree of pathology, defines the relationship. He led the dance."

Wraith saw that he had lost me. He shrugged. "Well, I think that's true. What we did was more about him than me. But I went along. And I could still find beauty in it."

"Then you have part of his soul. You must have the potential to do this, too. Not just participate. To initiate it."

"I don't know. Maybe. But he fed off my pain. That's what set him in motion. He was excited by it."

"How?"

"He vampirized me while he vamped our victim. He was getting a double high. I can remember things he would do just to injure me, for the sake of sucking from my suffering for his own pleasure. Christian found it more exciting to see me abuse Adam than to see me squirm while he damaged him, because it hurt me more. I feel other people's pain—all of my life I have been able to feel it. Christian thought he'd eventually turn me and we'd have a great time together. I'd create the scenarios with my imagination and he'd find ways to play them out."

"That sounds a lot like how the British killer, Dennis Nilsen, described what he was doing," I pointed out. "He said he created dreams into which real men stepped, and they never really got hurt because the laws of the dream were unreal. Is that what you think?"

Wraith looked at me as if measuring how much more he wanted to say, and I had the alarming impression that he'd barely begun to reveal the full extent of Christian's "beautiful madness."

"You don't really believe this, do you?" he remarked.

I was about to protest that of course I did, but I had to concede, "I don't really know. It sounds a bit fantastic. Jared. Michael. And now your lover of several years a sociopath."

"We can stop, if you like. I don't feel that I really have to tell you anything more."

I'd been a therapist long enough to spot the hidden challenge in these words. I could get in the car and leave now. I had enough material. And I was beginning to think that my childhood fear of the emergence of the hidden monster was about to happen. So I could just go ahead and get out of there.

Yet the same thing that had inspired me to become a therapist was working on me. I still didn't know why we'd come to that spot. I didn't really know why Wraith had begun this little game with me. I wasn't sure what he was getting out of confessing—and I wanted to know.

"No, don't stop," I said. "I want to hear it. It's just that, well . . . I mean, there's something about this that doesn't quite make sense. Why didn't Christian find that kind of thing in the others? In Michael, for instance. He sounds like he'd have been a more willing partner for Christian than you were. Whatever happened to him? Where was he during all this?"

"Michael . . ." Wraith took a deep breath before he told me. "Not long after I met him, Michael was found stabbed to death on the floor of his home."

CHAPTER EIGHTEEN

vampire crimes

I

In 1986 a young woman accepted a ride from a friendly businessman, who then held her prisoner for twenty-two hours. He needed her blood, he said, and he drained it from her into a glass jar and drank it. "I'm a vampire," he told her. She managed to escape and notify police, who arrested a man they suspected in numerous slayings in neighboring states. The following year in San Francisco, a jogger was grabbed and held in a van for an hour while a man drank his blood.

I knew about these things. Since I'd started this venture in response to a potential crime, I'd been reading about how some people develop a blood-lust and impose their need on others to the point of violence. In my opinion, it's not what vampire culture is about, but there will always be those on the edge who make a bad mark that gets generalized to others. I knew there were kids who wanted desperately to be vampires, and some of them were going to carry it too far.

Apparently, the National Clearinghouse on Satanic Crime in America (NCSCA) associates vampiric acts with satanism, because among the publications offered on their Web site is a *Vampirism Awareness Manual*. In fact, in 1993 three teenagers in West Memphis, Arkansas, formed a satanic cult that reportedly killed and ate dogs, orchestrated orgies, and finally killed three eight-year-olds and drank their blood. Ringleader Damien Wayne Echols claimed that he also drank blood from his sex partners to gain power for his sorcery and to "feel like God."

Not all—not even most—people who view themselves as vampires also see themselves as satanists, though some claim to have rituals in their gatherings that show a darker occult influence. The vampire image was once thought to be satanic, and that's why it cast no reflection in a mirror—the vampire had no soul that God might be able to save. This association still inspires people who want to do evil, to do it in the name of vampirism.

Norine Dresser, Richard Noll, Gordon Melton, and others who write about the vampire scene have documented vampire crimes going back several centuries. Fritz Haarmann, John George Haigh, Elizabeth Bathory—these are names that every vampirologist knows well. They did their bloody deeds in Europe, but we've had a few notorious vampire killers right here.

Richard Trenton Chase was known in the late seventies as the "Vampire of Sacramento." He began by killing a woman, cutting out her entrails, stuffing her mouth with dog feces, and drinking her blood. He also smeared his face with it. Next he killed a family, including an infant, and was quickly identified. In his apartment, police discovered evidence that he seemed to be planning to kill over forty more times that same year. He killed near his own home, and his criterion for entering a house was merely whichever door was not locked, because into those homes that were locked he was not invited. How vampiric!

During the second of Chase's incarcerations in psychiatric facilities, he purchased rabbits and drank their blood. At times he tried to inject rabbit blood into his own veins. He also bit the heads off birds and was known to the hospital staff as Dracula. Once he was free and without supervision, he also purchased or stole dogs and cats to torture them and drink their blood. He did these things because he believed that he was being poisoned by soap dishes. That is, if the bottom of a piece of soap in his dish was wet, it meant his blood was turning to powder and he would need to replenish it. Otherwise, all of his energies would be depleted.

Chase was sentenced to die, but was found dead in his cell in 1980 after swallowing an overdose of antidepressants.

James Riva, who claimed to hear the voice of a vampire, shot his grandmother four times with bullets that he had painted gold, and drank her blood from the wound in order to get eternal life. To some degree, he claimed, it was self-defense, because he was convinced she was drinking his blood while he was asleep, as were other vampires. He believed that everyone was a vampire and that he needed to do something to become like everyone else. The secret, he was told, was to kill someone and drink the blood. Fascinated with vampires since the age of thirteen, he drew pictures of violent acts and began to eat things with a blood-like consistency. He killed animals, including a horse, to drink their blood. He also punched a friend in the nose and tried to spear another in order to get blood from them, and claimed that he had attacked strangers to get it. He stopped drinking blood in prison, he said, because he couldn't get enough and he thought his body, adapted to human tissue consumption, was metabolizing his.

The cases of vampire crimes go on and on. Some obviously have other agendas besides just drinking blood.

Early in January of 1997, Jon C. Bush, a thin, brown-haired, twenty-six-year-old man who called himself a vampire, was sentenced in Virginia Beach to twenty-six years in prison for sexually molesting eight teenage girls whom he had invited into his vampire "family." First he had recruited high school boys, whom he had urged to bring in the girls, the youngest of whom was thirteen. The girls said that Bush had told them about a role-playing card game called "The Masquerade: Eternal Night," in which participants assumed the roles of ancient vampires in the thirty-member vampire family, all under Bush's leadership. Members sometimes painted their faces white and their lips and fingernails black for excursions to local malls. Bush told the girls they could become vampires by having oral sex or sexual intercourse with him, or by letting him bite them hard just below the breasts. He also insisted that he needed to drain energy from them through sexual contact.

The game-playing community was angry at media suggestions that role-playing causes such acts. In fact, no physical contact is permitted in legitimate groups. Greg Fountain, director of games marketing for White Wolf, which makes the "Masquerade" products, says, "No form of media from role-playing to movies to books is going to cause an aberrant or deviant behavior in a healthy, normal person. We don't feel the Beatles were responsible for the Manson murders because they sang 'Helter Skelter.' We don't think Stephen King was responsible for the murders where 'Redrum' was written."

Even so, there are those who believe that enacting evil through a game can give someone the idea, and even the courage, to carry out violence in real life. On November 24, 1997, the television program *Dateline* profiled the murder trial in Springfield, Missouri, of thirty-five-year-old schoolteacher Jon Feeney, accused of brutally killing his wife Cheryl and two children—including an eighteen-month-old daughter. The prosecution claimed that he was a man with a secret life. He'd had several extramarital affairs, and one of the prosecution's arguments was that, since the seventies, Feeney had been an avid member of local role-playing chapters. In recent years, he had moved from "Dungeons and Dragons" to sponsoring teenagers at the high school who played "Vampire: The Masquerade." Game sheets were found in his desk at school, although he denied any participation. The prosecution pointed out that "Vampire" explicitly recognizes the psychotic acts of some vampires—they "attempt to destroy everything and anything in sight"—and that Cheryl Feeney had been left in a posed position, suggestive of someone playing a degrading game. Two marks slit into her cheek looked like the bite of a vampire, and Manson-esque letters written on the wall were attributed to Feeney as part of the game. The letters, scrawled in paint, looked like an *m* and a *v*, which they interpreted as "master vampire." Kim Rey, one of the women with whom Feeney had had an affair, claimed that she felt controlled by him—that he had convinced her to participate in a kinky sexual party and had used mind control to teach her how to lie, which he called "eraser memory."

Although the jury found Feeney not guilty, several of those who spoke out afterward indicated they didn't think him innocent, either. In fact, some on the jury believed he was indeed the brutal murderer, but felt that the prosecution had not proven its case.

Feeney is not the only one to bring this game to national attention via a high-profile crime; yet a group led by sixteen-year-old Rod Ferrell in 1996, which also cast a bad light on "The Masquerade," only indicated that the game itself didn't encourage these extreme behaviors. Ferrell had to actually disengage from White Wolf's parameters and create his own scenarios to fully motivate and justify certain brutal acts.

Ferrell, from Murray, Kentucky, home of the national Boy Scout

Museum, had lived briefly in Eustis, Florida, where he had met Heather Wendorf. Back in Kentucky, he got involved with a chapter of "Vampire: The Masquerade," but he wanted something decidedly more dangerous, so he formed the Vampire Clan. A friend of his and reportedly a fellow clan member, John Goodman, recalled that Ferrell had become obsessed with opening the Gates of Hell, which meant to him that he would have to kill a large number of people in order to consume their souls. Ferrell had also claimed to be able to smell blood through walls.

Ferrell was arrested but not held for breaking into a local animal shelter, freeing the dogs, injuring many of them, and ritually killing two puppies. "They apparently like to suck blood," said police detective Mike Jump about the Clan. "They cut each other's arms and suck the blood. They cut up small animals and suck the blood. They honestly believe they're vampires." According to an Associated Press report, the legs were pulled off of one of the dogs.

But they didn't stop with that. Richard Wendorf, forty-nine, and Naoma Ruth Queen (Wendorf), fifty-three, of Eustis, Florida, were found beaten to death by a crowbar in their home on November 25, 1996, Thanksgiving Day. Wendorf had been beaten more than twenty times about the head and face. Cigarette burns in the shape of a *V*, with two dots on either side, were found on Wendorf's body, and Ferrell had told friends that his sign was a *V*, with dots on each side to signify clan members. A bloody bootprint and skin beneath Queen's fingernails also tied Ferrell to the crime. The early news reports suggested that the Wendorfs' fifteen-year-old daughter Heather had plotted with Ferrell and three of his friends to murder her parents. Wendorf and the others were subsequently arrested in Baton Rouge, Louisiana, after leaving Eustis. Roderick Ferrell, Howard Scott Anderson, seventeen, Charity Lynn Keesee (also known as Sara Remington), sixteen, and Dana Cooper, nineteen, were caught in the Wendorfs' stolen Ford Explorer when one of the girls called her parents and revealed their whereabouts. In the trunk, police found vampire novels, a book called *The Ultimate Vampire*, a book on magic (*Necronomicon*), and three Disney movies.

Ferrell confessed on videotape, in a bored manner, just how he had killed both people. He said it gave him a "rush" that made him feel "like a god." He also said that killing is a way of life and that humans are the worst predators of all.

In a grand jury hearing, Heather, fifteen, was cleared of all charges, although the other four were still held for trial—Ferrell and Anderson for murder and Keesee and Cooper as accessories. Heather claimed that she and Keesee were riding in Anderson's car when the murders took place. She had no idea what Ferrell was planning, and was not even sure that he had actually done it until she saw him playing with her mother's pearl necklace. Later, however, she admitted that Ferrell had discussed the murder with her and she had told him not to harm them.

The same day her parents were murdered, she had exchanged blood with Ferrell in a cemetery ritual in order to "cross over" and become a vampire. Because of this, she believed that "it's kind of like they made you and you're kind of under them." He was her sire. He was the boss. Reportedly, she had also told friends that she had been a demon in a past life and that she talked with spirits during blood-drinking rituals. When dating Ferrell, she viewed him as a kindred spirit and awaited the day when he would return to Florida so they could be together. She named her cat Vesago, a name that Ferrell had adopted after a prince of hell. She had dyed her hair purple and at school dangled a Barbie doll from her backpack on a noose. She allegedly had confided to a friend she wished her parents were dead, especially after they stopped Ferrell's collect calls to her, and had once asked her older sister Jennifer if she ever thought about killing their parents. She supposedly mentioned that Rod could kill people, if Jennifer ever needed that done. Heather later denied all of this, although letters she had written showed that she believed part of her soul was "the essence of vengeance, hate, and destruction."

Apparently, Ferrell had decided to kill Wendorf's parents before arriving. He had visited another girl in Eustis and had alluded to "unfinished business" and the "fun" they were going to have the following night.

Prosecutors said they would seek the death penalty for Anderson and Ferrell. Initially Ferrell told reporters from the *Orlando Sentinel*—at whom he stuck out his tongue when taken to jail—that a rival vampire clan had done the killings. Then he claimed to have been treated by psychiatrists for multiple personality disorder and to have experienced blackout episodes. The defense prepared to argue that Ferrell was borderline psychotic, had been sexually abused as a child, and was under the influence of vampirism and practices of the occult.

Then from Murray, Kentucky, came news of another bizarre but related case. Rod Ferrell's mother, Sondra Gibson, thirty-five, was indicted in November 1997 for allegedly writing sexually explicit letters to a teenage boy to entice him into sex as an initiation rite. She pleaded guilty to a felony charge of unlawful transaction with a minor. In the letter she stressed how she longed to be near him and to become a vampire so she could be his forever. She asked him to "cross me over and I will be your bride for eternity and you my sire." Her defense attorney claimed that she was mentally ill at the time. She told psychologists that members of the Vampire Clan would come to her home for group orgies. One member allegedly raped her during vampire ritual sessions and insisted she "cross over." She believed the group had supernatural powers and claimed that they had drugged her. She had allowed Ferrell to set up his room as a satanic shrine, with pentagrams on the floor.

Despite all of this, shortly before Ferrell was scheduled to be tried, his maternal grandparents claimed he was a good boy led astray by a bad girl, and that not only was he innocent of these deeds, but had the makings of a great spiritual leader.

As preparations began for the trial, some details emerged in the press of what apparently had happened the day of the murders. Anderson was in the house, but it was Ferrell who swung the crowbar at a sleeping Richard Wendorf. Ferrell then hit Queen in the head when she walked into the room and threw hot coffee on him. The girls (who had not been present) then met up with Ferrell and Anderson, and they all piled into the Ford Explorer to run away to New Orleans. Heather reportedly claimed it was Keesee who told her that her parents were dead, after conferring with Ferrell, and he later told her some of the gruesome details of the slaying. When they were caught, there were fresh scars on the arms of these Clan members, as if they'd been drinking blood that day.

Florida does not have a "diminished capacity" law that would allow for some kind of mental illness from occult influences. Thus, when a private lab found a DNA match between Ferrell and the blood found under Queen's fingernails, defense attorneys came up with a variety of possible psychiatric syndromes that would mitigate the penalty, such as suffering from a schizotypal personality disorder (a pattern of impaired capacity for close relationships and of perceptual distortions) and from his belief in vampirism.

During jury selection for Ferrell's trial, which was to take place first, Ferrell drew gargoyles with crayons and paid little attention. Then on February 5, 1998, just as the prosecutor began his introductory remarks, Ferrell pleaded guilty to the charges of murder, armed burglary, and robbery. Outside the court, his mother alluded to the vampire's immortality when she proclaimed, "We live forever!" The following week, the penalty phase began.

One of the defense witnesses was a boy, Steven Murphy, to whom Ferrell's mother also wrote love notes, who claimed that vampirism was a chosen lifestyle. He himself was "Prince of the City" (a White Wolf–inspired title of vampire royalty). He had known the murders were not about vampirism, he said, because Ferrell hadn't bled the victims. Before leaving the courtroom, he blew Ferrell a kiss.

Ferrell's father, who had not seen him in ten years, took the stand, but reports indicated that he would not even look at his son. Ferrell's mother was also a witness, but had little credibility. Some people felt she should be on trial, too, though she later insisted she "was a better mother than most."

It did not take long for the jury to recommend the death penalty. The circuit judge agreed, and on Friday, February 28, he sentenced Ferrell to the chair. He also recommended that the grand jury reconvene and look more closely at Heather Wendorf's involvement. "There is genuine evil in this world," he said. "There's a dark side and a light side competing in all of us."

Only a week later, on March 7, the Associated Press ran a story that indicated that Heather Wendorf had accepted one thousand dollars from true crime writer Aphrodite Jones in good faith toward a book to be called *The Embrace* and a possible movie deal.

In March, Anderson pleaded guilty to his part in the murders in exchange for two life sentences. Ferrell's lawyers argued in court for a reduced sentence for him to life imprisonment, but the judge blocked their bid. Dana Cooper's lawyers succeeded in moving her trial to St. Augustine, Florida. As of this writing, her trial and that of Charity Keesee were pending.

The vampire connection led to a flurry of media attention directed at the White Wolf Game Studio. On December 9, White Wolf posted a statement to a number of Internet groups urging anyone contacted to give calm, rational explanations of role-playing. They pointed out that there had never been any official connection between these murders and the game, and that largely, role-playing was safe.

Role-players do understand that vampires, by definition, are required to assault people to survive and grow in power. When players become members of a vampire clan, they are fantasizing that they are blood-sucking monsters. Most can walk away, knowing it's only a game that can have cathartic value, but a few enter the game arena *because* it expresses feelings they already have of rage, self-hatred, or any number of violence-supporting emotions. They bring their illness in with them.

2

With all of that in mind—that adopting the vampire identification in its full antisocial manifestation can encourage a mentally ill person to do real violence—I wanted to know more about Michael, the vampire leader who was murdered. He had been in a cult full of people who viewed themselves as vampires. Although they (if they were real) hadn't been playing a structured, commercial game, they'd been acting out a dangerous identity through rituals and mythologies; and now one of them was dead. That was a turning of the tables, surely. A murdered vampire. Was it a vampire hunter or inter-vampire rivalry?

"What happened?" I asked Wraith.

"He was found lying stabbed and bloody on the floor of his living room, on his beautiful oriental rug." Wraith's demeanor was nonchalant, as if this death was to be expected, or was just one of the side effects of being involved in such activities. "A gorgeous royal purple and white rug. I loved that rug."

"I'm sure you did. Now, what happened?"

"The knife was not at the scene and was never found, but that's because the killer took it with him. Michael was stabbed in the rib cage and the heart numerous times."

"Who did it? Do you know?"

"The rumor was that, since I had something to gain, I was the one who killed him. So I could have his house and be the cult leader. The police ruled it a crime of passion, a murder unsolved. Some of the Others said that Jared had killed him through me. Of course, this wasn't true."

"No? You didn't kill him?"

He shook his head, still looking away. "No."

"Have you ever killed someone?" I asked.

His eyes met mine, his face impassive. "It upsets me to even think about an animal dying. I once saw a bird on the road and I got out of the car and cried over it. I couldn't bear it."

"But you said you liked the violence that Christian committed."

"That's not the same."

He hadn't really answered, but I wasn't sure I wanted an answer. I was getting a little more nervous about him. Even if he was making it all up, these were rather savage thoughts. And I wasn't so sure he was making it up. I'd become more convinced of that as the night had progressed.

"So, then, did anyone ever discover who killed Michael?"

He inclined his head and pursed his lips. Then he said, "I believe . . . that it was Christian."

"Christian! Why?"

"To have complete access to me, to get rid of competition. Christian claimed he needed what I possessed, which was an intuitive manipulation ability. I could bend the will of others to my own."

"But I thought he had his own psychic powers. And I thought he bent your will to his."

"He did, but he didn't believe in himself. He always looked to me. He wanted to be me. And he didn't want Michael to claim me."

"But he never told you? You never asked?"

Wraith shook his head. "We never talked about it."

"You *never* discussed Michael's murder?"

"No."

This was so bizarre, but clearly he wasn't going to yield, so I asked, "What happened to the coven? Did you take over?"

"No. I withdrew."

"Wasn't that a betrayal?"

"No. I had attained a certain untouchable status. I had given them structure and ritual. It didn't matter that I cut my ties with them. I can always go back."

"I don't understand why you thought it was Christian, though. He seems mean, but why do you think he's a killer?"

"Come with me." He pushed himself away from his car. "I'll show you something."

The moment was at hand. I was to find out now what we were doing there, but suddenly I didn't want to go anywhere. I didn't want to leave the car. It was dark out there and we were in the woods somewhere. If he led me too far away, I'd be lost. And he was giving me the impression that there was a body buried out there somewhere.

"It's just down by the river," he said, as if reading my thoughts. "It's not far. You want to know the heart of a vampire or not?"

There wasn't any real reason not to go, and that was a rather provocative question, so I said, "You lead the way." I vowed not to let him get behind me, not to turn my back to him at any time. I touched the little charm on my earring to be sure it was still there, and followed him.

He took a trail through some weeds down to the river's edge and pointed out toward the glistening water. I spotted a loon and remembered a play I'd seen in which a loon had been used as a symbol for suicide. Its long, wailing night cry is often mistaken for a human scream. I wished it would fly away.

Wraith walked a few steps away and leaned against a rock. He was quiet for a while, as if thinking about something that had happened there. I was starting to shake a little. I didn't like this, any of this. Then he started telling a story that I was in no way prepared to hear.

"Listening to the crickets is one of my favorite things," he said softly, "and I was lying in the grass one evening behind our apartment, looking into the sky—just listening to the bugs and thinking. Christian was on his way home and supper was ready, a spicy chicken and rice, á la New Orleans. Christian loved it. He said it made him feel sexy and passionate.

"I heard those keys—he always twirled his keys. I looked up and he was standing over me, looking down and smiling. 'Let's go,' he said.

"'Where?'

"'Just for a ride.'

"I was a little irritated, because I'd made a great supper and planned a romantic evening. But Christian was always surprising me with something or other, so I just got up and went with him.

"'Where are we going?' I asked as we pulled out of the complex.

"'I've got something to take care of,' he said, 'and I want you with me.'

"This was a little disconcerting. I thought to myself: 'He's taking you to see or do something you really don't want to be involved in.'

But I didn't say another word, just small talk about our respective days, until he drove out to a wooded area. I tried not to cross him. He scared me sometimes."

Wraith gestured around him. "He brought me here. I couldn't figure out why. We'd only come here once or twice together. I asked him where he thought he was going this time of night. He just looked over at me and grinned. He stopped the car right up there, where our cars are parked. He got out and walked down this way. I stayed in the car, as I had no intention of getting out without knowing what was going on.

"Almost immediately a man appeared from the brush and started to talk to Christian. The sun was very low, but I could see the man was heavyset and scruffy-looking. They seemed to know each other. Christian glanced in my direction, so I decided to get out and have a closer look. Really I just wanted to wander in the trees for a bit while he settled whatever business he had with this character. As I stepped out of the car, I heard the tone of the conversation. It wasn't pleasant. Christian said, 'This is the end of it.' And with that, he pulled out a knife and quickly thrust the blade into the man's throat, slicing across the neck completely, from one side to the other."

Wraith stopped talking and looked at me.

I was stunned. He had just described a murder—one that had taken place right here where we were standing. A hideous, cold-blooded murder, done by his lover. My heart started to pound. I felt as if Christian might be somewhere close by, lurking and listening to what we were saying. Maybe in some kind of tandem setup that was meant to trap me. I felt, somehow, that I was in danger. I took a step back. Wraith seemed not to notice as he continued:

"The other man staggered after Christian, but I could see he was bleeding all over his shirt. Pressing his hands against his neck to try and stop the blood, he was reaching into his pocket for what I thought was a gun. I darted toward the two of them, in a panic, not knowing what to do or say. I screamed, 'Christian, what the hell are you doing? Oh my God . . . you've murdered him. What are you doing?'

"He just looked at me, smiled, and then turned back on the man. By now the bleeding figure had fallen to the ground. He was dying and Christian hovered over him, watching. Then, to my astonishment, he bent toward his neck and licked some of the blood from the wound. The man was aghast at what Christian was doing, but he was too weak to do anything about it. He wasn't dead yet, but he was in no condition to resist. I could hear him gasping and choking, through garbled sounds of blood and air.

"I didn't know what to do. I fell to my knees, right where you're standing, and started to cry. I was sobbing so hard I couldn't see anymore. Then I felt a hand on my neck, which startled me. Christian was trying to comfort me. I couldn't believe it. He'd just killed this man, and the body was lying a hundred feet from me, probably not even cold yet, and he was there telling me that this is no big deal.

"I got up and start running into the woods, up that way." Wraith pointed up the path down which we'd just come. "I knew my way around so I figured I could outrun him and hide. I was feeling strange, confusing things inside and it scared me." He stood up straight and gestured. "Come on," he said. "I'll show you where I went."

By this time, I nearly couldn't breathe. I didn't want to go anywhere except back to the car. I certainly didn't want to go deeper into the woods with Wraith. But he was already walking back up the path, and I wasn't about to be left behind. I glanced at the loon. It was still there, watching me.

I followed Wraith until he came to a large oak tree with huge outspread branches. He scrambled up the damp trunk until he was seated in the tree, some fifteen feet up. I looked around, feeling vulnerable. The car was not that far away. I could go. I could just leave. But I didn't. Instead, I went partway up the tree and seated myself in a position that would allow me to jump down easily and run if I needed to. Wraith looked down at me and I could barely see his face. He seemed to be in a state of turmoil, but I could not really tell.

"I came up here," he said. "I used to come to this same spot as a boy and sit in this tree. Jared would talk to me here, so this is where I went. I leaned over and vomited down on the ground and then started crying uncontrollably. I was numb all over. I didn't want to speak to Christian, didn't want to see him or ride back with him. I was scared of him. I thought that now he was going to kill me. If he found me, he'd kill me—I knew it. I was thinking all kinds of thoughts and I was curling up in a ball and leaning against my favorite knot. I didn't know what to do or think."

"So you really saw this," I said. "You saw Christian murder someone, just like that. And drink his blood. Why would he do that in front of you? Why would he do it at all?"

"I don't know."

I thought he did, but I didn't press it right then. He seemed caught up in the memory of his horror. He seemed to want very much to impress me with his reaction to what had happened, that he'd been truly horrified.

"So, there I was, in love with a boy who murders as easily as he breathes."

Now I had a real chill, and it wasn't from the night air. I didn't say anything as he went on, but I was growing physically ill.

"Christian found me," he said. "He climbed up to where you're sitting and told me I'd misunderstood. He came closer, gripped my arm, and took my hand while I was crying. He rubbed gently across my fingers, telling me, 'It's just business. Please get down. Please?'

"I didn't know what he meant by 'business,' but I could guess. I'd always thought he was doing these things, that maybe he was hurting or even killing people for money. He always seemed to have money, but I didn't know where it came from. I realized that must have been some kind of deal gone bad and it was his job to finish it. He was some kind of hit man, and it conveniently fed his vampire appetites.

"Christian dropped down out of the tree and pleaded with me again. I slowly made my way down and walked back to the car. He grabbed me around the waist, but I wouldn't talk. We got into the car and started to drive away. I couldn't help it, I had to look back—and all I could think of was the harsh penalty for Lot's wife when she looked back. But I did it anyway. The man was still lying there, jellied blood around his throat like raspberry jam. I was sure the flies had found him.

"'Are you just going to leave him there?' I asked.

"'No, I'll have it taken care of,' Christian said. 'Don't you worry your pretty little face, baby boy.' He proceeded to explain that it was business and he was just doing his job. The man knew he had it coming. It was nothing.

"'Fine,' I said, 'but why did you bring me with you?'

"Christian put his hand on my knee, turned, and with the most haunting eyes—beautifully bizarre—said, 'Because I knew you would secretly love it. You're me, just with a different face, sweetheart. We are the same.'

"And with that I said nothing else, just sat staring into the passing woods. The fireflies were everywhere, little torches flitting all over a thick carpet. It was beautiful."

Wraith stopped talking and looked away. I was a little stunned.

"You mean you just went home?" I asked.

"Yes. We went home and Christian left. I don't know where he went. I went to bed and cried some more. I fell asleep, and when I woke up, I was convinced it was a dream. I wanted him to tell me it was a dream. I asked him to, and he got annoyed. He wouldn't talk about it. I never knew what happened to the body. I never saw anything in the papers. I guess Christian or someone went back there and dumped him into the river. I thought someone might find him, but I never heard anything else about it. So I just let it be a dream, until . . ."

I didn't want to ask, but I had to. "Were there others?"

Wraith looked back at me. Then he said, "About six weeks later, Christian took me with him to another scene, an abandoned warehouse on the edge of town. We took off our clothes before we entered. We often did things naked, but I didn't realize what we were about to do that night."

"Really? You really didn't guess? No hint of it from him after what you'd seen here?"

"No. I didn't think he'd do it again, not like that. And he was always surprising me with things. Good things. He knew I liked unusual experiences, things that pushed the boundary. So that night he took me to a musty old place and there hanging upside down, his feet tied by a rope, was a young male. That wasn't such a surprise, because we often played games like this with willing males. But this, apparently, was another 'enforcer' situation. I didn't realize that until afterward. The boy was wearing only his Levi's and his face was red, every capillary engorged with blood. Christian walked over and chewed on his neck so hard that he tore a small hole in his artery. Blood began to pour quickly from this boy. Christian knelt below him and let the blood drop onto him. He bathed his face in it. He drank what he wanted and then insisted I drink while he gave the boy sexual pleasure. So, Christian unzipped him and worked on him while I drank. The boy actually had an orgasm of sorts, much like that of the hanging victim who cums when the body is stressed. Remember the mandrake legends? When a man dies by hanging, he cums hard. Where the semen hits the ground and soaks in, a mandrake grows. Even in the throes of death, orgasm is very powerful. That's what dangerous sex is all about—going right to the edge.

"I expected Christian to cut him down before the situation got truly dangerous, but he let the boy drain and then turned and led me back to the car. I knew the boy was dying or dead. I was not surprised. I halfway expected something like this. But I was surprised at how aroused I had become during the experience. And Christian knew that it would have an effect on me."

"Wait, wait!" I said. "You knew that guy was dying, and you were excited? You'd just helped to murder him!"

"I didn't feel that I was. I mean, I didn't put him in that position. I just participated. And I didn't know it was about killing him."

"But you guessed, didn't you? I mean, you weren't surprised. And it excited you?"

"His blood was like any other, but there was a stronger sense of excitement in what we were doing. We were doing it together. I really wasn't aware that we were killing him. I thought we would stop before he died and turn him loose. He didn't scream or struggle or beg us to let him down. In fact, that's why I thought he would live. I thought this was what he wanted. And I was entranced with Christian. I'd do anything he wanted, even if I didn't like it.

"I tried asking questions afterward, but as usual, Christian told me not to be concerned with such things. We left the warehouse and went to a bar on the beach for drinks, and then had sex. It was especially passionate, but I felt numb, just numb. I was aware that we had done something terrible, but I couldn't access the part of me that was outraged. I buried it."

I didn't quite believe him. In fact, this whole thing was beginning to seem a little too contrived. I was an audience being played toward some end. I wasn't sure why I thought that, but perhaps it was his impassivity. Something about his indifference in the way he described these events. Like he'd simply told me about what kinds of movies he likes to see.

"But how did you get to the place, psychologically, where you were horrified by the first murder, but just numb and dissociated with the second?" I asked. Then something occurred to me. "Or *was* this the second one?"

His response was quiet, but creepy, "No."

"No. There was someone else? Another?" I took a deep breath. "Okay. Back up. Something's missing. The steps . . . what made you change and accept this behavior? Tell me about the second one."

I'm not sure why I was pushing for this. I was in dangerous territory here—especially if he'd chosen to skip that episode. It was one thing for Wraith to tell me about a murder that he'd witnessed. Quite another to press him into admitting his complicity. Once he did, how would he treat me? Thus far he had presented himself as an unwilling participant. I might find out something I didn't want to know—something *he* didn't want me to know. And then we would have this . . . this *thing* between us with which we might not know what to do. But there was a puzzle here, a psychological maze through which I wanted to find my way.

"He was really crazy," Wraith said. "I told you that. He liked the taste of blood. He thought it was the closest he'd ever get to God. The very soul of our experience, he would tell me, rested within secrets. Secret longings and secret journeys into forbidden territory were what awakened the soul to its destiny. He thought it was his destiny to find me and to wed our madness, Katherine. You already know it. You obviously sense that. I can tell from your questions."

"I really don't see how this kind of treatment of people has any beauty to it. You think this is the heart of the vampire? Is that what you're saying? It's . . . it's disgusting!"

"You had to know him, Katherine. You would have seen what he'd have wanted you to see. The soul of your work must bring forth the sweet fragrance of his insanity. Insanity as fresh as early clover, crisp and cool. There is no smarter look than that of the insane. I'm convinced that your work is important; furthermore, I'm convinced that you are tuned to the screams of the crazy ones. You are. That's why I'm telling you this. I know he was crazy. He enjoyed the taste of blood, the sensation of quivering muscle and nerve between his teeth. It was such an elevated experience. But you get it, I know you do."

"You really believe that. That Christian's madness was exquisite."

He was quiet, searching for the right words. "I didn't want to hurt anyone, but I understood him. I understood what he was trying to get to."

"How? What happened with the second one that turned you?"

"I don't know."

"Did you know he was going to do it?"

"No. Not really. I didn't think he'd expose me to that again, after I'd reacted so badly. But he knew me better than I did. He set it up. I knew someone who operated a funeral home, so he told me to meet him there and let him in. It was after hours and there wasn't much chance of getting caught. He'd found a guy in a nearby gas station, just sitting in his car, waiting for something. Christian figured that was his destiny—that they had crossed paths for a reason. He walked up and asked for directions to the nearest cool club. The guy said he was on his way to one and told Christian to follow him. Christian noticed he was drunk, so he told him he had some really hot porn at his place, along with all the beer he could down, and he said, 'I'm there, dude.' Christian had something to use to knock him out and brought him to the home. He pulled the guy out of the car and put him on a wheelchair that he kept in his trunk for his grandmother.

"I was shocked to see him wheeling this boy into the prep room. I didn't know what he had in mind. I thought he was just going to experiment a little. I mean, this was just a pickup, not 'business,' like the guy by the river had been. But Christian sank the scalpel into the boy's chest, shearing away the pink flesh. He slurped at the thick clots of blood that began to leak from the laceration. I just watched. I didn't know what to do. The boy didn't even flinch. Christian made an incision in the neck, just below the ear, raising the carotid. Carefully clamping the artery, he sliced into the lumen and jabbed the end of the scalpel into the channel to clear away any clots. The boy began to bleed quickly. Soon it was evident that Christian planned to kill him. I left the room, but I knew what he was doing. He was slicing into the body and finding ways to get rid of the parts. He ground them in the aspirator and stuffed them into the hydro.

"Then he found me and put the boy's liver under my nose, but I pushed him away. I knew then that he was truly evil, and so was I. I wasn't doing anything to stop him. There's evil inside every soul, I believe that. We're all at the threshold of evil and all that's needed to enter is the right trigger. I am possessed with evil. I have to fight to keep it in check. Christian was for me the facilitator, the conduit. He was right; I was just like him, although I didn't want to believe that. We had established some powerful patterns of hunting and dominating others, and these incidents fit that pattern. They changed me."

"I still don't get it," I said. "How did this change you?"

"My life is a dream within a dream—this is what it is to touch the hem of madness, to don the mysterious shroud. When blood assumes the priority of night—when others become less valuable—when situations become fluid—when imagination becomes reality—madness becomes your life."

I shook my head. The tree felt hard beneath me and I wanted to move. I wanted to leave. I was exasperated by his philosophical dissociations. "This is crazy . . ." But he was on a roll.

"Yes," he said. "It is. When Shakespeare pondered whether a man is 'to be or not to be,' he was unwittingly inviting insanity—for the real question for the human mind is 'to be or not to be . . . sane.'

"There's no life more real than the insane life. The unfettered descent into madness is the true rite of the sentient human being.

"I was mad when I was with Christian—simply mad. We were lovers howling at the wonder of the night that insulated our crimson world. We suffered no remorse for our dreams, pleaded no contest to charges made by the ignorant—for all who were not like us . . . were *not* like us. What have we to do with them?

"This is how it is in madness—pure exclusion. We drank the blood of others, siphoning away their lives as gifts. They were relieved of their duties in a dim universe that sees no specters. We passed through their hearts and liberated them from the tyranny of the ordinary. Their rules and regulations did not touch us, did not smudge our silken souls. We drifted between civilization and madness as carelessly as wind wisps through trees.

"There is genius in madness. Some are born to music, like Mozart. Still others are born to murder, like Dahmer, Gein—and Christian. He thought that the soul of a murderer is a beautiful light, waiting to find its place in the darkness. A killer must kill, of necessity, for this is what killers do."

This whole conversation seemed to be spiraling out of control, but I wasn't sure how to stop it. "So Christian was really just a killer," I remarked. "He'd do it anytime, anywhere."

"I think so. I'm sure he killed people that I didn't even know about."

"How old was he when he first did this?"

"Well, he tortured animals first, but I think he might have been as young as sixteen. It was before he met me."

"So you think he instantly recognized in you the perfect partner?"

"He recognized an opportunity to enhance his skills."

"Skills?"

"He saw me as a natural charmer who could get next to anybody. He wanted me to teach him how to provoke an immediate sense of trust. He thought it would facilitate the eventual killing."

"And you bought into it all. You went along with Christian, even though you claim you were reluctant."

"I can't emphasize enough that there really was something very attractive about him when he did this stuff. His madness was streamlined for perfection, a royal flush in the house of pain. He knew how to bring suffering to the zenith of harmony. He could wed pain and ecstasy in each of our victims. He really could do that. And often, it's what they wanted. There was one guy, JB, whom he hung upside down naked and absolutely tortured with boiling water, but JB loved it. He came back for more. And I facilitated some of the misery of our relationship because I need pain. I always have. Our victims were that way, especially those who wanted the vampire to drink from them. Some of them really wanted to die. Some of them were *in love* with death."

"In love with death?" I'd read about this concept in Rice's novels. The vampire Armand talks about finding his victims among Those Who Want to Die. People who just can't bear life anymore. Rice herself had been among them after the death from leukemia of her five-year-old daughter. But I didn't think that could be a justification for killing them. "And you think your victims felt that way?"

Wraith nodded. "They were at least fascinated, or they wouldn't have been playing dangerous games. But yes, there were those who wanted it. For them, death was the ultimate romantic experience."

I leaned back against the tree. In that moment, nothing seemed real. I wasn't sure how we'd gotten to this point. First he was talking about murder and death as if they were commonplace events, and now I was listening to the details in a similar frame of mind. But I did know that there were those in vampire culture who played with fire and some of them secretly hoped to get burned. Wraith was not the first one to bring this to my attention.

CHAPTER NINETEEN
the glorious exit

It is in death that the individual becomes at one with himself, escaping from monotonous lives and their leveling effect; in the slow, half-subterranean, but already visible approach of death, the dull, common life at last becomes an individuality; a black border isolates it, and gives it the style of its truth.

—MICHEL FOUCAULT

I

Poppy Z. Brite, in *Lost Souls*, calls them "Deathers"—kids who embrace the night, who listen to music that speaks of "dark beauty and fragile mortality," for whom the vampire image is vital. Vampires are "their dream come true, their ideal to aspire to."

Some of the people who look for their souls in the vampire image do so because they believe they love death. They love to think about it, look at it, wish for it, taste it. Others claim they truly wish to die, so they don't mind unprotected sex, drinking blood, or dangerous people because they secretly hope to get ambushed. They want to flicker out while they're still young and beautiful. Some just get close and discover it's not what they want.

I met one vampire who loved death so much that he felt a deep affinity with corpses. Thirty-year-old "Anubis"—so named for the Egyptian deity who presided over the process of embalming and death rites—practices vampirism as a means to get close to the "theater of death" because he was exposed to so much of it early in life. He spoke with enthusiasm of his experiences, although he often hesitated when he remembered how his taste for death had sometimes earned him quick rejection or horrified skepticism. He apparently expected the same from me, and I'll admit, it wasn't easy to listen to some of his stories.

He was dark-haired with blue-gray eyes, a sweet, almost feminine face, and a gentle manner. It was hard to believe that serial killers—especially blood-drinkers and cannibals—fascinated him.

"I remember as a boy going to funeral homes with my father," he told me. "I was five, and my job was to hand him the tools he needed to repair things, but before he asked for them. I prided myself on my ability to anticipate his needs, but it wasn't long before I would wander off into the casket rooms, running my fingers against the linings. I used to imagine how it would feel to sleep in there—I always wanted to try it out.

"After visiting the staff and charming my way into their hearts, I'd slip into the prep room to see Frank. He would let me watch him embalm, even asking for instruments, like my dad. I learned a lot about the business of embalming. I knew all about the arteries, where every major artery and vein system ran and how to access them. I loved the smells, the sights, and the sounds of the prep room. The embalming fluids and tables excited me. I remember the first time I saw the rich flow of dark, almost black blood creeping down on the shiny stainless steel table. It was the most beautiful thing I had ever seen. I wanted to take a picture of it so I could go home and paint it. I thought it was sad to see the blood of a dead girl ease towards the sink drain and disappear. I remember thinking something like: 'All that she is, is just sliding away into the ground.' She was dead, and I knew it, but her life was in her blood.

'I wanted to taste it because I thought that if I could sip a little before it was all gone, I could save her memory. I felt very sad that she was draining away and there was no one to remember her. I knew that the family would come and that there would be a memorial of some kind, but that wasn't what she needed, at least not to my mind. She needed someone who loved her to witness the Vanishing."

"What's that?" I asked. "The Vanishing." In fact, I was trying to recover from what he'd just described.

He smiled sweetly, and then proceeded to explain. "When I was little, I wrote a story about the moment in life when the soul vanished, a moment that I thought occurred with the disappearance of the blood. As long as the blood was still in the body, there was some semblance of life substance. But once the blood was all gone, removed from the host, it was over. This was the saddest part of death to me—not the funeral or burial. It was when the blood began to vanish."

Other kids wrote stories about dogs and horses. He wrote about blood.

"So this guy, Frank, let you just hang around?" I asked.

"He encouraged me to learn all that I could about everything in life. He was patient with me, answering all of my questions—no matter how complex. Dad had told him that I was intelligent and he could discuss anything with me that he thought I could handle. I was afraid to ask Frank if I could taste that girl's blood. I thought he wouldn't understand my belief in its power, so I didn't ask him.

"One time, in another funeral home, I was with a guy named Don, and he was more in tune with the forces in the blood. I was older by now, eight or nine, and I asked if he would let me taste the blood of a teenage male we were working on at the time. Don said it would be dangerous to taste microbial blood . . . so he sterilized some for me. He heated a beaker full of blood and said I could taste all I wanted."

"You're kidding! He gave you blood from a body?"

"Well, he did warn me that I should probably not tell anyone about tasting human blood, just because people don't understand the natural curiosity. He said something like: 'It's not wrong to be curious and to want to understand everything. In fact, it's not even wrong to taste or eat blood. It's just that in our world there are things that are supposed to be right and wrong and people think that everyone should stick to those things.' He was very open-minded.

"Everyone there liked me. I was a little boy who felt the power of having adults cater to my intellect, stimulating my curiosities. I felt grown-up. I know that my love for things associated with blood and death was fed in these funeral homes. When I could read, I scoured journals of dying prisoners and embalming procedure manuals, medical books and nursing books, read theology journals and spent all of my free time in cemeteries and funeral homes. It wasn't long before I discovered the vampire. I sat daily in front of the television to watch Barnabas Collins on *Dark Shadows*. I was completely immersed in all that he was—a human monster. But a personal one. He frightened me, but also fascinated me. He was me, all grown up. The connective link between my soul and the tortured soul of Barnabas was immediate. He represented my own future self. It was the deep-seated need to survive regardless of dark secrets that attracted me to the vampire."

"So for you," I observed, by now almost dizzy from what I was hearing, "the vampire is a rogue figure, a source of dark energy."

He nodded. "Every genre of vampire mythology contains collective elements of human despair. The vampire is my chance to be recognized and loved for my own despair. I can be linked with him. I know it's 'cool' to be a vampire now. People are very excited by it. They want to know if I'm a vampire and they want me to say yes. They want me to drink from them or transform them. They want to be near me and take from me the power of my life. It's easy to woo people as a vampire."

"And you drink blood?"

"Yes. As often as I can. Sometimes I feel remorse and try to turn away from it, but not for long. If I do, I'll die inside, cease to be who I am. So the vampire is sacred to me; he's my kindred spirit. We share need as a common bond. The need is deeply rooted and will not be denied. The vampire understands what no one in normal society understands. We see the same fires and drink the same wine. I'm at home in him. Identifying with vampires makes my misery both acceptable and even delightful. It's victimization in glory."

"Glory?"

"Death fascinates me, especially suicide. I'm riveted by its chaos. I look at a hole through the flesh, an eyeball dangling, detached tendons and brain matter, and sometimes imagine the relationship among neurotransmitters, firing mechanisms, nerve impulses, and soul. Just where in this oozing intelligence did the first cue to kill originate? In what manner did it travel? What pathway did the feelings pursue? To just stand there and absorb what you see . . . it's profoundly moving when you can recognize your own life lying there on the table. It reduces my self-image to a raw examination of life's mysteries unraveling before me."

"Okay." I held up my hand to stop him. "I get the picture. So were there other associations with death besides those funeral homes?"

He smiled, as if he thought I was trying to change the subject a little. "There were other funeral directors. People who really loved their work and who wanted me to join them in their enthusiasm for it. I'll tell you about John. He was a fanatic. Once he had this incredible experience of meeting the very person he was going to embalm. Her name was Laurie. She was only twenty-four and very beautiful. John arranged her appointment for a time when he knew the other directors were busy because he wanted her all to himself. Laurie had an advanced case of leukemia. Two weeks before, she had been fine, laughing and playing tennis with her boyfriend. She had just won her match when she fainted, falling face forward into the grass court. She was rushed to a hospital and the diagnosis came quickly. Her case was rare and too advanced for any reasonable therapy, so she came to us. 'I went right from the doctor's office to my grandma's house to inquire what funeral home handled Papa's arrangements,' she said, her eyes nervously darting between John and me. John shot me a look. I knew what it meant.

"He was a real pro. His performances with the clients were legendary, but he reminded me of the Grinch, Dr. Seuss's evil villain who tried to steal Christmas. John's lips curled up with delight at the thought of Laurie's helpless naked body lying flat against the cold steel of his embalming table. He already knew what I was only beginning to understand—dead men tell no tales. Nor dead women.

"John stood to seal the arrangements with the customary handshake and escort Laurie to the car. He played the sensitive gentleman, of course, opening her door and then gently closing it. She opened her window and thanked him for his kindness. John patted her arm in mock consolation, an insidious stall tactic designed to aid his memorization of her body movements. All the while he was transferring these mental images to the holding tank in his brain. He would need these 'life-pictures' later.

"I arrived late the night Laurie's body came in. Mostly, I cleaned up the place, you know . . . a little vacuuming, dusting, and emptying the trash. I had to inspect all the doors and windows for security, then go to the Ready Room. The Ready Room is where all removals are stored upon arrival. This room is marked by brilliant white tiled floors and walls, stainless steel tables and instruments, and lots of shelved bottles filled with red, blue, and brown chemicals. There were glass bottles and jars of specimens, e.g., toes, intestines, and a severed breast nipple or two. John was working late. My job was to sterilize the instruments he used in embalming procedures, so I went in and started. He looked up at me and appeared startled at my presence, but then he told me he was glad I was there.

"John scared me. He taught me some basics of embalming procedure, explaining every possibility in painful detail. In the beginning, I thought it was normal for an embalmer to palpate cold flesh, searching vaginal and anal cavities for abnormalities that could obstruct arterial flow. He noted the importance of assessing each body to eradicate impediments to the centrifuge. After doing my own research, it became clear to me that, while John was an exceptional craftsman, he was taking unauthorized luxuries with the dead. He had moved beyond his professional calling into a morbid necrophilia. At first I thought his indiscretions to be an aberration, a fluke restricted to a select few LFDs. I was wrong. I would later discover that John's erotic desecration was shared with an elite club of practitioners."

"Wait," I said. "I don't know if I want to hear what's coming."

Anubis shrugged and smiled like he had a special secret.

"Okay, tell me what's coming."

"That night John directed my attention to the tabled remains. Rules of conduct require that sheets completely cover all arrivals. His hands caressed the body through the sheet, predicting difficulties with preservation before even glimpsing the flesh. Then he yanked the sheet down, dramatically revealing the as yet unchiseled work of art. I gasped. It was Laurie.

"Her body was ashen gray. There were a variety of black and blue marks dispersed over the surface of her swollen form. Her facial tissue was unusually clear, with only a couple of depressions. Her eyes were open, a stunt coordinated by John to enhance his dramatic unveiling. The eyes of the deceased are typically closed by the time they reach a funeral home, a fact unknown to me then. John had planned for me to be present at Laurie's debut. He had already initiated the preparation of her remains and had been waiting for me to come in.

"As I watched, he ran his fingers around her blue lips, giving special attention to the area just below her nostrils. He stroked her arm and gazed into her empty eyes. I backed away but watched closely as John spooled his 'life-pictures' of Laurie onto his hard drive, reenacting the moments between them two weeks earlier. This was the most fascinating phenomenon my twenty-year-old eyes had ever seen. And although I felt a little guilty, I took a seat in the corner to watch.

"John leaned down and pressed his lips against Laurie's cold flesh. His kiss was passionate, suggestive of some response. I surmised that this interactive play was imaginary, but set in John's head so vividly that his body was behaving as though the dead girl were really alive. He treated her as though she were kissing him back. He spoke to her softly, nibbling her blue earlobes and smiling. He fondled her breasts and ran his hands across her belly, while his fingers slid in and out of her navel. He became increasingly aroused, removing his shoes and clothing. When fully naked, he leaped upon the table and straddled the corpse, with feet and hands ceremoniously placed on her thighs and shoulders. He was like a mosquito positioning itself for the insertion of its stinger, psychically linking himself with Laurie's spirit. John was trying to pass some of his own energy into her cold body, a stab at jump-starting his lifeless lover.

"After a few moments of this silent ceremony, he lowered himself into Laurie and began grinding his sweaty body against her icy frame. I was appalled. Never had I imagined that any man would be turned on enough to do this. But here it was—right in front of me.

"John was adept at keeping himself balanced on the precarious embalming table. As he slammed into this helpless, lifeless body I began to feel horrible about watching them. I felt sorry for Laurie, to see her remains so desecrated. John seemed an unholy demon eagerly feasting upon the dead like a vulture picking at a carcass. His orgasm was violent, a literal blast from his loins into the cold, dry, and nonresponsive receptacle. He then dismounted from his icy lover, and kissing her sweetly, said good-bye.

"Turning to me, sweating profusely, he simply said, 'Well, what did we learn tonight?' Too stunned to reply, I swallowed hard and shrugged. John, calmly dressing, walked over and whispered in my ear, 'We learned that there is so much more to be learned.' As I stood to collect the instruments for sterilization, it occurred to me that John, too, might need to be sterilized."

When Anubis was finished with his account, I swallowed hard, a little overcome. I didn't want him to think I couldn't take this, but I was beginning to think that some things were better left behind closed doors. I didn't even care anymore about Anubis's vampirism, though I did wonder if he would have become a vampire had he never set foot inside a funeral home as a child. Finally I asked, "Wasn't he at all self-conscious that you were there?"

"No. He enjoyed it."

"This is incredible! To have met this girl and sized her up while still alive just makes it all that much more morbid. How did he become this way? I wonder what happens to a person when he or she first decides to do that. What goes through their minds? Really, it's just amazing."

"I did ask myself how John slipped into necro. I thought I understood. His life was nothing outside of the funeral home . . . no family, friends, nothing. People were surprised and a little disturbed that he so quickly took to me. But I loved being around him. He's a very special human being. I do not agree with his actions—a lot of them—but his is a rare genius. John had no warm lovers—he could not relate with anything outside the purview of death. He always left very late at night, and arrived very early in the morning and quickly secured himself in his Ready Room. If there were no bodies, then he hung out there alone. He was literally in love with his bodies and needed to be more for them than just their embalmer. He created a very safe world for himself. He was happy there.

"John invited me to watch his after-hours activities because it turned him on to have me watch. It increased his sexual energy during cold copulation. And he believed that I was one of his kind. He thought he saw in my eyes a steaming curiosity for the forbidden, and he was impressed with my intimate knowledge of the physical body, post-death. He saw me as another artist, like himself, because I was passionate about the stages of the cessation of body functions. I had studied every medical journal I could find associated with post-mortem anatomical alterations, and had gotten to where I could examine any corpse and be fairly accurate about probable cause of death. So he was trying to become my mentor and induct me into the club. It's a short step from enthusiasm to necrophilia. He gives them an embrace that no one else will. John sometimes would even lick the inside of the skin after he made the chest incision. He liked to see what they tasted like. He invited me to do this, but I wouldn't."

Now, this was really too much, but Anubis kept talking and didn't even notice that I was nearly gagging.

"Embalmers sometimes become like their subjects—cold, insensible, impervious. In their world, the forbidden easily moves in. Voyeurism, kinky sex. I heard that sometimes hot bodies of young victims are shared from one funeral home to another. Phone calls are made and those who are into the scene arrive after hours for their voyeuristic fix. They might jerk off on top of the bodies, or physically penetrate some body cavity. Alcohol and drugs are almost always involved, and coffins are popular places in which to have sex—with the lid closed.

"Necros know each other through a sort of radar. They know their own. There is a body of slang among funeral directors, and some words are peculiar to kinky stuff. Innuendo plays a very strong role. And they protect each other. It's a secret network. Some do it solo, some in groups."

"So you just took this all in and adapted to it."

"I began to notice death early, paying close attention to the way people died on television. If they died of a heart attack or stroke, I'd go immediately to my room and get my medical books so I could understand what had happened. I also researched any kind of murder or foul play. I spent all day in the library digging into vertical files explaining the deaths. I read all the documents on autopsies. I used to have recurring nightmares about my favorite family members being tortured with meat hooks or bleeding to death. The dreams terrified me, and I was using research and knowledge to take the fear out of my dreams. But around adolescence, I concluded that I was really interested in torture and death. I thought those dreams were my subconscious giving me permission to explore my ideas about death. I loved the crucifixion. I saw a connection between Jesus' love for us and his pleasure of dying for us through torturous suffering.

"I carried on my secret research from my first television experiences until I volunteered to assist embalmers in a local funeral home. I was totally fascinated with the fragile thread separating life from death."

"You had no qualms about viewing corpses? Not even at first?"

"No. I was totally into them. Few people are born to that kind of work, but I was. It felt natural to me."

2

Okay, this was not all that unusual among vampires. Some of the earliest documented cases of vampirism involved people who loved corpses. Some vampires were also cannibals. But it was one thing to read about historical cases and another to listen to someone talk like this.

"I am a born necrophile," Abubis said. "I have loved concepts of death since childhood. I'd love to experience my own death, the actual feel of the process of embalming. I believe that, with the knowledge I have, I'll be able to feel what it's like for them to handle my organs. I want the whole package—to see death from this side and the other. I've planned the whole process, exactly how I want it done, and given the directions to a friend who'll follow them to the letter. I know I'll experience it and I can't wait. That's probably why I love the idea of the glorious exit."

I'd never heard of this, so I asked, "What's the glorious exit?"

"Just what you think. Dying because it's beautiful to die. It's about going into the sunset—dancing one's way into one's own end, seducing the possibilities. It's difficult being an outsider and it's difficult to think about growing old, being sick, getting wrinkled. And with the advent of AIDS and other blood diseases, that makes the vampire lifestyle risky. So rather than just not doing it, we endow the risk with a romantic factor. And some of us even desire the end. We want to die.

"Sometimes that's the emotional response to fear and depression over things like AIDS. And not all cases of AIDS or the like are necessarily genuine. There's a sort of hysteria that happens among those who want to be included among the dying. They think they have it. They want it so badly that they see the signs of their death—even if they're not really dying. They have such anxiety over life that death seems a welcome escape, and they transmit the negative energy of their anxiety into their bodies. It's a state of being induced by the pain of existence itself. And for some, dying is a way to become Somebody, if only briefly and painfully. People pay attention to the dying."

"Then why not just kill themselves?"

"I think it's more subtle than that. They aren't perceiving the risk as suicidal, but as a way to challenge the gods, so to speak. And if they lose, well, at least they got into the fray. They want to flee, but they don't want to believe that they're in fact doing that."

"Is that what you want? The glorious exit?"

He crossed his arms and nodded. "Maybe. I'm fragile. I once read about an experiment in which physicians volunteered to become guinea pigs for a virus, and I wanted to be one of them. It would be wonderful to sacrifice my life like that, to die for the good of humankind. Mostly, of course, just to die, but then to do something good with it, too. Who I am has been constructed out of years of denial, covert existence, secret longings unfulfilled. Disenfranchised, alone. That's how it feels. At least when I'm young, I can enjoy health and sex. What kind of life will I have when I get old? Contracting something fatal from unhealthy blood is a perfect escape—a chance to exit in a blaze of glory from an unfriendly world."

I actually felt some sympathy for him, for his feeling of disenfranchisement. It's not easy to feel isolated.

"I'm wondering," I interjected, "about your complete lack of hesitation about death. It seems sort of . . . well, a bit antisocial. I mean, if you fell in love with someone, what would prevent you from killing that person in order to have their death process all to yourself? From the things you say, it seems a natural next step." I thought I might be going too far here, but his face registered no surprise or hostility, so I continued. "I have to tell you, if I were a sick person in your care and I knew you were eager to see my death, I'd be pretty nervous. Your attitude feels objectifying . . . and worse. It would feel like I'm a vulture's prey."

"Your concerns are natural, of course, and these questions aren't entirely unexpected. I don't think I can explain it to your satisfaction—or anyone's. I thought you could see the difference between fascination with death and application. I've shown you who I am, but I'm tilted in favor of compassion. I wouldn't kill someone for the joy of it, but if they died from other causes, I'd enjoy watching the process of deterioration. But I wouldn't want to own the death process of someone I loved. That's unthinkable!"

Interesting what he viewed as unthinkable. "Doesn't this love of death and dying ever bother you? I mean, don't you feel like a total outsider?"

"My secrets bother me at times. But I get into an objective mode. I stand away from it and observe it in myself. And I find ways to make myself feel good about being an outsider. I use charm and deception to maintain friendships because I feel that people won't want to be around me as I really am. I probably need counseling, but I won't go because I have strong feelings about being pronounced sick. I don't trust another's hearing of them for what they are. So I tell it to you objectively. It's a way to disconnect the secrets from me, to intellectualize them and place an artificial distance between myself and the secret. I can tell it to you without implicating myself."

"What about your own death process? I mean, for all your talk about the glorious exit and your wish to experience death, aren't you attracted to suicide?"

"Very much. And I might act on that someday. Maybe soon."

"You might kill yourself, or just try to contract something so you can die slowly?"

He shrugged. "Who knows? If I killed myself, I'd do it in a way that would allow me to see some of it. I wouldn't do it quickly. I'd want to experience it."

"You know, Jeffrey Dahmer was like that. He developed a preoccupation with death early in his life. In grade school, he collected skulls from roadkill and he was obsessed with controlling others. He wasn't abused. In fact, he was pampered."

"So was I."

"And look what his obsessions grew into. He killed and dismembered seventeen young men. He ate some of them. He coexisted with their rotting body parts. He wasn't psychotic or disoriented or dissociative. He just wanted to do these things. He just disconnected himself from the language of evil. He refused to recognize the horror of what he was doing. He became inured to the moral framework."

Anubis shrugged. "Well, I haven't done anything like that."

3

He was not the only one to describe this attraction. Although it's a social taboo, a fascination with death, particularly among those who love vampires, takes many forms. Theoretically, necrophilia is divided into three classifications: violent, fantasy, and romantic. The violent types include those who have such overpowering urges to be near a corpse that they kill in order to have one. Fantasy necrophiles are those for whom death figures prominently in their erotic imagery, and some brothels even provide "mortuary chambers" for acting out such fantasies. The romantic types feel such a strong bond with their lovers that they keep their corpses around after death. Some people have even had their former lovers preserved. Those who have a death fetish, as Anubis does, seek to discover every aspect of the process as they might know a lover. It makes sense that they might one day wish to merge with the object of their most fervent desire. No one else had developed such an elaborate and poetic framework as the glorious exit, but I heard about more than one person who actually had taken his belief in the blood spirit past the point of no return. And others who felt that their victims were being sacrificed for their own glorious exit.

Yet has anyone gone the distance? Really believed so firmly that suicide was the way toward empowerment that the final act of self-violence became inevitable? Wraith had said that Christian believed in this. Christian had discussed it with him many times, had urged him into a blood-pact of doing it together, had examined numerous mystical beliefs about blood and its power.

So out in the woods that night, after he told me how their victims really *wanted* to be victimized and had experienced their own glorious exit, I put the question to him. "And Christian. Whatever became of his idea to do this blood exit himself? Where is he now? Does he still want to do it?"

Wraith looked down at his hands, then up at me. "We have to go someplace else," he said quietly.

"We do?"

"Yes. You can follow me in your car. That's the last place I want to show you. Christian and I used to go there all the time together."

I knew better than to ask him to just to tell me, so I jumped down from my perch in the tree and went over to the cars. I heard Wraith come down, too, and stepped up my pace. I was already in my car before he got to his. He gave a little wave and got in. As if we hadn't just talked about his part in several murders. As if he was just some normal guy.

I followed him for a few miles, half-afraid that Christian himself might be waiting for us, worried that this was the plan—bring her over there and we'll finish her together. Then Wraith pulled up by a bridge. I hoped there weren't any loons here and I didn't like the fact that there was water. He got out of his car and waited for me to join him. My heart was pounding again. I wanted to stay close to the car. This place was darker still, but there was a little moonlight.

He walked before me along a grassy path until we came to an area that looked like some kind of abandoned building, mostly torn down or rotted away. There were large boulders scattered around and Wraith stopped next to one. He looked up at me.

"This is where they found him," he said.

"Found him?"

"Christian. He's dead. He killed himself."

I was stunned. I don't know why I hadn't expected this, and in fact, I felt an immediate sense of loss. For some reason, I wanted him to be alive. Bad as he was, he'd become almost a mythic figure to me. He was *it*. He was the vampire at its most extreme, charged with all the horror and resonance that the image holds for me. It didn't seem possible that he could be dead.

"How?" I asked.

"Late one night, he brought it up over coffee. He told me what he intended to do. I started to cry right there because I knew that once he got an idea, he would eventually make it happen. He told me he was going to join me away from his body. I argued with him for months, but I knew I couldn't change his mind. Christian was my stronger self. We were both dominators, but he led the dance.

"We had made a blood-pact that we would always be together. Two years later, on the anniversary of the pact, Christian came out here, took off all of his clothes, and sliced open both of his carotid arteries."

"And you didn't know?" I asked. As distraught as I was over hearing the details of his sadistic activities, this was really gruesome.

"That day we'd made plans, but he was behaving strangely, making mysterious allusions to being together in spirit, joining as one. And . . . he'd left our apartment. He'd moved back home. Things were shifting, changing. He said he was leaving me, but I thought he was just trying to torture me. It was just one more way to drink from my suffering. When I couldn't find him, I was in a panic. Then a friend came and told me he was dead. Two hunters had found him.

"I felt utterly dead inside. I didn't know what I would do without him. I stopped eating and sleeping. I couldn't function. He was part of me and he had killed himself. I went to the funeral, but in my mind, he wasn't there. It was very hard to look upon his beautiful face in the coffin. I wanted to have him back.

"He'd been unhappy without me always at his side—he wanted to be together forever. He believed that in dying, he would pass into me, come into me in the night, and walk with me. Now he is."

"What do you mean?"

"He comes to me at night. I feel him. I'm haunted by him. He directs me now in the hunt."

"You hear voices?"

"No, not that, really. But he speaks to me; he makes his wishes known—inside. Sometimes I even take his name when I'm on the prowl. I become him."

"I'm sorry," I said. "I don't follow you. He's a vampire ghost?" I'd heard of this. Anne Rice had put one in her novels. I'd even heard of a ghost hunter who'd claimed to have had a vampire experience. But the concept seemed, well, a bit far-fetched.

"A few days after he took his life," Wraith said, "I came to this spot to be with him. I brought a sharp knife, thinking that I would do the same, in the same place. Without him, I wanted to die. I'd been miserable with him, because he would hurt me. But he was a familiar misery. I didn't think I had the strength to reestablish myself in the world on my own. He'd kept me from going insane."

"He kept you . . . ?" I interrupted. "He was a killer, a sociopath, yet you think he kept you from going insane?"

"He was the stabilizing element in our equation. Since I was nine, I believed I was going mad. When he died, when I knew he was truly gone, I believed I'd slip slowly into that. It just seemed inevitable.

"So I came here and sat on the bloodstains on our rock and cried. I'd never cried so hard. Eventually I went over to the ruin and slid away a brick that hid our secret place. There I found his suicide note, addressed to me. It said simply, 'We are one now. I am with you always. Christian.' Then I felt a sensation of something running through me and there he was. He was standing in the woods, looking at me with a smile. I freaked out and ran as fast as I could to the car, but he was already there, in the passenger seat. He began to speak to me, telling me not to cry, that he hadn't left me. He said I'd now feel him inside me for the rest of my life and that we were more powerful together as vampires. So he's my secret power now. He's integrated his life force into mine."

"You believe you have a vampire familiar, a ghost companion?" I asked.

"Yes," he insisted. "He helps me select my prey. We communicate telepathically. I hunt because it's what he wants."

"Okay, but you said he did this because he wanted to be with you, and a minute ago, you said he was trying to leave you."

Wraith looked away. Then he whispered, "He *was* trying to leave me. He'd already moved out. I was devastated. He wanted to be with someone else. But I knew he still loved me."

"Wait, this isn't adding up. This..." Then I had a startling thought. "Did *you* kill him?"

Wraith shot me a surprised look. "No!" he protested. "I *loved* him. I wouldn't have killed him. I needed him."

"But it doesn't make sense, then. If he was leaving you, he wouldn't do something romantic like kill himself to join your spirit."

"He left a note. He said he'd be with me now."

I wondered. "So you think he wanted to die. That this beautiful twenty-four-year-old man wanted to end his life, just like that."

"Yes. I possessed the magic he needed to complete himself. He saw my power as significant, and so he attached himself to it. That's why he wanted to die—to attach himself to me in a permanent way. He wanted to graft himself onto my soul."

I wasn't entirely convinced, but I mentioned this glorious exit idea, and Wraith was quick to say, "Many gay males have a desire to disappear in a blaze of glory. The vampire image fits us because we want perpetual youth and beauty. To lose that is to die. I wanted to do what he did. I still want to, but I'm trying to stay in this world and paste my unique impression against the wall. And part of me fears that, upon death, Christian and I will be separated forever. But the allure to just be gone, to never get old and lonely, is strong. Christian is forever caught in the cycle of his suicide, a perpetual rehearsal of his own death through me. He brings me to the edge, savors the aroma, and then holds my head under water, pushing me into the deep blackness he calls home. If Christian were to leave me, I can't say what I would do. He is my night. I don't know how I would function. I think I would have only oblivion. I hunt because he's with me. I don't want to do it without him."

"What happened to all his money and possessions?"

"His possessions went straight to his family."

"All of it? He made no provision for you, though you'd been his lover?"

"He left me a note. Some personal things. That's all. I burned all photos of him, at his request."

"The ghost?"

"Yes."

"And he hunts with you now. He's with you when you drink blood."

"Yes. He often wants more than I do, so when I hunt, it's intense. I wish I could believe that his current presence in my life is nothing more than twisted anger and remorse at not having saved him, or maybe a sentimental memory, or some other psychological impairment that could be corrected with therapy. But he's inside me. I believe he will haunt me all of my life. And I think he wants me to die. I think that's where he's leading me." He grinned. "I know how absurd that sounds. But that's the reality of my life. A lot of my vampire life seems like one long day. Every event seems to just dump itself into a single pool of experience. It's him who wants me to tell you all this and I don't know why. Maybe he wants you to help him justify his deeds, or maybe he thinks your probing will upset me and lead to my destruction."

I didn't like the feeling that this vampire ghost was aware of me. "Does anyone else ever see him?"

"A genuine seer could. Last year, I picked this boy up and we spent an hour in conversation. Christian showed up, I felt the warmth he always brings, and this boy pointed at my head and said, 'Hey, man, there's a ring around your skull.' He said he could feel its heat. People often comment on the fact that there is something about me they can't resist. I believe that's Christian's effect. My security with him felt like a prison most of the time I was with him, and it still does."

"What do you mean?"

"I spent most of my time thinking of ways that I could escape him."

This was truly getting confusing. "I thought you loved him."

"I did . . . and I hated him. You can only passionately hate someone that you also love. I wish I could put your hand to my beating heart and let you imbibe of Christian's essence."

I stepped back. "No, I don't think so." I wasn't interested in picking up any hitchhiking vampire ghost. "But tell me what you mean."

"I loved him, but he tormented me. Once I was angry with him over something—I don't recall just what it was. I sulked all afternoon, sitting on a chair in my room, just staring out the window at the little oak tree. I got angrier by the second, especially since he was not responding to my suffering. I reached for my knife, sat on the bed, and began to slice my bed sheets, starting at the other side of the sheet and raking the blade across the mattress to where I was sitting. Each plunge was his heart and each rip was his bones being raked by the steel. That's how much I could hate him."

No matter how much I'd heard that night, each new description of violence was unsettling. And Wraith's anger was feeling more immediate. If Christian had suddenly materialized, I was sure Wraith would plunge a dagger into him. I felt my leg muscles tense to run.

"But you didn't kill him?"

"No. But I might have. If he'd lived and left me, really left me, I might have."

Something about this contradiction troubled me. I went back over some of the things he'd revealed, and asked, "Do you think you have the power to intuit what would destroy another person?"

"What do you mean?"

"I mean that maybe your feeding Christian's hunger for knowledge about the esoteric connection between blood and spiritual power inspired his suicide. It seems to me, from the way you talk, that some part of you knew how to trigger it and even knew that you *were* triggering it, and yet you continued to tell him things. Like you were feeding him, pushing him toward the edge. At some point, maybe you started to want him to die."

He shrugged, but didn't seem surprised by this possibility. "I do seem to know what destroys another person. I can remember in school sizing up other kids all the time, watching, observing, and then using my insight to gain advantage. I knew precisely which words would slice open and expose their raw selves. I saw their deeper fears, and I could heal or harm them. But even if I triggered Christian's suicide, I didn't necessarily win. He might be dead, but he still has power over me. There's still a struggle for domination between us. Our bond has twisted itself into a bizarre existence for me. I wouldn't do these things if he didn't make me.

"We had an intense rivalry. Things got bitter between us because of our attraction for each other. We wanted to be each other. Ours was a fierce hateful love born in jealousy. We wanted to crawl inside of each other and beat as one heart, and hatred kept a necessary balance.

"We had this force of invisible suffering, but also of deep affection. There were times between me and Christian, in the midst of everything going wrong, that good moments marked the end of our day.

The pain has grown dull and the suffering has faded, so much so that sometimes I cannot remember the truth."

I held up my hand for him to stop. "So you actually created much of the pain of your relationship, then," I suggested.

"I bounced off of Christian like a crazy lightning bolt, inciting him to riot. I magnified his pain. I instinctively knew where to touch to hurt someone. I did it with him all the time. I think it contributed to his drifting—or running—away, but he also knew he was inspiring me to hurt him."

"So it's possible then . . ."

"Yes, it's possible something inside me knew what to do. He wouldn't pay attention. He wouldn't . . ." He stopped, and I knew there was something dark and nasty behind that abrupt confession. "But I didn't want him dead. Not really. There was something of beauty in him. Something utterly unique and electrifying. No matter what Christian did, he was never disgusted. He didn't care what he was supposed to feel according to the rules of normal society. That was all so bland and weak to him. His madness was his treasure. He was free. And I loved him as I love myself. But Christian wanted to take me over, and I refused to allow it. I was not trying consciously to kill him—never! But subconsciously, I think I was bothered by his obsessive attachment to being me."

This guy was a chameleon. No matter what I said, he'd take it, roll himself in it, and present it back to me as truth. I really didn't know what to believe anymore.

"But I'm him now," Wraith said. "I'm elusive, mysterious, irregular, highly unpredictable, and fluid. I am Christian."

Okay, yes, I felt as if I were standing there with a crazy person, and why didn't I just leave? Because I have a weakness for this kind of conversation. There was more I wanted to know. "But he was actually leaving you? He was trying to get out of the relationship?"

Wraith nodded as if unable to articulate the reality of this. Somehow this story was falling apart. The Great Romance was flawed. Christian had actually wanted out. I wondered. I decided to try another theory.

"Have you ever thought," I said, "that with all the strange things he was involved with, and with the mean things he did, that maybe someone came after him? Maybe he was murdered. Maybe some deal went bad for him or someone finally got him back."

He was quiet for a moment.

"I've thought of it," he admitted. "There *are* people who believe that Christian was murdered. One guy claims that Christian knew it was going to happen and did nothing to prevent it. He remembers Christian saying something like, 'Everything is as it should be . . . and it will be fine in the end.' It's cryptic, but Christian was always cryptic. Apparently the local mob and Christian had some sort of partnership. It seems that Christian picked 'marks' for them from his stash of boys, and he'd kill as needed and make people disappear."

"And you might have been one."

"Yes. As I remember back, there were so many innuendoes that make sense now. That maybe he might have killed me one day."

"But you stayed with him."

"Yes. I'd rather have died than left him. So in the end, it doesn't much matter. He'd have killed me or I'd have killed him, or one of us would die in some other way. It would have all come to this kind of end."

He was right. It seemed pointless to argue the truth of the situation. And as I thought it over, it seemed to me that Christian may indeed have killed himself, but only because he knew he was going to die. He might have watched a drug deal go bad or heard a rumor that he was in trouble, and he might have gone through with the plan he had rehearsed with Wraith so many times that it glowed with a romantic light. Having no choice and wanting to go in his own way, he may have written the note as a sort of reconciliation with Wraith and then slit his own throat out there on that lonely rock.

4

The glorious exit. Enticing death. Suicide. Sacrifice. Red Roulette.

Whether or not Christian continues his existence in another form, he certainly lives on. Wraith told me of an even more insidious connection.

"Years later, some of the people Christian was involved with are still in this vampire cult. It's all very mystical. Some of them think he's even still alive in the flesh, but they think they can get some kind of power from him. This year, they're going to do a full Samhein-type of ceremony for several nights leading up to Halloween. They claim it will be a blood sacrifice, and the victims are aspiring young vampires seeking entry into an elite club of blood-drinkers.

"This cult is comprised of old and young members, a few from my own time. The rituals and regulations are much the same as when I was young, but with one difference: These vampires swear allegiance to a ghost master. It is their belief that Christian comes to them in their dreams and their unconscious minds. He tells them the things he desires them to do. For example, two teenagers were mutilated and drained of blood at the county pits near here, and there were bite marks on their necks and thighs. They appear to be transients. It wasn't in the papers, but I heard it from a friend on the police force. I think the killers are members of this cult, doing what they think Christian wants them to do.

"There's a strange hushed reverence that falls over them when Christian's name is spoken. I was startled by the reception I received upon meeting them. They treated me as if I were him. Apparently, word had leaked out that he'd killed himself in order to inhabit lesser vampires through me, his 'soul-house.' I was viewed as the place where he lived and labored for the cause of vampirism. I was immediately offered a position in the group. I calmly and respectfully declined to lead them, saying that I did not possess the spirit of Christian. It was a lie, but I didn't trust them. Several of the vampires accused me of not being aware of my own powers.

"The ranking leader pulled me aside and begged me to reconsider, noting that I was the only one who could bring Christian's spirit to them on the night of the Dark One. I asked him to allow me time to consider his proposal. After a few questions about the ritual, I left. I have received a few calls since then inquiring if I intend to partake of the ritual. I have yet to respond, but the time is growing closer and I need to give them an answer. They intend to offer fresh, flowing blood for sacrifice in return for being filled with Christian's spirit.

"I'm suspicious of this ritual, believing somehow that Christian might be able to return to these people and live again through them. I believe it's possible, yet I don't believe these vampires have the power to achieve it. If it happens, Christian will make it so. It will be by his hand that he returns, not theirs. But they've found a willing sacrifice, the best kind."

"Willing?"

"This boy wants to die at the hands of bloodthirsty vampires. He thinks, as you put it, that it would be a glorious end. I am to meet him to give my approval—but only if I'm to participate in the ritual."

"Why don't you just go look him over and tell them he's not appropriate? They'd trust your judgment. You'll save him, and maybe he'll come to his senses."

"It wouldn't work."

"Why not?"

"Because . . . they have more than one."

CHAPTER TWENTY

the tao of the
vampire

Unutterable and nameless is that which torments and delights
my soul and is also the hunger of my belly.

—NIETZSCHE, *Thus Spoke Zarathustra*

I

Wraith's story appeared to be at an end, but I kept questioning what
he'd told me. I'd noticed that he had cleverly described the murders
out of the order of their actual progression, and I knew cleverness of
this kind for what it was: a method for getting something while it
appeared that he was giving. I had not fallen for it, not altogether. The
problem was, I didn't know why he'd done it. In my head, I went over
the details in chronological order and kept asking for more refinement. I wasn't recording any of this. I was just trying to get it all
straight.

Sometimes this irritated him, but he did not allow himself to get angry enough to lose his own grounding. He was working me, I could feel it, but could not quite articulate what I needed to know. I'd first been tipped off to something when he'd led me from the river to the tree where he claimed to have wept and vomited over what Christian had done. Right then I'd begun to sense something theatrical afoot: He had climbed the tree to a certain spot, and I had climbed after him. Wraith had vividly described how sickened and afraid he was the evening that Christian had first murdered someone in front of him, and how he had spurned Christian's mocking insistence that they were two of a kind. Then he'd mentioned the other blood crimes just as I told them in previous chapters. He hinted that there had been others, but I didn't want to hear it. I'd heard enough.

I said, "Tell me again about the second murder. The one that followed this." He was evasive and I had sensed that something wasn't quite right, but in that moment, I just didn't know what was bothering me. I only knew that something was missing from his account.

Finally, when the "tour" into his terrain had concluded, he walked me back to the car. I had no idea if I'd ever hear from him again and it seemed odd just saying good-bye. I knew so much about him now, and most of it was pretty awful. But he seemed to have no problem. Apparently, he'd gotten what he wanted or had figured he wasn't going to. Clearly, he no longer wanted to talk. I shook his hand, thanked him for meeting me, and found my way (not easily) back to my hotel. I had a hard time believing I still had my tapes—and my life.

I had a few drinks that night as I pondered my feelings over the various things Wraith had described—and my feelings about vampire culture in general. Somehow it all related. I began to understand one thing about the kind of vampire Christian was: His method was based in deception and theft. He used beauty, charm, and lies to maneuver himself into positions that gave him the best advantage for feeding off others. Fluid fiction, the minister had said. Pretty phrase for an ugly behavior. Wraith had claimed that Christian had deceived him and had taken advantage of his vulnerability, had vamped off him repeatedly until he had no more resources for resistance. But was Christian's portrait, as presented by Wraith, the vampire's true essence? Was it really that simple? Something about it didn't quite gel.

I thought about this whole idea of what the true heart of the vampire is. Once I'd left the Susan Walsh story behind, I'd been looking for what to me was a real vampire. I had found myself increasingly troubled by how the vampire had evolved to suit this new generation of vampire lovers. Viruses, mortality, clan rules, and a host of other changes just didn't sit well with me. I know that vampires take many forms in different cultures, and some of the "new" dimensions are not new at all, but ancient. They may even be closer to the truth about vampires, if there is such a thing. But that didn't matter to me.

Among all those I spoke to who want to alter the vampire for a new age, I had failed to find the disturbing mystery and eroticism that I really wanted. Odd as it may sound, only Wraith had come close. Even as I'd been in his presence, listening with horror to what he was saying, I'd felt that braided tension of seduction, energy, and dread that seemed to me were indispensable to a vampiric experience. Which is not to say he had "the truth," but only that he touched on the aspects of the vampire that resonated for me.

But I still didn't know what exactly he'd shown me, aside from some places that were branded into his conscience, and the idea of beauty in madness. He'd said that I'd get it. He was confident that I would. Or rather, what he'd said was that *Christian* was confident that I would know—and ultimately depict—what a vampire really is.

I had another drink and thought about a story I'd read by Douglas Clegg. At the time it had made a strong emotional impact, but I didn't know how it related to anything I was witnessing. It was called "White Chapel," and I'd come across it in Poppy Z. Brite's *Love in Vein* anthology. Since the protagonist was a woman on a quest into the heart of darkness, I'd immediately identified with her. As I'd read, I'd become increasingly aware that Clegg knew something important.

In the story, the explorer, Jane Boone, hears about a man whose savagery has become legendary—a "white devil" who went to White Chapel in India (echoing Jack the Ripper in London), collecting human skins along the way off victims who were still alive. He even tortured children. Jane learns that a woman who had suffered extensively at his hands, her entire face peeled off, was so deeply grateful that she blessed him. Jane then becomes obsessed with finding this Nathan Merritt to hear from his own lips how he has developed a taste for the most unconscionable of crimes, yet can perform them with such artistry that his victims thank him. She pretends that she has a writer's interest, but there is something more personal at stake. Jane soon learns that those who hunt vampires quickly become the prey.

Merritt is aware of her search for him, and finding her capable of unique pain, he traps her and shows her the beauty of his evil. Despite what she "believes," she finds herself seduced, and even as he rips off her skin with his teeth during a sexual frenzy, she discovers the meaning of what she both fears and needs: absolute transcendence through extreme pain of the limitations of her identity. The only way to get that, she realizes, is to become a temple to the god: to be transformed from human flesh into boundlessness by being pushed over the edge.

In this story, the vampire is the keeper of the forbidden, the consort of the god. Those who seek it must endure his ego-shattering savagery before they're worthy and able to embrace the rending transformation of their souls. "When he finds you . . . you are no longer who you were. You become."

These were Wraith's sentiments—how he felt about his experience with Christian.

In this story, the vampire gives context to suffering; his extreme sensuality loosens soul from body through the blood, and transforms what would otherwise be unendurable pain into a radiant experience off which both vampire and victim can feed. Jane gives Merritt his "moment of mastery" through her submission to brutal suffering, and he gives her the openness she needs to lose herself totally. "The gift of suffering was offered slowly, with equal parts delight and torment . . ."

Yes, that was it! No matter what I felt about him, I sensed that Wraith had shown me the heart of a vampire in the way I personally understand it best. Beyond the black clothes, fake fangs, dramatic eyes, and theatrical poses, I still yearn for the vampire's exquisite savagery. I want this creature to be the seductive, calculating, sociopath that I think it is. I want to feel fear when I get close to that. We seek out vampires because they exploit us for their own needs and take everything we've got. They force surrender, but oh so sweetly. They use us and discard us, and even when they choose one among us for something special, that changes nothing about their nature. Life-takers, heat-seekers, ravishing devourers.

The vampire takes from us what it doesn't have and punishes us for what we do—our humanity. But we want what the vampire has—immortality, perception, and power—so we offer up our souls to the consecration of pain in the hope of getting the ultimate treasure. Wraith had sought that from Christian.

At the time I'd read the story, I had asked Doug Clegg why he made his vampire so savage. I'll never forget what he said.

"That image to me is much closer to the heart of the vampire than modern vampire culture shows it to be," Clegg had told me. "My savage god of that story wanted what may be the greatest gift that humans have: the ability to suffer. I really wonder, if there's an afterlife, whether we won't all be sitting around saying, 'You know what I miss? Pain. I miss the hurting and longing.' Animals suffer, but what sets humans apart is that they make an art of it. I think all the beautiful iconography of Christianity, such as Saint Sebastian, Saint Teresa, and Christ on the cross in Mexican churches, is the beauty of human suffering. Sometimes I think we have a huge capacity to inflict and sustain suffering because it's the only thing that makes us know we're alive."

2

This is what Wraith had been trying to convey about Christian's madness. And thinking about "White Chapel," I knew why I had walked out on Diogenes, but had stayed to hear about Christian, even as I shuddered at the ghastly details. Diogenes had a blood-lust, but it was ordinary and overly explicit. There was no poetry in it, no symbolism. Christian had known those finer nuances in the coagulation of pain, sexuality, and submission.

As I looked into the deep red of my Merlot at the hotel bar, I knew one thing: Had Christian still been alive and living in some White Chapel of his own, I'd have done what Jane did. I'd have gone into the heart of darkness and sought him out. Just to see it for myself. Wraith's description of him had horrified me, but had aroused something in me, too. Nothing else in vampire culture had shimmered with the enticing feel of the experience that could seduce me toward my own destruction—and surrender to it utterly. Nothing else had reverberated with the tension of resisting something that also compelled me toward it. Nothing had seemed so potentially enlarging of my knowledge and experience. I'm no masochist, but I do believe that one cannot easily fuse with the gods. There's a price to be paid. A dear one.

With blood-fetishists and vampire ritualists, I had learned the boundaries of my own preferences, but with Christian I had sensed the possibility of the annihilation of something in my own identity, and I began to understand why Wraith had remained with him. They had given each other the gift of suffering *and* the moment of mastery.

Yet Christian had moved beyond all limits and had lured Wraith into the very thing that Wraith feared most—his own desire to be *able* to do it. Wraith wanted to transform himself *into* the forbidden. And like the most unique and cherished of the vampire's victims, he had succumbed, died to himself, and then risen from the dead to become, himself, a vampire—or so he'd said. Whether he had just sensed what I wanted to hear and had adapted some fantasy to it, or whether he'd told me his own truth, it seemed to me that he'd certainly held the beating heart of the vampire in his hands. And he had frightened me with it in just the right way.

It was that fear, that gripping dread that still ran through me even though I was safe in my hotel. I didn't know why I was so anxious. Christian was dead. Wraith had let me leave without any attempt to stop me. Something still wasn't quite all there.

The answer to the riddle completely escaped me, no matter how often I went over the details of Wraith's story. So I finished my third glass of wine, went back to my room, and lay down on the bed to think about it some more. I must have fallen asleep because I dreamed I was on a ship, watching passengers scurry around. The atmosphere was tense, as if something was about to happen. One man was standing against a wall near the lifeboats and I recognized him as Wraith, but there was something different about him. He was staring straight at me with an angry expression and his eyes shifted and changed color. They seemed to deepen in dimension, as if someone else was inside him looking out at me. It was Christian, sending me a silent warning. I was not safe.

I woke up and had to sit up straight to assure myself that I was actually in my room, alone. My heart was thumping in my chest and I felt very disturbed. I didn't even dare look at the window for fear I'd see someone there. Yet there was something still just beyond my awareness, something I had a real *fever* to know.

Then I realized. The power of the vampire. It's not just deception, but something more: It's the *need* of the prey, and the naiveté. *My* naiveté. It had all been a deflection. Wraith had gotten me to look where he wanted me to look, rather than at the truth. What a devil he was!

I got up, got in the car, and went looking for him. I don't even recall what I was thinking. I didn't know if I'd find him. But I felt absolutely crystalized, hyper-focused on what I had to do. I had to confront him. I had to. This was not wise, I knew. In fact, it was downright stupid. But there was momentum in me. There was no turning back.

I knew why I was still afraid, even back at the hotel. Because for some six or seven hours, I'd been searching for the white whale and all along, I'd been riding on its back.

If Wraith was still around, he'd be in one of those places, and it seemed logical to look for him first at the spot where Christian had died. I made a few wrong turns and thought I'd never find it, but finally I saw the bridge—and Wraith's car. Amazingly, he was still there. I figured he'd be by the rock where Christian had sliced his throat. And that's exactly where he was, standing in the dark against a tree. I could just see him in the moonlight. It wasn't very smart to get out of my car and walk down there without all my faculties intact—I was tired, angry, a little intoxicated—but I had something to say.

3

Wraith did not seem surprised to see me. I stopped a few feet from him and said, "I had a dream."

He folded his arms, looked down at Christian's rock, and nodded. He listened as I described the details of my dream about the ship.

"On a ship," he murmured. "Must have been the *Edmund Fitzgerald*. That was Christian's favorite shipwreck."

"What?"

"There was a song about it by Gordon Lightfoot. Christian would lay on his bed with his hands resting over his chest and listen to it over and over while he meditated. That ship went down into Lake Superior one day in November, and no one knows how or why."

I knew that song. Something about the lake that never gave up its dead. "You're saying you think your ghost actually came to me?"

Wraith nodded, still watching the rock. "That's his signature. That's but a taste of what I've endured for the past decade. He's intense, scary, even terrifying. I know the sensations you had. He's playing with you, obviously. He brought you back here."

"I don't think so."

That statement made him look up.

"I know what the vampire is," I told him. "Or rather, who."

"Do you?"

"Yes, and it's not what you wanted me to think. It's not Christian. He's just a sociopath, attuned to his own demons. He's just a simple sadistic killer. *You* are the vampire. You're the manipulator. You've wanted me to believe it was him, that you were just some helpless accomplice who needed him so much that you went along with it all. But that's a lie."

"It is?" Wraith asked. His expression remained the same. "How did you come to that conclusion?"

"You've been trying to deceive me all along, trying to beguile me into presenting the wrong picture. You wanted me to write the story of Christian the vampire who terrorized people, drank their blood, killed them, and forced you to watch so he could vamp off your horror as an added bonus. You're sacrificing him."

He shrugged, not ready to admit to anything.

"But the clues were there. You've been hinting at the truth. It's about what happened between the first and second murders. Or rather, what *didn't* happen. Nothing happened. There was no shift, no collapse in you of some psychological boundary that allowed you to participate again. No wrestling with your conscience. No attempt to dissuade Christian. You knew what he was up to and you were *ready*. You wanted it. And you wanted the next one, and the next. You stayed with him, not because you were hopelessly in love with someone whose brutality you struggled to overlook, but because he was doing what you wanted him to do. And he knew it. He knew *you*, that you'd do anything to keep him going."

Wraith smiled slightly in the shadows, but still said nothing.

"You encouraged him," I continued. "You supported him. You were attracted to Christian because he'd take you into this arena. He acted out what you couldn't do yourself. You set him in motion and fed off him. You were *worse* than him because you exploited his sickness—you amplified it. You made him think he was working you into his game, when you were really working him. Just like you've been doing to me."

His dark eyes widened. "And that makes me more reprehensible?"

"Yes, because you fired up his sadism by acting reluctant when you really weren't. You heightened it."

He smiled. "Really? And that's worse? Worse than killing people? Christian had killed people before I came along, and he killed people without my assistance. And I'm worse than him?"

I had to think about this. I didn't know why, but I still felt that his moral crimes were darker.

"He was sick. You exploited that for your own appetites. It's like two compulsive killers who meet. One of them will eventually kill the other, and the one who triumphs is the one who's more calculating. And you're the one who's still alive. In fact, I think you did kill him. You finessed him right into it. You put the ideas into his head, you got him excited about the possibilities of some after-death power. You probably planted some trigger in all of that, just in case you ever needed to use it. And when he wanted to leave, you used it. He couldn't just go. He belonged to you. If he was finished, then he had to die."

Wraith found this amusing. "If you think I'm so powerful, aren't you afraid I might have done that with you? Planted some kind of trigger? I've been talking to you for some time now."

I didn't say anything. I hadn't thought of that.

Wraith tilted his head a little and seemed to want to laugh at my intense reaction. "Maybe you're right. Maybe I'm the vampire. But isn't it better that you came to this on your own? What good would it have been if I'd have just told you? Isn't your book better this way?"

I was shaking from the cold night air, from being alone in his presence, and from the force of this revelation. He'd been seducing me the entire night into thinking that the heart of the vampire was a compulsive thirst that made him almost as much a victim as his prey, when in fact that victim facade was just part of the deception. Covert vampirism, like my manipulative friend Paul.

I'd found myself liking Wraith, even feeling protective of him, wanting to believe he'd fallen in with a bad seed who'd entranced him and who still trapped him into a life he didn't want.

But he was no victim. He'd wanted it. He surely did. I just hadn't wanted to see that. I'd been charmed by his beauty, his childlike manner, his vulnerability, and had not seen what he was really after. He'd pretended to be struggling with his soul, knowing I'd be drawn in by that, and all the while he'd had another agenda. He had made me feel that I was special, that I had unique gifts that could help him find some sort of redemption. I had been tempted to offer my resources—only, I suspect, to lose them when he moved on to his next victim. And he'd used a third party—the classic projective entrapment of the covert vampire—to try to dupe me.

Wraith moved closer and I suddenly realized how stupid I was to be out there with him alone, not altogether steady, flinging angry accusations. I backed away, but kept my eyes on him.

"But think about this," he said. "Christian is still here. Now he inspires what I do. He feeds off me. So ultimately, isn't he the real vampire? Maybe he inspired this revelation of yours to deflect your attention away from him onto me. Maybe he's doing *exactly* what you're accusing me of doing."

I was astonished. "Is that what you think? That it's him?" Somehow I hadn't quite believed that he really thought he had a ghost.

"The vampire is immortal," he said smoothly. "The cycle never dies. Whether it's me or him, it will always continue."

"So you're not going to answer me."

"I did answer."

In that moment, I felt like a tennis ball being hit from one court to the other, and each player was using me to score a point. Wraith saying Christian was the vampire, Christian indicating that Wraith was, and neither being clearly forthcoming. I was dizzy and a little sick.

Wraith then gripped his fingertips around a silver ring on the forefinger of his left hand, removed it, and offered it to me. I didn't understand.

"Hold out your hand," he said.

I did so.

He placed the ring in my palm, closed my fingers over it, and said, "That was Christian's. I give it to you. He wants you to have it. A souvenir of the night."

I expected to feel some kind of heat from it, but it seemed like an ordinary silver band. My first impulse was to hand it back, but instead I put it in my pocket. Then I did what I had vowed not to do. I turned my back on Wraith and walked away through the damp weeds to my car. I just wanted to get away.

I imagined him following me, grabbing me, maybe hitting me with something to silence me. I had an urge to just start running. I listened for footsteps, ready to bolt, but all I heard were Wraith's final haunting words.

"You'll see him in your dreams," he promised from somewhere behind me. "He's not going to leave you alone. I give him to you. Now he's all yours."

EPILOGUE

I

My final event before turning in this book was the Vampyre Valentine's Day Ball in Manhattan. I took along another "mundane"—the naïve observer, hapless mortal, blank slate, whatever you want to call him. By this time I was pretty immersed and would surely have no clear perspective.

Stuart Lee Brown, blond with eyes the color of maple syrup, loves vampire movies but had never been to a vampire club. When I picked him up, I noticed that he wore a thick, studded dog collar around his neck—"a strategic move," he explained, "a preemptive strike." He was eager to go, and so visually oriented that he kept picking imaginary lint from my velvet pants on the train ride up. He had the right credentials. He'd be observant.

He also presented me with two antique rings that had belonged to his deceased aunt, a former diva of the night, and a fetish whip with a handle wrapped in black lace with a crimson rose. Very feminine. I accepted the whip—in case I ran into my friends from the fetish ball—but took the rings with some trepidation. I'm not too keen on gypsy ghosts that inhabit objects. Still, they were unusual and occultic.

As we walked away from his house he told me that his roommate had my name and number, should anything happen to him. This stopped me dead. "What do you mean?" I asked.

"You know . . . he's just worried."

"Worried? You mean, like I'm dangerous?"

"Yes," said Stuart.

I was astonished. Well, that was a turnaround. Usually people were asking me to give the names and addresses of the people *I* was going out with, for that very reason! Suddenly I was potentially the vampire. That showed me how things had changed since this all began, and being at the club made this even more obvious. My first experience had been rather exciting, a little scary, and utterly enlightening. Now it was all old hat. Been there, done that. It had lost the edge.

The Vampyre Valentine's Day Ball was at the Bank at 225 East Houston Street in Manhattan, and when we arrived, the lines of people dressed in black went around the building. Father Sebastian of Sabretooth had put it together and the evening featured two fashion shows and two rock bands: the Empire Hideous and from England, the mystical pagan/vampire band Inkubus/Sukkubus.

There were merchants all around the dance floor exhibiting jewelry, Goth CDs, books, and fetish wear. Sophie Diamantis was there with *Delirium* magazine, packed with information about the Goth/vampire community. She was real competition for our own *Vampyre Magazine*, which was also on display. She looked the part, with her long black hair and black dress, and she was friendly and happy to see me. I'd met her before at Tony Sokol's Vampyr Theatre. Tony was also there, and he introduced me to Vlad, the tarot reader. The crowds packed in fast and the music was blaring so loud, there was no possibility of talking. I checked into the back room—a former bank vault—and saw one guy dancing alone, muttering to himself with his eyes closed.

We went to the balcony overhead to watch the show. The room was largely dark, with candles set up behind the bar areas. Below us was an unsettled sea of black—hair and clothing—with the occasional valentine red appearing on roses and brocade jackets. There was one bride, and a couple of angels, a peasant girl, and a few Victorians, but mostly the dress for the evening was Goth. Three women formed a dancing circle with their palms pressed together, looking like the three Graces. The music ranged from Celtic to Industrial to house beat, with some *Carmina Burana* thrown in.

The first event was a fashion design show put on by Angel Power. There were half a dozen models—only one guy—sporting everything from rubber pants to animal-skin bodysuits to transparent plastic skirts. Ian Ford, the disc jockey, played seductive music over the stage while the young women cavorted in sexual poses to show off their unusual attire to advantage. The show was a crowd pleaser to the young girls pressing close to the front.

Then came the Empire Hideous, featuring Myke Hideous as lead singer. It was their final performance before breaking up, and they used reverb and fog machines to great mystical effect. From the microphone hung what looked like a cut-off arm. Reminiscent of the seventies rock groups Kiss and Alice Cooper, Hideous had garish Egyptian vampire makeup to accent his eyes, and long black strands of hair that fell down his back from wherever his head wasn't shaved. Red, green, and yellow strobe lights kept the feel of constant motion. For the most part, I couldn't make out the lyrics, except for him being our fantasy, but there was plenty of anger in his tone as Hideous bent forward at the waist and yelled out to the packed crowd.

Toward the end of his show, as a loudspeaker blared the repetitive chant, "Warning! The self-destruct sequence has been activated," a "surgeon" and "nurse" came onstage and proceeded to weave long hypodermic needles through his skin, over the eyebrows, until there were about a dozen that formed this bizarre decoration. He sang another song and then pulled the needles out, one by one, and let the blood stream down his face. Then he said something in a deep Darth Vadar voice about darkness being our destiny. There was a time when I'd have been shocked. Now it was just an interesting performance piece. But Stuart spoke like a true mundane as he leaned toward me and commented, "His mother must be proud."

We couldn't stay for the rest of the show, and on the way home, I asked Stuart to make an assessment. He was thoughtful and almost hesitant to say that much of it seemed stagy. In fact, he felt the whole thing was a bit demystifying of the image of a vampire club. On the way there, he'd been in a state of anticipation, but being there had shown him it's just a lot of kids dressed in black or some other vampiric fashion, listening to music. He'd never seen merchants pushing their wares at a dance club before, and thought it gave the place the flavor of a Renaissance fair, or—in reference to the overwhelming Goth atmosphere—"an alternate universe version of one." He found the dancing unusual, referrring to that anchored, almost motion-less—and *emotionless*—stylized movement of bodies, arms, and hands that I saw each time I went to a club. To him, it looked detached and fairly noninteractive. He also noticed a lot of science fiction references in the lyrics of the band, which seemed to him a puzzling way to present vampires. In fact, as he spoke, he was helping me to articulate what disturbed me about how the vampire was being transformed by this scene. The garish makeup, the needles, and the staged atmos-phere seemed to corrupt the vampire's mystery. It made me feel part of another era altogether, where the love of vampires was a more soli-tary pursuit—where my own imagination reigned and no one offered props. If there had been vampire clubs around when I was a kid feast-ing on the image, I wonder whether I'd have felt at home.

What surprised Stuart was that there were only two blond women in the place, me and a very sad-looking girl. He was also disturbed that no one returned his smile, except for a porcelain beauty of a man dressed smartly in Victorian garb. Aside from the angry and energetic music, there seemed little affect in the atmosphere. "It was largely sta-tic," he said. "Instead of a *tableau vivant*, it was more of a *tableau mourant*." He was glad he had come but a little disturbed by the lack of vampiric mystique.

2

Now we return to where we began: the mystery of Susan Walsh. Had some vampire group abducted her, or had she fallen into a vampire's trap? From what I knew, it seemed unlikely. The interesting thing about my involvement in this research was that no one, aside from those who knew Walsh, told me of any vampire conspiracy (though I did hear about government investigations of vampires and govern-ment manipulations of brain waves toward the end of creating antiso-cial psychosis among those who would become like vampires). No one seemed to think I was gathering dangerous information that would necessitate getting rid of me—and I certainly went deeper into this world than she had.

The fact that I took up where Walsh left off, that I spoke with people whom she had interviewed, and that I went so far into the vampire scene as to edit a magazine that made me a clear target, and *still* no one harassed or threatened me, indicated that perhaps there was no real foundation for her fears. I admit, I didn't uncover every possible lead as some detective might (although the police officer on the case said there *were* no leads), but that's because, once I was in the vampiric realm, other things became more interesting. I figured if there was a vampire holding her somewhere, I'd have heard about it. Surely, if there were dangerous secrets in the vampire realm that involved control of the world, I'd have garnered at least one late-night warning call, or even just a nasty e-mail. Particularly since people knew I was asking about Walsh.

Even so, I believe that, should she remain in hiding or change her identity and thus leave behind an unsolved mystery, she will be part of our culture's mythology of the vampire for some time to come.

On the other hand, maybe I *have* come into some secret knowledge, but since it makes me one of the elite—the Others—I'm not allowed to reveal it.

As for myself and my own conclusions, I can appreciate to some extent how the vampire is evolving. "This monster is mine"—it's the ultimate pull of our culture: Make everything fit *my* needs. The vampire metaphor can certainly be stretched in many directions, but I'm afraid if we stretch it too much, it could lose its elasticity and its value. In fact, the monster is not mine or yours or anyone's. There is no single truth about the vampire. To believe that it can be contained in the limited mind of a single individual or group is to disempower it, demystify it, shrink it into a life-size creature.

Yet for me, there's little in the nineties' version of vampires who eat food, steal energy, devise rules of conduct, and dance at clubs to draw me away from the traditions of terror and pulsing mystery that I prefer. Thus if I placed my own ad, it would run like this:

"Desperately Seeking Vampire. Must be sensual and seductive, drink blood, thrive in the shadows, and know how to stir my inner chaos into an erotic charge that will propel me into ecstasies heretofore unknown. Experience with immortality necessary. Only serious applicants need apply."

ACKNOWLEDGMENTS

Many people assisted me on this project, whether it was to send me articles, make introductions, suggest new directions, agree to interviews, tease me, encourage me, or accompany me to some vampiric event.

I wish to thank the following: Acacia, Lisa Alexander, Allison, Angel, Annie, Anubis, Sandrine Armirail, Donna Askren, Vincent Audigier, Axel, John Bardy, Kimberly Barker, Vincent Beers, Marianne Bergès, Sam Bergman, Blu, Robert Brautigam, Briglouis, Poppy Z. Brite, Stuart Lee Brown, Catharene, Nina Chatelain, Christian, Clarence, Cleo, Clint Catalyst, Douglas Clegg, Catrina Coffin, Conan, Frank Corey, Jessica Courtemanche, Dan Cox, Crazephile, Jack Dean, Tracy Devine, Sophie Diamantis, Diogenes, Norine Dresser, D'Shan, Johnny Dynell, Madame Elisandrya, David Farrant, Miss Mary Farrelly, Greg Fountain and White Wolf, Susan Garrett, Charles Gatewood, Leonard George, Fred Gobi, Virgil Greene, Lindig Harris, Jesse and Michael Hazel, Denise Heep, Manu Heiz, Eric Held, Nancy Holder, Jami Holmes, Georges Horhat, Alex Janke, Viola Johnson, Barbara Johnston, Tom Jolly, Stacy Kirk, Barbara Kirwin, Konstantinos, Susan Krzepisz, Steven Langguth, Catia Lattanzi, Barbara Leigh, Lynda Licina, Liriel McMahon, Jana Marcus, Jeanne Marchal, Jean Marigny, Raymond McNally, Robert McCully, Angie

McKaig, Yohan Meheu, J. Gordon Melton, Brad Middleton, Michael, Elizabeth Miller, Dave Mitchell, Moonfalcon, Morella, Mozart, Les Mulkey, Asif Murad, Blair Murphy, NiteTrain, Richard Noll, Nutley Police Department, Ruth and Doug Osborne, Carol Page, Lori Page, Pandora, Joe Petty, Tim Powers, Andrea Price, Martin and Denise Riccardo, Lisa Rowe, Jami Russell, Lisa Rutter, Sabine, Wiley Saichek, Philip Schlesinger, Father Sebastian, Shadow, Shifter, Elaine Showalter, Lea Silhol, Nancy Smith, Tony and Tina Sokol, Mark T. Spivey, Sarah Faye Starr, Stephanie, Nicolas Strathloch, Suntide, T. J. Ter, Lilith and Darryle Toney, Barbara Trimmer, Charon Ustick, Chi Chi Valenti, Maria A. Vega, Vincent, Vergil, Vlad, Yasmine Vogelwede, Joe Wilderman, Jud Wilhite, Deanna Woodall, Wraith, Chelsea Quinn Yarbro, Jeanne Youngson, Gail Zimmerman, and all the vampires or vampire lovers who helped but wished to remain unnamed.

Dean Koontz, who stood ready to take over should something "happen" to me.

Anne Rice, who changed the vampire for the better, and whose work with me gave me access to many people.

Donna Johnston, my sister, who accompanied me to Paris and encouraged my forays into dark worlds.

Ming Johnston, who kept track of the vampire trial.

Noelle La Corbiniere at HarperPrism, for boldly venturing where she might never have gone when she agreed to be second reader.

Gene Mydlowski, whose artistry inspired a cover that captures the vampire of these times, and Carl Galian, for venturing out to the clubs.

Lori Perkins, my agent, whose love of vampires has kept us on this track for many years, and who was willing to listen to any and all of my adventures.

Caitlin Blasdell, intrepid editor, who insisted I give Buffy a chance, and whose editorial instincts made this a more readable book. I admire her professionalism and was happy to have her personal support throughout this project.

It was John Silbersack's initial vision that started this book, and his constant support that fueled my ventures into the unknown. I'm grateful to him for making it happen, because it was a far greater adventure than I'd anticipated.

BIBLIOGRAPHY

Abrams, Jeremiah, ed. *The Shadow in America: Reclaiming the Soul of a Nation.* Mill Valley, CA: Nataraj, 1994.

Apter, Michael. *The Dangerous Edge: The Psychology of Excitement.* New York: The Free Press, 1992.

Auerbach, Nina. *Our Vampires, Ourselves.* Chicago: University of Chicago Press, 1995.

Barber, Paul. *Vampires, Burial, and Death: Folklore and Reality.* New Haven/London: Yale University Press, 1988.

Brite, Poppy Z. *Lost Souls.* New York: Delacorte, 1992.

—————*Love in Vein: Twenty Original Tales of Vampire Erotica.* New York: HarperPrism, 1995.

—————*Love in Vein II: Eighteen More Original Tales of Vampire Erotica.* New York: HarperPrism, 1997.

Bruni, Frank. "A Modern Bite of the Occult: Dracula Wasn't on Cable." *The New York Times,* August 10, 1996.

Bunson, Matthew. *The Vampire Encyclopedia.* New York: Crown, 1993.

Carter, Margaret L. *Dracula: The Vampire and the Critics.* Ann Arbor, MI: UMI Research Press, 1988.

Cheney, Margaret. *Why: The Serial Killer in America.* Saratoga, CA: R&E Publishers, 1992.

Christian. "The World Is a Vampire." *Vampyre Magazine,* no. 1 (fall 1997).

Copper, Basil. *The Vampire.* New York: Citadel, 1973.

Daraul, Arkon. *A History of Secret Societies.* New York: Carol Publishing, 1995.

Diamantis, Sophie. "The Vampyr Theatre." *Delirium*, no. 3 (1996).

Dresser, Norine. *American Vampires: Fans, Victims, Practitioners.* New York: W.W. Norton, 1989.

Evans, Fred. *Psychology and Nihilism.* Albany, NY: State University of New York Press, 1993.

Florescu, Radu R. and Raymond T. McNally. *Dracula: Prince of Many Faces.* New York: Little, Brown & Co., 1989.

Franzini, Louis R. and John M. Grossberg. *Eccentric and Bizarre Behaviors.* New York: John Wiley & Sons, Inc., 1995.

Friedman, C. S. "Come to the World of Darkness." *Vampyre Magazine*, no. 1 (fall 1997).

Gatewood, Charles, and David Aaron Clark. *True Blood.* San Francisco: Last Gasp Books, 1997.

Gelder, Ken. *Reading the Vampire.* London/New York: Routledge, 1994.

George, Leonard. *Alternative Realities: The Paranormal, the Mystic, and the Transcendent in Human Experience.* New York: Facts on File, 1995.

———"Visions, Dreams, Realities: The Problem of Imaginal Revelation." In *The Anne Rice Reader*, edited by Katherine Ramsland. New York: Ballantine, 1997.

Gordon, Joan, and Veronica Hollinger. *Blood Read: The Vampire as Metaphor in Contemporary Culture.* Philadelphia: University of Pennsylvania Press, 1997.

Griffin, John H. *Black Like Me.* New York: Signet, 1962.

Guiley, Rosemary Ellen, *Vampires Among Us.* New York: Pocket, 1991.

Guiley, Rosemary Ellen, and J. B. Macabre. *The Complete Vampire Companion: Legend and Lore of the Living Dead.* New York: Macmillan, 1994.

Guinn, Jeff, and Andy Grieser. *Something in the Blood: The Underground World of Today's Vampires.* Arlington, TX: Summit, 1996.

Harris, Helaine Z. *Are You in Love with a Vampire? Healing the Relationship Drain Game.* Encino, CA: An Awakening Publishing, 1997.

Hort, Barbara. *Unholy Hungers: Encountering the Psychic Vampire in Ourselves and Others.* Boston/London: Shambhala, 1996.

Johnson, V. M. *Dhampir: Child of the Blood.* Fairfield, CT: Mystic Rose Books, 1996.

Kaplan, Stephen. *Vampires Are.* Palm Springs, CA: ETC, 1984.

Kirwin, Barbara. *The Mad, the Bad, and the Innocent.* New York: Little, Brown & Co., 1997.

Konstantinos. *Vampires: The Occult Truth.* St. Paul, MN: Llewellyn, 1996.

Koontz, Dean. *Sole Survivor.* New York: Alfred A. Knopf, 1997.

Lane, Brian. *Chronicle of Twentieth-Century Murder,* Vols. I and II. New York: Berkley, 1995.

Lester, David. *Serial Killers.* Philadelphia: Charles Press, 1995.

Marcus, Jana. *In the Shadow of the Vampire.* New York: Thunder's Mouth Press, 1997.

Marigny, Jean. *Vampires: Restless Creatures of the Night.* New York: Abrams, 1994.

McCully, Robert. "The Nature of Collective Movements: The Hidden Second Force." *American Journal of Psychotherapy* 37, no. 2 (April 1983).

————"Vampirism: Historical Perspective and Underlying Process in Relation to a Case of Autovampirism." *The Journal of Nervous and Mental Disease* 139, no. 5 (November 1964).

McNally, Raymond T., and Radu R. Florescu. *In Search of Dracula.* Rev. ed. New York: Houghton Mifflin, 1994.

Melton, J. Gordon. *The Vampire Book: The Encyclopedia of the Undead.* Detroit: Visible Ink Press, 1994.

————*Vampires on Video.* Detroit: Visible Ink Press, 1997.

Mercer, Mick. *Hex Files: The Goth Bible.* Woodstock, NY: Overlook Press, 1997.

Noll, Richard. *Bizarre Diseases of the Mind.* New York: Berkley, 1990.

————*Vampires, Werewolves, and Demons: Twentieth-Century Reports in the Psychiatric Literature.* New York: Brunner/Mazel, 1992.

O'Kane, Francoise. *Sacred Chaos: Reflections on God's Shadow and the Dark Self.* Toronto: Inner City Books, 1994.

Page, Carol. *Bloodlust: Conversations with Real Vampires.* New York: HarperCollins, 1991.

Person, Ethel. *By Force of Fantasy.* New York: Basic Books, 1996.

Ramsland, Katherine. *Prism of the Night: A Biography of Anne Rice.* New York: Dutton, 1991.

————*The Anne Rice Reader.* New York: Ballantine, 1997.

————"Hunger for the Marvelous." *Psychology Today,* October 1989.

————"Let the Flesh Instruct the Mind." *Quadrant* 24, no. 2 (1991).

————"The Lived World of Anne Rice." In *The Gothic World of Anne Rice,* edited by Gary Hoppenstand. Bowling Green, OH: Popular Culture Press, 1997.

————"Monster in the Mirror." *Magical Blend*, January 1991.

————*The Roquelaure Reader.* New York: Plume, 1996.

————*The Vampire Companion: The Official Guide to Anne Rice's "The Vampire Chronicles."* New York: Ballantine, 1993; Rev. ed. 1995.

Rein-Hagen, Mark. *Vampire: The Masquerade.* Atlanta: White Wolf, 1991.

Rhodes, Daniel, and Kathleen Rhodes. *Vampires: Emotional Predators Who Want to Suck the Life Out of You.* Amherst, NY: Prometheus Books, 1998.

Riccardo, Martin. *Liquid Dreams of Vampires.* St. Paul, MN: Llewellyn, 1996.

————*The Lure of the Vampire.* Chicago: Adams Press, 1983.

Rice, Anne. *Armand.* New York: Alfred A. Knopf, 1998.

————*Interview with the Vampire.* New York: Alfred A. Knopf, 1976.

————*Memnoch the Devil.* New York: Alfred A. Knopf, 1995.

————*Pandora.* New York: Alfred A. Knopf, 1998.

————*The Queen of the Damned.* New York: Alfred A. Knopf, 1988.

————*The Tale of the Body Thief.* New York: Alfred A. Knopf, 1992.

————*The Vampire Lestat.* New York: Alfred A. Knopf, 1985.

Ridgeway, James. Photographs by Sylvia Plachy. *Red Light: Inside the Sex Industry.* New York: Powerhouse Books, 1996.

Roth, Andrew. *Infamous Manhattan.* New York: Citadel, 1996.

Rushkoff, Douglas. *The GenX Reader.* New York: Ballantine, 1994.

Simmons, Dan. *Carrion Comfort.* New York: Warner, 1989.

Skal, David. *Hollywood Gothic: The Tangled Web of "Dracula" from Novel to Stage to Screen.* New York: W.W. Norton, 1990.

————*The Monster Show: A Cultural History of Horror.* New York: W.W. Norton, 1993.

————*V is for Vampire: The A-to-Z Guide to Everything Undead.* New York: Plume, 1996.

Spivey, Mark Thomas. "The Postmodern Vampire Archetype: A Pastoral Perspective for Healing the Wounded in Generation X." Unpublished master's thesis, 1996.

————"Vampires and Generation X." *Vampyre Magazine*, no. 1 (fall 1997).

Stein, Murray. *Jung on Evil.* Princeton, NJ: Princeton University Press, 1995.

Summers, Montague. *The Vampire in Europe.* New Hyde Park, NY: University Books, 1968.

Tithecott, Richard. *Of Men and Monsters: Jeffrey Dahmer and the Construction of the Serial Killer.* Madison, WI: University of Wisconsin Press, 1997.

Toth, Jennifer. *The Mole People*. Chicago: Chicago Review Press, 1993.

Varma, Devendra P., ed. *Voices from the Vault: Authentic Tales of Vampires and Ghosts*. Toronto: Key Porter Books, 1987.

Wolf, Leonard. *Blood Thirst: One Hundred Years of Vampire Fiction*. New York/Oxford: Oxford University Press, 1997.

Yarbro, Chelsea Quinn. *Hotel Transylvania*. New York: St. Martin's Press, 1978.

Youngson, Jeanne Keyes. *Private Files of a Vampirologist*. Chicago: Adams Press, 1997.

Zimmerman, Gail. "The World of the Vampire: Rice's Contribution." In *The Anne Rice Reader*, edited by Katherine Ramsland. New York: Ballantine, 1997.

The account of the arrest and trial of Roderick Ferrell is from articles printed by the Associated Press and in the *Orlando Sentinel*, Lake County Edition, FL.

A SELECTION OF
VAMPIRE RESOURCES

Count Dracula Fan Club
29 Washington Square West
Penthouse North
New York, NY 10011

Vampire Studies
P.O. Box 151
Berwyn, IL 60412

Vampire Information Exchange
c/o Eric Held
P.O. Box 290328
Brooklyn, NY 11229-0328

Highgate Vampire Society
P.O. Box 1112
London, N10 3XE
England

The Anne Rice Vampire Lestat Fan Club
P.O. Box 58277
New Orleans, LA 70158-8277

Official Anne Rice Web Site
http://www.anne-rice.inter.net/

Temple of the Vampire
Box 3582
Lacey, WA 98503

The Camarilla
50 S. Main Street, #25 Suite 8
Salt Lake City, UT 84144

Vampirism Research Institute
LirielMc@aol.com

Vampiric Studies
http://members.aol.com/SeekerSA/index.html

Delirium Magazine
779 Riverside Drive #A-11
New York, NY 10032

Sabretooth/Vampyre Magazine/Syn Factory
175 Fifth Avenue, Suite 2669
New York, NY 10010
http://www.sabretooth.com/

Tony Sokol
Vampyr Theatre
P.O. Box 6012
South Hackensack, NJ 07606

Count Dracula Society
c/o Donald Reed
334 West 54th St.
Los Angeles, CA 90037

The Dracula Society
Bernard Davies, chairman
36 Elliston Street
Woolwich, London SE18
England

The Bram Stoker Society
c/o Albert Power
227 Rochester Avenue
Dun Laoghaire, County Dublin
Ireland

Secret Order of the Undead
155 East "C" Street, Suite 323
Upland, CA 91786

Vampire Pen Pal Network
Penthouse North
29 Washington Square West
New York, NY 10011

The Black Rose
http://www.geocities.com/BourbonStreet/Delta/2689

DarkRose Manor
http://www.darkrose-bds.com/

Cercle d'Etudes Vampiriques (*Requiem*)
http://wwwperso.hol.fr/~vampyre/
5, rue Jacques d'Aragon
34000 Montpellier
France

International Vampire
http://www.xs4all.nl/~intrvamp

Association Vampire Story (Vampire Dark News)
22 allee Claude Monet
92300 Levaillois-Perret, France
http://perso.magic.fr/slasher/vampire.html

Austrialian Vampire Information Association
P.O. Box 123
Mt. Gravatt Plaza
QLD 4122
Australia

Vampire Archives (Jule Ghoul)
2926 W. Leland Avenue
Chicago, IL 60625–3716

NiteTrain's Home Page
http://www.wwnet.com/~train/index2.html

Vamps: Personal Home Pages
http://www.nosferatu.com/vampnet.html

Anne Rice List
artist@webvoodoo.com/annerice

Vampire Connection (White Pages)
http://www.cclabs.missouri.edu/~c667539/vwp/index.html

White Wolf Games
http://www.white-wolf.com/

Pathway to Darkness
http://www.pathwaytodarkness.com/index.html

Vampyres Only
http://doncaster.on.ca/~vampyre/

Blood Moon Social Club
P.O. Box 80537
Las Vegas, NV 89180

INDEX

Abba, 149–50

Abel, 160, 162–65, 272

Acacia (dissociative personality disorder victim), 205–6

Adam (victim), 283–88

AIDS, 3, 25, 57, 243, 318

Alienation, 94, 235, 242–48, 280. *See also* Generation X

Alternative Realities: The Paranormal, the Mystic, and the Transcendent in Human Experience (George), 67

Alucarda (band), 145

American Gothic Productions, 168

American Vampires (Dresser), 23

Anderson, Howard Scott, 293–96

Andromeda body-piercing shop, 104

Angel (character), 88

Angels, vampires as, 59, 125

Angel Orensanz Foundation, 106, 144, 216

Angel Power, 343

Anna (victim), 193–96

Anne Rice's Vampire Lestat Fan Club, 230

Anne Rice Reader, The (Ramsland), 67

Annotated Dracula, The (Wolf), 132

Anubis, 310–20

Antiveninne, 213

Apache blood rituals, 264–65

Armand (character), 72, 141, 222, 308

Armand (Rice), 72

Armirail, Sandrine, 226, 227

Askren, Donna, 77

Astral vampirism, 166, 202

Audigier, Vincent, 227–28

Australian Vampire Information Association, 230

Autovampirism, 25, 240, 257

Axel, 146–47

Baby Boomers, 235–39
    as psychic vampires, 240–41, 249

Backflash (club), 142

Bands. *See* Music; names of bands

Bank, The (club), 103, 342–45

Bar Bat, Le (club)

Bat Club, The (club), 232

Bathory, Countess Elizabeth, 153, 290

Bauhaus (band), 145, 232

Beats, The, 93

Bergès, Marianne, 222–25, 226

Bizarre Diseases of the Mind (Noll), 133

Bizarre World of Vampires, The (Youngson), 131

Blackened Angels (shop), 142

Black Like Me (Griffin), xii, 255

Black Pages, 32, 46, 142

Black Pearls (film), 92–93

"Black Rose" Web site, 77, 213

Black Sabbath (band), 145

Blade (film), 222

Blood. *See also* Blood-drinkers
  art and, 146–47
  attraction to, 153, 238, 264
  consecrated, 59
  fetishism, 109, 134, 141, 155, 157, 177, 185, 238, 257, 335
  imagery of, 26, 94–95
  as life energy, 3, 16, 153, 262, 310
  powers conferred by, 157, 219, 264, 290, 321, 326
  sacrificial use, 139
  spiritual element, 153, 265

Blood and Donuts (film), 90

Blood-drinkers, xi, 3, 13–16, 23, 30, 49, 55–58, 75, 81, 94, 99–101, 116, 122, 125–26, 128, 129, 146, 150–53, 157–58, 165, 167, 177, 178, 181, 183–87, 219–20, 253–68, 270–71, 274–78, 291, 311–12, 329. *See also* Feeding Circles
  AIDS danger, 3, 25, 57, 188, 280
  dangerous, 17, 25, 135, 159, 161, 253–68, 283–88, 291, 303, 309
  mates of, 185
  motivation, 3, 136, 152–53, 165, 238, 270
  number of in U.S., 151
  as pathology, 133–34

Blood Is Not Enough (Datlow), 27

Bloodists, 5

Blood-letting, 93, 109, 186, 238, 279–80

Blood Lust (club), 144

Bloodlust: Conversations with Real Vampires (Page), 23, 165

Blood Moon Social Club, 120–21

Blood pact, 264, 322

Blood sports, 2, 154, 238, 248–49

Blood Thirst (Wolf), 132

Blu, 174–76

Blue Lagoon (club), 141

Blue Moon Social Club, 213

Blue Sky (film), 191–92

Blue, Sonja (character), 82

Body-piercing, 11, 104, 171, 343

Bondage-a-Go-Go (club), 142, 143

Bondage-and-discipline. *See* Sadomasochism

Bone Room, The (shop), 142

Boone, Jane (character), 333–34

Boulder, Colorado, 96

Bram Stoker Memorial Association, 131

Bram Stoker's Dracula (film), 88, 90

Bram Stoker Society, 231

Brainstorm Productions, 214

Brautigam, Rob, 230

Brite, Poppy Z., 84, 109, 141, 309, 333

Bromley Contingent, The (band), 232

Brown, Stuart Lee, 341–45

Bruni, Frank, 1–2

Buffy (character), 88, 208, 212

Buffy, the Vampire Slayer (television series), 88, 122

"Building a Mystery" (McLachlin), 235

Bush, Jon C., 291

Camarilla, The (fan club), 105, 210, 211, 227

Campbell, Joseph, 167

Camus, Albert, 236

Candlemas, 127

Carmilla (character), 70

"Carmilla" (Le Fanu), 87

Carmilla (online correspondent), 39–40

Carrion Comfort (Simmons), 197

Catacombs, The (club), 142

Catalyst, Clint, 237–38

Cataphile, 224

Cave, The (club), 103

Cercle d'Etudes Vampiriques, 226

Chance (victim), 48–50

"Changeling: The Dreaming" (game), 210

Charnas, Suzy McKee, 82, 217

Chase, Richard Trenton, 290

Chicago, Illinois, 156–72. *See also* Shadow clubs, 144
  Halsted district, cult in, 159
  LARP, 213
  music subculture, 23, 167–72
  vampire meetings, 156, 158–65, 272
  vampire researcher, 165–67

Children of Lilith, 149, 150

Christian (friend of Susan Walsh), 3, 4, 55, 105, 197, 258

Christian (friend of Wraith) , 55, 258, 260–66,
    267–68, 274–78, 283–88, 297–308, 321–30,
    332–40
Christian Death (band), 145
Christianity, 107–8
Church, The (club), 185
Clark, David Aaron, 141
Classicals, 5, 51, 52
Claudia (character), 72, 222
Clegg, Douglas, 333–34
Cleo, 146
Click 'n Drag, 7
Cloisters (club), 213
Cocaine, 129
Coffin, 7, 121, 122. *See also* Vampire, characteris-
    tics of contemporary
Coffin, Catrina, 122
Collins, Barnabas (character), 21, 71, 90, 312
Collins, Nancy, 82
Commedia del Sangue, La. *See* Vampyr
    Theater
Complete Vampire Companion, The (Guiley &
    Macabre), 88
Conan, 142–44
Cooper, Dana, 293–96
Coppola, Francis Ford, 88, 90
Costumes and clothing. *See also* Fangs
    contact lenses, 5, 146
    Goths or S&M, 7–8, 9, 11, 74, 103, 127, 133,
        170–71, 184, 185, 228, 232, 251
    hair color, 29
    LARP, 217, 233–34
    Temple of Set, 271
    vampire, 7–8, 28, 29, 74, 95, 110–11, 120, 131,
        133, 136, 142, 143, 144–45, 146, 188, 228–29,
        248, 341, 342–43
    vampire clubs, 9
    wedding, 186
Count Dracula Fan Club, 23, 130–31
Coupland, Douglas, 242
Coven or coterie, vampire, 28, 159, 161–62, 255,
    266–68, 274–78, 298, 328–30
Coven 13 (club), 126, 127
Covert vampires, 191–96, 197, 339
Crimes, 289–308. *See also* killing and murder;
    specific criminals
"Crossing Over," 295
Crucifix, 15, 71
Cruise, Tom, 88

Crypt, The (club), 142
Cult, The (band), 232
Cult of the Psychic Fetus, 7
Cure, The (band), 232

Dahmer, Jeffrey, 278–79, 307, 320
Danger of vampire cults, 17, 25, 42, 135, 159,
    161, 220, 272, 280, 283–88, 291, 297–308,
    309
Dangerous sex, 26, 135, 159, 161, 188, 291,
    297–308, 309. *See also* Sexuality and
    eroticism
Daniel (character), xii
Daniels, Les, 82
Dark Angel, 273–74
Darkangel's Theatre des Vampire aux Goth,
    144
Dark Gift, The (boutique), 121
"DarkRose Manor" Web site, 77
Dark's Art Parlor, 130
Dark Shadows (television series), 21, 23, 71, 88, 90,
    132–33, 312
Dark Side of the Net, The, 32
"Dark Spiral," 213
Dark Theater, 145, 165, 169
Datlow, Ellen, 26–27
Dave (blood-drinker), 176–79
Davies, Bernard, 231
Day One (television program), 90
Dean, Jack, 127–30
Deathers, 85, 309, 329
Death Guild, The (club), 142
Death, love of, and vampirism, 309–20, 329–30
Deception, 336, 338, 339
    covert vampires and, 194–96, 339
Delirium magazine, 342
Demant, Chrissie, 231
Demant, Kev, 231
Dementia. *See* Jesse
Devil. *See* Satanism
Devil's Castle, The (film), 87
Devine, Tracy, 144
Dhampir, 212–13
Dhampir: Child of the Blood (Johnson), 149
Diamantis, Sophie, 342
Didi, 154, 155
Dillinger, John, 153
Diogenes, 29–31, 34, 68, 69, 117, 120, 153–55, 238
Dissociative identity disorder, 133, 204–6

DNA, 295

Domains, 109–10, 211

Dominance-submission. *See* Sadomasochism

Dominatrix, vampire. *See* Sadomasochism;
Vampire dominatrix

Donors, 62, 116, 129, 134–35, 155, 177, 178–79,
188–89. *See also* Victims

Dracula (character), 94, 136
in film, 87–88

Dracula (1931 film), 71, 87, 132

Dracula (Stoker), 21, 23, 38, 70, 73, 82, 83, 96, 136,
212, 231

Dracula Experience, The, 231

Dracula Exposition. *See* Paris, France

DraculaFest, 144

Dracula Museum, 23

Dracula '97 conference, 82–83, 119, 120, 130–37,
226
film of, 92

Dracula: Prince of Many Faces (McNally &
Florescu), 132

Dracula's Daughter (film), 87

Dracula Society, 231

Dracula Tape, The (Saberhagen), 71, 132

Draugr, 176

Dream of Dracula, A (Wolf), 132

Dresser, Norine, 23, 131, 290

D'Shan, 111–15

"Dungeons and Dragons," 27, 209, 214, 292

Dynell, Johnny, 6, 7

Ecce Homo (Nietzsche), 278

Echols, Damien Wayne, 290

Eco, Umberto, 35

Ecstasy (drug), 129, 180–81, 189

Edmund Fitzgerald, 337

Eldrich, Andrew, 172

Elisandrya, Madame, 138–42

Elrod, P. N., 82

Elvira (television vampire hostess), 132

Empire Hideous, The (band), 342, 343

Empyre Films, 92

Energy. *See* Psychic vampires

England, Goth/Vampire community, 231–32.
See also London, England; Whitby,
England

Eric (friend of Wraith), 258–60, 286

Eternal Sisters of the Damned, 144

Eustis, Florida, 293

Evil, and vampirism, 42, 71, 82, 88, 125, 240, 249,
273–74, 278, 292, 296, 297–308

"Excess is Ease" (S. Rice), 93

Exit (club), 169

Fang Club, LA, 109, 121, 127–30, 144

Fangmakers, 6, 104–5, 142–43

Fangs, 5, 8, 29, 103–6, 108, 141, 155, 172, 177–78

Fantasy, 2, 27, 65, 166, 182, 272. *See also*
Role-playing
blood-fetish and, 155
-prone personality, 66–69

Farrant, David, 231

Feeding Circles, 19, 25, 30, 150, 151

Feeney, Jon, 292

Ferrell, Roderick, 292–96

Fetishes and fetish culture, 8, 75, 107, 109, 117,
129–30, 134, 143, 155, 231, 237–38
restaurant, 111–14
squatters, 272
types, 8

Fevre Dream, 71

Firestone, The (club), 179–82

Florescu, Radu, 132

Florida. *See also* Orlando, Florida; South Beach
(Miami), Florida
clubs, 173, 179–82, 183, 185
murder trial in, 294–97

Fluid fiction, 58, 61, 62, 63, 65–66, 68, 332

Ford, Ian, 343

Forever Knight (television series), 88, 91, 200

Fossey, Diane, xii

Foucault, Michel, 219–20, 309

Fountain, Greg, 210–12, 213, 291

France. *See* International vampirism; Paris,
France

Frequent Flyer Productions, 96

Freud, Sigmund, 281

Fright Night (film), 87–88

From Dusk Till Dawn (film), 88

Fugue, 168

Further Perils of Dracula, The (Youngson), 131

Games, vampire-based, 27–28, 209, 210. *See also*
Role-playing; "Vampire: The
Masquerade"

Gangrel, 210

Gargoyle (Goth shop), 142

Garlic, 71, 106, 168. *See also* Vampire

Gatewood, Charles, 141, 237
Gedanken eines Vampirs (Mozart), 233
Generation X, 235–39
    alienation/boredom of, 235, 242–48, 280
    cultural influences, 241–44
    Rice influence, 244–45
    role-playing, 241
    vampiric, dark, or Goth obsessions, 50, 75
Generation X (Coupland), 242
Genetic Vampire, 5, 52, 53, 198
George, Leonard, 67–68
Gerber/Hart Library, 170
Germany, vampire and Goth culture, 232–34
    Marburg LARP, 232
    music, 233
    RPG and LARP, 233–34
Ghost Research Society, 166
Ghoul, Jule, 165
Gibson, Sondra, 295–96
Gilcrest, Ethan, 1–2
Giles, Rupert (character), 88, 144, 208
Glorious exit, 318, 321, 324, 328
Gobi, Fred, 228
Goodman, John, 293
Gorillas in the Mist (Fossey), xii
Gothic, 232
Goths, 5, 6–7, 342. *See also* Costumes and
        clothing
    blood-drinking and, 3
    Chicago music and club nights, 167–68
    clubs of, 3, 6, 29, 126–30, 142, 144, 228,
        251
    column on, 170–72
    databases, 32
    demographics of, 3, 77, 237
    French, 227–28
    Internet sites, 32–34, 77
    London music/community, 231–32
    sourcebook, 231
Grand Guignol theater, 96
Grant, Charlie, 82
Greene, Virgil, 32
Grieser, Andy, 34, 124, 165
Griffin, John Howard, xii, 255
Groove Jet (club), 185
Guiley, Rosemary Ellen, 88
Guinn, Jeff, 34, 36, 124, 165
Haarmann, Fritz, 290
Haigh, John George, 134, 290

Halloween, 100, 170
    Babylonian equivalent, 68
    club scene, 144
    party, LA, 127
    party, Manhattan, 106, 144–47, 216
    vampire rituals on, 14, 328–30
Hamilton, George, 87
Hammer Studios, 38, 87, 145
Handfasting, 186–87
Harris, Lindig, 83
Havens, 109–10
Heiz, Manu, 228
Held, Eric, 23
Helster (band), 245
Helter Skelter (club), 126
Hex Files: The Goth Bible (Mercer), 231
Hideous, Myke, 343
Highgate Vampire Society, 231
Holder, Nancy, 133
Holland, vampire interest in, 230
Homosexuality and vampirism, 14, 47–50,
        54–58, 59–65, 99–101, 206–7, 258–68, 282–83
    Chicago, 168–72
    Florida transvestite transgender vampire,
        182
    glorious exit and, 324
Horhat, Georges, 228
Horror Writers of America, 82
House of Dracula (film), 87
House of Usher (club), 142
Hotel Transylvania (Yarbro), 82
House Sabretooth, 108–9
Hugo, Victor, 270
"Hunger for the Marvelous" (Ramsland), 123
Hunger, The, 71, 87
Hunter. *See* Vampire hunter.

I am Legend (Matheson), 71
Illuminati, 149, 152
Immortality, 11, 91, 126, 136, 159, 190, 244, 296,
        340
Industrial music. *See* Music
Inheriters, 5, 51, 52
Inkubus Sukkubus (band), 342
Insanity. *See* Psychopathology
In Search of Dracula (McNally & Florescu),
        132
In the Shadow of the Vampire (Marcus), 75, 113,
        138

Internet
  Anne Rice links, 13, 76–81, 209
  Brad (website creator) interview, 37–40
  Camarilla Web site, 211, 213–14
  chat rooms, vampire and Goth, 18–21, 40–41, 50–51, 76–81, 174, 208–9
  e-mail interview with vampire, 13–16
  IRC channel, 77, 199–200
  NiteTrain site and interview, 41–46, 68
  Temple of the Vampire Web site, 124
  vampire resources on, 32–40, 46–47, 226, 227–28, 232
  vampires on, 4, 34, 46–50, 198–99
International Vampire newsletter, 230
International vampire culture, 221–34
Intervamp, 230
Interview with the Vampire (film), 76, 78, 88
Interview with the Vampire (Rice), xii, 21, 71, 79, 244, 254

Jack the Ripper, 122, 231, 333
Jakarr, 120–21
Janke, Alex, 232–33
Jared (vampire), 256–58, 267, 275, 276, 286, 297, 301
Jeff (Wraith partner), 219
Jennifer Welling's Extreme Scenes, 122
Jenny Jones (TV show), 4, 215
Jesse (Dementia), 183–87
Jessica (friend of Marianne Bergès), 222, 228
John, Elton, 237
Johnny (Master Storyteller), 214–17
Johnson, Viola, 149–53
Jones, Aphrodite, 296
Journal of Modern Vampirism, 34
Journal of Vampirism, 165
Jugular Wine (film), 92
Jung, Carl, 70
  shadow side and vampirism, 26, 59, 70, 71, 182
"Just Us Served" (Sokol), 98–99

Kaplan, Stephen, 24
Keep, The (Wilson), 82
Keesee, Charity Lynn, 293–96
Kerouac, Jack, 93
Killing and murder
  animal, 247, 289–90, 291
  serial, 50, 228, 310. See also specific killers

vampirism and, 133, 161, 272, 282, 289–308, 332–40
Kindred, The, 209, 210
"Kindred of the East" (game), 211–12
Kindred: The Embraced (television series), 88, 210, 216
King, Stephen, 26, 71, 82, 292
Kirk, Stacy, 213
Kirwin, Barbara, 197–98, 239–41, 248, 249
Kitchen, The (club), 185
Kleine Vamir, Der, 233
Konstantinos (psychic vampire consultant), 202–4
Koontz, Dean, 121
Kyle, 48–49

Lacy, Washington, 123
Lamiai, 196, 197, 199–202
Langella, Frank, 87
LARP (live action role playing). *See* Role-playing
Las Vegas, Nevada, 120–21
LARP organization, 213
Lattanzi, Catia, 227
Lavey, Anton, 125
League of Vampiric Bards, 122
Le Comte Dracula (club), 228–29
Lee, Christopher, 87
Le Fanu, F. Sheridan, 87
Leigh, Barbara, 133
Lestat (band), 145
Lestat (character), 36, 41, 59, 72, 73, 79, 86, 94, 136, 145, 185, 222, 273
Lestat (role-player), 80–81
Licina, Lynda, 168–72
Lightfoot, Gordon, 337
Limelight, The (club), 103
Limit experience, 219–20, 250
Liquid Dreams of Vampires (Riccardo), 165, 166
London, England
  clubs, 232
  Dracula Society, 231
  Goth community, 231–32
  Highgate Cemetery, 231
  music, Goth, 231–32
  sites from Stoker's *Dracula*, 231
Long Black Veil, 6, 104
Lori (psychic vampire), 198–99

Los Angeles, California, 119–37. *See also* Dracula '97 conference
  Goth attractions, 121–22
  Goth clubs, 126–30
  Hollywood Death Tour, 121
  Koontz's description, 121
  vampire organizations, 122
Los Angeles Hearse Society, 122, 130
Lost Boys, The (film), 87
Lost Children of the Blood, 125
Lost Souls (Brite), 84–85, 309
Lothos (character), 88
Louis de Pointe du Lac (Anne Rice character), 22, 41, 71–72, 73, 78, 222, 223, 244, 255
Love at First Bite (film), 87
Love in Vein, Vols I & II (ed. Brite), 85, 141, 333
Lugosi, Bela, 71, 94, 145, 197
Lumley, Brian, 82
Lure of the Vampire, The (Riccardo), 165
Lycanthropy, 147–49

McMahon, Liriel, 34–37
Macabre, J. B., 88
Mad, the Bad, and the Innocent, The (Kirwin), 239
Madness. *See* Psychopathology
"Mage: The Ascension" (game), 210
Magess (psychic vampire), 200–202
Malefika. *See* Ramsland, Katherine
Malkavian, 210
Manhattan, 102–18
  Caramilla/Sabbat split in, 214
  Count Dracula Fan Club, 131
  Halloween party, 106, 144–47, 216
  LARP, 213–18
  Lower East Side, 1, 3, *see also* Tompkins Square Park
  St. Mark's Place, 103
  underground/mole people, 5, 252, 273–74
  vampire clubs, 6–13, 103, 213, 341–45
  vampire events, 7
  vampire squatters, Tompkins Square Park, 2, 31, 97–98, 103–4, 272
  vampires in, 1–4, 51–52
  vampire theater, 2, 96, 98–99, 342
  Vampyre Valentine's Day Ball, 108, 341–45
  Walsh, Susan disappearance, xi, 6, 53–54, 55, 105, 253, 272, 344
  West Side docks, 63

Marcus, Jana, 74–75, 111, 113, 138, 142
Marie Laveau voodoo shop, 74
Marigny, Jean, 227
Marilyn Manson (band), 145
Marius (Anne Rice character), 41, 273
Martel, Lucius, 123
Martin (film), 88
Matheson, Richard, 71
Matters of Life and Death (album), 165
McCammon, Robert R., 26
McCully, Robert, 25–26, 240, 248
McKaig, Angie, 32
McLachlan, Sarah, 235
McNally, Raymond, 131–32
Meheu, Yohan, 222–25, 228
Melton, J. Gordon, 87, 130, 131, 212–13, 290
Memnoch Ball, 74, 144
Memnoch the Devil (Rice), 72
Memoire of a Mad Vampire (Elisandrya), 139
Mercer, Mick, 231
Merritt, Nathan (character), 333–34
Miami, 272. *See also* South Beach (Miami), Florida
Michael (groom of vampire), 184–87
Michael (vampire coven leader), 266–68, 275–77, 288, 297–98
Michael (vampire minister), 59–65
Michael (victim), 199–202
Milan, Italy, vampire exposition, 227
Miller, Elizabeth, 130, 131
Mind's Eye Theater, 210, 211, 214
Mole People, The (Toth), 5, 252, 273–74
Monster, Carrie, 168
"Moon over Bourbon Street" (Sting), 145
Morella, 10
Mother (Manhattan vampire club), 6–13, 103, 104, 109, 115, 213
  Versailles Room, 7
Mozart (band), 233
Multiple Personality Disorder. *See* Dissociative Identity Disorder
Mummy, The (Rice), 77
Mundanes, 110
Murad, Asif, 10
Murphy, Blair, 92–95, 145, 155
Murray, Kentucky, 292–93, 295
Music, and vampirism, 7, 10, 11–12, 129, 143, 180, 183, 343. *See also* names of bands
  Goth, 171–72, 231–32, 233, 343

Music, and vampirism (*cont.*)
  industrial sound, 145–46, 165, 172
  punk, 232
  rock musicians as vampires, 23, 145, 165,
    168–70

National Clearinghouse on Satanic Crime in
    America, 289
Near Dark (film), 88
Necromance boutique, 121
Necronomicon, 293
Necrophilia, 32, 133, 310–20
NEO (club), 168
Nephilim, 125, 222
Newark, NJ, LARP in, 214
New Orleans, Louisiana, Goth and vampire
    culture in, 73–76, 84–85, 272
  Memnoch Ball, 74, 144
Newsletters, fan and vampire-oriented, 23, 32,
    83–84, 122, 230
New York Times, The, 1
Nietzsche, Friedrich, 233, 278, 279, 331
Nightlines Weekly, 168
Night Poe. *See* Seeker
Nighttimers, 5, 51, 52–53
Nilsen, Dennis, 287
Nina C., 78–79
Nine Inch Nails, 79
NiteTrain or WidowMaker, 41–46, 68
Noll, Richard, 132, 133–37, 290
Nosferatu (film), 87, 130
Nosferatu website, 32–33
Nouvelle Justine, La (restaurant), 111
Nutcracker Suite, The (dungeon), 110,
    114–18

One World By Night, 229
Ophelia, 154–55
Orlando, Florida, 179–82
Other(s), The, 16, 21, 71, 255, 262, 266–68, 270,
    271, 345
Outlaw, 6, 9, 11–13, 111
Outsider, vampire as, 83, 84, 99, 114, 239,
    249–50, 319

Paganism, 125, 161
Page, Carol, 22–23, 25, 169
Pandora (character), 78
Pandora (Rice), 72

Pandora (SOUND), 122–23
Paris, France, 221–29
  Camarilla chapter, 227
  catacombs, 224–25
  Dracula Exposition, 225–28
  famous landmarks and literary sites, 222
  Goth community, 227
Pere Lachaise Cemetery, 222–25
  Ramsland's photos of, 221
  RPG in, 222–24, 226
  Rice, Anne, settings, 222
"Pathway To Darkness" online newsletter,
    32
Paul (covert vampire), 192–96, 339
Pen pal network, 23, 46, 226
Perkins, Lori, 89
Petty, Joe, 78
Phenomenological bracketing, xii
Pitt, Brad, 88
Plachy, Sylvia, 2
Poetry, vampire, 96
Pornography, 2, 89–90
Portrait of Dorian Gray, The (Wilde), 61
Powers, Tim, 133
Prism of the Night: A Biography of Anne Rice
    (Ramsland), xi, 22
Private Files of a Vampirologist (Youngson), 131
Pseudo-vampirism, 36
Psychic vampires, 30, 44, 54, 122, 123, 125, 148,
    166, 190–91, 196–206, 267
  consultant, 202–4
  number of, U.S., 203
  poltergeist activity and, 197–98
  symptoms of attack, 204
  versus psychological vampirism (covert),
    191
Psychology Today, xi, 22, 123
Psychopathology
  clinical vampires, 135–36
  dissociative identity disorder, 133, 204–6,
    294
  sociopathic vampires or madness, 25, 79,
    277, 278, 279, 281, 283–88, 294, 295, 297–308,
    323, 327, 335, 338
  vampire culture and, 240–41

Queen of the Damned, The (Rice), 22, 71
Quickening, The, 275
Rakowitz, Daniel, 104

Ramsland, Katherine
  address and paper, Dracula '97 conference,
    132
  British research on Anne Rice, 231
  childhood fear of, 253
  costumes, 110–11, 118, 144–45
  as dominatrix, 116–18
  fangs made for, 104–6
  French translations of works, 226
  Gabrielle Weyland (LARP name), 216–17
  investigative technique, xii
  LARP by, 214–18
  Malefika (vampire name), 18, 29, 119
  origins of vampire interest, 21–22, 27, 28
  Paul and, 192–96
  Rice, Anne, and, xi, 10, 21–22, 67, 72–73
  Walsh, Susan, hunt for, xii, 1–4, 6, 28, 29,
    52–53, 55, 105, 332, 344–45
  writings of, xi, 22, 67, 72–73, 123, 132, 221,
    226
Ravenloft, 209
Razor blades, 177, 189, 238, 257, 266, 279
Red Death trilogy (Weinberg), 210
Red Ink Pages, The, newsletter, 122
Red Light: Inside the Sex Industry (Plachy &
    Ridgeway), 2, 3
Reflections on Dracula (Miller), 131
Reilly, Mary, 122
Rein-Hagen, Mark, 209
Renfield (character), 134
Renfield Syndrome, 134
Requiem (fanzine), 211
Requiem (journal), 226
Revenant (film), 122
Rey, Kim, 292
Reznor, Trent, 79
Rhodes, Daniel, 196
Rhodes, Kathleen, 196
Riccardo, Denise, 165, 166
Riccardo, Martin, 165–67, 168
Rice, Anne
  appeal of, 28, 109, 183, 227, 280
  biography of, 22
  chat rooms (online), 13, 76–78, 209, 271
  fans, 74–81, 176, 183, 230, 233
  gay following of, 14
  gender, notion of, 164
  Kerouac influence, 93
  on Las Vegas, 120

  literary inspiration, 72–73
  New Orleans and, 74
  novels of:
    Armand, 72
    Interview with the Vampire, xii, 21, 71, 79,
      244, 254
    Memnoch the Devil, 72
    Pandora, 72
    Queen of the Damned, The, 22, 71
    Roquelaure series, 138
    Tale of the Body Thief, The, 72, 185, 222
    Vampire Chronicles, The, 71–72, 77
    Vampire Lestat, The, 36, 71, 113, 145, 273
  sadomasochism and, 89, 138
  South Beach and, 185
  spirituality of vampires, 27, 59, 244
  view of vampires, 73
Rice, Stan, 93
Ricki Lake Show, The, 204
Ridgeway, James, 2
Rituals
  blood, 125, 155, 163–64, 219, 255, 263, 264,
    274–78, 335
  blood-letting, 93
  for blood-thirst, 24
  cemetery, 294
  handfasting, 185–87
  human sacrifice, 272, 328–30
  initiation, 160–61, 271, 295
  of passage, 164
  satanic, 289–90, 295
  secret, 282
Riva, James, 25, 291
Rod, 154, 155
Roderick's Chamber (club), 142
Role-playing, and vampire culture, 28, 29, 68,
    136–37, 140
  "Black Rose" Web site, 77
  chat rooms online and, 18–21, 208–9,
    212
  games (RPG), 27–28, 47, 77–78, 93, 106, 110,
    120–21, 127, 201, 208–18, 222–24, 226,
    227–28, 233, 241, 269, 272, 291–92, 296–97
  live action role playing (LARP), 208, 209–18,
    229, 232, 233
  sadomasochistic, 114
Romania, 132, 228
Roquelaure Reader, The (Ramsland), 138
Rowe, Lisa, 76–77

RPG (role playing games). *See* Role-playing, and vampire culture
Ruthven, Lord (character), 70

Sabbat, 214, 216
Saberhagen, Fred, 71, 132
Sabine, 46–47
Sabretooth, Inc., 6, 107, 109
   Halloween vampire ball, 144–47
   LARP, 213–18
Sadomasochism, 154, 167
   blood sports and, 248
   bondage-and-discipline, 8
   dominance-and-submission, 8
   fetish restaurant, 111–14
   gay vampires and, 63
   humiliation and, 164
   pain, 19–20, 154, 167, 266
   Rice's, 89
   safe words, 116–17
   scarification, 9–10, 117, 154
   shadow side and, 26
   vampire clubs and, 8–9
   vampire fetish ball and, 111, 114–18
   Walsh, Susan and, 3, 8
Saint-Germain, Count de, 71, 82, 83
Salem, Massachusetts, 144
'Salem's Lot (King), 26, 71, 82
Salopek, Laurie, 76
Salt Lake City, Utah, 211
Sanctuary Vampire Sex Bar, 144
San Francisco, California, 141
   Folsom Street gay pick-ups, 63
   vampire and fetish scene in, 141–44, 237–38
   vampire and Goth clubs, 141
Santa Cruz, California, 140–41
   LARP, 213
Santino (character), 78
Satanic Bible, The (Lavey), 125
Satanism and vampires, 124–25, 289–97
Satan's Den, 274
Satan's Night Out (characters), 145
Savage Garden (band), 145
Scarification, 9–10, 117
Scary Lady, 168
Screem in the Dark, 168, 170
Screem Jams, 168
Sean (victim), 206–7

Seattle, Washington
   Camarilla, The, 105
   fangmakers, 105
   vampyres in, 152
Sebastian, Father, 6, 104–10, 115, 116, 145, 146, 235, 269, 342
Secret gestures, 162, 182, 270
Secret societies. *See* Underground (vampire)
Seeker, 51–54, 103
Sensitive, 37
Sex industry, and vampirism, 2–3
Sexual abuse, 205, 238–39, 291, 294
Sexuality or eroticism and vampirism, 2–3, 8–9, 11, 15–16, 26, 27, 29–30, 36, 45, 47–50, 54–58, 76, 80, 84, 85, 99–101, 138, 141, 159–60, 163–65, 167, 173–74, 184, 206–7, 219–20, 233, 248, 261–68, 270–71, 276, 304. *See also* Homosexuality; Sadomasochism
   fangs and, 107, 173, 174
   incubi or succubi and lamiai, 196, 197, 199–202
   necrophilia (with corpses), 32, 133, 310–20
   online, 32, 39
   Rice's vampires, 78
   romantic encounters, 173–76, 183–87, 189
Shadow (vampire), 156–65, 182, 269, 272
Shape-shifters, 147–49
Shelley, Mary, 130
"She Poison" column (Licina), 168, 170–72
Sherman's March (film), 93
Shifter, 147–49
Shurpu Kishpu, 123
Side Tracks bar, 159
Sightings (TV show), 4, 165
Silhol, Lea, 226–27
Simmons, Dan, 197
Siouxie and the Banshees (band), 232
Sisters of Mercy (band), 145, 172, 232
Skal, David, 132, 231
Skeletons in the Closet: The L. A. Coroner's Gift Shop, 121
Skin piercing. *See* Body-piercing
Smart Bar, 168
Smith, G. Clinton, 123
Smith, Nancy, 96
Smiths, The (band), 232
Sociopath. *See* Psychopathology
Sokol, Tony, 96–99, 119, 342
Sole Survivor (Koontz), 121
Something in the Blood (Guinn & Grieser), 34, 165

Sommer-Bodenberg, Angela, 233
Son of Dracula (film), 87
SOUND (Secret Order of the Undead) (Bat Pack), 122
South Beach (Miami), Florida, 182–87
Spirituality of vampires, 27, 59, 70, 107, 123
Spivey, Mark T., 242, 244–48
Springfield, Missouri, 292
Starr, Sarah Faye, 76
Stiffs, Inc., 7
Stigmata (club), 126
Stine, R. L., 85
Sting, 145
Stoker, Bram, 21, 38, 70, 71, 82–83, 93, 109, 130, 132, 134, 231
Story Teller, 211. *See also* specific individuals
Stranger, The (Camus), 236
Strathloch, Nicolas, 123, 124–26, 269
Stress of Her Regard, The (Powers), 133
Subterraneans, The (Kerouac), 93
Suffering, 266, 325, 327
Suicide, 299, 322, 326
   blood ritual and, 264
   cults, 68
   fascination with, 312
   Gen X and, 236
Swans, 110
Symbiotics (PsiVamps), 53
Syn Factory, 213, 214

Talamasca, 35
Tale of the Body Thief, The (Rice), 72, 185, 222
Tattoos, 11, 12, 104, 171
Television. *See also Dark Shadows; Sightings;*
   Buffy series, 88, 122, 212
   cable access, vampire programs, 10–11, 51
   talk shows, 25
   vampire shows, 88, 90–91
Temple of Set, 124, 271
Temple of the Vampire, 123–24
Terry (friend of Wraith), 56–58, 257, 260
Theater. *See also* names of theaters
   Chicago vampire, 145, 165, 169
   Los Angeles vampire, 122
   Manhattan vampire, 2, 96, 98–99, 342
   Syn Factory, 214–18
Theater of the Vampires (in Anne Rice), 96, 222
"Theatre of the Vampires" (Frequent Flyer productions), 96

Theatre des Vampyres. *See* Theater of the Vampires
They Thirst (McCammon), 26
Those Who Want to Die, 308
Thus Spake Zarathustra (Nietzsche), 331
Tompkins Square Park, New York, 2, 31, 97–98, 103–4
Toney, Darryle, 77, 213
Toney, Lilith, 77, 213
Toreadors, 210, 216
Toronto, Canada, 144
Toth, Jennifer, 5, 252, 273–74
Tower, The (fetish party), 141
Transitive Vampire, The, 23
Transubstantiation, 59
Transylvanian Society of Dracula, 131
True Blood (Gatewood & Clark), 141, 237
Tunnel, The (club), 103
Type O Negative (band), 145

Umbra et Imago (Mozart), 233
Ultimate Vampire, The, 293
Undead Poets Society, 122
Underground (vampire), 269–74
Unquiet Grave Press, 23

V is for Vampire (Skal), 132
Valenti, Chi Chi, 6, 7
Vampira, 233
Vampire. *See also* Blood fetishism; Bloodists; Classicals; Covert vampirism; Genetic Vampires; Inheriters; Nighttimers; Psychic vampires
   appeal of, 26, 91, 94, 95, 107, 113–14, 130, 184, 226, 236–37, 238, 244–48, 312
   attraction to, 37, 189, 239
   as bats, 34, 140
   beauty and, 156–57
   Christ parallels, 59, 95
   contemporary, characteristics of, 1–2, 24, 33–34, 37, 80, 123, 151, 152, 166, 167
   definition, 109, 157
   embodiment of dangerous sex, 26, 27, 80
   gender and, 19, 80, 151, 156, 164–65, 182, 237
   mythology and archetype of, 24, 25–26, 27, 75–76, 79, 167, 212, 247
   as outsider or "other," 83, 84, 99, 114, 239, 249–50, 312
   population, U.S., 2, 24

Vampire (*cont.*)
"real," xi, 19, 21, 24, 36, 46, 274, 281, 332–40
romanticism of, 72–73, 82, 167, 229, 308
savagery of, 334–35
traditional image, 71, 167
types, 5, 32, 80, 198–99
writers on appeal of, 26
Vampire Access Line (VAL), 5, 51
Vampire Archives, The, 165
Vampire Bible, The, 123
Vampire Book: Encyclopedia of the Undead, The
    (Melton), 131, 212
Vampire Chronicles, The (Rice), 71–72, 77
Vampire circus (event), 168
Vampire Circus (film), 96
Vampire Clan, The, 293
Vampire clans, 109, 149. *See also* Kindred
Vampire clubs, 5–13, 127–30, 141–47, 173,
    179–82, 183, 185, 188, 213. See also clubs
    by location or name
Vampire Companion, The (Ramsland), 22, 72–73,
    221, 226
Vampire Connection, 108
Vampire conspiracy, 24
Vampire culture, 28–29. *See also* Goth; specific
    locations; specific topics
    danger of, 17, 25, 42, 272, 280, 291, 297–308,
    309
    death, love of, and, 309–20
    defined, 28–29
    disguise, 18. *See also* Costumes and clothing
    fantasizers and, 68
    films, 87–93, 132
    names, 18, 41, 51, 172, 212
    rebirth and, 94
    role-players, 18–21, 28, 65
    size of, U.S., 24, 28
    stage performances, 96–99, 132
    values of, 93–94
    vampyre versus vampire, 19, 109
Vampire D (film), 213
"Vampire: The Dark Ages" (White Wolf), 210
Vampire Dark News, 226
Vampire dominatrix, 138–42
Vampire elite, 269–74
Vampire Esoteric Encounters, 23
Vampire events, 7, 108, 127, 141, 168, 226–27,
    231, 341–44
Vampire fetish ball, 8, 110–18

Vampire ghost, 323–30, 337–40
Vampire Haven, The, 122
Vampire hunters
    films featuring, 88, 213
    LARP, 212
    television series (*Buffy*), 88, 122, 212
Vampire Information Exchange (VIE), 23
Vampire Killing Kit, 71
Vampire Lestat, The (Rice), 36, 71, 113, 145, 273
Vampirella, 133
Vampire Mad Tea Parties, 127
Vampire mentor, 101, 271
Vampire pornography. *See* Pornography
"Vampire Probability Test" online, 33
Vampire Research Center, 24
Vampire Research Institute (VRI), 34–35
Vampires Among Us, 35, 201
Vampires and Victims Ball, 144
Vampires Are (Kaplan), 24
*Vampires: Emotional Predators Who Want to Suck the Life
    Out of You* (Rhodes & Rhodes), 196
Vampires: The Occult Truth (Konstantinos), 202–4
"Vampires 101," 51–54
Vampires on Video (Melton), 87, 131
Vampires: Restless Creatures of the Night (Marigny),
    227
Vampire Story society, 226
Vampire Studies center, 165
Vampire Studies Society, The, 23
Vampires Unearthed (Riccardo), 165
Vampires, Werewolves and Demons (Noll), 134
Vampire Tapestry, The (Charnas), 71, 217
"Vampire: The Masquerade" (game), 27–28, 47,
    105, 120, 127, 209–12, 213, 223, 227–28, 269,
    291–96
"Vampire Vulnerability Test" online, 33
"Vampire White Pages," 46–47
Vampiricus (club), 127, 144
Vampirism Awareness Manual, 289
Vampyre, 19, 21, 74, 150, 152
Vampyre Dreams TV, 10–11
Vampyre Magazine, 110
"Vampyres Only," 37–40
Vampyre Valentine's Day Ball, 108, 341–45
Vampyr Theatre, 96, 98–99, 342
Van Helsing, Professor (character), 70, 71, 212
Varney (character), 70
VAT magazine, 231
Vault, The (club), 103

Vega, Maria A., 96
Ventrue, 210, 214, 216
Verbal Abuse magazine, 7
Verzeni, Vincenz, 133
Victims (or prey), 13–17, 27, 55, 60, 99–101,
    123, 162–65, 189–207, 279–80, 283–88, 323,
    336
    rape, 190, 284, 295
Village Voice, The, 2
Vincent (GenX blood-sport behavior), 248–49
Virginia, LARP in, 213
Vergil, 47–50
Vlad (magician), 147
Vlad (rock musician), 23, 165, 168–70
Vlad (Tarot reader), 342
Vlad Tepes the Impaler, 38, 78–79, 93–94, 122,
    127, 132, 165, 166, 228
Vogelwede, Yasmine, 78
Voltaire (band), 145
"Voluptuous Captivity: Evolution of the
    Vampire Erotic" (Ramsland), 132
Voluptuous Horror of Karen Black, The, 145

Walsh, Susan, xi, 1–4, 6, 8, 17, 28, 29, 53–54, 55,
    58, 60, 69, 105, 119, 220, 253, 272, 344–45
Washington Square (club), 183
Watcher, 88
Weddings, vampire or Goth, 169–70, 174, 185–87
    handfasting, 186–87
Weinberg, Robert, 210
Wendorf, Heather, 293–96
Wendorf, Naoma Ruth Queen, 293, 295
Wendorf, Richard, 293, 295

"Werewolf: The Apocalyse" (game), 370210
Westchester County, NY, LARP, 213
Westenra, Lucy (character), 231
Westgate Museum, 73–74, 93
West Memphis, Arkansas, 289
Whitby, England, 231
    "The Dracula Experience," 231
    vampire ball, 231
    Vamps and Tramps centenary, 231
"White Chapel" (Clegg), 333–35
White Wolf, 27, 105, 209, 210, 213, 214, 291, 292,
    296–97
Wilde, Oscar, 61
Wilhite, Jud, 242–44, 248
Willis, Danielle, 141
Wilson, Colin, 35
Wilson, F. Paul, 82
Wilson, Gahan, 132
Witching Hour, The (Rice), 77, 231
Wolf, Leonard, 132
World of Darkness, 209, 213
Wraith (W.), 13–17, 54–58, 68, 99–101, 206–7,
    213, 218–20, 221, 233, 250–68, 273, 274–88,
    297–308, 321–330, 331–40
"Wraith: The Oblivion" (game), 210

Xeper, 271

Yarbro, Chelsea Quinn, 71, 82–83, 131
Youngson, Jeanne Keyes, 23, 36, 130–31

Zimmerman, Gail, 90